International Dispute Settlement

A guide to the techniques and institutions used to solve international disputes, how they work and when they are used. Many, often topical examples place the theory of how things are supposed to work in the context of real-life events so that you can understand the strengths and weaknesses of different methods in practice. The fully updated edition of this successful textbook includes the most recent arbitrations, developments in the WTO and case law from the International Court of Justice.

J. G. Merrills has taught international law all over the world for more than forty years. He held visiting posts at the Universities of Auckland and Toronto, twice served as Dean of the Faculty of Law at Sheffield University and for eight years was Alternate Member of the UN Sub-Commission on Prevention of Discrimination and Protection of Minorities. He is the author of various books and journal articles on international law, and is a member of the American Society of International Law and of the British Institute of International and Comparative Law. In 2007 he was elected an Associate Member of the Institut de Droit International.

International Dispute Settlement

Fifth edition

J. G. MERRILLS

University of Sheffield

CAMBRIDGE
UNIVERSITY PRESS

CAMBRIDGE
UNIVERSITY PRESS

University Printing House, Cambridge CB2 8BS, United Kingdom

Cambridge University Press is part of the University of Cambridge.

It furthers the University's mission by disseminating knowledge in the pursuit of education, learning and research at the highest international levels of excellence.

www.cambridge.org
Information on this title: www.cambridge.org/9780521199094

First published 2011
7th printing 2014

Printed in the United Kingdom by Clays, St Ives plc.

A catalogue record for this publication is available from the British Library

Library of Congress Cataloguing in Publication data
Merrills, J. G.
International dispute settlement / J. G. Merrills. – 5th ed.
    p.   cm.
Includes bibliographical references and index.
ISBN 978-0-521-19909-4 (hardback)
1. Pacific settlement of international disputes.   I. Title.
JZ6010.M47   2011
341.5′2 – dc22   2010051865

ISBN 978-0-521-19909-4 Hardback
ISBN 978-0-521-15339-3 Paperback

Contents

Preface

Since the fourth edition of this book was published in 2005 there have been several developments with a direct bearing on its subject. A new administration in the United States, the growing influence of China in the world and political developments in Africa and Europe all have a significant impact on the activity of both the United Nations and regional organisations. The World Trade Organization, already an established player in 2005, has maintained its prominence, and its arrangements for dispute settlement continue to be widely used. The complex system set up by the 1982 Law of the Sea Convention has been slowly consolidated as cases have been taken to the International Tribunal for the Law of the Sea or to arbitration, while the International Court of Justice is busier now than at any previous time in its history. It must, of course, also be noted that solutions to such long-standing international problems as Cyprus, Kashmir and Israel/Palestine seem as far away as ever, reminding us, yet again, of the distance to be travelled, if institutional provisions for dealing with the most serious disputes and situations are to be effective.

The aim of this new edition is to examine the techniques and institutions available to states for the peaceful settlement of disputes, taking full account of recent developments. Chapters 1 to 4 examine the so-called 'diplomatic' means of settlement: negotiation, where matters are entirely in the hands of the parties, then mediation, inquiry and conciliation, in each of which outside assistance is utilised. Chapters 5 to 7 deal with legal means, namely, arbitration and judicial settlement through the International Court of Justice, where the object is to provide a legally binding decision. To underline the interaction of legal and diplomatic means and to show how they are used in specific contexts, Chapter 8 reviews the arrangements for dispute settlement in the Law of the Sea Convention and Chapter 9 considers the provisions of the World Trade Organization's remarkable Dispute Settlement Understanding. The final part of the book considers the role of political institutions, the United Nations (Chapter 10) and regional organisations (Chapter 11), while the final chapter reviews the current situation and offers some thoughts for the future.

Those familiar with the previous edition will find significant new material in almost every chapter, including references to recent arbitrations, to the developing practice of the International Tribunal for the Law of the Sea, the jurisprudence of the International Court of Justice and practice under the WTO system, as well as new political material relating to peace-keeping and other activities of regional organisations and the UN. In discussing the various techniques and institutions, my object has remained to explain what they are, how they work and when they are used. As before, I have sought to include enough references to the relevant literature to enable the reader to follow up any points of particular interest. With a similar objective I have retained and updated the appendices setting out extracts from some of the documents mentioned in the text.

For permission to quote the material in the appendices I am again grateful to the editors of the *International Law Reports*. My thanks are also due to Julie Prescott at the University of Sheffield for preparing the manuscript, to Raihanah Begum and Sinéad Moloney at Cambridge University Press, and to my wife, Dariel, whose encouragement, as always, was invaluable.

Table of cases

Table of treaties and agreements

Abbreviations

AFDI	Annuaire Français de Droit International
AJIL	American Journal of International Law
Annuaire	Annuaire de l'Institut de Droit International
Archiv des Völk.	Archiv des Völkerrechts
Aust. Year Book Int. L.	Australian Year Book of International Law
BYBIL	British Year Book of International Law
Calif. Western Int. LJ	California Western International Law Journal
Can. Bar Rev.	Canadian Bar Review
Can. Yearbook Int. L.	Canadian Yearbook of International Law
CML Rev.	Common Market Law Review
Colum. J. Transnat. L.	Columbia Journal of Transnational Law
Denver J. Int. L. & Pol.	Denver Journal of International Law and Policy
Ga J. Int. & Comp. L.	Georgia Journal of International and Comparative Law
Global Community YBILJ	Global Community Yearbook of International Law and Jurisprudence
Grotius Soc. Trans.	Grotius Society Transactions
Harv. Int. LJ	Harvard International Law Journal
ICLQ	International and Comparative Law Quarterly
ILM	International Legal Materials
ILQ	International Law Quarterly
ILR	International Law Reports
Ind. J. Int. L.	Indian Journal of International Law
Int. Org.	International Organization
Int. Rel.	International Relations
Iran–US CTR	Iran–United States Claims Tribunal Reports
Israel L. Rev.	Israel Law Review
J. World Trade	Journal of World Trade
Leiden JIL	Leiden Journal of International Law
Melbourne JIL	Melbourne Journal of International Law
Mich. L. Rev.	Michigan Law Review
NTIR	Nederlands tijdschrift voor internationaal recht
NYUJ Int. L. & Politics	New York University Journal of International Law and Politics

Ocean Devel. & Int. L.	Ocean Development and International Law
Rev. Egypt. Droit Int.	Revue Egyptienne de Droit International
RGDIP	Revue Générale de Droit International Public
RIAA	Reports of International Arbitral Awards
San Diego L. Rev.	San Diego Law Review
Syr. J. Int. L. & Com.	Syracuse Journal of International Law and Commerce
U. Chi. L. Rev.	University of Chicago Law Review
U. Toronto Fac. L. Rev.	University of Toronto Faculty of Law Review
U. Toronto LJ	University of Toronto Law Journal
UKTS	United Kingdom Treaty Series
UNTS	United Nations Treaty Series
Va JIL	Virginia Journal of International Law
YBIEL	Yearbook of International Environmental Law
Yearbook of WA	Yearbook of World Affairs

Websites

African Union, www.africa-union.org
Arab League, www.leagueofarabstates.org
Council of Europe, www.coe.int
Economic Community of West African States, www.ecowas.int
European Court of Human Rights, www.echr.coe.int
European Court of Justice, www.curia.eu.int
Inter-American Court of Human Rights, www.corteidh.or.cr
International Centre for the Settlement of Investment Disputes,
    www.icsid.org
International Court of Justice, www.icj-cij.org
International Criminal Court, www.un.org/law/icc/
International Criminal Tribunal for Rwanda, www.ictr.org
International Criminal Tribunal for the Former Yugoslavia,
    www.un.org/icty/
International Tribunal for the Law of the Sea, www.itlos.org
Iran–United States Claims Tribunal, www.iusct.org
North American Free Trade Agreement Secretariat,
    www.nafta-sec-alena.org
Organization for Security and Co-operation in Europe, www.osce.org
Organization of American States, www.oas.org
Organization of the Islamic Conference, www.oic-oci.org
Permanent Court of Arbitration, www.pca-cpa.org
United Nations, www.un.org
UN Department of Peacekeeping, www.un.org/Depts/dpko/
UN General Assembly, www.un.org/ga/
UN Security Council Information, www.un.org/Docs/scinfo.htm
World Trade Organization, www.wto.org

1

Negotiation

A dispute may be defined as a specific disagreement concerning a matter of fact, law or policy in which a claim or assertion of one party is met with refusal, counter-claim or denial by another. In the broadest sense, an international dispute can be said to exist whenever such a disagreement involves governments, institutions, juristic persons (corporations) or private individuals in different parts of the world. However, the disputes with which the present work is primarily concerned are those in which the parties are two or more of the nearly 200 or so sovereign states into which the world is currently divided.

Disputes are an inevitable part of international relations, just as disputes between individuals are inevitable in domestic relations. Like individuals, states often want the same thing in a situation where there is not enough of it to go round. Moreover, just as people can disagree about the way to use a river, a piece of land or a sum of money, states frequently want to do different things, but their claims are incompatible. Admittedly, one side may change its position, extra resources may be found, or on looking further into the issue it may turn out that everyone can be satisfied after all. But no one imagines that these possibilities can eliminate all domestic disputes and they certainly cannot be relied on internationally. Disputes, whether between states, neighbours, or brothers and sisters, must therefore be accepted as a regular part of human relations and the problem is what to do about them.

A basic requirement is a commitment from those who are likely to become involved, that is to say, from everyone, that disputes will only be pursued by peaceful means. Within states this principle was established at an early stage and laws and institutions were set up to prohibit self-help and to enable disputes to be settled without disruption of the social order. On the international plane, where initially the matter was regarded as less important, equivalent arrangements have been slower to develop. The emergence of international law, which in its modern form can be dated from the seventeenth century, was accompanied by neither the creation of a world government, nor a renunciation of the use of force by states. In 1945, however, with the consequences of the unbridled pursuit of national objectives still fresh in the memory, the founder members of the United Nations agreed in Article 2(3) of the Charter to 'settle their international disputes by peaceful means in such a manner that international peace and security, and justice, are not endangered'. What these peaceful means are and how they are used by states are the subject of this book.

A General Assembly resolution of 1970, after quoting Article 2(3), proclaims:

> States shall accordingly seek early and just settlement of their international disputes by negotiation, inquiry, mediation, conciliation, arbitration, judicial settlement, resort to regional agencies or arrangements or other peaceful means of their choice.[1]

In this provision, which is modelled on Article 33(1) of the Charter, the various methods of peaceful settlement are not set out in any order of priority, but the first mentioned, negotiation, is the principal means of handling all international disputes.[2] In fact in practice, negotiation is employed more frequently than all the other methods put together. Often, indeed, negotiation is the only means employed, not just because it is always the first to be tried and is often successful, but also because states may believe its advantages to be so great as to rule out the use of other methods, even in situations where the chances of a negotiated settlement are slight. On the occasions when another method is used, negotiation is not displaced, but directed towards instrumental issues, for example the terms of reference for an inquiry or conciliation commission or the arrangements for implementing an arbitral decision.

Thus, in one form or another, negotiation has a vital part in international disputes. But negotiation is more than a possible means of settling differences, it is also a technique for preventing them from arising. Since prevention is always better than cure, this form of negotiation, known as 'consultation', is a convenient place to begin.

Consultation

When a government anticipates that a decision or a proposed course of action may harm another state, discussions with the affected party can provide a way of heading off a dispute by creating an opportunity for

---

[1] *General Assembly Declaration on Principles of International Law Concerning Friendly Relations and Cooperation among States in Accordance with the Charter of the United Nations*, GA Res. 2625 (XXV), 24 October 1970. The resolution was adopted by the General Assembly without a vote.

[2] For discussion of the meaning and significance of negotiation, see C. M. H. Waldock (ed.), *International Disputes: The Legal Aspects*, London, 1972, Chapter 2A (H. Darwin); F. S. Northedge and M. D. Donelan, *International Disputes: The Political Aspects*, London, 1971, Chapter 12; P. J. I. M. De Waart, *The Element of Negotiation in the Pacific Settlement of Disputes between States*, The Hague, 1973; United Nations, *Handbook on the Peaceful Settlement of Disputes between States*, New York, 1992, Chapter 2A; B. Starkey, M. A. Boyer and J. Wilkenfield, *Negotiating a Complex World*, Lanham, MD, 1999; I. W. Zartman and J. Z. Rubin (eds.), *Power and Negotiation*, Ann Arbor, MI, 2000; and V. A. Kremenyuk (ed.), *International Negotiation*, 2nd edn, San Francisco, 2002.

adjustment and accommodation. Quite minor modifications to its plans, of no importance to the state taking the decision, may be all that is required to avoid trouble, yet may only be recognised if the other side is given a chance to point them out. The particular value of consultation is that it supplies this useful information at the most appropriate time – before anything has been done. For it is far easier to make the necessary modifications at the decision-making stage, rather than later, when exactly the same action may seem like capitulation to foreign pressure, or be seized on by critics as a sacrifice of domestic interests.

A good example of the value of consultation is provided by the practice of the United States and Canada in antitrust proceedings. Writing of the procedure employed in such cases, a commentator has noted that:

> While it is true that antitrust officials of one state might flatly refuse to alter a course of action in any way, it has often been the case that officials have been persuaded to modify their plans somewhat. After consultation, it may be agreed to shape an indictment in a less offensive manner, to change the ground rules of an investigation so as to require only 'voluntary' testimony from witnesses, or that officials of the government initiating an investigation or action will keep their antitrust counterparts informed of progress in the case and allow them to voice their concerns.[3]

This policy of co-operation, developed through a series of bilateral understandings, has been incorporated in an agreement providing for co-ordination with regard to both the competition laws and the deceptive marketing practices laws of the two states.

Consultation should be distinguished from two related ways of taking foreign susceptibilities into account: notification and the obtaining of prior consent. Suppose state A decides to notify state B of imminent action likely to affect B's interests, or, as will sometimes be the case, is obliged to do so as a legal duty. Such advanced warning gives B time to consider its response, which may be to make representations to A, and in any case avoids the abrasive impact of what might otherwise be regarded as an attempt to present B with a *fait accompli*. In these ways notification can make a modest contribution to dispute avoidance, though naturally B is likely to regard notification alone as a poor substitute for the chance to negotiate and influence the decision that consultation can provide.

Obtaining the consent of the other state, which again may sometimes be a legal obligation, lies at the opposite pole. Here, the affected state enjoys a veto over the proposed action. This is clearly an extremely important power

---

[3] See B. R. Campbell, 'The Canada–United States antitrust notification and consultation procedure', (1978) 56 Can. Bar Rev. p. 459 at p. 468. On arrangements with Australia, see S. D. Ramsey, 'The United States–Australian Antitrust Cooperation Agreement: A step in the right direction', (1983–4) 24 Va JIL p. 127.

and its exceptional nature was properly emphasised by the tribunal in the *Lake Lanoux* case:

> To admit that jurisdiction in a certain field can no longer be exercised except on the condition of, or by way of, an agreement between two States, is to place an essential restriction on the sovereignty of a State, and such restriction could only be admitted if there were clear and convincing evidence. Without doubt, international practice does reveal some special cases in which this hypothesis has become reality; thus, sometimes two States exercise conjointly jurisdiction over certain territories (joint ownership, *co-imperium*, or *condominium*); likewise, in certain international arrangements, the representatives of States exercise conjointly a certain jurisdiction in the name of those States or in the name of organizations. But these cases are exceptional, and international judicial decisions are slow to recognize their existence, especially when they impair the territorial sovereignty of a State, as would be the case in the present matter.[4]

In that case, Spain argued that, under both customary international law and treaties between the two states, France was under an obligation to obtain Spain's consent to the execution of works for the utilisation of certain waters in the Pyrenees for a hydroelectric scheme. The argument was rejected, but the tribunal went on to hold that France was under a duty to consult with Spain over projects that were likely to affect Spanish interests. Speaking of the nature of such obligatory consultations, the tribunal observed that:

> one speaks, although often inaccurately, of the 'obligation of negotiating an agreement'. In reality, the engagements thus undertaken by States take very diverse forms and have a scope which varies according to the manner in which they are defined and according to the procedures intended for their execution; but the reality of the obligations thus undertaken is incontestable and sanctions can be applied in the event, for example, of an unjustified breaking off of the discussions, abnormal delays, disregard of the agreed procedures, systematic refusals to take into consideration adverse proposals or interests, and, more generally, in cases of violation of the rules of good faith.[5]

The role of consultation at different stages of a dispute may be seen in the *Land Reclamation* case.[6] Here, Malaysia brought proceedings against Singapore in response to reclamation activities being undertaken by the latter in the Straits of Johor, claiming that, as the activities were damaging

---

4 *Lake Lanoux Arbitration (France v. Spain)* (1957) 24 ILR p. 101 at p. 127. For discussion of the significance of the case, see J. G. Laylin and R. L. Bianchi, 'The role of adjudication in international river disputes: The Lake Lanoux case', (1959) 53 AJIL p. 30.
5 24 ILR p. 101 at p. 128. See further C. B. Bourne, 'Procedure in the development of international drainage basins: The duty to consult and negotiate', (1972) 10 Can. Yearbook Int. L. p. 212; and F. L. Kirgis, *Prior Consultation in International Law*, Charlottesville, VA, 1983, Chapter 2.
6 *Case Concerning Land Reclamation by Singapore in and around the Straits of Johor (Malaysia v. Singapore)*, Provisional Measures Order of 8 October 2003, 126 ILR p. 487; and see J. G. Merrills, 'New horizons for international adjudication', (2006) 6 Global Community YBILJ p. 47 at pp. 48–57.

and had been carried out without notification or consultation, Singapore had breached its obligations under the 1982 Law of the Sea Convention. Malaysia first sought provisional measures of protection from the International Tribunal for the Law of the Sea, and, in its order in 2003, the Tribunal put on record various undertakings from the parties with regard to the sharing of information and co-operation and required them to set up a group of independent experts to investigate the dispute and make recommendations. The group submitted its recommendations as requested, which provided the basis for an agreement settling the dispute which shortly afterwards was incorporated in an arbitration award on agreed terms. Under the settlement, the two states set up a joint mechanism designed to promote co-operation between them in the future. Thus, here consultation played a triple role, providing the basis for Malaysia's initial claim, then forming part of a transitional framework in the provisional measures order, and finally supplying a major component of the final settlement.

Another example of how the various ways of co-ordinating activities may be constructively combined is provided by the 'Interim Reciprocal Information and Consultation System', established in 1990 to regulate the movement of British and Argentine forces in the southwestern Atlantic.[7] The system involved the creation of a direct communication link with the aim of reducing the possibility of incidents and limiting their consequences if they occur. These facilities for consultation are supported by a provision under which at least twenty-five days' written notice is required for air and naval movements, and exercises of more than a certain size. This is a straightforward arrangement for notification, but two component features of the system are worth noticing. First, the notification provision is very specific as to the areas in which the obligation exists and the units to which it applies, and thereby minimises the possibilities for misunderstanding. Secondly, in relation to the most sensitive areas, those immediately off the parties' respective coasts, the notifying state must be informed immediately of any movement which 'might cause political or military difficulty' and 'mutual agreement will be necessary to proceed'. Here, therefore there is not only a right and a corresponding duty in respect of notification, but in some circumstances at least a need to obtain consent.

When arrangements for consultation are agreed upon in advance, questions may naturally arise as to whether they have been complied with if one party adopts measures to which the other takes exception. In the recent *Pulp Mills on the River Uruguay* case,[8] for example, Argentina took Uruguay to the

---

[7] Text in (1990) 29 ILM p. 1296; and see document A in the appendix below. For discussion, see M. Evans, 'The restoration of diplomatic relations between Argentina and the United Kingdom', (1991) 40 ICLQ p. 473 at pp. 478–80. For later developments, see R. R. Churchill, 'Falkland Islands: Maritime jurisdiction and co-operative arrangements with Argentina', (1997) 46 ICLQ p. 463.

[8] *Pulp Mills on the River Uruguay (Argentina v. Uruguay)*, Judgment [2010] ICJ Rep.

International Court of Justice claiming, *inter alia*, that the latter had failed to notify and consult with Argentina before authorising the construction of two large pulp mills on the river which forms the international boundary. The obligations in question were contained in a bilateral treaty, the 1975 Statute of the River Uruguay, and, after examining the parties' conduct, the Court ruled that Uruguay had indeed breached its procedural obligations under the Statute. Argentina further claimed that Uruguay had violated its substantive obligations under the treaty, on account of the ecological impact of the pulp mills, but the Court found that this claim was not made out. Co-operative arrangements for utilising shared resources such as boundary rivers are increasingly common nowadays, and this case is a good illustration of their significance.

The advantages of consultation in bilateral relations are equally evident in matters which are of concern to a larger number of states. In a multilateral setting, consultation usually calls for an institutional structure of some kind. These can vary widely and do not have to be elaborate in order to be useful. The Antarctic Treaty system, for example, now operates on the basis of annual meetings but until recently had no permanent organs. It nevertheless exemplified the value of what has been called 'anticipatory co-operation' in addressing environmental and other issues in a special regional context. When closer regulation is needed, more complex institutional arrangements may be appropriate. Thus, the International Monetary Fund at one time required a member which had decided to change the par value of its currency to obtain the concurrence of the IMF before doing so. It is interesting to note that the term 'concurrence' was chosen 'to convey the idea of a presumption that was to be observed in favour of the member's proposal'.[9] Even so, the arrangement meant that extremely sensitive decisions were subject to international scrutiny. As a result, until the par value system was abandoned in 1978, the provision gave rise to considerable difficulties in practice.

Consultation between states is usually an *ad hoc* process and, except where reciprocity provides an incentive, as in the cases considered, has proved difficult to institutionalise. Obligatory consultation is bound to make decision-making slower and, depending on how the obligation is defined, may well constrain a government's options. In the *Lake Lanoux* case, the tribunal noted that it is a 'delicate matter' to decide whether such an obligation has been complied with, and held that, on the facts, France had done all that was required. If consultation is to be compulsory, however, the circumstances in which the obligation arises, as well as its content, need careful definition, or an allegation of a failure to carry out the agreed procedure may itself become a disputed issue.

Whether voluntary or compulsory, consultation is often easier to implement for executive than for legislative decision-making, since the former is

---

[9] See J. Gold, 'Prior consultation in international law', (1983–4) 24 Va JIL p. 729 at p. 737.

usually less rigidly structured and more centralised. But legislative action can also cause international disputes; therefore procedures designed to achieve the same effect as consultation can have an equally useful part to play. Where states enjoy close relations, it may be possible to establish machinery for negotiating the co-ordination of legislative and administrative measures on matters of common interest. There are clear advantages in having uniform provisions on such matters as environmental protection, where states share a common frontier, or commerce, if trade is extensive. The difficulties of achieving such harmonisation are considerable, as the experience of the European Union has demonstrated, though, if uniformity cannot be achieved, compatibility of domestic provisions is a less ambitious alternative. In either case, the rewards in terms of dispute avoidance make the effort well worthwhile.

Another approach is to give the foreign state, or interested parties, an opportunity to participate in the domestic legislative process. Whether this is possible depends on the legislative machinery being sufficiently accessible to make it practicable and the parties' relations being good enough for such participation, which can easily be construed as foreign interference, to be acceptable. When these conditions are fulfilled, the example of North America – where United States gas importers have appeared before Canada's National Energy Board and Canadian officials have testified before Congressional committees – shows what can be achieved.[10]

Consultation, then, is a valuable way of avoiding international disputes. It is therefore not surprising to find that, in an increasingly interdependent world, the practice is growing. The record, however, is still very uneven. Although, as we shall see in Chapter 9, consultation is increasingly important in international trade, on other issues with the potential to cause disputes, such as access to resources and the protection of the environment, progress in developing procedures for consultation has been slower than is desirable. Similarly, while there is already consultation on a number of matters between Canada and the United States and in Europe, in other parts of the world the practice is scarcely known. Finally, when such procedures have been developed, there is, as we have noted, an important distinction between consultation as a matter of obligation and voluntary consultation which states prefer.

The author of a comprehensive review of consultation was compelled by the evidence of state practice to conclude that:

> Despite the growth of prior consultation norms, it is unlikely that there will be any all-encompassing prior consultation duty in the foreseeable future. Thus, to the extent that formal procedural structures for prior consultation may be

---

[10] See *Settlement of International Disputes between Canada and the USA* (Report of the American and Canadian Bar Associations' Joint Working Group, 1979) for a description of this and other aspects of United States–Canadian co-operation.

desirable, they should be tailored to recurring, relatively well defined, troublesome situations.[11]

The difficulty of persuading states to accept consultation procedures and the ways in which they operate when established are reminders of the fact that states are not entities, like individuals, but complex groupings of institutions and interests. If this is constantly borne in mind, the salient features of negotiation and the means of settlement discussed in later chapters will be much easier to understand.

Forms of negotiation

Negotiations between states are usually conducted through 'normal diplomatic channels', that is, by the respective foreign offices, or by diplomatic representatives, who in the case of complex negotiations may lead delegations including representatives of several interested departments of the governments concerned. As an alternative, if the subject matter is appropriate, negotiations may be carried out by what are termed the 'competent authorities' of each party, that is, by representatives of the particular ministry or department responsible for the matter in question – for example, between trade departments in the case of a commercial agreement, or between defence ministries in negotiations concerning weapons procurement. Where the competent authorities are subordinate bodies, they may be authorised to take negotiations as far as possible and to refer disagreements to a higher governmental level. One of the treaty provisions discussed in the *Lake Lanoux* dispute, for example, provided that:

> The highest administrative authorities of the bordering Departments and Provinces will act in concert in the exercise of their right to make regulations for the general interest and to interpret or modify their regulations whenever the respective interests are at stake, and in case they cannot reach agreement, the dispute shall be submitted to the two Governments.[12]

In the case of a recurrent problem or a situation requiring continuous supervision, states may decide to institutionalise negotiations by creating what is termed a mixed or joint commission. Thus, neighbouring states commonly employ mixed commissions to deal with boundary delimitation, or other matters of common concern. The Soviet Union, for example, concluded treaties with a number of neighbouring states, providing for frontier disputes and incidents to be referred to mixed commissions with power to

---

[11] Kirgis, *Prior Consultation*, p. 375. See also I. W. Zartman (ed.), *Preventive Negotiation*, Lanham, MD, 2001.

[12] See the Additional Act to the three Treaties of Bayonne (1866), Article 16, in (1957) 24 ILR p. 104.

decide minor disputes and to investigate other cases, before referring them for settlement through diplomatic channels.[13]

Mixed commissions usually consist of an equal number of representatives of both parties, and may be given either a broad brief of indefinite duration, or the task of dealing with a specific problem. An outstanding example of a commission of the first type is provided by the Canadian–United States International Joint Commission, which, since its creation in 1909, has dealt with a large number of issues, including industrial development, air pollution and a variety of questions concerning boundary waters.[14]

An illustration of the different functions that may be assigned to *ad hoc* commissions is to be found in the *Lake Lanoux* dispute. After being considered by the International Commission for the Pyrenees, a mixed commission established as long ago as 1875, the matter was referred to a Franco-Spanish Commission of Engineers, set up in 1949 to examine the technical aspects of the dispute. When the Commission of Engineers was unable to agree, France and Spain created a special mixed commission with the task of formulating proposals for the utilisation of Lake Lanoux and submitting them to the two governments for consideration. It was only when this commission was also unable to agree that the parties decided to refer the case to arbitration, though not before France had put forward (unsuccessfully) the idea of a fourth mixed commission which would have had the function of supervising execution of the water-diversion scheme and monitoring its day-to-day operation.

If negotiation through established machinery proves unproductive, 'summit discussions' between heads of state or foreign ministers may be used in an attempt to break the deadlock. Though the value of such conspicuous means of negotiation should not be exaggerated, summit diplomacy may facilitate agreement by enabling official bureaucracies to be bypassed to some extent, while providing an incentive to agree in the form of enhanced prestige for the leaders concerned. It should be noted, however, that summit diplomacy is usually the culmination of a great deal of conventional negotiation, and in some cases at least reflects nothing more than a desire to make political capital out of an agreement that is already assured.

A disadvantage of summit meetings is that, unlike conventional negotiations, they take place amid a glare of publicity and so generate expectations which may be hard to fulfil. The idea that a meeting between world leaders

---

[13] For details, see N. Bar-Yaacov, *The Handling of International Disputes by Means of Inquiry*, Oxford, 1974, pp. 117–19.

[14] For an excellent survey of the work of the International Joint Commission, see M. Cohen, 'The regime of boundary waters – The Canadian–United States experience', (1975) 146 *Hague Recueil des Cours* p. 219 (with bibliography). For a review of another commission, see L. C. Wilson, 'The settlement of boundary disputes: Mexico, the United States and the International Boundary Commission', (1980) 29 ICLQ p. 38.

has failed unless it produces a new agreement of some kind is scarcely realistic yet is epitomised by the mixture of hope and dread with which meetings between the leaders of the United States and the Soviet Union used to be surrounded. In an attempt to change this unhealthy atmosphere, in November 1989 President George H. Bush described his forthcoming meeting with Mr Gorbachev as an 'interim informal meeting' and emphasised that there would be no specific agenda.[15] It is doubtful if such attempts to damp down expectations can ever be wholly successful and even less likely that politicians would wish the media to treat their exploits on the international stage with indifference. However, as the solution of international problems is primarily a matter of working patiently with regular contact at all levels, there is much to be said for attempting to remove the unique aura of summit meetings and encouraging them to be seen instead as a regular channel of communication.

The public aspect of negotiations which is exemplified in summit diplomacy is also prominent in the activity of international organisations. In the United Nations General Assembly and similar bodies, states can, if they choose, conduct diplomatic exchanges in the full glare of international attention. This is undoubtedly a useful way of letting off steam and, more constructively, of engaging the attention of outside states which may have something to contribute to the solution of a dispute. It has the disadvantage, however, that so visible a performance may encourage the striking of attitudes which are at once both unrealistic and difficult to abandon. It is therefore probable that, for states with a serious interest in negotiating a settlement, the many opportunities for informal contact which international organisations provide are more useful than the dramatic confrontations of public debate.

Whether discussion of a dispute in an international organisation can be regarded as equivalent to traditional diplomatic negotiation is an issue which may also have legal implications. In the *South West Africa* cases (1962),[16] one of South Africa's preliminary objections was that any dispute between itself and the applicants, Ethiopia and Liberia, fell outside the terms of the International Court's jurisdiction (which rested on Article 7 of the Mandate), because it had not been shown that the dispute was one which could not be settled by negotiation. The Court rejected the objection on the ground that extensive discussions in the United Nations on the question of South West Africa, in which South Africa and the applicants had been involved, constituted negotiations in respect of the dispute and the fact that those discussions had ended in deadlock indicated that the dispute could not be settled by negotiation.

In their joint dissenting opinion, Judges Spender and Fitzmaurice disagreed. In their view, what had occurred in the United Nations did not

---

[15]   See L. Freedman, 'Just two men in a boat', *The Independent*, 3 November 1989, p. 19.

[16]   *South West Africa*, Preliminary Objections, Judgment, [1962] ICJ Rep. p. 319.

amount to negotiation within Article 7. Those discussions, they argued, failed to satisfy the requirements of Article 7 because such discussions had not been directed to the alleged dispute between the applicants and South Africa, merely to points of disagreement between the Assembly and South Africa. Even if this had not been so, proceedings within an international organisation could never be regarded as a substitute for direct negotiations between the parties because:

> a 'negotiation' confined to the floor of an international Assembly, consisting of allegations of Members, resolutions of the Assembly and actions taken by the Assembly pursuant thereto, denial of allegations, refusal to comply with resolutions or to respond to action taken thereunder, cannot be enough to justify the Court in holding that the dispute 'cannot' be settled by negotiation, when no direct diplomatic interchanges have ever taken place between the parties, and therefore no attempt at settlement has been made at the statal and diplomatic level.[17]

The *Northern Cameroons* case[18] raised a very similar issue. Article 19 of the Trusteeship Agreement for the Cameroons, like Article 7 of the Mandate, covered only disputes incapable of settlement by negotiation. The International Court, which decided the case on other grounds, did not discuss this aspect of Article 19. Fitzmaurice, however, examining the requirement in light of his opinion in the *South West Africa* cases, observed that 'negotiation' did not mean 'a couple of states arguing with each other across the floor of an international assembly, or circulating statements of their complaints or contentions to its member states. That is disputation, not negotiation',[19] and repeated his view that direct negotiations were essential. Finding that the only 'negotiations' in the present case had taken the form of proceedings in the General Assembly, Fitzmaurice upheld a British objection that the requirements of Article 19 had not been satisfied.

The issue here is clearly one that is unavoidable. International organisations, as already noted, provide an attractive forum for the airing of certain types of international disputes. How far it is appropriate to regard such exchanges as an alternative to conventional negotiation is a question which judicial institutions must expect to resolve as part of the larger process of settling their relationship with their political counterparts.

Substantive aspects of negotiation

For a negotiated settlement to be possible, the parties must believe that the benefits of an agreement outweigh the losses. If their interests are diametrically opposed, an arrangement which would require one side to yield all or most of its position is therefore unlikely to be acceptable. This appears

---

[17] *Ibid.*, p. 562.   [18] *Northern Cameroons*, Judgment, [1963] ICJ Rep. p. 15.
[19] *Ibid.*, p. 123.

to have been the situation in the *Lake Lanoux* dispute, where the various attempts at a negotiated settlement encountered an insuperable obstacle in the irreconcilability of Spain's demand for a veto over works affecting border waters with France's insistence on its complete freedom of action.

There are a number of ways in which such an impasse may be avoided. If negotiations on the substantive aspects of a dispute are deadlocked, it may be possible for the parties to agree on a procedural solution. This is not an exception to the principle that gains must outweigh losses but an illustration of it, as the *Lake Lanoux* case demonstrates. For there the parties' eventual agreement to refer the dispute to arbitration provided both states with the benefits of a definitive settlement to a question which had been under discussion for almost forty years, and the removal of a serious irritant in Franco-Spanish affairs.

Another approach is to consider whether the issue at the heart of a dispute can be split in such a way as to enable each side to obtain satisfaction. A solution of this kind was devised in 1978 to the problem of maritime delimitation between Australia and Papua New Guinea in the Torres Strait.[20] Having identified the different strands of the dispute, the parties succeeded in negotiating an agreement which dealt separately with the interests of the inhabitants of islands in the Strait, the status of the islands, seabed jurisdiction, fisheries jurisdiction, conservation and navigation rights. The virtue of this highly functional approach to the problem is underlined by the fact that earlier attempts to negotiate a single maritime boundary for the area had all ended in failure.

If splitting the dispute is not possible, a procedural agreement may be used to compensate one side for yielding on the substantive issue. In 1961, the United Kingdom and Iceland ended a dispute over the latter's fishing limits with an agreement which provided for the recognition of Iceland's claims in return for phasing out arrangements to protect British interests and an undertaking that future disputes could be referred to the International Court. The agreement provided that Iceland:

> will continue to work for the implementation of the Althing Resolution of May 5, 1959, regarding the extension of fisheries jurisdiction around Iceland, but shall give the United Kingdom Government six months' notice of such extension and, in the case of a dispute in relation to such extension, the matter shall, at the request of either party, be referred to the International Court of Justice.[21]

Two points are worth noting about this provision. First, while it is phrased in terms which permit recourse to the Court by either party, it is clear from

---

[20] See H. Burmester, 'The Torres Strait Treaty: Ocean boundary delimitation by agreement', (1982) 76 AJIL p. 321; also D. Renton, 'The Torres Strait Treaty after 15 years: Some observations from a Papua New Guinea perspective', in J. Crawford and D. R. Rothwell (eds.), *The Law of the Sea in the Asian Pacific Region*, Dordrecht, 1995, p. 171.

[21] See [1973] ICJ Rep. p. 8.

the *travaux préparatoires* that it was included at Britain's request. Secondly, the reference to the Althing Resolution shows how a compromise can be agreed without prejudicing what one side regards as an important point of policy or principle.

Agreements like the one just quoted in which the parties are able to bring their negotiations to a successful conclusion, while agreeing to differ on what may appear to be a major obstacle to agreement, are not uncommon. Like other diplomatic techniques, such 'without prejudice' clauses are as useful in multilateral as in bilateral negotiations, where the need to avoid sensitive issues may be even greater. A particularly good example may be seen in the Antarctic Treaty of 1959,[22] which succeeded in creating the basis for international administration of the area, while providing in Article 4 that:

1. Nothing contained in the present treaty shall be interpreted as:
    (a) a renunciation by any Contracting Party of previously asserted rights of or claims to territorial sovereignty in Antarctica;
    (b) a renunciation or diminution by any Contracting Party of any basis of claim to territorial sovereignty in Antarctica which it may have whether as a result of its activities or those of its nationals in Antarctica, or otherwise;
    (c) prejudicing the position of any Contracting Party as regards its recognition or non-recognition of any other State's right of or claim or basis of claim to territorial sovereignty in Antarctica.
2. No acts or activities taking place while the present treaty is in force shall constitute a basis for asserting, supporting or denying a claim to territorial sovereignty in Antarctica or create any rights of sovereignty in Antarctica. No new claim, or enlargement of an existing claim, to territorial sovereignty in Antarctica shall be asserted while the present treaty is in force.

A comparable bilateral example is the informal agreement between the United Kingdom and Argentina in 1989 to the effect that discussions between them would take place relating to various aspects of the Falkland Islands issue, but that the question of sovereignty would not be raised.[23] As in the case of Antarctica, the effect of this was that each side reserved

---

[22] Antarctic Treaty, 1959. Text in (1960) 54 AJIL p. 477. For discussion of this and other aspects of the treaty, see J. Hanessian, 'The Antarctic Treaty 1959', (1960) 9 ICLQ p. 436. Also J. Crawford, 'The Antarctic Treaty after 50 years', in D. French, M. Saul and N. D. White (eds.), *International Law and Dispute Settlement: New Problems and Techniques*, Oxford, 2010, p. 271.

[23] The parties agreed to place the sovereignty issue under a so-called 'umbrella', while other differences were discussed. See Evans, 'The restoration of diplomatic relations', pp. 476–7. For the text of the informal agreement, see (1990) 29 ILM p. 1291. The same formula was subsequently employed in the two states' *Joint Declaration on Co-operation over Offshore Activities in the South West Atlantic*, 1995; text in (1996) 35 ILM p. 301.

its position on the sovereignty question, in order that negotiations could proceed on other matters.

It is easy to appreciate why such arrangements are popular with negotiators and to recognise their value in not so much bridging, as creating a detour around, incompatible positions. It seems improbable that in 1959 the question of Antarctica could have been dealt with in an acceptable way without the ingenious formula of Article 4. Similarly, it is only necessary to recall that in 1984 a previous attempt to discuss the Falkland Islands broke down when Argentina insisted on raising the issue of sovereignty, to appreciate the importance of a 'without prejudice' arrangement in that context. Such arrangements are not a panacea however. The issues on which states agree to differ are unlikely to disappear and, to the extent that they are really important, far from being forgotten, will remain as a source of future problems. Within ten years of the 1961 agreement, Iceland was extending its fishing limits again, and it is scarcely necessary to point out that at present neither the status of Antarctica nor the future of the Falkland Islands can be regarded as completely settled. 'Without prejudice' arrangements should therefore be thought of less as a means of settling disputes by negotiation than as a way of managing them. By allowing attention to be focused on those matters which can be negotiated, they allow progress to be made until such time as other more intractable issues can be addressed.

It often happens that the nature of a dispute and the parties' interests are such that in an agreement one side is bound to gain at the other's expense. A possible way of providing compensation in such a situation is to give the less-favoured party control of details such as the time and place of the negotiations. The latter in particular can assume considerable symbolic importance and thus constitutes an element which may be used to good effect. A more radical solution is to link two disputes together so that a negotiated settlement can balance gains and losses overall and be capable of acceptance by both sides. Such 'package deals' are particularly common in multilateral negotiations such as the Third United Nations Conference on the Law of the Sea, where the large number of states involved and the broad agenda made the trading of issues a conspicuous feature of the proceedings.[24]

The fact that today the public dimension of diplomacy has much greater importance than in the past is another factor with a bearing on the substance of international negotiations. For, if negotiation is a matter of exchanging proposals and counter-proposals in an attempt to arrive at an agreement from which both sides can derive a measure of satisfaction, the parties' awareness of an audience consisting of the general public in one or both of the states concerned, and the international community as a whole, can

---

[24] See H. Caminos and M. R. Molitor, 'Progressive development of international law and the package deal', (1985) 79 AJIL p. 871.

seriously affect the outcome. The element of give and take which is usually an essential part of a successful negotiation is likely to be inhibited if every step is being monitored by interested pressure groups at home, while the suspicion that the other side may simply be interested in eliciting a favourable audience reaction may lead serious proposals to be dismissed as mere propaganda. The difficulty of negotiating arrangements for arms limitation and disarmament in the era of the Cold War illustrates both points.

It follows that, in sensitive negotiations, precautions may be necessary to ensure that the demands of the media do nothing to jeopardise agreement. In 1982, when the British military commander was negotiating the surrender of the Argentine forces in Port Stanley at the end of the conflict over the Falkland Islands, he insisted that the official photographer wait in an adjoining room until agreement had been secured. He explained afterwards that he had taken this step to avoid anything that might interfere with the final stages of the negotiations. While these were in progress, the British government imposed a news black-out on Port Stanley for the same reason.[25]

Besides inhibiting possible agreement, the real or supposed need to keep the public informed as to the state of negotiations can itself be a cause of avoidable controversy. In the *Aegean Sea Continental Shelf* case, the International Court was called upon to examine the legal significance of a joint communiqué issued to the press by the Prime Ministers of Greece and Turkey, following a meeting between them in May 1975. The key passage in the communiqué was the paragraph which stated that:

> In the course of their meeting the two Prime Ministers had an opportunity to give consideration to the problems which led to the existing situation as regards relations between their countries. They decided that those problems should be resolved peacefully by means of negotiations and as regards the continental shelf of the Aegean Sea by the International Court at the Hague.[26]

Greece argued that this constituted an agreement to refer the dispute over the continental shelf to the Court and that it permitted unilateral recourse in the event of a refusal by either side to conclude any subsequent agreement that might be needed to implement the obligation. Turkey denied that the communiqué had any legal force and argued that in any event it could not be said to contemplate recourse to the Court prior to the negotiation of a special agreement.

In its decision in 1978, the Court held that both the terms of the disputed instrument and the circumstances of its conclusion were relevant to its

---

[25] For an account of the negotiations, see L. Freedman and V. Gamba-Stonehouse, *Signals of War: The Falklands Conflict of 1982*, London, 1990, Chapter 23.

[26] [1978] ICJ Rep. pp. 39, 40. For a comprehensive review of this decision, see D. H. N. Johnson, 'The International Court of Justice declines jurisdiction again', (1976–7) 7 Aust. Year Book Int. L. p. 309.

interpretation. The background to the communiqué was, the Court found, a situation in which in previous diplomatic exchanges and at an earlier meeting of foreign ministers in Rome, the parties had discussed the possibility of a joint submission to adjudication. The Court found no evidence in the terms of the communiqué to suggest that at the meeting of Prime Ministers this situation had changed and that the possibility of a unilateral reference had been in the parties' contemplation. Indeed, a reference in the communiqué to a subsequent meeting of the parties' experts confirmed that only a joint reference of the matter had been envisaged. Further support for this construction was found in the parties' subsequent practice. From the first, Turkey had insisted that a special agreement must be negotiated, and even Greece had not sought to argue that the communiqué alone provided a basis for the Court's jurisdiction until the initiation of the present proceedings. Thus, the Court's conclusion was that the communiqué provided no basis for its jurisdiction.

In the *Maritime Delimitation and Territorial Questions* case[27] between Qatar and Bahrain, which raised a rather similar issue, the Court reached the opposite conclusion. The first question in that case was whether the minutes of a meeting of the Cooperation Council of Arab States, held in 1990, constituted an agreement between the two states capable of providing the International Court with a basis of jurisdiction. The Court decided that the minutes were an agreement, rather than a 'simple record of negotiations' as Bahrain maintained, and, having established this point, then had to determine the content of the agreement. This called for decisions as to both the subject matter of the dispute and how it should be submitted which presented considerable difficulties. When states discuss submission of a dispute to the Court, they therefore need to be clear about the nature and scope of their commitments if subsequent argument on these matters is to be avoided.

Negotiation and adjudication

Although negotiation is usually involved at some stage in every international dispute and in that sense is related to all of the other methods of settling disputes we shall be considering, its relation to one of them, adjudication, is particularly significant. Negotiation is a process which allows the parties to retain the maximum amount of control over their dispute; adjudication, in contrast, takes the dispute entirely out of their hands, at least as regards the court's decision. It is therefore not surprising that defining the point of transition from one to the other, and establishing the relation between

---

[27] *Maritime Delimitation and Territorial Questions between Qatar and Bahrain,* Jurisdiction and Admissibility, Judgments of 1 July 1994 and 15 February 1995, [1994] ICJ Rep. p. 112 and [1995] ICJ Rep. p. 6. For comment, see M. D. Evans, Note, (1995) 44 ICLQ p. 691.

them, when a court first becomes involved, then while it is functioning, have been matters to which states and international courts alike have had to give a good deal of attention.

One situation in which the connection is important is when states choose to make the exhaustion of attempts to settle a dispute by negotiation a condition of an adjudicator's jurisdiction. Questions which may arise here are, first, what is to be regarded as negotiation for jurisdictional purposes? And, then, how is it to be established that the possibilities of a negotiated settlement have been exhausted? We have already seen that the *South West Africa* cases posed the first question with reference to diplomatic exchanges in the United Nations and the issue can also arise in other contexts. In the *Border and Transborder Armed Actions* case,[28] for example, where the question was whether negotiations in a dispute between Honduras and Nicaragua were still in progress, the International Court decided that the multilateral diplomacy of the Contadora process constituted mediation rather than negotiation, and accordingly rejected an argument from Honduras to the effect that the Court's jurisdiction had not yet been established.

Whether the prerequisites for negotiation had been satisfied was also an issue in the *Armed Activities* case[29] between the Democratic Republic of the Congo (DRC) and Rwanda. Here, the DRC sought to base the International Court's jurisdiction on a number of treaties, including the 1971 Montreal Convention, which provides in Article 14 that any dispute between the parties 'which cannot be settled by negotiation' shall at the request of one of them be referred to arbitration and may then be referred to the Court if the parties cannot agree on the organisation of the arbitration. In its decision on admissibility and jurisdiction, the Court decided that this provision did not provide a basis for its jurisdiction because the DRC had failed to show that it had ever tried to begin negotiations and also did not appear to have suggested arbitration. In the earlier *Lockerbie* cases,[30] on the other hand, Libya was able to rely on Article 14 because its request for arbitration had been rejected by the United States and the United Kingdom and the Court agreed that the dispute could not be settled by negotiation.

Showing that the possibilities of a negotiation have been exhausted might seem to require a demonstration that negotiations of some kind have taken place. Usually this will be so, but, if one party to a dispute makes it clear

---

[28] *Border and Transborder Armed Actions*, Jurisdiction and Admissibility, Judgment, [1988] ICJ Rep. p. 69. The Court's decision on this point and the significance of the Contadora process are further discussed in Chapter 11.

[29] *Armed Activities on the Territory of the Congo (Democratic Republic of the Congo v. Rwanda)*, Jurisdiction and Admissibility, Judgment, [2006] ICJ Rep.; and see A. Orakhelashvili, Note, (2006) 55 ICLQ p. 753.

[30] *Questions of Interpretation and Application of the 1971 Montreal Convention Arising from the Aerial Incident at Lockerbie*, Preliminary Objections, Judgment [1998] ICJ Rep. 9 and 115; and see F. Beveridge, Note, (1999) 48 ICLQ p. 658.

that it is unwilling to negotiate, the absence of negotiations will not be regarded as an obstacle to an international court's exercising jurisdiction.[31] Consequently, when the parties to a dispute specify that negotiations are to have priority as a means of settlement, it will not be open to either of them to delay legal proceedings by the simple expedient of refusing to negotiate. While it is easy to appreciate that any other view would deprive the parties' reference to adjudication of its intended force, a more difficult situation arises when negotiations take place but fail to yield a solution. Here, the party which wishes to avoid litigation is likely to argue that further efforts at negotiation should be made, while its opponent will seek to persuade the court or tribunal that nothing more is needed to enable it to exercise jurisdiction. To spare the adjudicator the delicate task of deciding whether there is still a chance to reach a negotiated settlement, treaties such as the 1965 Convention on Transit Trade of Land-Locked Countries[32] lay down a time limit for use of the preferred procedure.

Under Article 283(1) of the UN Convention on the Law of the Sea, the parties to a dispute concerning the interpretation or application of the Convention 'shall proceed expeditiously to an exchange of views regarding its settlement by negotiation or some other peaceful means'. Accordingly, when a dispute is referred to a court or tribunal under Part XV of the Convention, an 'exchange of views' is a jurisdictional prerequisite, making the interpretation of this requirement potentially very important. Moreover, under Article 283(2), there is a similar obligation where a procedure 'has been terminated without a settlement or where a settlement has been reached and the circumstances require consultation regarding the manner of implementing the settlement'. Thus, an exchange of views is more than an initial requirement when a dispute first arises, but, depending on how it progresses, may be a continuing obligation.

Since an exchange of views is a condition of resort to compulsory procedures entailing binding decisions under the Law of the Sea Convention, it is not surprising that the fulfilment of the requirement has often been the subject of argument. At the provisional measures stage of the *Southern Bluefin Tuna* cases,[33] Japan denied that sufficient efforts to resolve the dispute by negotiation had been made and similar arguments were put forward by the United Kingdom in the *MOX Plant* case[34] and by Singapore in the *Land*

---

[31] See, for example, *United States Diplomatic and Consular Staff in Tehran*, Judgment, [1980] ICJ Rep. p. 3.

[32] 597 UNTS p. 3. Article 16(1) of the Convention provides: 'Any dispute which may arise with respect to the interpretation or application of the provisions of this Convention which is not settled by negotiation or by other peaceful means of settlement within a period of nine months shall, at the request of either party, be settled by arbitration.'

[33] *Southern Bluefin Tuna* cases, Request for Provisional Measures, Order of 27 August 1999, (1999) 38 ILM p. 1624.

[34] The *MOX Plant* case, Request for Provisional Measures, Order of 3 December 2001, (2002) 41 ILM p. 405.

Reclamation case. In all three cases, however, the International Tribunal for the Law of the Sea (ITLOS) reviewed the communications between the parties and concluded that they satisfied the requirements of Article 283. In the last case, for example, finding that Malaysia had informed Singapore of its concerns, the Tribunal ruled that 'in the circumstances of the present case Malaysia was not obliged to continue with an exchange of views when it concluded that this exchange could not yield a positive result'.[35]

Even if the parties are not required to explore the possibility of a negotiated settlement as a condition of international jurisdiction, diplomatic exchanges will usually be necessary to focus a disagreement to the point where it can be treated as an international dispute. In relation to adjudication this is particularly important because, as we shall see later, adjudication is a rather specialised way of resolving conflicts, and cannot be regarded as appropriate for every sort of disagreement. One reflection of their specialised function is that courts, unlike international political institutions, cannot be asked to deal with situations in which there is pervasive tension, but no specific questions to be resolved. It follows that one of the functions of negotiation is to bring such situations into focus so that any issues which might be put to a legal tribunal can be identified. Thus, quite apart from its jurisdictional significance, negotiation will often be needed to make the points of disagreement sufficiently concrete for reference to a court or tribunal to be possible.

Although this screening or concretising function is another significant facet of the relation between negotiation and adjudication, it would be wrong to see a linkage between the two processes as vital, or to believe that negotiation is indispensable. To prove that a dispute exists, it is necessary to show that the claim of one party is positively opposed by the other. Usually this will be done by using the parties' diplomatic exchanges to demonstrate that official representations have defined the points in issue and that efforts to resolve the matter by negotiation have failed. However, there is no rule of law to the effect that a dispute exists only if it is reflected in a formal exchange of representations. If the subject of a disagreement is perfectly clear, then the International Court has indicated that it will be prepared to hold that a dispute exists, even if there has been no official contact. This was the situation in the *Diplomatic Staff in Tehran* case, where the actions of Iran had caused a break in relations but the Court had no hesitation in finding that there was a dispute with the United States, arising out of the interpretation or application of the relevant international conventions.

Referring a case to a court or tribunal is merely one way of attempting to settle international differences and, as several of the cases we have been considering demonstrate, even when judicial settlement has been agreed on

---

[35]   126 ILR p. 487, para. 48. See also on Article 283 the *Barbados/Trinidad and Tobago* case, Award of 11 April 2006, (2006) 45 ILM p. 798.

by the parties in advance, there is no guarantee that it will appeal to them equally when a dispute arises. A further question to be considered therefore is whether, as a matter of principle, the competence of an international court is affected if negotiation is also under way. To avoid misunderstanding it should be emphasised that the issue here is not whether it is open to the parties to agree to give negotiation formal priority. For, as we have seen, this can easily be arranged by including an appropriate provision in the instrument establishing jurisdiction. Rather, the question is whether the relation between negotiation and adjudication is such that it is inappropriate or impermissible for the two methods of settlement to be pursued simultaneously; whether in short the judge must be ready to defer to the negotiator.

This issue was one of the preliminary matters considered in the *Aegean Sea Continental Shelf* case. Certain observations by the Turkish government were interpreted by the International Court as perhaps suggesting that it ought not to proceed while Greece and Turkey continued to negotiate, and that the existence of active negotiations was a legal impediment to the exercise of its jurisdiction. All this the Court emphatically rejected. It drew attention to the fact that negotiation and judicial settlement are enumerated together in Article 33 of the Charter and pointed out that on several occasions both methods have been pursued simultaneously. Moreover, in some cases judicial proceedings have been discontinued when negotiations resulted in a settlement. In light of this, said the Court, 'the fact that negotiations are being actively pursued during the present proceedings, is not, legally, any obstacle to the exercise by the Court of its judicial function'.[36]

Thus, while negotiation is a basic means of attempting to settle disputes, any priority or privileged status which it is to enjoy depends on the parties, and not on considerations of principle bearing on justiciability. This is a sensible approach because it avoids placing unnecessary constraints on the actions of states and recognises that, as international disputes are complex, the chances of a peaceful settlement are enhanced by allowing different procedures to be employed simultaneously. Though relevant to the relation between negotiation and adjudication, this point is no less pertinent in other contexts. For, as we shall see in later chapters, the approach adopted in the *Aegean Sea Continental Shelf* case has been followed in cases where the relation between adjudication and other political procedures was in issue.

The final aspect of negotiation which needs to be mentioned concerns what may be termed the substantive relation between negotiation and adjudication. When the parties to an international dispute attempt to deal with it by diplomacy, they may say and do things in the course of negotiation which could prejudice their case if the dispute is subsequently referred to adjudication. Although the dangers here should not be exaggerated and a

---

[36] *Aegean Sea Continental Shelf*, Judgment, [1978] ICJ Rep. p. 3 at p. 12.

state's actions can sometimes have the effect of improving its case, if such a prejudicial link exists (or is thought to exist) it may make a state reluctant to refer a dispute to adjudication. The answer to this type of problem is to insulate the judicial proceedings from the previous negotiations concerning the substance of the dispute. An example of how this can be done is provided by the Special Agreement under which the United States and Canada agreed to refer the *Gulf of Maine* case[37] to a chamber of the International Court. Article 5(1) of the Agreement stated:

> Neither party shall introduce into evidence or argument, or publicly disclose in any manner, the nature or content of proposals directed to a maritime boundaries settlement, or responses thereto, in the course of negotiations or discussions between the parties undertaken since 1969.[38]

This type of provision is rather rare, which perhaps suggests that excluding the evidence of diplomatic exchanges is only likely to be important when negotiations have been prolonged, or when criteria of reasonableness or acceptability are expected to play a significant part at the judicial stage. In the first situation, however, the value of being able to move from profitless negotiation to a definitive settlement is particularly marked; moreover, the tendency to use equitable criteria for certain kinds of decision means, as we shall see, that, in some areas of international law, the line between adjudication, based on rules, and conciliation, emphasising accommodation, has become somewhat blurred. If, therefore, negotiation is not to be a barrier to adjudication, prohibitions on referring to diplomatic material at the stage when a dispute is being litigated may be increasingly necessary.

Limitations of negotiation

Negotiation is plainly impossible if the parties to a dispute refuse to have any dealings with each other. Serious disputes sometimes lead the states concerned to sever diplomatic relations, a step that is especially common when force has been used. Prominent examples include the severance of relations between the United States and Iran, following the seizure of the embassy in Tehran in 1979, and the breaking of diplomatic relations between Britain and Argentina after the invasion of the Falkland Islands in 1982. Of course, the termination of official relations need not entail the elimination of all contact between the states concerned. It does, however, preclude the

---

[37] *Delimitation of the Maritime Boundary in the Gulf of Maine Area*, Judgment, [1984] ICJ Rep. p. 246. This case is discussed in Chapters 6 to 7.

[38] Text in (1981) 20 ILM p. 1378. A further reference to negotiations is to be found in Article 7(1) which provided that: 'Following the decision of the Chamber, either party may request negotiations directed toward reaching agreement on extension of the maritime boundary as far seaward as the Parties may consider desirable.'

use of the various standard arrangements for diplomatic contact, described earlier, and thus places a substantial obstacle in the path of negotiation.

Similar consequences flow from the use of non-recognition to deny standing to the other party to a dispute, or as a general mark of disapproval. Here, the problem is that official channels are never established. The consequences of this are demonstrated by the Arab–Israeli situation, where for many years the refusal of the Arab states to recognise Israel and Israel's refusal to acknowledge the PLO prevented direct negotiations. It is again possible for the absence of official communication to be mitigated by alternative means, as the extensive discussions between US and Chinese representatives in the years before American recognition of the Beijing government demonstrate. But, where non-recognition is essentially a reflection of the substantive issues in dispute, as in the case of the Arab states and Israel, there may be little reason for such links to be established.

Negotiation will be ineffective if the parties' positions are far apart and there are no common interests to bridge the gap. The variety of ways in which an agreement can be constructed so as to satisfy both sides has already been pointed out. But it must be frankly recognised that in many situations no arrangement, however ingenious, is capable of fulfilling this function. In a territorial dispute, the party in possession may see no reason to negotiate at all. In any dispute, if one party insists on its legal rights, while the other, recognising the weakness of its legal case, seeks a settlement on some other basis, there is little room for agreement on matters of substance, and even a procedural agreement, to refer the dispute to arbitration, for example, may be difficult to negotiate without seeming to prejudice one side or the other.

Disagreement on the agenda for discussion, which may mean that negotiations never get beyond the stage of 'talks about talks', is usually a reflection of a wide gulf between the parties on some such substantive matter. For example, the reluctance of the United Kingdom to place the issue of sovereignty on the agenda of its discussions with Spain on the subject of Gibraltar is a clear indication of unwillingness to yield on the crucial issue of legal title. While it is true that relations between states are not static and that concessions which are unthinkable today may be regarded with equanimity tomorrow, in many disputes, including some of the most serious, until the time is ripe, negotiation can have little to offer.

Even when it is obvious that negotiation has only a small chance of success, it is commonly assumed that the parties to a dispute are duty bound to try. Whether this assumption is correct depends on whether negotiation is ever to be regarded as an inappropriate means of settlement. The answer must be yes. If a different arrangement has already been agreed between the parties, a state which demands negotiation and refuses to use the agreed procedure is in breach of its obligations and has no reason to complain if its demands are refused. This was the position in the 1972 'Cod War' when Iceland repudiated the provisions for judicial settlement in the treaty quoted earlier and the United Kingdom referred the dispute to the International Court.[39]

A more general objection is that the idea that states should always be prepared to negotiate ignores the fact that the terms of any agreement will generally reflect not the merits of each party's case, but their relative power.[40] Admittedly, 'a less powerful party in an international negotiation is not necessarily at the mercy of a more powerful party',[41] and the concept of power itself is a complex one. The fact remains, however, that a state with a completely unjustified claim may well be able to secure a favourable negotiated settlement by bringing superior power to bear. A party which possesses this kind of advantage will naturally tend to demand negotiations and to portray any resistance as unreasonable. But, since it is clear that to negotiate in such a situation is to guarantee that the solution will be unjust, the weaker party has excellent grounds for refusing the invitation.

Another drawback appears if we consider the possibility that the attempt to resolve a dispute by negotiation may be unsuccessful. For negotiations which are unsuccessful do not, as might be thought, simply leave a dispute where it was to begin with. On the contrary, although they can sometimes improve matters by demonstrating that the parties are slowly moving closer together, they can also have the opposite effect. Indeed, because negotiations involve exploring the possibilities for resolving a dispute peacefully, lack of progress may encourage the use of force by seeming to eliminate every alternative. As a commentator on the Falklands dispute put it:

> While negotiations can control a conflict for a certain time while alternatives are being considered, every time an alternative is considered and discarded by mutual agreement, the dispute . . . has less and less room to evolve toward settlement. The successful control of a conflict – not necessarily its resolution – seems to lie in the ability to avoid running short of viable alternatives.[42]

Events in the twenty-year period preceding the war of 1982 appear to bear out this analysis. Initially, the United Kingdom denied that there was any dispute with Argentina, then, when this was no longer feasible, delayed formalising negotiations for as long as possible. The wisdom of this strategy became apparent when negotiations eventually began, because, as one alternative after another was discussed and rejected, the prospects of securing a settlement which both sides could accept soon receded to vanishing point. This does not mean that Argentina was justified either legally or

[39] See *Fisheries Jurisdiction (United Kingdom v. Iceland)*, Jurisdiction of the Court, Judgment, [1973] ICJ Rep. p. 3.

[40] See Northedge and Donelan, *Political Aspects*, p. 282.

[41] J. W. Salacuse, 'Lessons for practice', in Zartman and Rubin, *Power and Negotiation*, p. 255 at p. 257.

[42] R. de Hoyos, 'Islas Malvinas or Falkland Islands: The negotiation of a conflict, 1945–1982', in M. A. Morris and V. Millán (eds.), *Controlling Latin American Conflicts*, Boulder, CO, 1983, p. 185 at pp. 192–3.

morally in attempting to seize the islands by force, nor that the failure of the parties' negotiations should be thought of as making the war inevitable. It does, however, suggest that the ending of negotiations can sometimes be the signal for a dispute to enter a new and more dangerous phase and, as a corollary, that an awareness of these implications can make governments reluctant to become involved with them.

A state can of course bind itself to negotiate by treaty, or find itself in a situation where an obligation to negotiate arises under the general law. In 1997, for example, the International Court decided that Hungary and Slovakia were under a legal obligation to negotiate in good faith to determine how the objectives of a treaty concerning a project on the Danube could best be carried out.[43] In an earlier case, it decided that, according to customary international law, the delimitation of continental shelf boundaries between neighbouring states 'must be effected by agreement in accordance with equitable principles'.[44] Similarly, in 1974 it found that the United Kingdom and Iceland were 'under mutual obligations to undertake negotiations in good faith for the equitable solution of their differences'[45] concerning their respective fishery rights in the waters of Iceland. In all three cases, what the Court was saying was that, since the rights of more than one state were in issue, the matter in question was not open to unilateral regulation, but had to be negotiated.

In the above situations, like the cases of consultation considered earlier, the duty to negotiate exists even before there is a dispute. Often, however, negotiation is laid down as a requirement when a dispute arises and forms either the exclusive procedure, or, more commonly, a necessary preliminary to the use of other methods. An illustration of this type of obligatory negotiation may be seen in Article 41 of the 1978 Vienna Convention on Succession of States in Respect of Treaties,[46] which provides:

> If a dispute regarding the application or interpretation of the present Convention arises between two or more Parties to the Convention, they shall, upon the request of any of them, seek to resolve it by a process of consultation and negotiation.

It is clear, then, that, in some situations, there is a duty to negotiate. Moreover, in others, as we have seen, the parties to a dispute may have a lesser obligation such as to 'proceed expeditiously to an exchange of views' regarding the means of settlement to be adopted. However, it is worth emphasising that, just as there is no general duty to consult other states before taking action which may affect them, so there is no general duty to attempt to settle disputes by negotiation. The various means of

---

[43]   *Gabcikovo-Nagymaros Project (Hungary/Slovakia)*, Judgment, [1997] ICJ Rep. p. 7.

[44]   *North Sea Continental Shelf*, Judgment, [1969] ICJ Rep. p. 3.

[45]   *Fisheries Jurisdiction (United Kingdom v. Iceland)*, Merits, Judgment, [1974] ICJ Rep. p. 3.

[46]   See R. Lavalle, 'Dispute settlement under the Vienna Convention on Succession of States in Respect of Treaties', (1979) 73 AJIL p. 407.

settlement in Article 33 of the Charter are listed as alternatives, and so, in the absence of a specific obligation to negotiate, a state is entitled to suggest that another procedure should be used. In a dispute concerning sovereignty over territory, for example, a state which is confident of its legal title may well advocate judicial settlement, as the United Kingdom did in the case of Gibraltar. Naturally, the offer is unlikely to be accepted if the other party's claim is political rather than legal. But that is hardly the point. Negotiation is simply one means of settlement and, in the absence of a legal duty to negotiate, states are entitled to use it or not as they see fit.

None of the above is intended to imply that negotiation is not an extremely important means of dealing with international disputes. In almost all cases, diplomatic exchanges will be necessary before a disagreement becomes sufficiently specific to be called a dispute, and, once a dispute has arisen, negotiation will often provide the best prospect of a solution. We have seen, however, that, although negotiation must be regarded as basic, it may also be impossible, ineffective or inappropriate. As a consequence, use of the methods described in the following chapters may be essential if any progress is to be made.

2

Mediation

When the parties to an international dispute are unable to resolve it by negotiation, the intervention of a third party is a possible means of breaking the
impasse and producing an acceptable solution. Such intervention can take
a number of different forms. The third party may simply encourage the dis-
puting states to resume negotiations, or do nothing more than provide
them with an additional channel of communication. In these situations, the
intermediary is said to be contributing 'good offices'. On the other hand,
the assignment may be to investigate the dispute and to present the parties
with a set of formal proposals for its solution. As we shall see in Chapter 4,
this form of intervention is called 'conciliation'. Between good offices and
conciliation lies the form of third-party activity known as 'mediation'.[1]

Like good offices, mediation is essentially an adjunct to negotiation,
but with the mediator as an active participant, authorised, and indeed
expected, to advance fresh proposals and to interpret, as well as to transmit,
each party's proposals to the other. What distinguishes this kind of assistance
from conciliation is that a mediator generally offers proposals informally and
on the basis of information supplied by the parties, rather than independent
investigations, although in practice such distinctions tend to be blurred. In
a given case, it may therefore be difficult to draw the line between mediation
and conciliation, or to say exactly when good offices ended and mediation
began.

Mediation may be sought by the parties or offered spontaneously by
outsiders. Once under way, it provides the governments in dispute with
the possibility of a solution, but without any prior commitment to accept
the mediator's suggestions. Consequently, it has the advantage of allowing
them to retain control of the dispute, probably an essential requirement

---

[1] Useful discussions of mediation are to be found in F. S. Northedge and M. D. Donelan (eds.),
   International Disputes: The Political Aspects, London, 1971, Chapter 13; C. M. H. Waldock (ed.),
   International Disputes: The Legal Aspects, London, 1972, Chapter 2B; K. V. Raman (ed.), *Dispute
   Settlement through the United Nations*, New York, 1977, Chapter 3; S. Touval and I. W. Zartman
   (eds.), *International Mediation in Theory and Practice*, Boulder, CO, 1985; United Nations,
   Handbook on the Peaceful Settlement of Disputes between States, New York, 1992, Chapter 2C;
   D. J. Bercovitch and J. Z. Rubin (eds.), *Mediation in International Relations*, London, 1992;
   J. Bercovitch (ed.), *Resolving International Conflicts: The Theory and Practice of Mediation*,
   London, 1996; M. Kleiboer, *The Multiple Realities of International Mediation*, Boulder, CO,
   1998; and M. C. Greenberg, J. H. Barton and M. E. McGuinness (eds.), *Words over War*,
   Lanham, MD, 2000.

if negotiations are deadlocked on a matter of vital interest. On the other hand, if a face-saving compromise is what is needed, it may be politically easier to make the necessary concessions in the course of mediation than in direct negotiation. If a dispute concerns sensitive issues, the fact that the proceedings can be completely confidential is an advantage in any case. As with other means of dispute settlement, however, not every international dispute is suitable for mediation. The first requirement is a willing mediator.

Mediators

Mediation may be performed by international organisations, by states or by individuals acting independently. For the United Nations and a number of regional organisations, the settlement of disputes is a basic institutional objective, and, as a result, the Secretary-General and his regional counterparts are often engaged in providing good offices and mediation. In certain situations, non-governmental organisations can act as mediators. The International Committee of the Red Cross (ICRC), for example, avoids involvement in political disputes, but regularly intervenes where armed conflict or the treatment of detainees raise humanitarian issues.[2] Since it offers the opportunity to become involved in a dispute and to influence its outcome, the role of mediator also has attractions for states concerned to see a dispute resolved peacefully, or with an interest in a particular solution. Thus, it is not unusual to find the course of an international dispute punctuated by offers of mediation from one or more outside parties.

In the dispute between Britain and Argentina over the invasion of the Falkland Islands in 1982, first the United States, in the person of Secretary of State Alexander Haig, offered to mediate, then the United Nations Secretary-General, Javier Pérez de Cuéllar, tendered his good offices.[3] From the American perspective, war between a NATO ally and a leading member of the OAS would force a choice between allies which it strongly wished to avoid. The Secretary-General, on the other hand, was involved in the dispute because Argentina's invasion had already been condemned by the Security Council and almost all members of the United Nations were anxious for a fresh initiative to avert the threat of further bloodshed.

In 1978, when war between Chile and Argentina seemed to be imminent over the implementation of the *Beagle Channel* award,[4] the Pope offered

---

[2] See D. P. Forsythe, 'Humanitarian mediation by the International Committee of the Red Cross', in Touval and Zartman, *International Mediation*, p. 233.

[3] For an excellent account of these initiatives and the attempt by President Belaunde of Peru to develop the results of the Haig mediation, see L. Freedman and V. Gamba-Stonehouse, *Signals of War: The Falklands Conflict of 1982*, London, 1990, Chapters 12–18; and Kleiboer, *Multiple Realities*, Chapter 5.

[4] *Beagle Channel Award* (1977), 52 ILR p. 91. Text also in (1978) 17 ILM p. 634. For discussion of this case, see Chapter 5.

the services of Cardinal Antonio Samoré as mediator, a proposal which both governments accepted. As in the Falklands crisis, the motives for intervention are not hard to identify. For the concern naturally aroused by the prospect of war between two Catholic states was here reinforced by both the promptings of the United States and a tradition of Papal involvement in South American affairs stretching back over five centuries.

In an earlier territorial dispute, the conflict between India and Pakistan over Kashmir in 1965, the mediation of the Soviet Union was instrumental in securing a cease-fire when war had already broken out. The historical and religious connections which inspired the offer of mediation in the previous example were here replaced by a political interest in restoring stability to an area close to the southern borders of the Soviet Union and avoiding the risk of Chinese intervention, while at the same time advancing Soviet influence in the region.[5]

The desire to extend influence is by no means confined to major powers. Indeed, mediation can provide small or middle-rank states with an opportunity to improve relations with larger states, while also safeguarding other interests. In 1980, for example, Algeria pursued a combined good-offices and mediation role in the diplomatic hostages dispute between the United States and Iran. The dispute, after some very complex negotiations over Iranian assets in the United States, was eventually settled. The settlement not only enhanced Algeria's reputation in the eyes of Americans, but, more importantly, resolved a crisis which could have led to war between a superpower and a Muslim state.[6] In a similar way, Algeria's constructive intervention in the dangerous tension between Iran and Iraq in 1975 again served to increase the mediator's prestige and influence in the Muslim world, while also preserving the unity of OPEC, an organisation in which Algeria, as an oil exporter, had a major interest.[7]

In the crisis which accompanied the break-up of Yugoslavia between 1991 and 1995, mediation was attempted by a number of intermediaries, including at various times the European Community (EC), the United Nations working in conjunction with the EC, and the United States. Incentives for EC involvement were the historical and geographical links of many

---

[5] See T. P. Thornton, 'The Indo-Pakistan conflict: Soviet mediation at Tashkent, 1966', in Touval and Zartman, *International Mediation*, p. 141. Similar motives probably lay behind an unsuccessful Soviet attempt to mediate in the Gulf crisis of 1990: see L. Freedman and E. Karsh, *The Gulf Conflict 1990–1991*, London, 1993, pp. 175–9.

[6] See G. Sick, 'The partial negotiator: Algeria and the US hostages in Iran', in Touval and Zartman, *International Mediation*, p. 21; and R. M. Slim, 'Small state mediation in international relations: The Algerian mediation in the hostage crisis', in Bercovitch and Rubin, *Mediation*, p. 206. For Algeria's unsuccessful attempt to mediate when Iraq invaded Kuwait, see Freedman and Karsh, *The Gulf Conflict*, p. 248.

[7] See D. Lieb, 'Iran and Iraq at Algiers, 1975', in Touval and Zartman, *International Mediation*, p. 67.

of the member states with Yugoslavia[8] and for the UN a combination of humanitarian considerations and the issue of peace and security which led the Security Council to adopt measures under Chapter VII of the Charter. The United States, which became involved in mediation at a relatively late stage, had throughout been closely concerned with the crisis in its capacities as a member of the Security Council and NATO and had witnessed the failure of earlier efforts to deal with a critical threat to regional stability.

The cases just considered indicate the kinds of concerns that may induce an offer of mediation. It should be noted, however, that in a significant number of disputes mediation will be out of the question because no mediator is able or willing to act. Third states are unlikely to regard themselves as qualified to act as mediators between superpowers, which are moreover rarely willing to entertain the idea of outside intervention in their disputes. In most situations, too, mediation is an exhausting and often thankless task, which therefore requires a correspondingly strong incentive. Shuttling between Buenos Aires and London in an effort to reconcile the governments of General Galtieri and Mrs Thatcher called for more than patience and an iron constitution. As the Haig mission demonstrates, a state which puts itself forward in the role of mediator may antagonise an erstwhile ally, while sacrificing its own freedom of action. Yet, there can never be any guarantee that these and other diplomatic costs will be repaid by a successful outcome to the mission. In such circumstances, the calculations that must temper an inclination to mediate and the result – that in some disputes a willing mediator may be hard to find – are not difficult to understand.

Consent to mediation

Mediation cannot be forced on the parties to an international dispute, but only takes place if they consent. So, unless they have taken the initiative and appointed a mediator already, their unwillingness to consider this form of assistance may prove a major stumbling block. This is because, although a mediator's proposals are not binding, the very act of mediation has implications which may be unacceptable to either or both of the governments concerned.

By accepting mediation, a government acknowledges that its dispute is a legitimate matter of international concern. If, therefore, a question of international accountability lies at the heart of the controversy, as in the furore over South Africa in the apartheid era, mediation will be out of the question. Moreover, a mediated settlement is always likely to be a

---

[8] See K. Webb, V. Koutrakou and M. Walters, 'The Yugoslavian conflict, European mediation, and the contingency model: A critical perspective', in Bercovitch, *Resolving International Conflicts*, p. 171; and M. C. Greenberg and M. E. McGuinness, 'From Liston to Dayton: International mediation and the Bosnia crisis', in Greenberg, Barton and McGuinness, *Words over War*, p. 35.

compromise of some kind. So, if a government believes either that it can win the dispute, or that the time to make concessions has not yet arrived, there is again unlikely to be room for mediation. The clearest example of the former situation is when a state's position is effectively unchallengeable, as when the Soviet Union refused to accept the mediation of the United Nations Secretary-General following its intervention in Hungary in 1956. An example of the 'no compromise' situation is provided by Nigeria's refusal to accept mediation over the secessionist war in Biafra, which it also claimed was a matter of domestic jurisdiction.

The elements that may induce a government to accept mediation may be illustrated from the disputes already considered. In the Falklands crisis, both Britain and Argentina were anxious to secure and maintain the sympathy of regional allies and to avoid alienating outside states, whose political or economic support might be useful in the event of armed conflict. Here, then, acceptance of mediation was motivated by a desire to project an image of political reasonableness as much as by any expectation of success. In the Yugoslavia crisis, on the other hand, Serbia was under severe pressure from economic sanctions imposed by the UN, the beleaguered Bosnian government desperately needed outside support and neither Croatia, nor the Serbian minority in Bosnia, was in a position to challenge international involvement. These factors made mediation possible from an early stage, although the complexity of the situation and its constantly changing character meant that only the final effort, led by the United States and culminating in the Dayton Peace Agreement of 1995, was successful.

In many disputes, outside opinion is not as important, but other inducements may be present. Unlike the Falklands dispute, where the forcefulness of the British response appears to have taken the Argentine government by surprise, the *Beagle Channel* controversy concerned a situation in which the use of force by Argentina was certain to lead to war. Since Argentina was ruled by a military junta, war could have radical domestic repercussions. In light of this, and the fact that, by setting up the ill-starred arbitration, Chile and Argentina had sought an external resolution of this dispute once already, it is perhaps not too surprising that, following the Pope's timely intervention, they were willing to accede to mediation and try again.[9]

In the Kashmir dispute, on the other hand, war, the product of two decades of hostility between India and Pakistan, had already broken out. What seems to have been the main incentive to accept mediation here was that, having used force to make the point that their respective claims would

---

[9] See M. Laudy, 'The Vatican mediation of the Beagle Channel dispute: Crisis intervention and forum building', in Greenberg, Barton and McGuinness, *Words over War*, p. 293; T. Princen, 'International mediation – The view from the Vatican', (1987) 3 *Negotiation Journal* p. 347; T. Princen, 'Mediation by a transnational organisation: The case of the Vatican', in Bercovitch and Rubin, *Mediation*, p. 149; and G. R. Moncayo, 'La mediation pontificale dans l'affaire du Canal Beagle', (1993) 242 *Hague Recueil des Cours* p. 197.

be defended, neither side had the power to go further and impose its own solution unilaterally. Thus, if hostilities cannot always be avoided, a military stalemate may provide a convenient opportunity for second thoughts.

Mediation is likely to be particularly relevant when a dispute has progressed to a stage which compels the parties to rethink their policies. A stalemate is clearly one such situation; another is when the parties come to recognise that the risks of continuing a dispute outweigh the costs of trying to end it. In the dispute between Iran and Iraq, for example, Iraq's determination to crush the Kurds presented Iran with a choice between increasing its support, leading, almost certainly, to war with Iraq, and offering to withdraw its support for the Kurds in return for Iraq's recognition of Iran's boundary claims. Since Iraq had concluded that the Kurds were currently a more pressing issue than the disputed boundary, the way was clear for the two states to accept a fact-finding mission from the United Nations, a diplomatic initiative by Egypt and finally Algeria's mediation.

In the diplomatic hostages dispute between Iran and the United States, where Algeria was also involved, there had been deadlock for almost a year when Iran eventually made approaches to the United States. A significant factor here was that the domestic turmoil which had accompanied the Islamic Revolution, and which was to complicate the dispute throughout, was beginning to subside. If this made a new policy towards the hostages easier to formulate and put into effect, such a move was also becoming increasingly necessary. Politically, the hostages had probably served their purpose, a presidential election in the United States was imminent and Iran was suffering from financial and diplomatic isolation. When Iraq seized the opportunity to attack Iran in September 1980, the pressure to seek a deal which would release Iranian assets in the United States was further increased. Much hard bargaining would be needed before a settlement was secured, but the United States and Iran were now both in a frame of mind to accept an offer of mediation.

For mediation to get under way, the parties in dispute must do more than accept that it is a good idea. They must also agree upon the mediator. If the governments concerned believe that a would-be mediator has little understanding of their position, is unsympathetic, wholly committed to the other party, or less concerned with their interests than with a selfish agenda, the candidate is unlikely to be acceptable, though if there is no objection to mediation in principle, an offer from a different quarter may be more successful.

An individual's ability to pose as a prospective mediator depends on relevant personal qualities and reputation; a state's on the circumstances, including the time and place of the dispute. In the *Beagle Channel* controversy, for example, not only was the Pope a singularly appropriate mediating authority, but his envoy revealed himself as an immaculate exponent of the art of personal diplomacy. Described as 'tireless, bubbling over with humour and goodwill, a beaming Pickwickian prelate who was also the soul of discretion',[10] Cardinal Samoré was clearly a shrewd choice for this exacting role.

It is sometimes suggested that mediation will only be acceptable if the mediator is perceived to be strictly neutral. Neutrality is certainly important for some mediators and in some situations. The ICRC, for example, is always careful to avoid taking sides in political disputes and recognises that its standing to act on humanitarian issues depends on preserving its neutrality. The same is true of the wider type of intervention practised by the Secretary-General of the United Nations. As we shall see in Chapter 10, the Secretariat has a power of initiative in dispute situations, as well as a role in carrying out functions assigned by the political organs; in both cases, it must act impartially. Elsewhere, however, acceptability is likely to depend more on what a mediator can offer and on being in a position to talk to both sides. Thus, Algeria, an uncommitted Muslim state, was in an ideal position to mediate between Iran and Iraq in 1975, and, as the state which had been entrusted with the representation of Iran's interests in Washington since diplomatic relations were broken off, was also well placed to mediate in the hostages crisis.

In the Kashmir dispute, neither the United States nor the United Kingdom was in a position to act as mediator. The first was too closely aligned with Pakistan, and though the United Kingdom had successfully mediated in the same parties' dispute over the Rann of Kutch only a few months earlier, it had now cut off military aid and was attempting to have India condemned in the United Nations. In contrast, the acceptability of the Soviet Union rested on its interests and influence as a regional power, and the fact that, though more attention had been paid to developing relations with India than with Pakistan, this policy had recently been modified. When war broke out, the Soviet Union refused to condemn Pakistan and so, despite maintaining its military assistance to India, was able to satisfy Pakistan as to its suitability as a mediator.[11]

When states offer to mediate, it is usually because they see either a settlement in itself, or a settlement on particular terms, as furthering some interest of their own. This is well recognised and is therefore not a disqualification, provided the mediator can offer the parties something which they want, or cannot afford to refuse. Thus, the fact that a state has interests of its own and may have close relations with one party to a dispute will not normally be an objection so long as it is on speaking terms with the other party. Indeed, a special relationship with one side may actually be an advantage, for, as a leading commentary notes, when a state which is close

---

[10] *The Economist*, 13 January 1979, p. 54.
[11] See N. Schwiesow, 'Mediation', in E. Luard (ed.), *The International Regulation of Frontier Disputes*, London, 1970, pp. 161–2.

to one party offers to act as mediator, 'the closeness that implies a possibility to "deliver" its friend may stimulate the other party's co-operativeness'.[12]

The inducements to accept particular mediators are well illustrated by the Falklands crisis. There, neither side could challenge the authority of the Secretary-General, who could explore the possibilities of a settlement on behalf of the United Nations, while the situation of the United States bore some resemblance to the Soviet position in the Kashmir dispute. Allied with Britain through NATO, and a potential source of logistical support for the British task force, the United States had also recently sought to develop closer relations with Argentina. Any doubts the latter may have had as to the objectivity of the United States were outweighed by the influence it was in a position to exercise over its ally[13] and by another consideration that may have been present in the previous case – the political cost of rejecting mediation, especially when offered by a powerful neighbour.

Functions of mediation

If mediation becomes possible when the parties suspect that a settlement on their own terms may no longer be achievable at an acceptable cost, then the mediator's task is to devise or promote a solution from which both can devise a measure of satisfaction. This may, of course, be impossible, in which case mediation will fail. But a resourceful mediator has a variety of means at his disposal to avoid this result.

Much can be achieved by simply providing good offices and facilitating communication between the parties. If a dispute is serious enough to call for the services of a mediator, it is possible that events have already had the effect of restricting the parties' contact, or have made it difficult for them to deal with each other openly. In the diplomatic hostages crisis, for example, formal relations between the United States and Iran were broken off following the seizure of the American embassy in Tehran in November 1979 and a subsequent unsuccessful rescue mission. Moreover, since the revolutionary authorities had presented the United States as the enemy of Iran, and corrupter of its spiritual values, it was impossible for Iran to deal directly with the United States, even when Iran had decided that it was in its interests to end the crisis. The elimination of official contact therefore meant that the task of re-establishing communication was performed by a highly

---

[12]   Touval and Zartman, *International Mediation*, p. 257. See also P. J. Carnevale and S. Arad, 'Bias and impartiality in international mediation', in Bercovitch, *Resolving International Conflicts*, p. 39.

[13]   Indeed, according to a leading study, 'The Argentines were generally pleased with the idea of American mediation: securing it had been one of the original objectives behind the occupation of the Islands.' Freedman and Gamba-Stonehouse, *Signals of War*, p. 168.

diverse group of intermediaries and ultimately by the Algerians, whom the parties were prepared to entrust with good offices and mediation.[14]

Once the parties are in contact, a mediator can be useful in loosening the tension which may have developed in the course of the dispute, and creating an atmosphere conducive to negotiation.[15] Such an intermediary can also be an effective channel of information. Thus, in the hostages crisis, Algeria was able to suggest how certain proposals from Washington could be modified to improve their chances of acceptance and in a subtle way convey the message from Tehran that, though Iranian assets in the United States were of great symbolic importance, the financial implications of the arrangements for dealing with them were a secondary consideration.[16] It is naive to believe that all international disputes can be solved by the removal of misunderstandings, but, since the attitude of a party is determined by its appreciation of its own position in relation to its adversary's capabilities and intentions, a mediator's reports may be important in encouraging a realistic assessment of the situation and inducing a conciliatory frame of mind. In the Falklands crisis, for example, there is good reason to believe that one of Mr Haig's first tasks was to convince the Argentine government that Britain's threat to use force to recover the islands was not a bluff, and that the price of intransigence on the terms of a possible settlement would be correspondingly high.[17]

The value of mediation as a source of information should not be over-stated. Mediators are not infallible and, as we have seen, often have interests of their own which may influence what they say and how their messages are received. It is therefore as well to remember that,

> Governments generally do not lend absolute credibility to mediators (or to any other sources or channels). Instead, information received is interpreted in light of the assumed motives and interests of the source or the channel, and in terms of its usefulness in furthering the recipient's own goals.[18]

There is therefore no guarantee that the information brought by a mediator will always be believed; nevertheless, its presence will certainly tend to discourage wishful thinking, while sometimes providing critics of official policy (whose pressure may be important in encouraging a settlement) with a source of valuable intelligence.

[14] For a vivid account of the unconventional arrangements preceding Algeria's involvement, see P. Salinger, *America Held Hostage*, London, 1982.

[15] See H. G. Darwin, 'Mediation and good offices', in Waldock, *Legal Aspects*, p. 83 at p. 85.

[16] Sick, 'The partial negotiator', p. 35. For an excellent account of the value of mediation in situations of this type, see R. Cohen, 'Cultural aspects of international mediation', in Bercovitch, *Resolving International Conflicts*, p. 107. See also G. O. Faure, 'International negotiation: The cultural dimension', in V. A. Kremenyuk (ed.), *International Negotiation*, 2nd edn, San Francisco, 2002, p. 392.

[17] See Freedman and Gamba-Stonehouse, *Signals of War*, p. 176.

[18] Touval and Zartman, *International Mediation*, pp. 15, 16.

What of the mediator's substantive contribution? The aim, as already noted, must be to satisfy both parties. In some situations it will be possible to do this by giving each state all or most of what it wants. This is because the aims of the parties in an international dispute are rarely identical and often quite different. Of course, the fact that there is a dispute indicates that the parties' aims are not entirely compatible, but unsuccessful negotiations may cause these differences to become the exclusive focus of attention. A mediator who can remind the parties of their essential objectives (or cause them to be redefined) may therefore be in a position to suggest a mutually satisfactory arrangement.

In the *Beagle Channel* controversy, for example, Argentina's main interest evidently lay in the effect of the controversial award on its maritime sovereignty, while Chile's centred on respect for the decision and the territorial consequences. The settlement promoted by Cardinal Samoré's mediation therefore confirmed Chile's sovereignty over the disputed islands, in return for relinquishing its rights in South Atlantic waters.[19] Similarly, in the Iran–Iraq dispute of 1975, Iran's support for the Kurds was evidently regarded by the Shah as a means to an end, rather than an essential interest. Consequently, when Iraq decided that its main concern was to secure an end to Iranian intervention, Algeria was able to arrange a settlement containing concessions by Iraq on the border issue.

A state in a strong position will naturally expect a settlement to reflect its aims, though acceptance of mediation usually denotes a readiness to make at least some concessions. If both parties regard themselves as relatively strong and their aims are truly incompatible, then mediation, if it is possible at all, will generally fail. To reduce this risk, the mediator may be able to put extra inducements into the scale of the parties' calculations. In both the Falklands crisis and the Kashmir dispute, the fact that the mediating state was a substantial source of military support for one party was clearly capable of manipulation as an incentive to both sides to make concessions. Moreover, in the Kashmir dispute, India relied on Soviet influence to protect it from condemnation in the Security Council. The possibility of Soviet protection being withdrawn, whether or not the threat was actually made, accordingly increased the leverage which Mr Kosygin could exercise as mediator.[20]

One of the reasons why powerful states are so often called upon to act as mediators is this ability to influence the parties' behaviour by exploiting the strength of their own position. In the negotiations over the future of

---

[19] For the Papal Proposal of 1980 and the 1984 Treaty of Peace and Friendship, which settled the dispute, see (1985) 24 ILM p. 7 and p. 10.

[20] Thornton, 'The Indo-Pakistan conflict', pp. 158–9. The possibility of the Soviet veto being used against Pakistan meant that Mr Kosygin was also in a good position to put pressure on Pakistan. On the value of this type of influence see further Carnevale and Arid, 'Bias and impartiality', *passim*.

Namibia, for example, a prominent role was played by a Contact Group consisting of representatives of five Western members of the Security Council.[21] By acting together, the members of the Group were in a position to threaten South Africa with the prospect of economic sanctions, a form of leverage which requires concerted action if it is to be credible. An illustration of the opposite technique, the rewarding of co-operation, is the settlement of the Indus waters dispute through the mediation of the International Bank for Reconstruction and Development in 1960. By providing Pakistan with the resources needed to control its own water supply, the Bank in effect bought one party its objective, while relieving the other, India, of the burden of the dispute: a settlement in which, with the aid of outside intervention, both parties were able to realise their aims.[22]

Although a mediated settlement must be a compromise of some kind, it does not follow that the parties must be treated equally. Each must be given something, but need only receive whatever it is ready to settle for as the price of ending the dispute. A state in a relatively weak position may be prepared to sacrifice its original objective and accept some substitute satisfaction as a way of cutting losses and saving face.[23] Thus, a party may be content with some symbolic or token recognition of its claims. Here, mediation can be useful in improvising such expedients, especially when there are obstacles to direct negotiation. In the Falklands mediation, for example, there was talk of dual flags and a symbolic Argentine presence on the islands, either of which in other circumstances might have been a suitable inducement for withdrawal.

Because the costs of a dispute end with its settlement, the fact that a dispute has been settled peacefully can itself be treated as an achievement, regardless of the terms obtained. This is often a key factor in promoting the peaceful settlement of disputes, and a skilful mediator is likely to emphasise the credit which a settlement will reflect on the parties, while reminding them of the serious consequences of any failure. The Iran–Iraq agreement was announced to general acclaim at the closing session of the first OPEC summit in 1975, and shows how a successful outcome can be orchestrated. On the other hand, as the 1938 Munich agreement demonstrates, a desire for peace at any price may enable what is really nothing more than the appeasement of an aggressor to be presented as a diplomatic masterstroke.

---

[21] See M. A. Spiegel, 'The Namibia negotiations and the problem of neutrality', in Touval and Zartman, *International Mediation*, p. 111.

[22] For an account of the background to the dispute and the details of the Indus Waters Treaty (1960) by which it was resolved, see A. H. Garretson, C. J. Olmstead and R. D. Hayton (eds.), *The Law of International Drainage Basins*, New York, 1967, Chapter 9. See also S. C. McCaffrey, *The Law of International Watercourses*, Oxford, 2001, pp. 248–50.

[23] See F. Edmead, 'Analysis and prediction in international mediation', in Raman, *Dispute Settlement*, p. 221 at pp. 260–7.

Closely related to peaceful settlement as prominent values are observance of international law and the United Nations Charter, and compliance with judicial decisions and the resolutions of international organisations. These work best when backed by other pressures and even then may not be enough to produce a settlement. Their force, however, should not be under-estimated. The humanitarian mediation practised by the ICRC relies very heavily on the desire of governments to secure the Red Cross 'good house-keeping seal of approval'[24] and the odium which attaches to those who seem to have something to hide. These factors are also relevant to the mediation of political disputes. In the Falklands crisis, for example, if Argentina had wanted to avoid hostilities, Security Council Resolution 502, which called for Argentine forces to leave the islands, would have provided a respectable reason for withdrawal.

In a dispute which neither side can win, both may be looking for such a way out. In the Kashmir dispute, the military stalemate meant that both parties were more concerned with cutting their losses than with achieving their initial objectives. There, mediation provided an honourable escape route in the form of a cease-fire and arrangements for continuing discussions between India and Pakistan on issues of outstanding concern. Agreements like this on future procedure are among the most important kinds of substitute satisfaction. They provide the parties with respite and a sense of progress, while postponing the day of reckoning. Such an arrangement may lead eventually to the resolution of a dispute, as when the mediation of the United Kingdom inspired a successful arbitration in the Rann of Kutch dispute.[25] The difficulty, however, is that, by failing to grapple with the substance of the dispute, a procedural agreement points the parties in the direction of a solution, while leaving scope for second thoughts.

The limits of mediation

Enough has been said to indicate that, as a means of dispute settlement, mediation is subject to important limitations. The readiness to mediate and the need for a mediator have already been considered. Once mediation has begun, its prospects of success rest on the parties' willingness to make the necessary concessions. Although this can be encouraged by a skilful mediator in the ways described, the chances of a successful mediation often hinge on its timing.

In the Falklands crisis, the aims of the parties were diametrically opposed. Argentina's objective was to rule the islands. Although Britain was not committed to retaining the Falklands indefinitely, it was prepared to relinquish sovereignty only on condition that the wishes of the inhabitants

[24] Forsythe, 'Humanitarian mediation', p. 242.
[25] *Rann of Kutch Arbitration*, 50 ILR p. 2. For further discussion, see Chapter 5.

were respected, which in the circumstances made Argentine rule extremely unlikely. A mediated settlement therefore depended on whether either party was prepared to abandon its original aim and cut its losses. But mediation took place before the battles between the Argentine Air Force and the Royal Navy had established who had the military advantage. Thus, mediation had to be tried at a time when both sides could still think in terms of a military solution and in that situation had little chance of success.[26]

In the diplomatic hostages dispute, on the other hand, Algeria was called upon to act when Iran had decided that it was time to end the crisis. Since this was what the United States had been trying to do from the beginning, the mediator's role was to bring the parties into contact and help them to work out the details of a settlement. The timing of Algeria's intervention in the Iran–Iraq dispute was equally felicitous. There, too, the parties were ready for a settlement; moreover, the ground had already been prepared by a diplomatic initiative taken by Egypt and the constructive assistance of a UN fact-finding and mediation mission.

A well-timed offer of mediation will often be able to exploit the efforts of others who may have been involved at earlier stages, or who may still be present in the background. In the Kashmir negotiations, for example, both sides were aware that, if they failed to agree, the dispute would go to the Security Council. In that event, the Soviet attitude would be crucial, which, as we have seen, gave Mr Kosygin considerable leverage as mediator.

Exhaustion or the risks of escalation are other factors which can help the mediator. Thus, in the Kashmir and Rann of Kutch disputes, military action had been tried and the offer of mediation could be timed to take advantage of the parties' search for some alternative. These disputes were therefore ripe for mediation. It is worth recalling, however, that, despite this critical similarity, the effect of mediation in the two disputes was quite different. In the Rann of Kutch dispute, as already noted, mediation led eventually to a binding arbitration. In the Kashmir dispute, however, following the agreement on a cease-fire, no progress was made in resolving the basic issue. When important interests are at stake, as in Kashmir, it will generally be much easier to negotiate a provisional solution than to achieve a permanent settlement. A cease-fire is better than nothing, of course, but, like a temporary filling in a bad tooth, it may mean even more trouble in the future if steps are not taken to get to the root of the problem.

A related point is that, if an agreement concerns future procedures, it may be ineffective unless there is someone to ensure its implementation. The mediator should therefore recognise that, 'left to their own devices,

---

[26] It has also been suggested that, for the Argentine leadership, 'the prospect of defeat in battle was preferable to dishonor. Anglo-Saxon material commonsense, in this instance, did not coincide with the imperative requirements of Argentinean *machismo* and *dignidad*'. See Cohen, 'Cultural aspects' p. 120.

the parties may fall out of an agreement just as it is being made or implemented'[27] and to forestall this possibility may seek to extend the mediator's role. In the Iran–Iraq dispute, Algeria not only supervised the negotiation of the 1975 peace treaty, but also arranged for its representative to be present when the mixed commissions which the parties had agreed upon were created and subsequently during the commissions' deliberations.[28] At all three stages, the presence of a third party helped to maintain the parties' commitment to the agreement and avoided the stalemate and recriminations which had characterised their earlier negotiations.

Despite the negotiation of the Algiers Accord and the careful arrangements for its implementation, in September 1980 Iraq attacked Iran and attempted to recover the territory conceded in the earlier agreement. The war, which lasted for eight years, ended only when both sides were exhausted and again ready to accept outside mediation, on this occasion by the UN Secretary-General. The fact that the war took place is not, of course, a ground for criticising the 1975 settlement, which achieved all that was possible at that time. It is, however, a reminder that there are two types of temporary settlement: those like the Kashmir agreement, which never purport to be anything more than interim arrangements, and those like the Algiers Accord which, though addressed to the basic issues in dispute and intended to be permanent, are unable to withstand the pressure of changing circumstances.

Sometimes, then, mediation may only be able to achieve a partial solution. Even that degree of progress will be impossible if the parties cling tenaciously to fundamentally incompatible positions – if, for example, they are not prepared to acknowledge that a political solution is what is needed, rather than an endorsement of existing rights. In the *Beagle Channel* dispute, Cardinal Samoré's proposals would have been still-born if Chile had insisted on implementation of the original award with all its jurisdictional implications, just as a mediation in the Falklands crisis would have been pointless had Britain refused to discuss the future status of the islands.

In the same way mediation is likely to be ineffective in situations where any solution would require one side to abandon its main objective and receive little in return. This was the position during the crisis which led to the Gulf War of 1991.[29] Following Iraq's invasion of Kuwait in August 1990 and the imposition of sanctions by the UN Security Council, the Secretary-General, France, the Soviet Union and a number of others made several attempts to bring about a peaceful solution. All were unsuccessful, essentially because a key demand was that Iraq should withdraw from Kuwait and not be rewarded for its aggression. This clearly restricted what

---

[27] Touval and Zartman, *International Mediation*, p. 268.
[28] Lieb, 'Iran and Iraq at Algiers', pp. 83–4.
[29] See Freedman and Karsh, *The Gulf Conflict*, pp. 430–2.

Iraq could be offered as an inducement and meant that the main incentive for withdrawal was that it would remove the threat of military conflict. It is therefore perhaps not surprising that, from the very beginning, this was a crisis in which few considered that mediation would produce a solution.

Mediation may also founder if a dispute has become an issue in the domestic politics of one or both of the parties. A government may have adopted a position from which it cannot retreat without attracting accusations of betrayal, or the subject matter of a dispute may be so emotive that the very act of negotiating will be contentious. The situation is even more difficult if either of the parties has a government which is unstable or divided. In the former case, a government is likely to be particularly sensitive to criticism, and in the latter may find it impossible to follow a consistent policy. The fact that an international dispute is a major issue in domestic politics need not preclude effective mediation, as the settlement of the hostages crisis demonstrates. However, it is clear that, where there are domestic repercussions, strict confidentiality is essential during the negotiations. Moreover, since mediation is in this respect subject to the same limitations as other means of dispute settlement, in some cases of this type the gulf between the parties' respective positions will simply be too wide to be bridged.

Thus, mediation can only be as effective as the parties wish it to be, and this is governed largely by their immediate situation. Although this is a major limitation on the usefulness of mediation, it is important to retain a sense of perspective. It would be quite wrong to think that a mediator is merely someone who lends authority to an agreement that is already virtually made. On the contrary, by facilitating the parties' dialogue, providing them with information and suggestions, identifying and exploring their aims and canvassing a range of possible solutions, mediation can play a vital role in moving them towards agreement. Although success will often be incomplete and failure sometimes inevitable, the mediators job is to spare no effort for the parties, and trust that they will reciprocate.

3

Inquiry

When a disagreement between states on some issue of fact, law or policy is serious enough to give rise to an international dispute, their views on the matter in question may be difficult or impossible to reconcile. In such a case, either or both of the parties may refuse to discuss the matter on the ground that their position is 'not negotiable'. Alternatively, negotiations may drag on for years until one side abandons its claim or loses patience and attempts to impose a solution by force. It follows that negotiation, even if assisted by good offices or mediation, cannot be regarded as an adequate means of resolving all international disputes.

With states, as with individuals, experience demonstrates that the risks of stalemate are greatly reduced when a disinterested third party is brought into a dispute to provide the parties with an objective assessment. Internationally, a number of methods of achieving this have been developed. The method with which this chapter is concerned is called 'inquiry'.

'Inquiry' as a term of art is used in two distinct, but related, senses. In the broader sense, it refers to the process that is performed whenever a court or other body endeavours to resolve a disputed issue of fact. Since most international disputes raise such issues, even if legal or political questions are also present, it is clear that inquiry in this operational sense will often be a major component of arbitration, conciliation, action by international organisations and other methods of third-party settlement.

The place of inquiry in the work of the United Nations, the International Court and other bodies will be examined in later chapters. Our present concern is with inquiry in another sense, not as a process which any tribunal may be required to perform as part of its work, but as a specific institutional arrangement which states may select in preference to arbitration or other techniques, because they desire to have some disputed issue independently investigated. In its institutional sense, then, inquiry refers to a particular type of international tribunal, known as the commission of inquiry and introduced by the 1899 Hague Convention.

The 1899 Hague Convention

On 15 February 1898, the United States battleship *Maine*, at anchor in Havana harbour, was destroyed by an explosion which killed 259 of her officers and crew.[1] Relations between the United States and Spain were already strained, and American opinion needed little encouragement to see the *Maine* disaster as the work of the European power. Although Spain denied liability and held a commission of inquiry which found the explosion to have had an internal cause, American suspicions were confirmed when a rival commission, composed of US naval personnel, decided that the *Maine* had been destroyed by a submarine mine.

While it would be wrong to suppose that the *Maine* incident was the fundamental cause of the Spanish–American war which followed, the precipitating effect of what was really no more than a disagreement about the interpretation of evidence sufficiently impressed the delegates to the Hague Peace Conference of 1899 for them to give serious attention to the issue of fact-finding in international disputes. The focus of debate at the conference was a proposal from the Russian delegation for the replacement of national commissions of inquiry of the kind that had proved so unsatisfactory in the *Maine* episode with international commissions for the impartial investigation of the facts and circumstances of international disputes.

After discussion had revealed, among other sources of doubt, a fear on the part of some of the smaller states that inquiry commissions might be used as a cloak for foreign intervention, the conference eventually agreed that such commissions were acceptable, provided a number of important conditions were fulfilled. These were that inquiry commissions should only be used for disputes 'involving neither honour nor essential interests', that they should handle only questions of fact and not questions of law, and finally that neither the creation of a commission nor the implementation of its findings should be regarded as obligatory. With these qualifications, arrangements for the creation and operation of inquiry commissions were outlined in six articles of the 1899 Hague Convention.[2] Their value was soon to be demonstrated.

The *Dogger Bank* inquiry

In the early hours of 9 October 1904, a squadron of Russian warships, on their way from the Baltic to the Far East to take part in the Russo-Japanese war, unwittingly steamed into the Hull fishing fleet near the Dogger Bank. In the ensuing confusion, the Russian admiral formed the erroneous impression that he was being attacked by Japanese torpedo boats which were rumoured to be in the area, and opened fire. The firing, which lasted about ten minutes, caused considerable damage. One of the trawlers was

---

[1] For details of the *Maine* incident, see *Annual Register*, 1898, pp. 362–3.

[2] Hague Convention for the Pacific Settlement of Disputes, 1899, Articles 9–14. See also A. Eyffinger, *The 1899 Hague Peace Conference*, The Hague, 1999, Chapter 10.

sunk and five others were damaged; and two crew members were killed and six wounded.[3]

When news of the incident reached England, feelings ran high and preparations were made to intercept the Russian fleet which, in ignorance of its error, was by now approaching Gibraltar. Before matters could deteriorate any further, intense diplomatic activity by France, which strongly desired to avoid a rupture of Anglo-Russian relations, persuaded the two states to establish a commission of inquiry in accordance with the Hague Convention.

The commission, which was set up in November 1904, was composed of an admiral from each of the parties, together with one each from France, Austro-Hungary and the United States. Its terms of reference were to:

> inquire into and report on all the circumstances relative to the North Sea Incident, and particularly on the question as to where the responsibility lies and the degree of blame attaching to the subjects of the two High Contracting Parties, or to the subjects of other countries, in the event of their responsibility being established by the inquiry.[4]

The Commission spent two months hearing witnesses and preparing its report, which was delivered in February 1905. In it, the Commission found that there had been no torpedo boats either among the trawlers or anywhere nearby and concluded that the Russian admiral had therefore had no justification for opening fire. It added, however, that these findings were not, in the Commissioners' opinion, 'of a nature to cast any discredit upon the military qualities or the humanity of Admiral Rojdestvensky, or the personnel of his squadron'.[5] Following acceptance of the report by both parties, Russia made a payment to Britain by way of damages of some £65,000 and the incident was closed.

The *Dogger Bank* episode furnishes a striking example of the value of the international inquiry commission as an instrument of dispute settlement. Had the issue been investigated by two national inquiries, it is almost certain that, as in the *Maine* case, they would have exacerbated matters by coming to opposite conclusions. Although it may be doubted whether such an outcome would necessarily have resulted in war, since neither Britain nor Russia had previously contemplated such a step, their decision to establish a commission of inquiry effectively removed the risk that a dispute involving issues of considerable sensitivity might get out of hand.

---

[3] For an account of the incident and the subsequent fate of Admiral Rojdestvensky, see R. Hough, *The Fleet That Had to Die*, London, 1975.

[4] Declaration between Great Britain and Russia, relating to the constitution of an international commission of inquiry on the subject of the North Sea incident, signed at St Petersburg, 12/25 November 1904, Article 2. See J. B. Scott, *The Hague Court Reports*, New York, 1916, p. 411. The original French text is *ibid.*, p. 614.

[5] *Ibid.*, p. 410.

In this respect, the inquiry also demonstrated that, provided no actual clash of policy was involved, even disputes involving 'honour' and 'essential interests' might be amenable to the inquiry process. Indeed, it is evident that it was the very sensitivity of the issue that prompted the setting up of the inquiry as a way of relaxing the tension.

In another way, too, the inquiry departed from the pattern envisaged by the Hague Convention. The duty to apportion 'blame' appeared to assign the Commission an arbitral as well as a fact-finding function. The admirals who made up the Commission, no doubt wisely, sought to underplay this aspect of their work and, in a decision of somewhat ambiguous legal import,[6] demonstrated what later experience was to confirm, that in the interests of dispute settlement, legal and factual issues need not always be sharply distinguished.

There was one further respect in which the *Dogger Bank* episode was significant. Before it could begin its investigation, the Commission had to spend precious time deciding upon its rules of procedure. With a view to expediting the work of future commissions, the Hague Convention of 1907 expanded the somewhat skeletal provisions of the 1899 Convention with a series of articles devoted to organisation and procedure.[7] As a result, it was these new arrangements that were followed when the next international inquiry commission was convened.

Inquiries under the 1907 Hague Convention

The first case under the new Convention concerned a series of incidents off the Tunisian coast during the Turco-Italian war of 1911–12. Although France was neutral in that war, the Italian government strongly suspected that French vessels were involved in the shipment of Turkish contraband. The interception of French ships by the Italian navy had already led to two disputes which had been referred to arbitration[8] and when, on 25 January 1912, the French mail steamer *Tavignano* was arrested and two other vessels were fired on, according to Italy on the high seas, but according to France in Tunisian territorial waters, it was agreed to refer the matter to a commission of inquiry in accordance with the 1907 Convention.

The main question for the Commission, which consisted of a French, an Italian and a British naval officer, was to determine exactly where the controversial incidents had occurred. In an attempt to resolve the serious

---

[6] For an excellent summary and analysis of scholarly responses to the case, see N. Bar-Yaacov, *The Handling of International Disputes by Means of Inquiry*, Oxford, 1974, pp. 72–81. See also R. N. Lebow, 'Accidents and crises: The Dogger Bank affair', (1978) 31 *Naval War College Review* p. 66.

[7] Hague Convention for the Pacific Settlement of International Disputes, 1907, Articles 9–35. For commentary, see Bar-Yaacov, *Inquiry*, Chapter 4.

[8] The Franco-Italian disputes referred to arbitration were the *Carthage* and *Manouba* cases. For the Awards of 6 May 1913, see Scott, *Hague Court Reports*, p. 330 and p. 342.

conflict of evidence on this point, the Commission did not confine itself to an examination of witnesses and documents, but also visited the scene of the incident. In its unanimous report, however, it concluded that it could do no more than indicate the areas in which the incidents had taken place.[9] From the Commission's findings, it was clear that, though the arrest of the *Tavignano* may or may not have been in Tunisian waters, the firing incidents certainly were.

The decision to establish the commission of inquiry had been accompanied by an agreement which envisaged that the next step might be a reference of the legal aspects of the dispute to arbitration. Following receipt of the Commission's report, a decision to this effect was taken; but, before the case could be heard, the issue was settled out of court when the Italian government agreed to pay 5,000 francs in satisfaction of the claim. If the *Dogger Bank* case had demonstrated the value of inquiry in defusing an explosive situation, the *Tavignano* case showed how in other circumstances it could be used to provide the basis for subsequent arbitration.

By assigning the disputed issues of fact to a commission of inquiry, the parties ensured that the evidence was reviewed at the earliest opportunity by a tribunal with the requisite expertise. The *Tavignano* Commission, like its predecessor, was ideally constituted for the work in hand and, relieved by the provisions of the 1907 Convention of the need to settle procedural issues, it was able to complete its investigation in less than a month. Although, as we have seen, the Commission was compelled to leave a crucial issue unresolved, the French and Italian governments were sufficiently satisfied with its work to include in their arbitral agreement a provision requiring the use of its report.

Paradoxically, the fact that the dispute was not in the end resolved by arbitration is also significant. For it indicates that, though fact-finding may be envisaged as a preliminary to arbitration, and can certainly function in that way, in practice, as the sponsors of the Hague Convention foresaw, an elucidation of the facts, or even only some of them, may be all that is needed to induce a negotiated settlement.

The next inquiry to be held under the 1907 Convention concerned a situation not unlike the previous case. On 7 May 1917, during the First World War, a German submarine pursued and sank a Norwegian ship, the *Tiger*, off the northern coast of Spain. As in the *Tavignano* incident, the justification advanced was that the vessel was a neutral carrying contraband and the crucial question was the vessel's location. Spain, also a neutral, alleged that the arrest had taken place in her territorial waters; Germany maintained that it had taken place on the high seas.

Following lengthy diplomatic exchanges, Spain and Germany agreed to set up a commission of inquiry under the 1907 Convention, charged with

---

[9] See Scott, *Hague Court Reports*, p. 413.

the task of determining where the crucial events had occurred. The *Tiger* Commission, like its predecessor, was made up of naval officers from the parties in dispute, with a neutral (here, Danish) chairman. Once again, the evidence concerning the vessel's navigation sharply conflicted and the Commission experienced great difficulty in coming to a decision as to exactly what had occurred. In the end, however, it concluded that the pursuit and arrest had occurred in Spanish waters.[10]

Although similar in many respects to the previous case, the *Tiger* inquiry contains several points of interest. This was the first case in which the parties to an international inquiry agreed in advance to accept the report of the commission as binding. This departure from the Hague Conventions underlined the determination of the states concerned to use the fact-finding process to achieve a settlement of the dispute, and, like the inclusion of a legal question in the terms of reference of the *Dogger Bank* Commission, showed how in appropriate circumstances the inquiry procedure was flexible enough to act as a substitute for arbitration.

But, if the binding nature of the decision brought the *Tiger* proceedings close to arbitration in one respect, the Commission's treatment of the evidence served to emphasise the distinctive character of the inquiry procedure. The evidence concerning the location of the submarine and its victim at the material time proved exceptionally difficult to interpret. In part, this was because, as the *Tavignano* case had already shown, the location of a ship at sea is often difficult to determine with great precision and after the event; in part, it was because, unlike the earlier case, the lapse of time between the incident and the inquiry had resulted in the destruction of much important evidence including the submarine with its crew and vital log book, all of which had been lost on a subsequent operation. An arbitration in this situation might have been expected to generate a major argument over the burden of proof. The fact that the commission of inquiry was not a court of arbitration enabled it to assess the evidence and ultimately settle the dispute without addressing this notoriously thorny legal issue.[11]

The last case also involved a German submarine. On 16 March 1916, the Dutch steamer *Tubantia* was sunk by a torpedo on the high seas. The Dutch government claimed that the sinking was the work of a U-boat and that, since Holland was neutral, Germany must pay compensation. Germany, on the other hand, though unable to deny that the sinking had been caused by a German torpedo, since identifiable fragments of the torpedo had been

---

[10] See Bar-Yaacov, *Inquiry*, pp. 156–71. The Commission's report was not published; the documents are in the Library of the Permanent Court of Arbitration at The Hague.

[11] The importance which the burden of proof argument might have assumed is clear from the separate opinion of the German commissioner who examined the issue in some detail. On the general significance of such evidential factors in the work of inquiry commissions, see the comments of H. Darwin in C. M. H. Waldock (ed.), *International Disputes: The Legal Aspects*, London, 1972, p. 169.

recovered, maintained that the torpedo in question had actually been fired at a British destroyer, which it had missed, and must have remained afloat to claim the *Tubantia* some ten days later.

When the war was over, the two governments established a commission of inquiry with the aim of establishing the cause of the sinking. The Commission, consisting of naval officers from Denmark, Sweden, the Netherlands and Germany, together with a Swiss jurist as chairman, heard a variety of witnesses and experts and delivered its report in February 1922.[12] In it, the Commission decided that the *Tubantia* had indeed been the victim of a submarine attack. This was a clear finding of German responsibility, though the Commission was careful to add that it was not in a position to determine whether the torpedoing had taken place knowingly or as a result of error. The German government accepted the conclusions of the report and paid an indemnity of 6.5 million florins to the Dutch government in satisfaction of the claim.

This was the first case in which a commission of inquiry had included a lawyer among its members. Although the Commission's interpretation of its mandate was broad enough to include questions of knowledge and motive among the 'facts' to be investigated, it is clear that there were no specifically legal issues to be decided in this case. The inclusion of a jurist has been seen therefore as a reflection of the seriousness of the matter under investigation – virtually a criminal charge – and an indication that, in view of the exceptional quantity of very diverse technical evidence, the parties regarded a legally qualified chairman as essential.[13]

The *Tubantia* inquiry is also notable for the extent to which the proceedings resembled arbitration. For, although, as we have seen, no legal issue was in dispute and, in contrast to the *Tiger* inquiry, the parties had not undertaken to accept the Commission's report in advance, the exchange of memorials and the handling of the oral evidence were both more reminiscent of a judicial proceeding than of the inquiry provisions of the Hague Conventions.

Treaty practice 1911–40

The desire of states to depart from the pattern of the Hague Conventions, which was so evident in the *Tubantia*, had already inspired a number of important developments on the other side of the Atlantic. In 1911, the United States negotiated treaties with France and the United Kingdom which provided that all differences or controversies between the parties must be submitted either to arbitration or to a Joint High Commission of Inquiry. These treaties, known as the Taft (or Knox) treaties of arbitration,

---

[12] See J. B. Scott, *The Hague Court Reports* (Second series), New York, 1932, p. 135.
[13] Bar-Yaacov, *Inquiry*, p. 178.

laid down that the organisation and procedure of the commissions were in general to be governed by the relevant provisions of the 1907 Hague Convention. However, in a series of significant departures from the latter, the new treaties contained no limitations as to the kinds of dispute which could be investigated, authorised the commissions to make recommendations as well as findings of fact and went so far as to lay down that decisions by a commission as to whether a dispute was subject to arbitration were binding on the parties.

Between 1913 and 1940, the United States concluded a further series of treaties, known as the Bryan treaties, again based on the Hague Convention. Though unrestricted as to subject matter, these treaties conferred no power to make recommendations, but contained another innovation in that the commissions provided for by the treaties were to be permanent rather than *ad hoc* bodies. Inspired by the early Bryan treaties, Argentina, Brazil and Chile concluded the so-called ABC Treaty in 1915, the United Kingdom made rather similar agreements with Brazil and Chile in 1919, and in 1923 sixteen American states concluded the Gondra Treaty with arrangements for inquiry along the same lines.[14]

Though quite extensive, the treaty practice just described did not produce a series of inquiries like those generated by the Hague Conventions.[15] But, if its significance in that sense is negligible, it represents an important step in the development of dispute settlement. For these treaties were an early recognition of the three principles essential to further progress: that permanent or standing commissions offer significant advantages over *ad hoc* bodies like the *Dogger Bank* Commission; that the types of disputes which can be investigated should be unrestricted; and that the ability of commissions to contribute to the settlement of disputes could be increased by authorising them to make recommendations. As we shall see in the next chapter, when these elements were finally brought together, the product was the institutional technique known as conciliation.

The *Red Crusader* inquiry

After the *Tavignano* inquiry in 1922, almost forty years passed before the next international commission was appointed. This was the inquiry set up by the United Kingdom and Denmark to investigate the *Red Crusader* incident in 1961.

As in the other cases we have considered, the incident arose out of events at sea. On 29 May 1961, the Danish fisheries protection vessel *Niels Ebbesen*

[14] See D. V. B. Galeano, 'The Gondra Treaty', (1929) 15 Grotius Soc. Trans. p. 1.

[15] The Taft treaties never came into force, and the procedures laid down by the Bryan treaties have so far been used only once, in the *Letelier and Moffitt* case (1992), discussed below. For further discussion of these treaties and their significance, see Bar-Yaacov, *Inquiry*, pp. 113–17; and J.-P. Cot, *International Conciliation*, London, 1972, pp. 66–74.

encountered the British trawler *Red Crusader* close to the Faroe Islands and with its fishing gear in the water. Accusing the trawler of illegal fishing, the Danish commander forced it to stop and effected an arrest by putting two members of his crew on board. While en route to a port in the Faroes, the crew of the *Red Crusader* succeeded in incapacitating their guards and reversed course. Pursued by the Danish vessel, the trawler was fired at with solid shot and suffered damage to its prow, masts, wireless aerials and radar installation. A British frigate came on the scene, and, after the abducted Danes had been returned to their ship, all three vessels headed for Aberdeen.

In the diplomatic exchanges which followed, it was clear that the Danish government took a serious view of the incident, not least because the Danish boarding party had been unarmed in accordance with a previous request from the British government that this step would reduce tension when British trawlers had to be arrested. With a view to settling the dispute, the United Kingdom and Denmark, after some negotiation, eventually agreed to establish a commission of inquiry to investigate the incident.

The three-member commission was composed of distinguished international lawyers from Belgium, France and the Netherlands Inspector-General of Shipping. Its terms of reference were to investigate and report to the two Governments:

(i) the facts leading up to the arrest of the British trawler *Red Crusader* on the night of the 29th of May, 1961, including the question whether the *Red Crusader* was fishing, or with her fishing gear not stowed, inside the blue line on the map annexed to the Agreement between the two Governments concerning the regulation of fishing around the Faroe Islands constituted by the Exchange of Notes of the 27th April, 1959;

(ii) the circumstances of the arrest, and

(iii) the facts and incidents that occurred thereafter before the *Red Crusader* reached Aberdeen.[16]

The Commission received written submissions from Britain and Denmark and held oral hearings at The Hague. Its sizeable report was delivered to the parties in March 1962. In it, the Commission set out a detailed description of the events which comprised the incident and drew the following main conclusions:[17]

1. There was no proof that the *Red Crusader* had been fishing within the forbidden area, although the vessel was within the area with her gear not stowed.

---

[16] Exchange of Notes of 15 November 1961, para. (b), UKTS No. 118 (1961, Cmnd No. 1575), also in Bar-Yaacov, *Inquiry*, p. 185.

[17] See 35 ILR p. 485 and document B in the appendix below.

2. The *Red Crusader* was arrested, but the skipper, having changed his mind, 'attempted to escape and to evade the jurisdiction of an authority which he had at first, rightly, accepted'.
3. In opening fire after the escape, the Danish commander 'exceeded legitimate use of armed force' because the circumstances did not 'justify such violent action'.
4. The British naval officers 'made every effort to avoid any recourse to violence' between the Danish vessel and the *Red Crusader*, and exhibited an attitude and conduct that were 'impeccable'.

As in the cases already considered, the report of the commission of inquiry facilitated the settlement of the dispute, though on this occasion only after some delay since it was nearly a year from the delivery of the Commission's report to the announcement that Britain and Denmark had agreed to settle the issue by a mutual waiver of their claims.

If inquiries under the Hague Conventions had shown how the desire of states for highly specific types of third-party settlement could be accommodated by investing the procedure of pure inquiry with overtones of arbitration, the *Red Crusader* inquiry displays the process of assimilation taken a good deal further. For, in respect of its composition, its procedure and its findings, the *Red Crusader* Commission was a fundamentally judicial operation.[18] A majority of the Commission were jurists, and had the tribunal been a court of arbitration its blend of legal and non-legal expertise would have been in no way unusual. Moreover, like many arbitral tribunals, but unlike any of the previous commissions of inquiry, no member of the tribunal was a national of either of the parties to the dispute.

As in the *Tubantia* inquiry, the *Red Crusader* proceedings were divided into a written and an oral stage. But an important innovation in the latter was that, as in an arbitration, the principal examination of the witnesses was conducted by the representatives of the parties instead of by the members of the Commission. Scarcely less significant was the parties' decision that the report of the Commission should not be published automatically, as had been the case with the reports of previous commissions of inquiry, but, like an arbitral award, should be published only with the consent of the two governments.

The findings of the Commission, though mainly devoted to the facts of the incident, clearly included important legal rulings. The Commission's findings that Danish authority had been 'rightly' accepted by the skipper of the *Red Crusader* and that the subsequent firing 'exceeded legitimate use of armed force' are, as has been pointed out,[19] legal judgments which, like other features of the case, suggest arbitration rather than inquiry.

---

[18] Bar-Yaacov, *Inquiry*, p. 192.
[19] E. Lauterpacht, *The Contemporary Practice of the UK in the Field of International Law* 1962 (I), London, 1962, p. 53.

What, then, was the difference between the *Red Crusader* inquiry and an arbitration? Two important distinctions can be identified and may well explain the parties' preference for this mode of settlement.

First, by creating a tribunal whose primary concern was to establish the facts, the parties were able to avoid debating the full legal implications of the case. Of course, legal issues of immediate significance, such as the lawfulness of the shooting, had to be considered. Had the matter been dealt with by arbitration, however, it is likely that the legality of the Faroese fishery limits would also have been the subject of argument, because this issue was currently the subject of a clear difference of opinion between Britain and Denmark.[20] Thus, by handling the matter by means of a commission of inquiry rather than by arbitration, the two states were able to obtain a solution to the immediate problem without the delay and precedential implications of a more broadly based adjudication.

Secondly, because the proceedings were in the form of an inquiry, the outcome was a report rather than an award. Despite the Commission's findings of fault on both sides, the question of the effect to be given to the report remained in the hands of the parties. The fact that it then took them almost a year to agree upon a settlement suggests that in this respect a binding arbitration award, specifying damages or some other remedy, might have provided a more expeditious solution. The delay is, however, also a reminder of the importance which governments attach to freedom of action even in relatively minor disputes, and, as a corollary, the usefulness of the inquiry procedure as a means of accommodating this demand.

The *Letelier* and *Moffitt* case

The *Red Crusader* inquiry was followed almost thirty years later by the decision in the *Letelier and Moffitt* case, the first, and so far the only, investigation by a commission established under one of the Bryan treaties.

The circumstances which gave rise to the case were unusual and account for a number of features which distinguish the work of this commission from that of its predecessors. The dispute had its origin in the murder in 1976 of Mr Orlando Letelier, a former foreign minister of Chile, who was killed in Washington DC when a bomb which had been placed in his car exploded. The explosion also killed an American lady, Mrs Moffitt,

---

[20] The 'blue line' mentioned in the terms of reference of the Commission was the six-mile fishery line which Britain had recognised in the 1959 agreement in return for Denmark's recognition of the British right to fish beyond the limit. By 1961, however, Denmark was seeking revision of this arrangement and, following the termination of the earlier agreement in 1962, unilaterally imposed a twelve-mile limit in March 1964. For a review of this episode and contemporaneous developments, see D. H. N. Johnson, 'European fishery limits', in *Developments in the Law of the Sea 1958–1964*, British Institute of International and Comparative Law Special Publication No. 6, London, 1965, pp. 48–92.

and seriously injured her husband, both of whom were also travelling in the car. Mr Moffitt, Mr Letelier's estate and relatives of the deceased then brought proceedings against Chile in the United States, alleging that the state was responsible for the explosion. Following the rejection of a plea of sovereign immunity, the claim was successful and the plaintiffs were awarded approximately US$5 million in damages.[21] However, the judgment was not satisfied and the US courts then rejected an attempt to obtain execution against the assets of the Chilean national airline.[22]

In 1988, the United States made an international claim against Chile in respect of the deaths and injuries, subsequently invoking the provisions of the Bryan–Suárez Mujica Treaty of 1914 between the two states.[23] Although Chile denied responsibility for the incident, it indicated that it was prepared to make an *ex gratia* payment to the US, on behalf of the families of the victims. In view of this concession, the United States and Chile were able to conclude an agreement in 1990 under which Chile agreed to make an *ex gratia* payment corresponding to the sum payable if liability had been established.[24] The agreement went on to provide that the amount of this payment was to be determined by a commission established under the 1914 treaty and that this was to be the sole question to be determined.

The five-member Commission, appointed in a *compromis* appended to the agreement, was composed of Judge Aguilar Mawdsley of the International Court of Justice, from Venezuela, as president, and four other jurists, including a national from each of the parties. The Commission received written submissions from the United States and Chile and at the parties' request had the benefit of facilities provided by the Inter-American Commission on Human Rights. In its decision, which was delivered in January 1992, the Commission reviewed the numerous legal and factual issues pertaining to the question of compensation, and, after considering the various individual claims, unanimously awarded sums amounting in total to just over US$2.5 million.[25]

In accordance with the parties' original intentions, the decision effectively settled the dispute. It will be recalled that the parties had already undertaken to treat the Commission's decision as binding and within a month of the ruling Chile agreed to pay the total sum awarded, to be divided among the relatives of those killed.

As in the *Red Crusader*, the task given to the Commission in this case was essentially judicial, and this was reflected in all stages of its work. Its membership included prominent international lawyers, and, though the

---

[21] See 63 ILR p. 378; see also the note in 88 ILR p. 747.   [22] See 79 ILR p. 561.

[23] Treaty for the Settlement of Disputes that May Occur Between the United States and Chile, 1914, US Treaty Series No. 621.

[24] Chile–United States: Agreement to Settle Dispute Concerning Compensation for the Deaths of Letelier and Moffitt, 1990, (1991) 30 ILM p. 422.

[25] See 88 ILR p. 727; also in (1992) 31 ILM p. 1.

nature of the issues made examination of witnesses unnecessary, the parties filed what in effect were written pleadings and could comment in writing on the other's observations. No arrangements for publication of the decision were made, although in the event it was not treated as confidential.

The Commission's decision, like the report in the *Red Crusader*, included several important legal rulings, as well as numerous findings of fact. Indeed, the former were much more important here than in the earlier case, because where compensation is in issue the principles governing assessment supply the framework for identifying the relevant facts. In this respect, it is notable that the *compromis* specifically required the Commission to give its decision 'in accordance with applicable principles of international law', which led it to refer *inter alia* to the decision of the Permanent Court of International Justice in the *Chorzów Factory* case,[26] and to the practice of judicial and arbitral tribunals with regard to non-pecuniary loss, as well as to questions such as remoteness and compensation for special expenses. The significance of the decision as a contribution to international law was further explored in Professor Orrego Vicuña's concurring opinion.

The Commission did not, of course, decide that Chile was responsible for the act of terrorism, but the fact that the sum involved was paid *ex gratia* affects neither the legal basis of the decision, nor the genuine nature of the argumentation. As Professor Orrego Vicuña observed, the parties argued their cases with professional skill and 'every relevant point of law and fact [was] controverted by the parties with precision during the proceedings'.[27] Thus, although the United States originally invoked the 1914 treaty 'to investigate and report upon the facts' surrounding the victims' deaths, the Commission which was eventually set up functioned less as a commission of inquiry of the traditional type and more like a court of arbitration, producing a binding decision and deciding issues of law as well as fact. The *Letelier and Moffitt* case thus confirms a general point made earlier that commissions of inquiry can sometimes be used in unexpected ways, and a specific point, as we shall encounter again in Chapter 5, that when a face-saving solution is wanted, procedures such as inquiry and arbitration can help by enabling certain issues to be resolved authoritatively, while leaving others, such as responsibility, undecided.

The value of inquiry

It is clear from the cases we have considered that, from its inception in the *Dogger Bank* case to its latest use in the *Letelier and Moffitt* case, the international commission of inquiry has compiled a worthwhile yet curiously ambivalent record. Envisaged by the Hague Conventions as an institution

---

[26] *Chorzów Factory* case, PCIJ Series A, No. 17.
[27] Orrego Vicuña, concurring opinion, section 5, 88 ILR p. 741.

for the management of a relatively narrow range of disputes, inquiry has been employed in cases in which 'honour' and 'essential interests' were unquestionably involved, for the determination of legal as well as factual issues, and by tribunals whose composition and proceedings more closely resembled courts than commissions of inquiry as originally conceived. On the other hand, this lateral extension of the role of the commission of inquiry has not, as might have been expected, generated a corresponding increase in business. On the contrary, the four inquiries between 1905 and 1922 were followed by a forty-year gap until the *Red Crusader* in 1962, and, despite the elaborate provisions of various treaties and a General Assembly resolution[28] urging the use of fact-finding procedures, there has been only one case since. These apparently contradictory tendencies tell us a good deal about the settlement of international disputes in the modern world.

The utilisation of inquiry for disputes as varied as the *Dogger Bank* and *Tavignano* cases is a reminder that, where sovereign states are concerned, form is subordinate to function. Since international disputes are infinitely various in their circumstances and subject matter, it is not surprising that in their search for acceptable procedures states have adapted the inquiry technique to provide a range of institutional solutions, from the 'pure' fact-finding of the *Tiger* inquiry, to the near arbitration of the *Red Crusader* and *Letelier and Moffitt* inquiries.

Why, then, if the inquiry procedure is so flexible, is it not more widely used? Here the answer is more complex.

First – and the point is so obvious it may easily be overlooked – it is sometimes unnecessary to set up an inquiry because a situation in which the facts are open to different interpretations proves amenable to negotiation. In May 1999, for example, during the eleven-week NATO air campaign against the Federal Republic of Yugoslavia, a US aircraft bombed the Chinese embassy in Belgrade, killing three Chinese nationals and wounding twenty others. The attack was evidently a mistake as those who planned the raid were under the impression that the building was a Yugoslav arms agency, having relied on incorrect intelligence information from the US authorities. As the attack was highly controversial and the circumstances initially unclear, the matter could in principle have been investigated through an international inquiry. In the event, however, it was resolved through discussions involving an explanation and apology and the payment of compensation by the United States.[29]

---

[28] Resolution 2329 (XXII), 18 December 1967. Text in Waldock, *Legal Aspects*, p. 175. See also United Nations, *Handbook on the Peaceful Settlement of Disputes between States*, New York, 1992, Chapter 2B.

[29] See (2000) 94 AJIL p. 127, and for another episode involving these states (2001) 95 AJIL p. 630. See also the acceptance by the United States in March 1989 of an offer of compensation by Iraq for the attack on the USS *Stark* while on station in the Persian Gulf in 1987. See (1989) 83 AJIL p. 561.

A second point is that, when an inquiry is needed, there are a number of ways in which it can be carried out without recourse to the machinery of the Hague Conventions. The League of Nations set up its own commissions of inquiry in seven cases, including the Åland Islands dispute between Finland and Sweden in 1921 and the Mosul dispute between Britain and Turkey in 1925.[30] These commissions, which did not include representatives of the parties, examined the circumstances of each dispute in considerable detail and in some cases also attempted conciliation. The United Nations has used inquiry in a similar way. In 1982, for example, the Security Council established a fact-finding commission to investigate an attempted coup led by foreign mercenaries in the Seychelles, and, when chemical weapons were used in the Iran–Iraq war in 1984, Secretary-General Pérez de Cuéllar sent a commission of Swiss, Swedish, Spanish and Australian experts to study the situation at the front and report back.[31]

An unusual procedure similar in some respects to inquiry is the process established by the Security Council to deal with claims arising from the invasion of Kuwait by Iraq in 1990. Using a body called the UN Compensation Commission,[32] the process enables governments, companies and international organisations to have claims for compensation assessed by expert panels and to receive payment from a special fund financed from a levy on Iraqi oil sales. A very large number of such claims have now been reviewed, resulting in the payment of several billion dollars of compensation. Contrary to what might be thought, the process involved here is not arbitration or adjudication, but administrative in nature as the broad issue of Iraq's liability was settled by Security Council Resolution 687 in 1991, and the proceedings before the Commission are not adversarial and are usually conducted through written submissions. Thus, in the words of the Secretary-General, the Commission 'performs an essentially fact-finding function of examining claims, verifying their validity, evaluating losses, assessing payments and resolving disputed claims'.[33]

The UN's specialised agencies can also conduct inquiries in certain situations. Thus, the ILO has on several occasions created commissions of inquiry to deal with complaints relating to labour conventions, and in September 1983 the ICAO instructed its Secretary-General to investigate the *KE 007* incident, which involved the shooting down of a South Korean jumbo jet

---

[30] See Cot, *International Conciliation*, p. 250.

[31] See R. R. Probst, '"Good offices" in international relations in light of Swiss practice and experience', (1987) 201 *Hague Recueil des Cours*, p. 211 at p. 372.

[32] For a description of the Commission, see J. R. Crook, 'The United Nations Compensation Commission – A new structure to enforce state responsibility', (1993) 87 AJIL p. 144; and, for an account of some of its recent work, see M. Kazazi, 'Environmental damage in the work of the UN Compensation Commission', in M. Bowman and A. E. Boyle (eds.), *Environmental Damage in International and Comparative Law*, Oxford, 2002, p. 111.

[33] UN Doc. S/2259, 2 May 1991, para. 20, quoted in J. Collier and V. Lowe, *The Settlement of Disputes in International Law*, Oxford, 1999, p. 42.

in Soviet airspace. The inquiry report,[34] which was ready by the end of the year, complained of the lack of Soviet co-operation and was unable to shed light on all aspects of the incident. It did, however, serve to establish many of the facts and provided the basis for a resolution in which the ICAO Council condemned the Soviet attack. The resolution in turn facilitated the adoption in May 1984 of an amendment to the Chicago Convention on Civil Aviation, designed to reduce the risk of such incidents in the future. Here, then, an inquiry by an organisation was possible without the consent of one of the states involved, and, though the report cannot be said to have settled the dispute, had an important bearing on its consequences.

In 1993, the World Bank created a kind of standing inquiry procedure when it established an Inspection Panel[35] to receive and review requests from communities, organisations or groups who believe they may be adversely affected by a project funded by the Bank and claim the project may contravene the Bank's operational policies and practices. The Panel's task is first to recommend to the Executive Directors whether the matter should be investigated and then, if asked to do so, to carry out an inspection. The findings of the Panel are not binding, but, based as they are on impartial investigation, utilising visits and consultations, carry considerable weight. As evaluation has a quasi-judicial aspect, Panel reports go beyond inquiry in the strict sense, but clearly incorporate a significant fact-finding element. The World Bank's Panel has begun to develop a useful practice[36] and both the Inter-American Development Bank and the Asian Development Bank now have similar mechanisms.

Regional organisations also set up inquiry commissions from time to time and, as we shall see in Chapter 8, the 1982 Law of the Sea Convention has provision for inquiry in its articles on 'special arbitration'. It was noted earlier that inquiry in the operational sense is a frequent component of judicial settlement. Presumably, therefore, with the creation of standing judicial tribunals in the form of the Permanent Court of International Justice and its successor, the present International Court of Justice, litigation has been employed in a number of disputes which might otherwise have provided

---

[34] *Destruction of Korean Air Lines Boeing 747 over Sea of Japan 31 August 1983 Report of ICAO Fact-Finding Investigation*, (1983) ICAO Doc. C-WP/7764, Attachment, p. 1, reproduced in part in (1984) 23 ILM p. 864.

[35] For comment on the Panel and its significance, see C. Chinkin, 'Alternative dispute resolution under international law', in M. D. Evans, *Remedies in International Law: The Institutional Dilemma*, Oxford, 1998, p. 123 at pp. 134–7; and P. Sands, *Principles of International Environmental Law*, 2nd edn, Cambridge, 2003, pp. 210–11.

[36] See R. E. Bissell, 'Recent practice of the Inspection Panel of the World Bank', (1997) 91 AJIL p. 741; and A. N. Gowlland Gualtieri, 'The environmental accountability of the World Bank to non-state actors: Insights from the Inspection Panel', (2001) 72 BYBIL p. 213. Also D. French and R. Kirkham, 'Complaint and grievance mechanisms in international dispute settlement', in D. French, M. Saul and N. D. White (eds.), *International Law and Dispute Settlement, New Problems and Techniques*, Oxford, 2010, p. 57 at pp. 68–72.

subjects for inquiry. Likewise, we shall see in the next chapter that the early inquiry commissions were followed in the inter-war period and afterwards by commissions of conciliation, which suggests that the blending of inquiry with conciliation in the League of Nations era also had a diversionary effect.

The fact that there are now many alternatives to the traditional inquiry commission is therefore another reason for the relatively small number of cases. There is, however, a third and more fundamental explanation. All forms of third-party settlement have proved less popular than was once anticipated. States have no compelling reason to regard inquiry as more attractive than, say, judicial settlement, and, as will be seen later, they are prepared to refer disputes to international courts and tribunals only in somewhat exceptional circumstances. The fact of the matter is that states are often less interested in settling a dispute than in having their view prevail. The *KE 007* incident illustrates the point perfectly. This incident, in some ways reminiscent of the *Dogger Bank* affair, might be thought well suited to an inquiry commission of the traditional type. It is true that a dispute involving security interests, accusations of spying and perhaps questions about the Soviet chain of command, is not the kind of dispute which those who drew up the Hague Conventions had in mind. Yet, as we have seen, the commission of inquiry can be, and has been, adapted to deal with just this type of case. From the technical point of view, there would therefore have been no difficulty in establishing an international commission of inquiry to investigate the incident. What prevented this from being done was not any lack of flexibility in the procedures available for dispute settlement, but an unwillingness on the part of the Soviet Union to have its account of the incident or its actions challenged in an international forum. Although this could not prevent the matter from being investigated by the ICAO, it clearly ruled out any possibility of a consensual inquiry commission of the type we have been considering.

It is therefore only in situations in which certain special conditions are satisfied that there is scope for setting up an inquiry commission. As already indicated, these are that the disputed issue is largely one of fact, rather than law or policy, that no other procedure is being employed and, most important of all, that the parties are willing to accept that their version of events may be shown to be wrong. Such a combination of circumstances evidently does not occur very often. When it does, the highly satisfactory outcome of the two most recent cases demonstrates that as a means of dispute settlement the international commission of inquiry can still produce useful results.

4

Conciliation

Conciliation has been defined as:

> A method for the settlement of international disputes of any nature according to which a Commission set up by the Parties, either on a permanent basis or an *ad hoc* basis to deal with a dispute, proceeds to the impartial examination of the dispute and attempts to define the terms of a settlement susceptible of being accepted by them or of affording the Parties, with a view to its settlement, such aid as they may have requested.[1]

The eclectic character of the method is at once apparent. If mediation is essentially an extension of negotiation, conciliation puts third-party intervention on a formal legal footing and institutionalises it in a way comparable, but not identical, to inquiry or arbitration. For the fact-finding exercise that is the essence of inquiry may or may not be an important element in conciliation, while the search for terms 'susceptible of being accepted' by the parties, but not binding on them, provides a sharp contrast with arbitration and a reminder of the link between conciliation and mediation.

The emergence of conciliation

The first treaty to provide for conciliation was concluded between Sweden and Chile in 1920.[2] Its emphasis, however, was on inquiry and the only reference to conciliation is in an article putting it forward as an optional

---

[1] The quotation is from Article 1 of the Regulations on the Procedure of International Conciliation adopted by the Institute of International Law in 1961. See (1961) 49 (ii) *Annuaire* pp. 385–91. For comment on these provisions, see H. Fox, 'Conciliation', in C. M. H. Waldock (ed.), *International Disputes: The Legal Aspects*, London, 1972, p. 93. N. Bar-Yaacov, *The Handling of International Disputes by Means of Inquiry*, Oxford, 1974, Chapters 5 and 7, gives a good account of conciliation from the inquiry aspect. For general surveys, see J.-P. Cot, *International Conciliation*, London 1972; and United Nations *Handbook on the Peaceful Settlement of Disputes between States*, New York, 1992, Chapter 2E. Also S. M. G. Koopmans, *Diplomatic Dispute Settlement*, The Hague, 2008.

[2] For discussion of the treaty between the United States and Canada relating to boundary waters (1909) and the activities of the International Joint Commission, see Chapter 1. For detailed accounts of the development of conciliation, see J. Efremoff, 'La conciliation internationale', (1927) 18 *Hague Recueil des Cours* p. 5, and 'L'organisation de la conciliation comme moyen de prévenir les guerres', (1937) 59 *Hague Recueil des Cours* p. 103. See also C. C. Hyde, 'The place of commissions of inquiry and conciliation treaties in the peaceful settlement of disputes', (1929) 10 BYBIL p. 96.

procedure. A number of treaties at about this time dealt with conciliation in a similar way, though in others it was given a more prominent place. In 1921, for example, conciliation and arbitration were laid down as alternative means of settlement in a treaty between Germany and Switzerland. If conciliation were chosen, a Permanent Board of Conciliation would be charged with the two-fold task of investigating the facts and the law and formulating proposals for a solution. In 1922, the Assembly of the League of Nations, after some debate, adopted a resolution in which it recommended member states to conclude agreements providing for the submission of disputes to conciliation commissions, and with this encouragement more than twenty treaties providing for some form of conciliation were signed in the first five years of the decade.

The year 1925 was marked by two important developments. First, a treaty between France and Switzerland defined the functions of permanent conciliation commissions in terms which were to become the model for later treaties:[3]

> The duty of the Permanent Conciliation Commission shall be to elucidate the questions in dispute, to collect with that object all useful information by inquiry or otherwise, and to endeavour to bring the Parties to an agreement. It may, after examining the case, intimate to the Parties the terms of settlement which seem to it suitable, and lay down a time-limit within which they are to reach their decision.

> At the close of its proceedings the Commission shall draw up a report stating, as the case may be, either that the Parties have come to an agreement and, if need be, the terms of the agreement, or that it has proved impossible to effect a settlement.

> The Commission's proceedings must, unless the Parties otherwise agree, be concluded within six months of the day on which the dispute was laid before the Commission.[3]

Then, shortly afterwards, in the four bilateral Locarno treaties,[4] Germany agreed with Belgium, France, Czechoslovakia and Poland that, except where the parties agreed to refer a legal dispute to judicial settlement or arbitration, all disputes between them should be subject to conciliation. The powers of the Permanent Commissions provided for in the Locarno treaties were virtually identical to those provided for in the Franco-Swiss treaty, and this formula was again employed when the Locarno approach was endorsed by the Assembly of the League of Nations and embodied in the multilateral General Act for the Pacific Settlement of International Disputes in 1928.

---

[3] M. Habicht, *Post War Treaties for the Pacific Settlement of International Disputes*, Cambridge, MA, 1931, p. 226.

[4] There were seven Locarno treaties in total: the four mentioned in the text and three treaties of guarantee.

Under the General Act, the parties agreed to set up permanent bilateral commissions, or an *ad hoc* commission if no permanent commission was in existence at the time of the dispute. Conciliation was to be compulsory unless the states concerned had accepted the jurisdiction of the Permanent Court and if conciliation was unsuccessful the dispute had to be taken to arbitration. The General Act was revised in 1949, but no change was made in these arrangements, which had also been incorporated in a treaty between Czechoslovakia, Romania and the Kingdom of the Serbs, Croatians and Slovenes in 1929.

Although much influenced in its early period by the example of the Bryan treaties, conciliation acquired its prominence as a means of dispute settlement from treaty practice in Europe. It was not long, however, before the new process crossed the Atlantic. As early as 1923, the United States and five Central American states signed the Treaty of Washington, which provided for the creation of commissions with powers of conciliation as well as inquiry. As already noted, the Gondra Treaty of the same year reverted to the Bryan arrangements for enlarged inquiry, but, in response to the General Act and the vogue for conciliation in Europe, the Inter-American General Convention of Conciliation (1929) revised the Gondra Treaty to enable commissions of inquiry, established under Article IV, to exercise wide powers of conciliation. These developments were taken a stage further in 1933, when a protocol to the 1929 Treaty provided for the creation of permanent bilateral commissions, and at the same time the multilateral Saavedra Lamas Agreement[5] incorporated conciliation provisions modelled on those of the General Act.

The period between 1925 and the Second World War saw the climax of the worldwide movement in favour of conciliation, and by 1940 nearly 200 treaties had been concluded. The majority were patterned on the 1925 Franco-Swiss treaty, though there were significant differences of approach to such important matters as the function of commissions of conciliation and their procedure which, as we shall see, were subsequently reflected in their work.

The work of commissions of conciliation

In 1931, a Germano-Lithuanian Commission met to consider a dispute occasioned by the expulsion of five Germans from Memel. Three years later, a Belgium–Luxembourg Commission examined a dispute over contraband traffic, and in 1938 a dispute between Denmark and Lithuania over the construction of a railway was referred to conciliation. It is known that all three disputes were eventually settled on the basis of the commissions' recommendations, but information concerning the activities of these and

---

[5] See P. C. Jessup, 'The Argentine Anti-War Pact', (1934) 28 AJIL p. 538.

other commissions in the inter-war period is scant, owing to the confidential nature of the procedure and the fact that their reports were never published.[6] The work of later commissions is better documented, and, by studying some of the more prominent cases, it is possible to grasp the purposes for which the machinery described in the previous section has been employed.

The Chaco Commission[7] was set up after an outbreak of fighting at Fort Vanguardia on the border between Bolivia and Paraguay. Established as a result of the good offices of the Conference of American States, meeting to revise the Gondra Treaty, the Commission consisted of two delegates from each party to the dispute and one each from the United States and four other American states. Under the terms of the protocol creating the Commission, its functions were to carry out an inquiry and to submit proposals for a settlement. If its proposals were not accepted, it was to draw up a report and, if it was not able to effect conciliation, it was 'to establish both the truth of the matter investigated and the responsibilities which, in accordance with international law, may appear as a result of its investigation'.[8]

The Commission met for six months and studied a large quantity of evidence from each of the parties, as well as the testimony of both sides' prisoners. In September 1929, it unanimously adopted a resolution of conciliation, in which it was able to announce that the parties had agreed to a mutual waiver of their claims, to a restoration of the territorial *status quo* and to a resumption of diplomatic relations.

The success of the Commission meant that it had no need to draw up a report. It is clear, nonetheless, that a large part of the Commission's time was taken up with the investigation of how the fighting had broken out and other disputed questions of fact. In this respect, the Chaco Commission bears an obvious resemblance to the cases considered in the previous chapter, with the important difference that here inquiry was not the sole, nor even the primary, function of the commission, but simply a way of preparing the ground for the parties' reconciliation.

A very different kind of frontier dispute came before the Franco-Siamese Conciliation Commission in 1947.[9] Siam claimed that its frontier with French Indo-China should be altered for a combination of ethnic, geographical and economic reasons; France disagreed. An agreement between

---

[6] An outline of the work of pre-war commissions of conciliation can be found in Cot, *International Conciliation*, pp. 91–2; and Koopmans, *Diplomatic Dispute Settlement*, pp. 87–9.

[7] See *Proceedings of the Commission of Inquiry and Conciliation, Bolivia and Paraguay, March 13, 1929–September 13, 1929* (1929). For commentary, see L. Woolsey, 'Commission of inquiry and conciliation, Bolivia and Paraguay', (1929) 23 AJIL p. 110 and (1930) 24 AJIL pp. 122 and 573.

[8] See (1929) 23 AJIL p. 98.

[9] See S. Bastid, 'La Commission de conciliation franco-siamoise', in *Etudes en l'honneur de Georges Scelle*, vol. I, Paris, 1950, p. 1.

the two states established a conciliation commission, composed of one representative of each party and three neutral commissioners, to consider the question. Both the composition and the powers of the Commission were established in accordance with the 1928 General Act.

After hearing the parties' evidence and their replies to certain questions, the Commission tried to move the parties towards agreement. When this proved unsuccessful, the Commission drew up a report in which it summarised the parties' arguments and its own conclusions and made a number of specific recommendations. Although it suggested minor adjustments of the frontier, together with certain modifications to the frontier regime, the Commission's report was effectively a rejection of the Siamese claim. The Siamese request for the transfer of the whole of Laos was rejected as beyond the Commission's competence, while its examination of the ethnic, geographical and economic evidence led the Commission to conclude that there would be no advantage in moving the frontier in any of the other disputed areas.

In the Franco-Siamese dispute, the Commission's investigation of the facts was not concerned with specific events, as in the Chaco case, but rather with the whole ethnic, geographical and economic situation in the frontier region. Moreover, the Commission's concern was not merely to identify the relevant material on these matters, but also to determine its significance with respect to the issue of frontier rectification and conciliation, a matter of interpretation of the evidence with no counterpart in the earlier case.

The Franco-Siamese dispute was unusual in the sense that it was a straightforward conflict of political interests. In most disputes submitted to conciliation, law, as well as politics, has been involved. In 1952, the Belgian-Danish Commission[10] was asked to examine the circumstances in which two Danish merchant ships, the *Gorm* and the *Svava*, had been evacuated from Antwerp when Belgium was overrun by the Germans in 1940. Both vessels had subsequently been lost and the Commission, which was established in accordance with a Belgian-Danish treaty of 1927, was required to advise on whether Belgium should pay compensation. To answer this question, the Commission sought first to determine the legal character of the actions taken by the Belgian authorities. The Commission was agreed that the vessels had not been seized as prize, but was divided as to whether they could be said to have been requisitioned. If the Commission had been a court of arbitration, a ruling on this point would have been essential. However, since its task was conciliation, it was able to leave the issue unresolved, and to propose an agreement, which the parties accepted, under which Belgium paid a reduced amount of compensation to reflect the element of uncertainty in the Danish claim.

---

[10] See H. Rolin, 'Une conciliation belgo-danoise', (1953) 57 RGDIP p. 353.

In 1955, the Franco-Swiss Commission,[11] acting under the influential 1925 treaty mentioned earlier, handled another dispute with a significant legal dimension. Like the Belgian-Danish case, it arose from the traumatic events of 1940. When France surrendered to the Germans, a Polish division which had fought as part of the French army crossed into Switzerland and was interned. The internment lasted until 1945 and the dispute was over who should pay the cost. Switzerland maintained that, as the unit had been fighting for France, the responsibility was French; France stated that, as the soldiers were Poles, the responsibility was Poland's. Since the facts were not really in dispute, the Commission's investigation was largely concerned with legal issues. After hearing the parties' arguments, the Commission proposed that France should pay the costs of the internment up to February 1941, the date when French internees had been freed, and that for reasons of equity France should pay Switzerland a substantial sum as compensation for the remaining years. If the dispute had been referred to arbitration, this result, which was accepted by the parties, might have been different. As in the previous case, however, it is clear that the Commission's appreciation of the parties' legal rights formed the framework of its proposals for conciliation.[12]

Legal issues were even more prominent in the next case to be considered, a dispute which was brought to the Italo-Swiss Commission[13] in 1956 over whether Swiss nationals could claim exemption from a special Italian property tax. The nationals of allied states already enjoyed exemption under the Treaty of Peace with Italy (1947) and an earlier treaty between Switzerland and Italy contained a most-favoured-nation clause. The question therefore was whether that clause applied to the preferential arrangements contained in the Peace Treaty.

The Commission, set up in accordance with the Italo-Swiss Treaty of Conciliation and Judicial Settlement of 1924, took the view that its duty was 'to consider in the first place the legal aspects of the dispute'[14] and found that Swiss nationals were not entitled to exemption from the tax. However, it also decided that the treaty provision in question did entitle Swiss nationals to equality of treatment under Italian law, and that the disputed legislation violated this standard of equality by discriminating against foreign corporations. Taking this and the various facts which had

---

[11] See F. M. Van Asbeck, 'La tâche et l'action d'une Commission de conciliation', (1956) 3 NTIR p. 1, and 'La procédure suivie par la Commission permanente de conciliation franco-suisse', *ibid.*, p. 209. Also S. Bastid, 'La commission de conciliation franco-suisse', (1956) 2 AFDI p. 436; and A. Gros, 'Remarques sur la conciliation internationale', in *L'Evolution du Droit Public: Etudes Offertes à Achille Mestre*, Paris, 1956, p. 279.

[12] The Commission also succeeded in resolving another dispute at the same time. This concerned alleged violation of Swiss territorial sovereignty by French customs officials and appears mainly to have turned on the facts. See Bar-Yaacov, *Inquiry*, pp. 220–4.

[13] See M. Breton-Jokl, 'La Commission permanente de conciliation italo-suisse', (1957) 3 AFDI p. 210.

[14] (1958) 25 ILR p. 316.

emerged in the course of the proceedings into account, the Commission proposed as an 'equitable settlement' of the dispute that Swiss nationals should pay the tax, but that its impact should be lightened in various ways.[15] This proposal was accepted by the parties.

In the cases considered so far, conciliation was carried out by commissions containing several members, and this is the usual arrangement under bilateral or multilateral treaties. It is, however, open to states to refer a dispute to a single conciliator, and this was the procedure adopted in 1977 when Kenya, Uganda and Tanzania asked the experienced Swiss diplomat, Dr Victor Umbricht, to make proposals for the distribution of the assets of the former East African Community (EAC).[16] The dispute had arisen because the partner states, having integrated their economic activities both before and after independence, had now decided to go their separate ways. Before this could be done, it was necessary for an agreement to be reached on the extent of the EAC's assets and liabilities and, more contentiously, on their allocation. As the three states were unable to resolve these matters by negotiation, they were encouraged by the World Bank to give Dr Umbricht a wide-ranging brief to investigate the whole issue and bring forward proposals for its resolution.

From the first it was apparent that the conciliator's task was one of outstanding difficulty. The assets of the EAC included land, ships, aircraft, railways and rolling stock, as well as plant, machinery and spares and various non-physical assets. These were spread across East Africa and, along with the Community's liabilities, had to be located and valued. Less than a year had been allowed for compiling an inventory, but, not surprisingly, the process actually took four years and eventually revealed assets with a net value exceeding one billion dollars.

The conciliator then had to find appropriate criteria for distribution. Various possibilities were rejected as unsuitable, but at last a formula was found which gave Kenya 42.7 per cent of the assets, Tanzania 34.3 per cent and Uganda 23 per cent. When this was put to the parties, they did not immediately accept it, but, as they were entitled to do, used the conciliator's proposals as a basis for negotiation. With further assistance from Dr Umbricht, an agreement winding up the affairs of the EAC was finally concluded in May 1984. Although the division of assets under the agreement

---

[15] See the annex to the report of the Commission, *ibid.*, p. 322.

[16] For a comprehensive account of this case, see V. Umbricht, 'Principles of international mediation: The case of the East African Community', (1984) 187 *Hague Recueil des Cours* p. 307. Although termed by the parties a 'mediator', Dr Umbricht was clearly engaged in conciliation. For a less successful contribution by an individual mediator/conciliator, see K. R. Simmonds, 'The Belize mediation', (1968) 17 ICLQ p. 996; and J. G. Merrills, 'The Belize–Guatemala territorial dispute and the legal opinion of January 2002', (2002) Global Community YBILJ p. 77 at pp. 80–1 and 91–2.

differed slightly from that originally proposed, it is clear that the reports and findings of the conciliator made a vital contribution to the settlement.

A later dispute referred to conciliation involved a commission of the conventional type and, though it raised some difficult issues of law and fact, was more straightforward than the *East African Community* case. In 1980, Iceland and Norway set up a commission to make recommendations with regard to the dividing line for the area of continental shelf between Iceland and Jan Mayen Island. The Commission was directed to take into account Iceland's 'strong economic interests' in the sea areas in question, together with 'the existing geographical and geological factors and other special circumstances'. Following a detailed investigation of the evidence pertaining to these matters, the Commission proposed a joint development agreement covering substantially all of the area offering any significant prospect of hydrocarbon production. This recommendation (document C in the appendix below) was subsequently accepted by the parties, and in 1981 was incorporated into a treaty which ended the dispute.[17]

The practice of conciliation

All conciliation commissions have the same functions: to investigate the dispute and to suggest the terms of a possible settlement. However, as our review of some of the cases has already indicated, within this broad mandate, conciliation commissions have performed a variety of different tasks. What a commission does and how it goes about its work depend in the first place on the instrument setting it up. But much also depends on how the parties choose to present the particular case, and how the members of the commission see their role. Consequently, though the practice of conciliation commissions exhibits many common features, significant differences of approach to the most basic matters are also to be found.

What sort of process is conciliation? One view is that it is to be regarded as a kind of institutionalised negotiation. The task of the commission is to encourage and structure the parties' dialogue, while providing them with whatever assistance may be necessary to bring it to a successful conclusion. This approach, which proceeds from the premise that the resolution of disputes depends on securing the parties' agreement, finds an affinity between conciliation and mediation and can best be seen in the work of the Chaco Commission, the Franco-Siamese Commission and the Commission in the

---

[17] For the Commission's report, see (1981) 20 ILM p. 797 and 62 ILR p. 108. For the treaty, which substantially incorporated the Commission's recommendations, see (1982) 21 ILM p. 1222. For reflections on the case by the chairman of the Commission, see E. L. Richardson, 'Jan Mayen in perspective', (1988) 82 AJIL p. 443. And see also R. R. Churchill, 'Maritime delimitation in the Jan Mayen area', (1985) *Marine Policy* p. 16.

Jan Mayen dispute.[18] Another view is that conciliation is closer to inquiry or arbitration,[19] that the commission's function is to provide information and advice as to the merits of the parties' positions and to suggest a settlement that corresponds to what they deserve, not what they claim. This approach, which can be seen in the work of the Belgian-Danish Commission and the *East African Community* conciliation, reflects the historical link between conciliation and the procedure for enlarged inquiry contained in the Bryan treaties.

Clearly, a commission's views as to the nature of conciliation are likely to exercise an important influence on its work. A commission which sees conciliation as a form of quasi-arbitration, or which is required to perform this function by the parties, will naturally tend to operate more formally than one which sees itself primarily as a forum for negotiation. Thus, in the Belgian-Danish case, both written and oral proceedings were reminiscent of an arbitration. In the *Jan Mayen* case, on the other hand, the Commission decided that, since its purpose was to submit unanimous recommendations and its two national members had participated in all previous diplomatic negotiations, pleadings of any kind were unnecessary. An intermediate position was taken in the Franco-Siamese case where written and oral proceedings were intermingled and in the Franco-Swiss and Italo-Swiss cases where the oral proceedings were quite informal and the parties' agents sat alongside the members of the commission and participated fully in its work.

A conciliation commission has a duty to examine the nature and background of a dispute and so is usually equipped with wide powers of investigation. Unlike an inquiry, however, whose whole *raison d'être* is to illuminate the dispute, a conciliation commission has as its objective the parties' conciliation. Its investigative powers are thus simply a means to an end. As a result, if it becomes apparent that the exposure of some matter might make conciliation more difficult, that line of investigation is unlikely to be pursued. In 1958, a Franco-Moroccan conciliation commission was set up to investigate the French authorities' diversion of an aircraft carrying Ben Bella and four other leaders of the Algerian revolt from Morocco to Tunis.[20] The Commission was asked by Morocco to permit the questioning of all the passengers on the diverted plane, but refused to do so on the ground that 'to have taken this evidence would, in the opinion of the Commission, have been likely to embitter Franco-Moroccan relations and thus defeat the

---

[18] See also the 'Facilitation Process' initiated by Belize and Guatemala assisted by the OAS in 2000, discussed in Merrills, 'The Belize–Guatemala territorial dispute', pp. 81 and 93–4, and in Koopmans in *Diplomatic Dispute Settlement*, pp. 102–4.

[19] See the views expressed in Professor Rolin's report to the Institute of International Law in (1959) 48 (i) *Annuaire*, pp. 30–42.

[20] See Note, 'L'Affaire du F-OABV', (1958) 4 AFDI p. 282; and C. Rousseau, 'Echec de la procédure d'enquête et de conciliation dans l'affaire du dééroutement de l'avion transportant de Rabat à Tunis les chefs nationalistes algériens le 22 octobre 1956', (1958) 62 RGDIP p. 691.

purpose of the mission with which the Commission had been entrusted by the two governments'.[21]

A commission can obtain information in different ways. The commission in the *Jan Mayen* case obtained its evidence on technical matters by convening a meeting at Columbia University at which geologists and geo-physicists who had conducted research in the area described their findings. The Chaco Commission declined to carry out a survey to establish the location of Fort Vanguardia, but arranged for each side's prisoners to be questioned by neutral committees in Argentina and Brazil. The Franco-Siamese Commission neither visited the disputed area, nor took testimony from witnesses, but relied for its information on a questionnaire, devised in consultation with the parties.

In the *East African Community* case, the nature of the conciliator's remit was such as to make the gathering of information a vital part of his work. Identifying and listing the assets of the Community, and then putting a value on them, was, however, an enormous and complex task. Recognising that, if he was to carry this out, Dr Umbricht would need assistance, the partner states authorised him to appoint consultants and full advantage was taken of this facility.[22] One of the conciliator's first actions was to set up an auditing board composed of experts in accounting, finance and engineering to advise him on the formulation of guidelines and their application. In addition to this body, which met at regular intervals, Dr Umbricht also engaged more than forty technical and financial experts for limited periods to assemble and check information. These were organised into working groups and between them prepared draft reports on all the EAC institutions. The draft reports were passed to the governments for comment and eventually provided the basis both for the preparation of the conciliator's proposals relating to the distribution of assets and for the parties' subsequent negotiations.

As already noted, many of the disputes handled by conciliation commissions have raised questions of law, and this is reflected in their membership, which has usually been made up of lawyers, though diplomats, like Dr Umbricht, and individuals with technical expertise have also been employed. In a case involving the complex financial consequences of a prewar Japanese loan, the parties appointed the President of the International Monetary Fund as sole conciliator,[23] and, in a later case[24] with similar subject matter, the President of the International Bank for Reconstruction and Development served in the same capacity.

---

[21] Cot, *International Conciliation*, p. 193.

[22] See Umbricht, 'Principles of international mediation', pp. 328–41.

[23] See *In re Imperial Japanese Government 4% Loan of 1910 Issued in France – Methods of Resumption of Service*, 29 ILR p. 4. In the event, another expert, M. von Steyern, deputised for the IMF President.

[24] *In re City of Tokyo 5% Loan of 1912 – Plan for Resumption of Payment and Interest on the French Tranche of the Loan*, 29 ILR p. 11.

How active should the commission be in seeking to bring the parties together? In the earliest conciliation treaties, the duties of the commission were to hold its investigation and make its proposals, leaving the parties to perform the act of conciliation. Though this approach was followed by the conciliators in the two Japanese loan cases, other commissions have tried to play a more active role. Both the Franco-Siamese Commission and the Italo-Swiss Commission attempted to bring the parties together after the completion of the investigation and prior to the presentation of the report, and in the second case the Commission was successful. The Chaco Commission adopted a more radical approach and began its work of conciliation before it had begun its investigation, an unusual procedure, redolent of mediation rather than conciliation.

Whether a commission is engaged upon investigation, or the formulation of proposals and the work of conciliation, the confidentiality of its proceedings is essential to its prospects of success. Disputes invariably raise delicate issues; it is much easier for governments to offer concessions privately, and so secrecy has been the general rule. In the Ben Bella affair, a request by Morocco for public hearings was rejected, presumably on the ground that, in a case which had already aroused the bitterest feelings, the cause of conciliation would not be furthered by the spotlight of publicity.[25] Even the Chaco Commission, which did conduct some of its proceedings in public, held its most sensitive sessions behind closed doors.

As previously noted, one of the distinctive features of conciliation is that a commission's report takes the form of a set of proposals, not a decision. Thus, even in cases where law has been a major consideration, the report is quite different from an arbitral award and not binding on the parties. This feature of conciliation has presented commissions with something of a dilemma. On the one hand, they wish to make their proposals as persuasive as possible by supporting them with reasons; on the other hand, they are unwilling to provide the parties with legal arguments or findings of fact that may be cited in subsequent litigation. The Belgian-Danish Commission adopted the curious expedient of accompanying a written statement of its conclusions with an oral explanation of its reasons. The Franco-Swiss and Italo-Swiss Commissions adopted the more satisfactory practice of providing a written account of both conclusions and reasons, subject to a restriction that 'the opinion of the Commission on points of law may not be invoked by the parties before any tribunal, judicial or arbitral'.[26] A later treaty of conciliation[27] contains a provision to the same effect, indicating that the need for such precautions is well recognised.

[25] On the damaging consequences of the sensationalism of the French journal *L'Express* in this case, see Cot, *International Conciliation*, pp. 166–7.
[26] (1958) 25 ILR p. 321. See also Koopmans, *Diplomatic Dispute Settlement*, pp. 153–5.
[27] Treaty for Conciliation, Judicial Settlement and Arbitration between the United Kingdom and the Swiss Confederation (1965) Cmnd 2741.

Because the proposals of a conciliation commission can be either accepted or rejected, the usual practice is for the commission to give the parties a specified period of a few months in which to indicate their response. If its proposals are accepted, the commission draws up a *procès verbal* (agreement) recording the fact of conciliation and setting out the terms of the settlement. If the proposed terms are rejected, then conciliation has failed and the parties are under no further obligation. Thus, in the normal case, the functions of a conciliator come to an end with the presentation of a report, and everything thereafter is in the hands of the parties. It is, however, open to states to agree on a different arrangement and to ask the conciliator to perform a more extensive role. In this respect the *East African Community* case is again instructive.

After identifying the relevant assets and liabilities and valuing them, both processes in which the partner states were closely involved, Dr Umbricht heard their legal, economic and financial arguments, and, in October 1981, produced a report containing his proposals on distribution. A series of ministerial meetings was then held with a view to negotiating an agreement. At these meetings, it became apparent that the parties were divided as to the choice of criteria for distribution and the weight to be given to each. With a view to bridging the financial gap between what the parties wanted and what was available, Dr Umbricht approached a number of foreign governments to explore possible sources of financial assistance. These efforts, which had the consent of the partner states, were unsuccessful, and so, in February 1983, the conciliator, at the request of the parties, presented a further report to the Presidents of the partner states. Between the presentation of this report and the meeting of the Presidents in November, Dr Umbricht engaged in shuttle diplomacy in an attempt to bring the positions closer together. As noted earlier, this was successful, and the final agreement was signed in May 1984, seven years after the breakdown of the Community.[28] Thus, in this case, the conciliator's involvement was both varied and unusually protracted, first supervising a far-reaching inquiry and bringing forward proposals for a settlement, then acting as mediator in the final phases of the dispute.

The place of conciliation in modern treaty law

In the period since 1945, conciliation has retained a place in bilateral treaty practice, though on a much diminished scale. A handful of treaties were concluded in the years after the war, and more recently Switzerland, the

---

[28] For an account of events after the presentation of the conciliator's report, see Umbricht, 'Principles of international mediation', pp. 356–8. A rather similar function was performed by Sir Arthur Watts who was appointed Special Negotiator for Succession Issues by the High Representative for Yugoslavia in 1996. In that capacity he provided drafts of a framework for negotiation by the parties which eventually led to a settlement in 2001. See Koopmans, *Diplomatic Dispute Settlement*, p. 49.

leading exponent of conciliation, has concluded treaties with the United Kingdom and a number of other states. Apart from treaties of this kind, which establish general obligations, it is, of course, open to states to make an agreement setting up a commission for an individual dispute. *Ad hoc* arrangements of this type were the basis of the conciliators' jurisdiction in the *Jan Mayen* dispute and the *East African Community* case, and, in 1986, formed part of an agreement between Egypt and Israel relating to the settlement of a boundary dispute in the Taba area.[29] This latter treaty was unusual because, although it was primarily an arbitration agreement, it included detailed arrangements for conciliation while the arbitration was in progress. However, conciliation, when attempted, was unsuccessful and so in the end this dispute had to be settled by arbitration.[30]

If conciliation has rather fallen out of favour in bilateral treaty practice, multilateral treaties show a quite different pattern. The Pact of Bogotá (1948) provides for conciliation, along with a variety of other procedures and, as we shall see in Chapter 11, the relation between the provisions in the Pact dealing with conciliation and those providing for judicial settlement was one of the issues considered by the International Court in a case in 1988.[31] The European Convention for the Peaceful Settlement of Disputes (1957) similarly provides for conciliation in a provision modelled on the Franco-Swiss treaty of 1925. Other regional agreements containing references to conciliation include the Charter of the Organization of African Unity (1963) and the Treaty Establishing the Organization of Eastern Caribbean States (1981).[32] In the former, conciliation was one of the functions of the Commission of Mediation, Conciliation and Arbitration envisaged in a protocol of 1964;[33] in the latter agreement, on the other hand, conciliation is provided for in an annex to the treaty which establishes a panel of conciliators from which commissions can be drawn when required.

Conciliation is also available under the settlement provisions of a number of treaties on particular topics. It is not the purpose of this book to describe the arrangements for settling disputes in particular fields in any detail, but it is appropriate to mention that conciliation is a favoured procedure in agreements concerned with international trade[34] and is also prominent

---

[29] See Agreement to Arbitrate the Boundary Dispute concerning the Taba Beachfront, Egypt–Israel (1986), text in (1987) 26 ILM p. 1. Also, Koopmans, *Diplomatic Dispute Settlement*, pp. 63–6.

[30] See *Boundary Dispute concerning the Taba Area*, Arbitration Award, 1988, text in (1988) 27 ILM p. 1421, summarised in (1989) 83 AJIL p. 590. For further discussion, see Chapter 5.

[31] See *Border and Transborder Armed Actions*, Jurisdiction and Admissibility, Judgment, [1988] ICJ Rep. p. 69.

[32] Text in (1981) 20 ILM p. 1166.

[33] See Chapter 11. In the event, the Commission never became operational and was dropped when the OAU was replaced in 2001 by the new African Union: see C. A. A. Packer and D. Rukare, 'The new African Union and its Constitutive Act', (2002) 96 AJIL p. 365 at p. 376.

[34] See Chapter 9.

in treaties for the protection of human rights. Thus, under Article 38 of the European Convention on Human Rights, one of the functions of the European Court of Human Rights is to 'place itself at the disposal of the parties concerned with a view to securing a friendly settlement of the matter on the basis of respect for human rights as defined in the Convention and the protocols thereto', and equivalent provisions are to be found in other instruments.[35]

Under the Convention in its original form, the promotion of friendly settlements was one of the responsibilities of the European Commission of Human Rights, a group of human rights experts which dealt with all cases taken to Strasbourg. Since the restructuring of the system and the abolition of the Commission in 1999, this function has passed to the Court which in practice means that it is now carried out by the Registrar.[36] Although the vast majority of cases, and consequently friendly settlements, involve claims brought by individuals, in the rarer inter-state cases the same possibilities are available. Thus, in 2000, the case of *Denmark* v. *Turkey*[37] was settled in this way. The claim, which involved alleged maltreatment of a Danish citizen, was resolved following an agreement in which Turkey acknowledged various incidents of wrongdoing, undertook to pay a substantial sum by way of compensation and committed itself to certain human rights projects. This was fundamentally a bilateral settlement to which the Registry, acting under Article 38, contributed advice on drafting.

In the present context, two general points are particularly worth noting about Article 38. One is that, as part of a functioning system of rights protection, this is a type of conciliation provision which is regularly used. The other is that, by referring to a friendly settlement 'on the basis of respect for human rights', the Convention makes it clear that the purpose of this provision is not simply to achieve a settlement without further recourse to Strasbourg, but to enable cases to be disposed of informally, while at the same time observing the Convention's basic values. The fact that here, and in other human rights treaties, conciliation is more than a means of securing a settlement which the parties can accept, but has an additional – and crucial – substantive component, is clearly something which distinguishes

---

[35] See the International Covenant on Civil and Political Rights (1966), Articles 41 and 42; the International Convention on the Elimination of All Forms of Racial Discrimination (1965), Article 12; the American Convention on Human Rights (1969), Articles 48 and 49; and the African Charter on Human and Peoples' Rights (1981), Article 52. For discussion of conciliation in these and other human rights treaties, see A. H. Robertson and J. G. Merrills, *Human Rights in the World*, 4th edn, Manchester, 1996.

[36] On the evolution of the friendly settlement procedure, see Koopmans, *Diplomatic Dispute Settlement*, pp. 184–99.

[37] *Denmark* v. *Turkey*, ECtHR (Friendly Settlement), 5 April 2000, Case No. 34382/97. On an earlier inter-state case brought by Denmark, France, the Netherlands, Norway and Sweden against Turkey and also resolved by a friendly settlement, see Koopmans, *Diplomatic Dispute Settlement*, p. 190.

friendly settlement under these arrangements from conciliation as generally understood.

Conciliation in the conventional sense is provided for in numerous treaties on other topics. Indeed, the inclusion of arrangements for conciliation either in combination with, or as an alternative to, other procedures, has become almost a routine feature of modern multilateral treaties. The 1969 Vienna Convention on the Law of Treaties,[38] for example, provides for disputes concerning the interpretation or application of the articles on *ius cogens* to be referred to the International Court and for other disputes relating to the validity or termination of treaty obligations to be dealt with by compulsory conciliation. The arrangements for setting up a commission are set out in some detail in an annex to the Convention. The annex provides for the Secretary-General to maintain a list of qualified jurists as available conciliators. Commissions are created by each party nominating two members, not necessarily from the list; the four members so appointed then appoint a fifth, who acts as chairman. A feature of the procedure is that any appointment not made within the specified period can be made by the Secretary-General, so preventing frustration of the process. The commission 'hears the parties, examines the claims and objections and makes proposals to the parties with a view to reaching an amicable settlement of the dispute'[39] and must submit its report within twelve months of its constitution. In light of a point raised earlier, it is interesting to note that the annex envisages a commission's report including 'conclusions regarding the facts or questions of law', but, as well as stating that it is not binding on the parties, lays down that it 'has no other character than that of recommendations submitted for the consideration of the parties in order to facilitate an amicable settlement of the dispute'.[40]

The 1975 Convention on the Representation of States in Their Relations with International Organizations of a Universal Character[41] and the 1978 Vienna Convention on Succession of States in respect of Treaties[42] contain arrangements for conciliation along lines which are generally similar. In both conventions, consultation is a prerequisite for activating the conciliation machinery and, as in the 1969 Convention, the setting up of a commission cannot be prevented by default. The 1975 Convention is unusual in that it provides for commissions of three, rather than five members and also mentions the possibility of a commission recommending that the international organisation concerned seek an advisory opinion from the International Court. The 1978 Convention, on the other hand, is unique in providing for the expenses of its conciliation commissions to be borne by the United Nations. Both conventions provide in the usual way that the recommendations of a commission shall not be regarded as binding. However,

---

[38] Text in (1969) 63 AJIL p. 875.   [39] Annex, para. 5.   [40] *Ibid.*, para. 6.
[41] Text in (1975) 69 AJIL p. 730.   [42] Text in (1978) 72 AJIL p. 971.

the earlier convention adds the words 'unless all the parties to the dispute have accepted them'[43] and also provides for a party to declare that it will abide by such recommendations unilaterally.

Striking examples of the use of conciliation in combination with other methods of settlement can be seen in a number of treaties concerned with the environment. For example, the 1985 Vienna Convention for the Protection of the Ozone Layer[44] provides that, in the event of a dispute relating to the interpretation or application of the Convention, the parties must first attempt to settle the dispute by negotiation. If negotiation is unsuccessful, they may jointly seek the good offices or mediation of a third party. To deal with disputes which are still outstanding, states may further declare that they accept either arbitration or the jurisdiction of the International Court. Finally, if the parties have each accepted a different procedure, or if they have accepted no procedure, they are obliged to submit the dispute to conciliation, unless they can agree on some other means of settlement. The Convention deals rather briefly with the arrangements for constituting a commission, but the essential points are covered.

Similar arrangements are to be found in the 1992 Convention on Biological Diversity,[45] the 1992 Framework Convention on Climate Change[46] and the 1994 Convention to Combat Desertification.[47] The Biodiversity Convention sets out its conciliation procedure in an annex, whereas in the other conventions this is left for later adoption at a Conference of the Parties. On the other hand, the latter conventions provide for conciliation to begin twelve months after the notification that a dispute exists, whereas the Biodiversity Convention, like the 1985 Vienna Convention, simply requires conciliation to be used without specifying a time-limit. Conciliation, then, has a role to play in all these conventions and in the event of a dispute relating to their interpretation or application, which cannot be resolved by other means, a compulsory, though non-binding, procedure is available.

Related to the above are the arrangements for dispute settlement to be found in the 1997 United Nations Convention on the Law of the Non-Navigational Uses of International Watercourses.[48] After providing in Article 32 for non-discriminatory access to domestic remedies by private parties, the Convention establishes a staged procedure in Article 33 for dealing with disputes at the inter-state level. This involves first negotiations, then various other options, followed, if necessary, by a compulsory fact-finding process which can be invoked by any party. The process, which is carried out by a

---

[43] Article 85(7).
[44] Text in (1987) 26 ILM p. 1516. It should be noted, however, that Article 8 of the 1987 Montreal Protocol to the Vienna Convention provides for the creation of a non-compliance procedure which has made the dispute settlement provisions described above much less important. See the text accompanying note 59 below.
[45] Text in (1992) 31 ILM p. 818.   [46] Text in (1992) 31 ILM p. 849.
[47] Text in (1994) 33 ILM p. 1332.   [48] Text in (1997) 36 ILM p. 700.

three-member commission, one of whom is from a third country and acts as chair, results in a non-binding report and is primarily conceived as a form of inquiry. Its relevance in the present context is that the commission's report, in addition to its findings (with reasons), is also to include 'such recommendations as it deems appropriate for an equitable solution of the dispute, which the Parties concerned shall consider in good faith'. Commissions under Article 33 thus also have a significant conciliatory function since their reports, as an authority on water resources has pointed out, 'could point to solutions not foreseen by the parties, or that they, for domestic political or other reasons, would otherwise have difficulty in adopting on their own initiative'.[49]

Finally, it should be pointed out that an elaborate and potentially very important treatment of conciliation is to be found in the 1982 Law of the Sea Convention. However, these arrangements can most conveniently be studied alongside the extensive provisions of the Convention concerned with other means of settlement. Discussion of this aspect of conciliation will therefore be postponed until Chapter 8.

Further developments

Interest in conciliation as a possible means of handling disputes is evident in a number of further developments. The first of these is the effort within the United Nations to produce a code of rules on the subject. In 1990, the Sixth Committee submitted a report to the General Assembly containing a set of Draft Rules for the Conciliation of Disputes between States. The General Assembly asked the Secretary-General to circulate the draft rules for comment, and decided that they should be examined as part of the programme of the UN Decade of International Law and in the Special Committee on the Charter of the United Nations and on the Strengthening of the Role of the Organization. The Special Committee completed its work in 1995 and submitted its report, containing a revised version of the Model Rules, which was approved by the General Assembly.[50]

In their revised form, the Model Rules contain twenty-nine articles covering all aspects of conciliation from the initiation of proceedings to the submission of the report. As Model Rules they have no binding force, but are intended as a set of norms which states between whom a dispute has arisen can agree to adopt, either by simply referring to them in a bilateral agreement, or, if they wish to amend them, by making the desired changes.

---

[49] S. C. McCaffrey, *The Law of International Watercourses*, Oxford, 2001, p. 444.

[50] See GA Res. A/50/50 (1996); and V. Morris and M. C. Bourloyannis-Vrailas, 'The work of the Sixth Committee at the Fiftieth Session of the UN General Assembly', (1996) 90 AJIL p. 491 at p. 497. The Permanent Court of Arbitration adopted a set of Model Rules in the same period. For discussion and comparison of the two approaches, see Koopmans, *Diplomatic Dispute Settlement*, pp. 106–20.

The Model Rules may be particularly useful where states are already parties to a convention which lays down conciliation as a mandatory procedure, but which does not prescribe the necessary arrangements. Naturally, if the convention does contain its own arrangements, the Model Rules are less useful, although it is worth noting that, even here, the parties can, if they wish, use the Model Rules instead by following the appropriate formalities. There is likewise no difficulty if the parties to a dispute are already under an obligation to submit a dispute to the International Court or to arbitration, since it is normally open to states to agree that they will first try conciliation, and to postpone recourse to binding procedures until alternative methods have been explored.

Unless states decide to employ conciliation more frequently than hitherto, the Model Rules seem unlikely to have a major impact on the way international disputes are handled. However, as a modest step forward, they are useful in supplying a framework for conciliation and in drawing attention to its potential.

Developments of a more far-reaching nature are to be found in various initiatives utilising conciliation taken by the Organization for Security and Co-operation in Europe (OSCE), formerly the Conference on Security and Co-operation in Europe (CSCE). We shall see in Chapter 11 that this is a quasi-regional political organisation with its origins in the Helsinki Agreement of 1975. Although that Agreement itself committed the participating states to settle their disputes by peaceful means, it was not until the Vienna Follow-Up Meeting, which concluded in 1989, that measures were adopted to implement this principle. That this was possible was a consequence of the ending of the confrontation between East and West which had held up progress across the whole range of issues. Now, however, significant steps have been taken to address the issue of dispute settlement and, although their effect should not be exaggerated, the central place assigned to conciliation is certainly of interest.

The first step was the creation of a CSCE Dispute Settlement Mechanism involving a combination of mediation and conciliation.[51] The Concluding Document of the Vienna Follow-Up Meeting accepted the concept of 'mandatory involvement of a third party in certain categories of disputes' and the details were agreed at a meeting of experts at Valletta in 1991, then endorsed at the Berlin Meeting of the CSCE in the same year and in the Helsinki Document of 1992. The Valletta Procedure, as it is known, provides for disputes to be dealt with in two stages. At the first stage, the parties to a dispute which they have failed to resolve establish a 'Mechanism' by

---

[51] See K. Oellers-Frahm, 'The mandatory component in the CSCE dispute settlement system', in M. W. Janis (ed.), *International Courts for the Twenty-First Century*, Dordrecht, 1992, p. 195. The text of the CSCE Procedure for Peaceful Settlement of Disputes can be found in *ibid.*, p. 206, and in (1991) 30 ILM p. 390.

selecting one or more individuals from a central register to provide 'comment or advice' on the procedure to be adopted to deal with the dispute.[52] At the second stage, the individual or panel is authorised to comment or advise on the substance of the dispute. At either stage, the parties can, by agreement, modify or adapt the procedure to perform fact-finding or other functions.

It is important to note that the process can be initiated by any party to the dispute and does not depend on agreement. In that sense, submission to the procedure is mandatory and there is a provision to ensure that a Mechanism can be established even if a party refuses co-operation. However, although comments or advice emanating from the Mechanism must be considered 'in good faith and in a spirit of co-operation', they are not binding. Thus, the process is essentially one of conciliation, with elements of mediation, particularly at the first stage, and also inquiry if the parties so desire. A further limitation to the Mechanism is that, if another party 'considers that because the dispute raises issues concerning its territorial integrity, or national defence, title to sovereignty over land territory, or competing claims with regard to jurisdiction over other areas, the Mechanism should not be established or continued' (Section XII). This is clearly a major exclusion.

At the Stockholm Meeting of the Council of the CSCE in 1992, the participating states decided to complement the Valletta Procedure by creating a formal conciliation procedure.[53] The arrangements agreed enable the parties to a dispute to refer it to a conciliation commission either by agreement, or unilaterally where both have accepted its jurisdiction in advance by making declarations analogous to those under Article 36(2) of the Statute of the International Court of Justice.[54] A commission consists of one conciliator selected by each party from the Valletta register, who then select a third person from the register as chairman. The powers and procedure of the commission are set out in provisions rather like those of the UN Model Rules, but there are some significant differences. Thus, while the parties are normally free to reject the commission's proposals, a party may declare either generally, or in relation to a specific dispute, that it will accept them as binding on a condition of reciprocity. Likewise, to reflect the institutional setting of its work, a commission must forward a report to the Senior Council of the OSCE.[55]

---

[52] The procedure for appointing a Mechanism was simplified at the third meeting of the CSCE Council at Stockholm in 1992. See Annex 1 to the Council's Decision on Peaceful Settlement of Disputes, text in (1993) 32 ILM p. 551 at p. 556.

[53] See Annex 3 to the Council's Decision on Peaceful Settlement of Disputes, *ibid.*, p. 568.

[54] The procedure established by Article 36(2), known as the 'optional clause', is described in Chapter 6.

[55] Formerly known as the Committee of Senior Officials of the CSCE.

Another decision taken at Stockholm was intended to take the use of conciliation even further. Whereas the procedure just described is essentially voluntary, at the Stockholm Meeting the Council of Ministers decided that it, or the Senior Council, can direct any two participating states to seek conciliation if they have been unable to settle a dispute within a reasonable time.[56] Such 'directed conciliation' is therefore mandatory and to ensure that the new power can be used, the parties to the dispute are not allowed to participate in the initial decision. Directed conciliation uses the same procedure as if the parties had made a joint request, subject to minor variations, and, although the process itself is not optional, the parties remain free to reject the conciliation commission's recommendations. Furthermore, not all disputes are subject to directed conciliation. In addition to those which are already covered by other processes, conciliation may not be ordered with regard to disputes falling within the categories excluded from the Valletta Process. As before, this is a crucial limitation.

A general point about all the arrangements mentioned so far is that, in so far as they can be thought of as creating obligations for OSCE states, these obligations are of a political and not a legal character. This stems from the fact that, from the 1975 Helsinki Agreement onwards, CSCE undertakings took the form not of treaties, but of political commitments. This does not make such developments meaningless, or mean that they can safely be ignored,[57] but when surveying current arrangements for dispute settlement it is at least something to be borne in mind. The remaining OSCE development to be considered is different, however, because it is in the form of a treaty and thus comparable to the various conventions already discussed. This is the Stockholm Convention on Conciliation and Arbitration within the CSCE,[58] another achievement of the 1992 Meeting.

As the name indicates, this Convention is concerned with two distinct methods for dealing with disputes: arbitration, which is further discussed in Chapter 5, and conciliation. The Convention provides for the creation of a panel of conciliators and arbitrators, nominated by the states parties, and collectively known as the 'Court of Conciliation and Arbitration'. The Court, which is based in Geneva, establishes its own rules of procedure, and is competent to provide conciliation for cases which are referred either by agreement or unilaterally by the states parties. A commission is appointed for each case, and includes one member chosen by each party from the

---

[56] See Annex 4 to the CSCE Council's Decision on Peaceful Settlement of Disputes, text in (1993) 32 ILM p. 570.

[57] As regards the issue of human rights, for example, the signature of the Soviet Union and the communist governments of Eastern Europe to the 1975 Helsinki Agreement had far greater consequences than their ratifications of the 1966 UN Covenants on Human Rights. See further Robertson and Merrills, *Human Rights in the World*, pp. 179–90.

[58] Text in (1993) 32 ILM p. 557. The Convention forms Annex 2 to the CSCE Council's 1992 Decision on Peaceful Settlement of Disputes.

panel, together with an uneven number (normally three), selected by the Court's Bureau. The commission's function is 'to assist the parties to the dispute in finding a settlement in accordance with international law and their CSCE commitments' (Article 24). If the dispute is not settled in the course of the proceedings, the Commission draws up a report containing its proposals which the parties are free to accept or reject. However, if the Commission's proposals are not accepted, its report is forwarded to the OSCE Council.

The Convention came into force in 1994 when it had been accepted by twelve, mainly Western European, states. Although it creates obligations only for the parties, it is significant, at least potentially, because a state which has accepted the Convention can be obliged to submit to conciliation unless another procedure for settling the dispute has been agreed. In this respect, it is particularly important that there is no category of excluded disputes, in sharp contrast to the Valletta Process, and that the Convention contains no provision enabling states to make reservations which would exempt specific types of dispute from conciliation. Becoming a party to the Convention thus entails a general and unqualified commitment to conciliation by the OSCE state concerned. However, none of these elaborate arrangements for OSCE conciliation has so far been used, suggesting perhaps that here, as elsewhere, the need is not so much for new mechanisms and procedures, as for a readiness on the part of governments with unresolved disputes to use established arrangements wisely.

The last development which should be noted concerns the emergence of novel 'compliance procedures' constituting a special form of conciliation in recent environmental agreements. The first agreement of this kind was the 1987 Montreal Protocol on Substances that Deplete the Ozone Layer,[59] under which an Implementation Committee consisting of ten parties to the Protocol has been established to hear submissions relating to a party's non-compliance which may be put forward by the Secretariat or any other party. The Committee may then make recommendations 'with a view to securing an amicable resolution of the matter on the basis of respect for the provisions of the Protocol'. Implementation of the ozone regime is reviewed through a number of institutions, of which the compliance procedure is only one. But,

---

[59] Text in (1987) 26 ILM p. 154. See D. G. Victor, 'The operation and effectiveness of the Montreal Protocol's non-compliance procedure', in D. G. Victor, K. Raustiala and E. B. Skolnikoff, *The Implementation and Effectiveness of International Environmental Commitments*, Laxenburg, 1998, p. 137; C. Chinkin, 'Alternative dispute resolution under international law', in M. D. Evans (ed.), *Remedies in International Law: The Institutional Dilemma*, Oxford, 1998, p. 123 at pp. 128–34; and P. Sands, *Principles of International Environmental Law*, 2nd edn, Cambridge, 2003, pp. 205–10. Also J. Klabbers, 'Compliance procedures', in D. Bodansky, J. Brunnée and E. Hey (eds.), *The Oxford Handbook of International Environmental Law*, Oxford, 2007, p. 995; and K. N. Scott, 'Non-compliance procedures and dispute resolution mechanisms under international environmental agreements', in D. French, M. Saul and N. D. White (eds.), *International Law and Dispute Settlement: New Problems and Techniques*, Oxford, 2010, p. 225.

by dealing with disputes both 'in house' and informally, the new procedure is particularly suitable for an evolving regulatory regime, as it can reflect the expectations and understandings of the parties, but at the same time avoid crystallising the law in a fast-changing area. Not surprisingly, therefore, following this example, non-compliance procedures have been introduced or provided for under a number of other environmental treaties.

A good example of the non-compliance procedure in operation may be seen in the case of Russia, the issue of whose record under the Montreal Protocol was raised before the Implementation Committee in 1995. By 2002, following public scrutiny and the provision of funds and assistance, Russia had achieved compliance. While not all cases have been so successful, there are clear advantages in supervisory arrangements which engage all parties to a treaty and are aimed at providing incentives for compliance, rather than grounds for recrimination. The traditional law of state responsibility, though necessarily the basis of treaty obligations, is at the same time a crude and unsatisfactory instrument for encouraging performance. With environmental treaties in particular, it has been suggested that traditional methods 'simply do not work: they are hardly ever applied, are antagonistic and ... offer little scope for win-win solutions'.[60] The emergence of non-compliance procedures to rectify these deficiencies may thus be seen as a logical progression.

In addition to the Montreal Protocol, more than twenty other treaties now provide for non-compliance procedures, including the 1997 Kyoto Protocol,[61] for which a compliance regime was established in 2001, the 1998 Aarhus Convention,[62] the parties to which set up a Compliance Committee in 2002, and the 2000 Cartagena Protocol on Biosafety,[63] where a non-compliance procedure was adopted in 2004. Equivalent arrangements for other treaties are currently under negotiation. As a relatively new means of monitoring states' international commitments and resolving disagreements, non-compliance procedures represent an important development, but raise a number of issues which have yet to be resolved, not least their relation to more traditional ways of handling disputes. Nevertheless, non-compliance procedures are a type of multilateral conciliation with unique advantages, and as such are likely to be increasingly prominent.

The significance of conciliation

In the ninety or so years in which conciliation has been available, less than twenty cases have been heard. Although this is rather more than the number of cases handled by commissions of inquiry over a slightly longer period, it is hardly an impressive record. When one bears in mind the more than

---

[60] Koopmans, *Diplomatic Dispute Settlement*, p. 227.   [61] Text in (1998) 37 ILM p. 22.
[62] Text in (1999) 38 ILM p. 517.   [63] Text in (2000) 39 ILM p. 1027.

200 bilateral treaties and the various multilateral instruments with similar provisions, it is clear that conciliation has failed to become the routine procedure that its promoters expected. Why?

The treaties themselves suggest one set of explanations. Some bilateral treaties are restricted to particular categories of disputes; some multilateral treaties, the General Act, for example, are subject to wide-ranging reservations, which have the same effect of restricting the parties' obligations. Moreover, the significance of some treaties was always likely to lie more in the example they set than in their application, since disputes between, say, Sweden and Chile, or Brazil and Poland,[64] have never been very common.

As in the case of inquiry, the influence of other means of dispute settlement must also be taken into account. We shall see in later chapters that a government which is interested in settling a dispute can be helped to do so through informal conciliation within an international organisation. Likewise, a government which merely wishes to ventilate a grievance has in the United Nations a forum which a conciliation commission cannot hope (and should not try) to match. The more bilateral conciliation acquires the overtones of arbitration, the more the tendency to take disputes of a political character to international organisations will be encouraged. But, since to convene and operate a conciliation commission is neither easy nor cheap, even states with legal disputes will often have reason to prefer the tried and tested procedures of arbitration to the uncertainties of conciliation.

In the *Interhandel* case,[65] the United States rejected a proposal for conciliation on the ground that the facts were clear. This suggests that sometimes the possibilities of conciliation may not be fully appreciated, a problem which is exacerbated by the limited amount of practice and the paucity of published material. The fact that conciliation is a relatively elaborate procedure probably discourages its use for minor disputes; but a conciliation commission, unlike a mediator, usually has no political authority to back up its proposals and so, quite apart from other considerations, conciliation is not a particularly attractive option for major disputes either.

In 1938, Czechoslovakia's request for conciliation in the Sudeten crisis was ignored by Nazi Germany. Goodwill and a readiness to compromise are clearly prerequisites of conciliation and in virtually all the cases in which it has been attempted the parties have been neighbours, or near neighbours, with an interest in maintaining friendly relations. Conciliation, like inquiry, can provide the parties with a better understanding of their opponent's case and an objective appraisal of their own, and, like mediation, with the assistance of a third party in negotiation and an opportunity to make concessions without loss of face.

---

[64] Brazil and Poland signed a treaty of conciliation in 1933.
[65] See *Interhandel*, Judgment, [1959] ICJ Rep. p. 6.

Conciliation has so far proved most useful for disputes where the main issues are legal, but the parties desire an equitable compromise. The Belgian-Danish, Franco-Swiss and Swiss-Italian cases were all of this type, as were the two Japanese loan cases, the *Roula* case[66] (1956) between Italy and Greece, and the more recent *Jan Mayen* case. In cases of this type, conciliation would appear to offer two advantages over arbitration *ex aequo et bono*, the obvious alternative.

First, because of the way conciliation is conducted – through a dialogue with and between the parties – there is no danger of it producing a result that takes the parties completely by surprise, as sometimes happens in legal proceedings. Secondly, a commission's proposals, as already noted, are not binding and, if unacceptable, can be rejected. The importance which states attach to retaining control of a dispute has been mentioned earlier, and would appear to be equally relevant here.

In all the cases just mentioned, conciliation was successful. Significantly, all involved issues that were both legal and of secondary importance. The difficulties that have been experienced in utilising conciliation for other types of disputes indicate its limitations. The Chaco Commission was instructed to confine its attention to the incident at Fort Vanguardia, and, though it subsequently obtained authority to investigate the whole of the long-standing border dispute in the area, its proposals for a solution were not taken up. The Franco-Siamese Commission prudently sought to limit its brief by excluding the issue of Laos; even so, its report was rejected by Siam. In the Ben Bella affair, the Moroccan delegate resigned when the commission refused to allow the passengers on the diverted aircraft to be called as witnesses. And, in the *Vitianu* case (1949), an attempt to achieve a conciliated settlement in a dispute involving a Romanian diplomat collapsed when the Swiss authorities refused to discontinue proceedings for espionage.[67] In all these cases, a substantial interest of a political nature was in issue, and strong feelings made it difficult for the parties to accept a compromise.

It is worth noting, however, that the *East African Community* case was resolved by conciliation, though substantial sums were at stake, and that, even when it is less successful, conciliation can still have significant results. Although the Chaco Commission failed to resolve the underlying issue, it succeeded in patching up the immediate quarrel. Likewise, despite the rejection of the Franco-Siamese Commission's report, when a new government came to power in Siam, it indicated that it regarded the border dispute as over. While it is tempting to believe that there ought to be ways of resolving disputes once and for all, partial or step-by-step solutions may often be the best that can be managed.

---

[66] See J. P. A. François, 'Le Palais de la Paix en 1956', (1957) 4 NTIR p. 69 at p. 71.

[67] See Cot, *International Conciliation*, p. 93.

When assessing the significance of conciliation, it is also worth bearing in mind that, while the conciliation provisions in many treaties have still to be utilised, this does not, as might be thought, make such arrangements meaningless. A former legal adviser, who was closely involved with the negotiation of the Vienna Convention on the Law of Treaties, has observed that:

> the chief value of the automatic procedures for settlement of disputes now written into the Convention lies not in their precise content but in their mere existence. Paradoxically, the less they are utilised the more effective they will be. No state is anxious to indulge in lengthy and expensive international conciliation or litigation. This imposes a very heavy burden upon Foreign Offices and upon their legal advisers, with the outcome far from certain. What is important – what is indeed crucial – is that there should always be in the background, as a necessary check upon the making of unjustified claims, or upon the denial of justified claims, automatically available procedures for the settlement of disputes.[68]

The comment is, of course, equally applicable to other multilateral conventions, whether general or particular, and indeed to arrangements for conciliation in bilateral treaties, whether or not they are employed in practice.

Currently, then, conciliation is regularly included in provisions dealing with dispute settlement and retains a modest place among the procedures actually used by states when disputes arise. While the number of cases handled by conciliation is small and there can be no guarantee that if attempted the procedure will be successful, the *Jan Mayen* case and the *East African Community* case have provided timely reminders of its value. As these cases demonstrate, the *ad hoc* use of conciliation is no less handy in practice than the standing arrangements laid down in treaties, and, as noted above, informal conciliation through organisations is a further possibility. Like inquiry, the process from which it developed, conciliation offers a procedure adaptable to a variety of needs, and demonstrates the advantage to be derived from the structured involvement of outsiders in the settlement of international disputes.

---

[68] I. Sinclair, *The Vienna Convention on the Law of Treaties*, 2nd edn, Manchester, 1984, p. 235.

5

Arbitration

The means available for the settlement of international disputes are commonly divided into two groups. Those considered so far, namely, negotiation, mediation, inquiry and conciliation, are termed diplomatic means, because the parties retain control of the dispute and may accept or reject a proposed settlement as they see fit. Arbitration and judicial settlement, on the other hand, are employed when what is wanted is a binding decision, usually on the basis of international law, and hence these are known as legal means of settlement.

Judicial settlement involves the reference of a dispute to the International Court or some other standing tribunal, such as the International Tribunal for the Law of the Sea or the European Court of Human Rights. Arbitration, in contrast, requires the parties themselves to set up the machinery to handle a dispute, or series of disputes, between them. Historically, arbitration was the first to develop and provided the inspiration for the creation of permanent judicial institutions. The focus of this chapter will therefore be on the earlier institution.[1]

Forms of arbitration

Whether states are drafting a general undertaking to refer future disputes to arbitration, or negotiating a *compromis* (agreement) for the submission of a dispute that has already arisen, the first step is to decide the kind of tribunal to be appointed. One possibility is to set up a commission consisting of equal numbers of national arbitrators, appointed by the parties, and a neutral member (or umpire) to whom cases are referred if the national

---

[1] For general reference, see J. G. Wetter, *The International Arbitral Process: Public and Private*, 5 vols., New York, 1979, an outstanding collection of cases and materials; J. L. Simpson and H. Fox, *International Arbitration: Law and Practice*, London, 1959; C. M. H. Waldock (ed.), *International Disputes: The Legal Aspects*, London, 1972, Chapter 2; United Nations, *Handbook on the Peaceful Settlement of Disputes between States*, New York, 1992, Chapter 2F; C. Gray and B. Kingsbury, 'Developments in dispute settlement: Inter-state arbitration since 1945', (1992) 63 BYBIL p. 97; and S. Muller and W. Mijs (eds.), *The Flame Rekindled: New Hopes for International Arbitration*, Dordrecht, 1994. See also J. Collier and V. Lowe, *The Settlement of Disputes in International Law*, Oxford, 1999, Chapters 3, 4 and 8; and R. Y. Jennings, 'The differences between conducting a case in the ICJ and in an ad hoc tribunal – An inside view', in N. Ando, E. McWhinney and R. Wolfrum (eds.), *Liber Amicorum Judge Shigeru Oda*, The Hague, 2002, p. 893.

members cannot agree. The origins of this form of tribunal, frequently used to deal with claims arising out of injury to aliens, can be traced back almost 200 years. In the Treaty of Ghent (1814), the United States and the United Kingdom agreed that certain disputes between them should be arbitrated by national commissioners with reference to a disinterested third party in the event of disagreement. Under the earlier and more famous Jay Treaty (1794), on the other hand, national commissioners alone were employed. These early Anglo-American commissions were not judicial tribunals in the modern sense, but were supposed to blend juridical with diplomatic considerations to produce (in effect) a negotiated settlement. In the modern form of mixed commission, however, the juridical element predominates, with the result that cases like the *Bolivar Railway Company* claim[2] (1903), decided by the British–Venezuelan Commission, and the *Youmans* claim[3] (1926), decided by the United States–Mexican General Claims Commission, are regarded as authoritative applications of international law.

Another form of arbitration derives from the long-established practice of referring a dispute to a foreign head of state or government for decision. Examples can be found in classical times and also in the medieval period when the Pope was often called upon to act in this capacity. Because the effect is to involve an influential outside party in the dispute, arbitration in this form has some of the same advantages as mediation. A powerful arbitrator, like a powerful mediator, can be useful when pressure or inducements are needed to encourage a party to accept an unfavourable decision, or expertise and resources are needed to implement a settlement by carrying out tasks such as mapping or surveying. One disadvantage of this form of arbitration was that it used to be common for sovereign arbitrators to answer the parties' question without giving reasons. It was therefore impossible to know what part, if any, juridical considerations had played in the decision. Towards the end of the nineteenth century, however, as arbitration came to be recognised as an essentially judicial process, reasoned decisions, based on advice tendered by jurists, became the norm. As a result, by 1931, arbitral decisions like that of the King of Italy in the *Clipperton Island* case,[4] were regularly settling disputes on the basis of international law.

Although sovereign arbitration is now a rarity, its flexibility and adaptability to modern circumstances were demonstrated in two contemporary arbitrations. Under a treaty of 1902, the Queen, as successor to her great-grandfather King Edward VII, was empowered to act as arbitrator in

---

[2] *Bolivar Railway Company Claim (Great Britain v. Venezuela)* (1903), 9 RIAA p. 445.

[3] *Youmans Claim (United States v. Mexico)* (1926), 4 RIAA p. 110. For discussion of the significance of cases of this type, see B. J. Bederman, 'The glorious past and uncertain future of international claims tribunals', in M. W. Janis (ed.), *International Courts for the Twenty-First Century*, Dordrecht, 1992, p. 161.

[4] *Clipperton Island Case (France v. Mexico)* (1931), (1932) 26 AJIL p. 300.

territorial disputes between Chile and Argentina. In the *Palena* case[5] between these two countries in 1966, these powers were delegated to a tribunal consisting of a jurist, Lord McNair, and two geographical experts. In the *Beagle Channel* case[6] (1977), in contrast, Argentina would have preferred a reference of the matter to the International Court and so the tribunal appointed was composed entirely of jurists, all of them members of the permanent body.

If neither a mixed commission nor a sovereign arbitrator is considered appropriate, another possibility is to refer the dispute to a specially qualified individual for a decision. The 1899 Hague Convention established a list of arbitrators, styled, inappropriately, 'the Permanent Court of Arbitration', and created a bureau with premises, library and staff, which still exists and plays a major role in facilitating arbitration and other forms of peaceful settlement.[7] Provided a suitable individual can be found, using a single arbitrator can be quicker and less expensive than convening a larger body, though the demands on the person chosen are correspondingly increased. For this reason, it cannot be regarded as appropriate for all types of case, though the decisions of Chief Justice Taft in the *Tinoco* arbitration[8] and Max Huber in the *Island of Palmas* case[9] show what can be achieved. A variant of this method was employed in the *Monetary Gold* arbitration,[10] where the single arbitrator, George Sauser-Hall, was a member of the Permanent Court of Arbitration and appointed in response to a request from the parties by the President of the International Court. Normally, where a single arbitrator is appointed, he or she will be a jurist. Exceptionally, however, an arbitrator with other qualifications may be chosen. Thus, in 1986, France and New Zealand asked the Secretary-General of the United Nations to act as arbitrator in the *Rainbow Warrior* case,[11] and his ruling, which was unreasoned, but covered the outstanding issues, settled the dispute.

---

[5] *Argentine–Chile Frontier Case*, (1966) 38 ILR p. 10; 16 RIAA p. 109. For discussion, see H. Fox, 'Arbitration', in E. Luard (ed.), *The International Regulation of Frontier Disputes*, London, 1970, pp. 172–91.

[6] *Beagle Channel Arbitration (Argentina v. Chile)* (1977), 52 ILR p. 93. For discussion, see M. Shaw, 'The Beagle Channel Arbitration Award', (1978) 6 Int. Rel. p. 415.

[7] After a period of neglect the role of the PCA has recently been given renewed attention; see J. L. Bleich, 'A new direction for the PCA: The work of the expert group', in Muller and Mijs, *The Flame Rekindled*, p. 17; and W. E. Butler, 'The Hague Permanent Court of Arbitration', in Janis, *International Courts*, p. 43. See also P. Hamilton, H. C. Requena, L. van Scheltinga and Bette E. Shifman (eds.), *The Permanent Court of Arbitration: International Arbitration and Dispute Resolution*, The Hague, 1999.

[8] *Tinoco Arbitration (Great Britain v. Costa Rica)* (1923), 1 RIAA p. 369.

[9] *Island of Palmas Case (The Netherlands v. United States)* (1928), 2 RIAA p. 829.

[10] *Gold Looted by Germany from Rome in 1943 (United States, France, United Kingdom, Italy)* (1953), 20 ILR p. 441.

[11] *Ruling Pertaining to the Differences between France and New Zealand Arising from the Rainbow Warrior Affair* (1986), 74 ILR p. 241. Text also in (1987) 81 AJIL p. 325, (1987) 26 ILM p. 1346 and document J in the appendix below. For discussion, see M. Pugh, 'Legal aspects of the Rainbow Warrior Affair', (1987) 36 ICLQ p. 655.

The form of tribunal most commonly found in modern treaty practice is the collegiate body consisting of an uneven number of persons, generally three or five, with the power to decide the case by majority vote. This type of tribunal was first used in the famous *Alabama Claims* case[12] (1871–2), which concerned the United Kingdom's responsibilities as a neutral during the American Civil War. There, the British and American governments established a five-member tribunal, containing only two national members, and it is this feature, together with the fact that the tribunal followed a strictly juridical procedure and issued a reasoned award, which makes the case a decisive step in the development of arbitration. Cases in which a five-member court has been employed include the *Taba* dispute[13] (1988) between Egypt and Israel, the earlier *Channel* arbitration[14] between the United Kingdom and France (1976–7), the two-stage *Eritrea/Yemen* arbitration[15] (1998–9) and the *Iron Rhine Railway* arbitration[16] between Belgium and the Netherlands (2005). On the other hand, in the *Maritime Delimitation* cases[17] between Guinea and Guinea-Bissau (1985) and Guinea-Bissau and Senegal (1989), the *Heathrow Airport* case[18] between the United States and the United Kingdom (1992–3) and the *OSPAR (Article 9)* arbitration[19] between Ireland and the United Kingdom (2003), a smaller three-member tribunal was used.

The selection of arbitrators

The membership of a collegiate tribunal, like the appointment of a single arbitrator, is a matter for negotiation between the parties, with each side generally appointing one or more 'national' arbitrators and the remaining 'neutral' members being agreed between them. If the parties can settle the

---

[12] J. B. Moore, *History and Digest of the International Arbitrations to Which the United States Has Been a Party*, London, 1898, vol. I, p. 653; also in A. G. La Pradelle and N. Politis, *Recueil des Arbitrages Internationaux*, Paris, 1957, vol. II, p. 713. The award and a valuable collection of background material can be found in Wetter, *The International Arbitral Process*, vol. I, pp. 27–173. See also T. Bingham, 'The *Alabama* Claims Arbitration', (2005) 54 ICLQ p. 1.

[13] *Arbitral Award in the Dispute concerning Certain Boundary Pillars between the Arab Republic of Egypt and the State of Israel* (1988), 80 ILR p. 224, summarised in (1989) 83 AJIL p. 590.

[14] *Delimitation of the Continental Shelf (United Kingdom of Great Britain and Northern Ireland and the French Republic)* (1977), 54 ILR p. 6. For analysis and commentary, see J. G. Merrills, 'The United Kingdom–France Continental Shelf Arbitration', (1980) 10 Calif. Western LJ p. 314.

[15] *Eritrea–Yemen Arbitration*, Phase I (1998), Phase II (1999), (2001) 40 ILM pp. 900 and 983. For discussion, see N. S. M. Antunes, (1999) 48 ICLQ p. 362 and (2001) 50 ICLQ p. 299.

[16] *Iron Rhine Railway Arbitration (Belgium/Netherlands)* (2005), www.pca-cpa.org.

[17] *Guinea–Guinea-Bissau Maritime Delimitation Case* (1985), 77 ILR p. 636; *Guinea-Bissau–Senegal Maritime Delimitation Case* (1989), 83 ILR p. 1.

[18] *United States–United Kingdom Arbitration concerning Heathrow Airport User Charges* (1992–3), 102 ILR p. 216. For analysis, see S. M. Witten, 'The US–UK arbitration concerning Heathrow Airport user charges', (1995) 89 AJIL p. 174.

[19] *Access to Information under Article 9 of the OSPAR Convention (Ireland v. United Kingdom)* (2003), (2003) 42 ILM p. 1118, summarised in (2004) 98 AJIL p. 330.

composition of the tribunal at an early stage, it will be possible to name the members in the arbitration agreement. In the *Channel* arbitration, for example, the *compromis* listed the five jurists who the parties had agreed should constitute the tribunal (see document D in the appendix below). Frequently, however, the identity of the members is left to be settled later. In the latter case, the agreement will simply define the membership of the tribunal and lay down the procedure to be followed in setting it up. A provision of this type may be seen in the agreement setting up the court of arbitration for the *Maritime Delimitation* case between Guinea and Guinea-Bissau.[20]

When setting up the Iran–US Claims Tribunal in 1981, following the diplomatic hostages crisis, it was necessary to create a plenary body from which smaller chambers could be created for determining particular cases. For this reason, the arrangements for the nomination of arbitrators had to be more elaborate than for a conventional arbitration. The instrument establishing the Tribunal therefore provides:

> The Tribunal shall consist of nine members or such larger multiple of three as Iran and the United States may agree are necessary to conduct its business expeditiously. Within ninety days after the entry into force of this agreement, each government shall appoint one-third of the members. Within thirty days after their appointment, the members so appointed shall by mutual agreement select the remaining third of the members and appoint one of the remaining third President of the Tribunal. Claims may be decided by the full Tribunal or by a panel of three members of the Tribunal as the President shall determine. Each such panel shall be composed by the President and shall consist of one member appointed by each of the three methods set forth above.[21]

For obvious reasons, the result of a collegiate arbitration often turns on the decision of the neutral member or members. Deciding who they shall be is therefore extremely important to the governments concerned, which may sometimes find it difficult to agree on suitable candidates. To take account of this, arbitration treaties often provide that, in the event of disagreement, the neutral members may be appointed by the President of the International Court or by some other disinterested party. Such arrangements have proved useful on a number of occasions. In the *Lake Lanoux* arbitration,[22] for example, the French and Spanish governments referred the selection of the president of the tribunal to the King of Sweden, and

---

[20] For the text of this agreement, see 77 ILR p. 642.

[21] Declaration of the Government of the Democratic and Popular Republic of Algeria Concerning the Settlement of Claims by the Government of the United States of America and the Government of the Islamic Republic of Iran, 1981, Article III(1), I Iran–US CTR p. 10; (1981) 20 ILM p. 230. For various reasons the composition of the Tribunal gave rise to a number of problems in practice. For discussion of these, see R. Khan, *The Iran–United States Claims Tribunal*, Dordrecht, 1990, Chapters 3 and 4; and G. H. Aldrich, *The Jurisprudence of the Iran–United States Claims Tribunal*, Oxford, 1996, pp. 9–44.

[22] *Lake Lanoux Arbitration (France v. Spain)* (1957), 24 ILR p. 101. See further Chapter 1.

in the *Rann of Kutch* case[23] the Secretary-General of the United Nations performed the same service for India and Pakistan.

Authorising a third party to take the steps necessary to complete the membership of a tribunal is beneficial in a double sense. In the above-mentioned cases, it enabled states which were experiencing genuine difficulties to avoid an impasse. However, it also prevents a state which has conceived an objection to the whole idea of arbitration from frustrating the process by a blank refusal to co-operate in the appointment of neutral members. But, suppose that a state which wishes to be obstructive refuses even to appoint its own members? The effect of this form of non-co-operation had to be considered in the *Peace Treaties* case.[24]

The peace treaties with Bulgaria, Hungary and Romania provided that disputes arising out of their interpretation or execution were to be referred to arbitral commissions. In accordance with the usual practice, these were to consist of a national member appointed by each side and a third member appointed by agreement, or, failing that, by the Secretary-General of the United Nations. Soon after the treaties came into force in 1947, the United Kingdom and the United States complained that the three former enemy states were violating their human rights obligations. However, when an attempt was made to set in motion the arbitral procedure, the respondent states refused to appoint their representatives to the commissions. In 1950, the whole matter came to the International Court, when the General Assembly asked for an advisory opinion as to the legal consequences of this action.

In the first phase of the case, the Court rejected the respondents' argument that there was no dispute to which the settlement provisions of the peace treaties could apply, and held that Bulgaria, Hungary and Romania were under an obligation to appoint their members of the commissions. When it became clear that, despite the opinion, this duty would not be performed, the Court had to consider whether the provision in the treaties for recourse to the Secretary-General could be invoked to save the arbitration. The Court was urged to decide that the term 'third member' in the treaties meant simply 'neutral member' and was not intended to make the appointment of both national members a prerequisite for the exercise of the Secretary-General's power. This was, however, held to be an unconvincing reading of the text which, the Court held, must be interpreted to cover only situations in which the parties had failed to agree. Consequently, although the respondents' failure to make their appointments incurred international responsibility, it could not in itself justify the creation of a commission by the method proposed.

---

[23] *Indo-Pakistan Western Boundary (Rann of Kutch) Case (India v. Pakistan)* (1968), 50 ILR p. 2. For commentary, see J. G. Wetter, 'The Rann of Kutch Arbitration', (1971) 65 AJIL p. 346.

[24] *Interpretation of Peace Treaties with Bulgaria, Hungary and Rumania*, Advisory Opinion, First Phase, [1950] ICJ Rep. p. 65; Second Phase, [1950] ICJ Rep. p. 221. For commentary, see K. S. Carlston, Note, (1950) 44 AJIL p. 728.

The *Peace Treaties* case is a striking illustration of the obstacles which an unwilling state can place in the way of arbitration and the care which must be taken to cover all contingencies when drafting provisions dealing with the appointment of arbitrators. As in the case of disagreement over the neutral members, the simplest solution is a provision to the effect that, after three months, or some other suitable period, the necessary appointment may be made by an outside party. Though not always included even today, such provisions have been a feature of bilateral treaties for more than fifty years and were endorsed by both the International Law Commission and the Permanent Court of Arbitration.[25] Similar arrangements have been incorporated into the major multilateral agreements on peaceful settlement, including the 1928 Geneva General Act (Article 23), the 1948 Pact of Bogotá (Article 45) and the 1957 European Convention for the Peaceful Settlement of Disputes (Article 21). As we shall see in Chapter 8, arrangements of this type are also to be found in the arbitral provisions of the 1982 Law of the Sea Convention.

When an arbitration is held before a standing body, such as the Iran–US Claims Tribunal, arbitrators will already have been appointed, and so the issue of default should not arise. On the other hand, it is still possible for the national arbitrators to disagree about the appointment of the 'neutral' members, or about selecting the president. To cover these possibilities, the instrument establishing the Tribunal provides for any outstanding appointments to be made by an 'appointing authority', chosen by the Secretary-General of the Permanent Court of Arbitration. The person designated to act in this capacity also has the task of resolving any challenges which may be made to the neutral members. In 1999, for example, Sir Robert Jennings, as appointing authority, reviewed a challenge to the Tribunal's president put forward by Iran and based on supposed doubts about his independence and impartiality. After looking into the matter, however, Sir Robert rejected the allegations, and, in 2001, reached a similar conclusion when another third party judge was challenged by the United States.[26]

Terms of reference

Just as the appointment of arbitrators is in the hands of the parties, so it is for them to determine how the proceedings are to be conducted and what

[25] See the ILC Model Rules of Arbitral Procedure (1958), ILC Year Book, 1958, vol. II, p. 12; text also in Simpson and Fox, *International Arbitration*, p. 295, and Wetter, *The International Arbitral Process*, vol. V, p. 232; and the Permanent Court of Arbitration's Optional Rules for Arbitrating Disputes between Two States (1992), text in (1993) 32 ILM p. 572. It is interesting to see that, in the *Dubai/Sharjah Boundary* arbitration, 91 ILR p. 543, the ILC Model Rules were regarded as an authoritative statement of customary international law and used to identify the salient characteristics of a true arbitral award. See D. W. Bowett, 'The Dubai/Sharjah Boundary Arbitration of 1981', (1994) 65 BYBIL p. 103 at p. 116.
[26] For accounts of these episodes, see (2000) 94 AJIL p. 378 and (2001) 95 AJIL p. 895.

question or questions the arbitrator will be asked to decide. The 1899 and 1907 Hague Conventions laid down rules which have provided the procedural framework for many subsequent arbitrations; more recently, these have been elaborated through the work of the International Law Commission, the International Law Association and other bodies. Ultimately, however, it is for the parties to agree the procedural arrangements, and so here, as elsewhere, they can exercise a high degree of control over the handling of their dispute.

The procedural arrangements determine the way in which the arbitration is to be conducted, where it is to be held and how the proceedings are to be paid for. It is usual to include quite detailed provisions relating to the number and order of the written pleadings, the oral stage of the proceedings and the important issue of time-limits. Other matters which are normally covered in the *compromis* are how the tribunal is to obtain evidence, whether it may appoint experts or conduct visits, whether it can order provisional measures, what languages will be used, how the decision will be taken, whether separate opinions are allowed and whether the decision will be published. Although each of these matters can be negotiated separately, it is clearly convenient if the parties can agree on the use of standard provisions. In the same way, when dealing with the finer procedural details, time can be saved by following established practice. In the 1985 *Maritime Delimitation* case, for example, it was agreed at the first session of the tribunal that the arbitration 'would follow the same rules of procedure as the International Court of Justice, and more specifically that Articles 30–31, 49–50, 52, 54, 56–58, 60–68, 71, 72, 94–95 and 98 of the Rules of the Court would be applicable *mutatis mutandis*'.[27]

Similarly, in the *Heathrow Airport* arbitration, the parties agreed that the tribunal should use rules of procedure adapted from those of the International Centre for Settlement of Investment Disputes.[28] The use of rules developed for international commercial arbitration is explained by the complex economic issues involved in this dispute and the same factor accounts for a number of other procedural innovations. Thus, the United States and the United Kingdom agreed that staggered, rather than simultaneous, pleadings should be filed,[29] while the tribunal decided that the proceedings should be divided into two phases: an initial phase to decide whether the US claims were well founded; then, if necessary, a remedial phase to determine compensation. In the event, the second phase was never concluded

---

[27] Award, para. 9, 77 ILR p. 647. A similar approach was employed in the *Dubai/Sharjah Boundary* arbitration where the vagueness of the *compromis* caused a number of problems; see Bowett, 'The Dubai/Sharjah Boundary Arbitration', pp. 108–9.

[28] See Witten, 'The US–UK arbitration', pp. 182–3.

[29] See *ibid.*, p. 183, n. 34. This departure from the procedure laid down in the 1977 'Bermuda II' Agreement, which prescribes two rounds of simultaneous pleadings, allowed the parties to respond to each other's submissions.

because the case was settled. However, it is interesting to note that, during the pre-hearing period of the remedial phase, the tribunal was persuaded by the United States to direct the United Kingdom to produce hundreds of pages of financial documentation for inspection. Pre-trial discovery is, of course, common in domestic civil litigation, but rather unusual in inter-governmental arbitration. The fact that it was used so extensively here again highlights the special nature of the issues in this case and, like the innovations already described, shows how the procedural framework of an international arbitration can be adapted to meet the parties' needs.

The definition of the issue is important because it establishes the scope of the arbitrator's jurisdiction. By defining the issue broadly, the parties can use arbitration to remove a major obstacle to good relations. Conversely (and more commonly), by defining the issue narrowly, they can prevent an investigation of wider questions which might create more problems than it would resolve, or exclude from arbitration particular issues for which negotiation or some other means of settlement is considered more appropriate. In the *Rainbow Warrior* case, for example, France and New Zealand asked the Secretary-General for a ruling on a number of aspects of the dispute, including the amount of compensation to be paid by France for sinking the vessel in Auckland harbour and the future of the two French intelligence agents who were serving prison sentences in New Zealand for carrying out this action. The Secretary-General was not asked to decide whether compensation was due, because this responsibility was admitted, nor whether New Zealand was justified in detaining the agents, because both states were more concerned with finding an acceptable solution to the dispute than with justifying their past actions. Although, therefore, the Secretary-General had to deal with a range of issues, in the interests of settling the dispute the parties chose to focus on certain matters, to the exclusion of others.

The framing of the question or questions is normally a matter for nego-tiation between the parties and, because of its importance, may be difficult to agree. This was the case in the *Beagle Channel* dispute where sovereignty over the islands of Picton, Nueva and Lennox was clearly the central issue, but Chile and Argentina were unable to devise a mutually acceptable for-mulation for the *compromis*. The solution was to include two versions of the question, and refer both to the tribunal for decision. A different solution was adopted in the *Eritrea/Yemen* arbitration, where territorial sovereignty was in issue, but the parties could not agree on whether certain islands fell within the scope of the arbitration. The two states therefore left the question for the tribunal itself to determine, asking it to decide this as a preliminary issue, taking into account 'the respective positions of the two Parties'. A mat-ter on which they did agree was that, as their maritime boundaries were also disputed, and largely dependent on their territorial titles, the arbitration should take place in two stages. They therefore included in their *compromis* a requirement that the issue of titles, along with the scope of the dispute, should be decided at the first stage of the arbitration, followed by a second on the question of maritime delimitation.

If the parties fail to define the issues on which they want a decision with sufficient particularity, damaging disputes over exactly what has been agreed are likely to arise. In the *Alabama Claims* case, for example, disagreement between Great Britain and the United States over whether the tribunal was authorised to award compensation for indirect damage almost led to a failure of the arbitration. On the other hand, defining the issue too narrowly can sometimes create difficulties of a different kind. In the *Taba* dispute, which concerned the location of certain pillars marking an international boundary, Egypt and Israel set out their respective submissions in an appendix to the *compromis* and asked the tribunal to decide the location of the pillars in dispute. However, in an annex to the agreement, they stated that the tribunal was not authorised to establish a location of a boundary pillar other than a location advanced by Israel or Egypt and recorded in the appendix to the agreement. In other words, the tribunal had to choose between the rival locations put forward by the parties and could not select a different solution. This type of directive was not unprecedented and is, of course, perfectly clear. It does, however, create a problem if neither party can make out a persuasive case. One of the arbitrators considered that, if Israel's argument was rejected, Egypt's was even less convincing and so the tribunal should declare that neither had proved its case.[30] Although the majority rejected this conclusion, there is no doubt that restricting the powers of a tribunal so severely can generate problems.

A rather similar difficulty has arisen in a number of recent cases concerned with the delimitation of maritime zones. Here, the parties must not only decide whether they wish the tribunal to draw a boundary line on a map, or to indicate merely the principles and rules applicable to the delimitation, or to do something in between.[31] They must also decide whether they wish the tribunal to deal with the continental shelf alone, or with the whole exclusive economic zone, and, if the latter, whether the tribunal must establish a single boundary for all purposes, or whether it is to be allowed to deal separately with jurisdiction over the sea and the sea-bed. The tendency in recent arbitral agreements has been to require a single boundary line and it is easy to see the advantages of this solution. From the juridical point of view, however, a directive of this kind can make it difficult for a tribunal to discharge its task adequately, because the considerations relevant to the sea

---

[30] See the elaborate dissenting opinion of Professor Lapidoth in 80 ILR p. 312 at pp. 347–8.

[31] For example, to identify the relevant principles and rules and 'to specify precisely the practical way in which the aforesaid principles and rules apply to this situation so as to enable the experts of the two countries to delimit those areas without difficulty', see the Special Agreement in the *Tunisia–Libya Continental Shelf* case in [1982] ICJ Rep. p. 21. The problems of interpreting this type of directive are discussed in the penultimate part of Chapter 7.

and the sea-bed will often be quite distinct and it might therefore be better to have different boundaries for different purposes.

Arbitrators only have authority to answer the question or questions referred, and if they exceed their jurisdiction the award can be challenged as a nullity. As a result, although jurisdictional questions are less prominent in the work of arbitral tribunals than in proceedings before the International Court, when such questions do arise they are treated with the same scrupulous regard for the principle of consensuality. For example, it emerged in the course of the proceedings in the *Channel* arbitration that to delimit a sea-bed boundary in the area between the Channel Islands and the coasts of Normandy and Brittany, it would be necessary to decide a number of disputed issues concerning each party's territorial sea. Since this would be to go beyond the terms of the *compromis* which the United Kingdom and France were evidently unwilling to extend, the court decided that a delimitation of this area was outside its competence and must be left for the parties themselves to determine. In the *Eritrea/Yemen* case, on the other hand, the tribunal, having identified certain islands as belonging to Yemen, went on to hold that this did not affect the traditional rights of Eritrean fishermen in the surrounding seas. Since the arbitration agreement asked only for a decision 'on sovereignty', the tribunal's approach might be questioned, but on practical grounds can be justified as a realistic interpretation of its remit.[32]

In the *St Pierre and Miquelon* case,[33] the issue of consent arose in relation to a third party. France sought a delimitation of the continental shelf appertaining to islands situated off the Canadian coast and also asked the tribunal to determine their entitlement beyond the 200-mile limit. However, the court held that this would involve determining France's rights *vis-à-vis* the international community which was not a party to the arbitration. It therefore decided that it had no jurisdiction to extend its ruling in the way requested. We shall see later that the International Court operates under a similar limitation. Thus, not only is the consent of the litigants essential to the arbitrator's competence, but so is the consent of any third party whose rights may be in issue.

In the above examples, the courts concerned were able to decide the main points in dispute, and so the limitations on their authority were not very important. Sometimes, however, the issue of jurisdiction goes to the root of the arbitrators' competence. In its decision in the case of *Haji-Bagherpour v. United States*,[34] the Iran–US Claims Tribunal decided that it had no jurisdiction over a claim by an Iranian national whose oil tanker

---

[32] See N. S. M. Antunes, 'The Eritrea–Yemen Arbitration: First stage – The law of title to territory re-averred', (1999) 48 ICLQ p. 362 at pp. 383–4. See also, however, the text accompanying note 53 below.

[33] *Case Concerning Delimitation of Maritime Areas between Canada and the French Republic (St Pierre and Miquelon)* (1992) 95 ILR p. 645, summarised in (1993) 87 AJIL p. 452.

[34] (1983), 2 Iran–US CTR p. 38; 71 ILR p. 600.

was destroyed by American forces during the abortive attempt to rescue the diplomatic hostages in April 1980. Similarly, in the case of *Grimm* v. *Iran*,[35] the Tribunal decided that it had no jurisdiction over a claim by a wife based on her husband's assassination on the ground that the claimant's 'property rights' were not in issue. In these cases, then, individual claims failed and were rejected on jurisdictional grounds.

Even more significant are those decisions in which the effect of a ruling is to settle the fate of a whole class of cases. In *Case No. A/18*,[36] for example, the Tribunal decided that, in view of the purpose for which it had been established, it had jurisdiction to entertain the claims of dual Iranian and United States nationals, provided they satisfied the dominant or effective nationality test in accordance with general international law. In an earlier ruling, the Tribunal decided that, under the terms of the Settlement Agreement, it had no general jurisdiction over claims which might be filed by Iran against nationals of the United States.[37] This, too, was a critical decision because it had the effect of limiting the Tribunal's competence to Iranian counter-claims against Americans with cases already before the Tribunal.

Basis of the decision

No less important than the definition of the issue is the parties' directive to the tribunal as to the criteria to be applied in making its decision. Frequently, the tribunal's instructions are to decide the matter in accordance with international law. The court was called upon to decide the boundary of the British and French portions of the continental shelf on this basis in the *Channel* arbitration, and the *compromis* in the *Beagle Channel* case, after formulating the rival versions of the point at issue, was in similar terms. When the directive is less explicit, the applicable law must be inferred. In the *Rann of Kutch* case, for example, the parties asked the court to decide the case in light of their respective claims and the evidence produced before it, and in the *Taba* dispute the *compromis* contained no reference at all to the applicable law, but merely asked the tribunal to decide the location of the boundary pillars 'of the recognised international boundary'. Despite these unhelpful instructions, the respective courts followed the usual practice in such cases, assumed that what the parties wanted was a decision based on international law and gave their judgments accordingly.

Sometimes, the parties want international law to provide the basis for the tribunal's decision, but wish particular aspects to be emphasised. For example, when Eritrea and Ethiopia set up a boundary commission to

---

[35] (1983), 2 Iran–US CTR p. 78; 71 ILR p. 650.
[36] (1984), 5 Iran–US CTR p. 25; 75 ILR p. 176. The scope of this decision was subsequently considered in *Saghi* v. *Iran*, (1993), 14 Iran–US CTR p. 3; 84 ILR p. 609.
[37] Iran–United States Claims Tribunal: Decision with regard to Jurisdiction over Claims Filed by Iran against US Nationals (1981), 1 Iran–US CTR p. 101; 62 ILR p. 595.

define their disputed frontier in 2000, they required it to perform its task on the basis of 'pertinent colonial treaties' and applicable international law, but explicitly laid down that 'the Commission shall not have the power to make decisions *ex aequo et bono*.[38] Similarly, in the *Eritrea/Yemen* case, the tribunal was asked to rule on territorial sovereignty 'in accordance with the principles, rules and practices of international law applicable to the matter, and on the basis, in particular, of historic titles'. Likewise, at the second stage of the arbitration, it was requested to delimit the maritime boundaries between Eritrea and Yemen in light of the decision reached in the first stage and 'taking into account . . . the United Nations Convention on the Law of the Sea and any other pertinent factor'. Given the matters in dispute and the parties' respective positions, no decision based on law could have ignored the elements mentioned even without these directives. By including them specifically, however, the two states indicated clearly what they saw as key features of the case and therefore expected the tribunal to deal with in its decision.

If the parties are agreed that a solution in accordance with international law would not be appropriate, they can instruct the arbitrator to decide the dispute on some other basis. This can sometimes be another way of isolating a dispute from surrounding complications. In the *Alabama Claims* case, for example, the parties instructed the tribunal to apply a particular set of rules concerning neutrality which the United States regarded as international law, but Great Britain did not. Here, then, the parties' willingness to have the rules applied as *lex specialis* meant that the wider disagreement as to their status was no longer an obstacle to settlement of the dispute. If, on the other hand, the arbitrators' remit is not extended, then the scope for such initiatives is restricted. Thus, in the *OSPAR (Article 9)* case, an arbitration founded on Article 32 of the 1992 OSPAR Convention, the tribunal held that the only applicable law was the Convention itself, and no less crucially that, when interpreting the Convention, it could not take account of evolving international law and practice, or developments that were 'almost law', in the absence of express authority to do so.[39]

The parties' ability to specify the law the arbitrator is to apply also enables them to employ municipal law, either alone, or in combination with some other system. In the *Trail Smelter* case,[40] the tribunal was instructed to

---

[38] On this and other aspects of the Commission's work, see J. G. Merrills, 'Reflections on dispute settlement in light of recent arbitrations involving Eritrea', in A. Constantinides and N. Zaikos (eds.), *The Diversity of International Law*, Leiden, 2009, p. 109. Also M. N. Shaw, 'Title, control and closure? The experience of the Eritrea–Ethiopia Boundary Commission', (2007) 56 ICLQ p. 755.

[39] The tribunal reached this decision by a majority of two to one. For criticism of its conclusion, see P. Sands, *Principles of International Environmental Law*, 2nd edn, Cambridge, 2003, pp. 857–8, but compare T. L. McDorman, Note, (2004) 98 AJIL p. 330 at pp. 337–9.

[40] *Trail Smelter Arbitration (US v. Canada)* (1938 and 1941), 3 RIAA p. 1905. For commentary, see J. E. Read, 'The Trail Smelter dispute', (1963) 1 Can. Yearbook Int. L. p. 213.

apply 'the law and practice followed in dealing with cognate questions in the United States of America as well as international law and practice'. Since the dispute concerned liability for trans-frontier air pollution, an issue on which international law had only recently begun to develop, authorising the use of municipal law here provided the tribunal with a recognisably legal basis for its decision, as well as an invaluable opportunity to advance the development of international environmental law.

Reference to municipal law is, of course, particularly common in commercial arbitration. The concession agreement involved in the important case of *BP* v. *Libya*,[41] for example, provided that:

> This concession shall be governed by and interpreted in accordance with the principles of the law of Libya common to the principles of international law and in the absence of such common principles then by and in accordance with the general principles of law, including such of those principles as may have been applied by international tribunals.

This kind of dispute, involving an entity other than a state, is strictly speaking beyond the scope of this study but similar provisions can be found in arbitration agreements between states. The Iran–US Claims Tribunal, for example, is instructed to 'decide all cases on the basis of respect for law', and to apply 'such choice of law rules and principles of commercial and international law as the Tribunal determines to be applicable, taking into account relevant usages of the trade, contract provisions and changed circumstances' – a directive which clearly reflects the predominantly commercial character of the Tribunal's business, as well as an intention to give it considerable freedom of action.[42]

If the parties wish to increase the arbitrator's freedom still further, they can authorise him to take into account what is fair and reasonable, as well as the rules of international or municipal law. There is a hint of this in the reference to 'changed circumstances' in the provision just mentioned, and the direction to the *Trail Smelter* tribunal to 'give consideration to the desire of the high contracting parties to reach a solution just to all parties concerned' was quite explicit. In the absence of such instructions, arbitral tribunals have frequently achieved the same result by using 'equitable' considerations of various kinds to qualify or expand their application and interpretation of the law. This technique has been particularly prominent in arbitrations concerning territorial and boundary disputes, where the best solution may sometimes be difficult to justify in strictly legal terms. Thus, in the *Rann of Kutch* case, the award of certain territory to Pakistan was

---

[41] *BP Exploration Company (Libya) Limited* v. *Government of the Libyan Arab Republic* (1973), 53 ILR p. 297. For analysis, see R. C. A. White, 'Expropriation of the Libyan oil concessions – Two conflicting international arbitrations', (1981) 30 ICLQ p. 1.

[42] See J. R. Crook, 'Applicable law in international arbitration: The Iran–US Claims Tribunal experience', (1989) 83 AJIL p. 278; and Aldrich, *The Jurisprudence*, Chapter 4.

held to be justified on the ground that 'it would be inequitable to recognise these inlets as foreign territory. It would be conducive to friction and conflict. The paramount consideration of promoting peace and stability in the region compels the recognition and confirmation that this territory, which is wholly surrounded by Pakistan territory, also be regarded as such.'[43]

It is worth noting that, in some situations, it is unnecessary to give arbitrators express authority to apply equity because such considerations are already incorporated in the relevant legal rule. In the *Heathrow Airport* arbitration, for example, the question before the tribunal was whether the UK had fulfilled its obligations under Article 10 of the 1977 Air Services Agreement with the United States, allowing the imposition of charges which were 'just and reasonable' and subject to 'equitable apportionment' among airport users. This very general language clearly gave the arbitrators a good deal of freedom, but at the same time made their task difficult because there was little in the way of international precedent to guide them.[44] Another example of this state of affairs is in the law relating to the delimitation of maritime zones, where, as a result of judicial pronouncements, developing state practice and international conventions, it is now accepted that the law requires delimitation in accordance with equitable principles, taking into account all relevant circumstances, so as to reach an equitable result. This clearly leaves a great deal of scope for argument as to the content of the applicable principles, the relevance of particular circumstances and the appropriate result in a specific case.

It is interesting, however, that in deciding the various cases which have arisen, international courts and tribunals have consistently made the point that their decisions must be based on law, and that without further authorisation they are not 'endowed with discretionary powers or . . . authorised to decide *ex aequo et bono*'.[45] It follows that, while certain criteria are accepted as relevant to delimitation, attempts to refashion nature or to compensate for the economic inequalities of states are not. In this way, tribunals dealing with maritime delimitation have sought to utilise the flexibility inherent in the idea of equity, while at the same time retaining their legal character and avoiding approaches which would smack of conciliation. Whether this delicate distinction can actually be sustained is an issue to which we shall return in Chapter 7.

---

[43] 50 ILR p. 530. For a penetrating analysis of the use of equity and related considerations by international tribunals in such cases, see A. L. W. Munkman, 'Adjudication and adjustment – International judicial decision and the settlement of territorial and boundary disputes', (1972–3) 46 BYBIL p. 1. On equity in other contexts, see C. W. Jenks, *The Prospects of International Adjudication*, London, 1964, Chapter 7.

[44] See Witten, 'The US–UK arbitration', p. 191. As the same writer points out, the general language of the terms which were being applied also had the effect of depriving the decision of most of its value as a precedent.

[45] *Maritime Delimitation* case, 77 ILR p. 635 at pp. 675–6.

When arbitrators are asked by the parties to have regard to equitable considerations, or take it upon themselves to do so, they are no longer simply adjudicators, applying the relevant rules, but begin to assume the role of legislators, creating law for the case in hand. In the cases considered above, equity was employed as part of the law, or as a supplement to it, and the arbitrator thus combined the two functions. Sometimes, however, what is wanted is a wholly legislative solution, a decision, that is, in which the question of current rights is completely subordinated to the search for a fair and reasonable solution. Arbitration is flexible enough to allow for such a solution, which the parties can obtain by asking the tribunal to render its decision *ex aequo et bono*.

Numerous examples of tribunals being given the authority to decide cases on this basis can be found in treaties of arbitration. The convention between Great Britain and Portugal of 1872 regarding claims to Delagoa Bay provided that 'should the Arbiter be unable to decide wholly in favour of either of the respective claims, he shall be requested to give such a decision as will, in his opinion, furnish an equitable solution of the difficulty'. And a treaty on the arbitration of boundary disputes concluded between Colombia and Ecuador in 1907 went even further in providing that 'the arbiters . . . may, leaving to one side strict law, adopt an equitable line in accordance with the necessities and convenience of the two countries'.[46]

In several of the cases decided on this basis, an arbitrator has been called upon to lay down the rules of a new regime to regulate aspects of the parties' relations, a matter which would normally be settled by diplomatic negotiation. In both the *Bering Sea* arbitration[47] (1893) and the *North Atlantic Coast Fisheries* case[48] (1910), a framework for the future conduct of the United States and the United Kingdom was created in this way, while in the *Brcko* arbitration[49] (1999) a tribunal set up under the 1995 Dayton Peace Agreement created a special regime for a disputed area of Bosnia and Herzegovina, and, in the *Free Zones* arbitration[50] (1933), a tribunal undertook the onerous task of laying down new customs regulations to govern the exchange of goods between the free zones and Switzerland 'in a manner more appropriate to the economic conditions of the present day'.

---

[46] See Munkman, 'Adjudication and adjustment', p. 24.

[47] *Bering Sea Arbitration (Great Britain v. United States)* (1893), Moore, *International Arbitrations*, vol. I, p. 935; also in (1912) 6 AJIL p. 233.

[48] *North Atlantic Coast Fisheries Arbitration (Great Britain v. United States)* (1910), 11 RIAA p. 173.

[49] *Arbitral Tribunal for Dispute over Inter-Entity Boundary in Brcko*, Final Award, (1999) 38 ILM p. 534; and see M. G. Karnavas, 'Creating the legal framework of the Brcko district of Bosnia and Herzegovina', (2003) 97 AJIL p. 111. It should be noted, however, that in setting up this regime the tribunal adopted an extremely broad interpretation of its terms of reference.

[50] *The Free Zones of Upper Savoy and the District of Gex*, Arbitral Award (1933), (1933–4) 10 PCIJ Ann. R. (Ser. E) p. 106; also in Wetter, *The International Arbitral Process*, vol. I, p. 596.

In the unusual circumstances of the *Rainbow Warrior* affair, the Secretary-General interpreted his function in a rather similar way. Here, the parties appear to have given no indication at all of the basis on which the case was to be decided, and the Secretary-General, whose decision was in the form of an elaborate set of conclusions, saw no necessity to explore the issue. However, in dealing with the crucial question of the future of the imprisoned French agents, he outlined the parties' opposing submissions, and then said that he saw his task as to 'find a solution in respect of the two officers which both respects and reconciles these conflicting positions'.[51] This certainly suggests that he considered that his function was to find an acceptable result, rather than to determine the parties' legal rights, and this is borne out by the solution which he arrived at. For, as well as settling the question of compensation and various other issues, the Secretary-General decided that the agents should be transferred from New Zealand and spend the next three years under military discipline on a base in a remote island in French Polynesia. This ingenious solution, which was subsequently implemented, would clearly not have been open to an arbitrator concerned only with the parties' legal rights, and in this respect the case resembles those in which arbitral tribunals have created new regimes. On the other hand, the explicit emphasis on reconciling the parties' positions suggests a process closer to conciliation than arbitration *ex aequo et bono*.

In the *Eritrea/Yemen* arbitration, having ruled at the first stage of the case that its decision on territorial title was without prejudice to the parties' traditional fishing rights, the tribunal then had to establish the scope and basis of such rights at the second stage, a matter on which Eritrea and Yemen, perhaps not surprisingly, expressed very different views. The tribunal thus found itself with the task of identifying, or (more accurately) creating, a regime for fishing, a consequence not of the arbitral *compromis* but of its own earlier decision. Although unusual, this self-imposed task, as already mentioned, can be regarded as both necessary and justified in the circumstances. Less easy to defend, however, is the tribunal's decision to account for the new regime in terms of Islamic law, a legal system which it had not been asked to apply. As one critic of the case has observed, tribunals in international arbitrations 'would be well advised to stick to international law, particularly when the parties have expressly indicated that they wish it to be applied and when it contains all the elements necessary for achieving the tribunal's objectives'.[52]

How significant is the distinction between, on the one hand, arbitration *ex aequo et bono* in a case like the *Free Zones*, or the 'binding conciliation'

---

[51] *Rainbow Warrior* ruling, 74 ILR p. 241 at p. 272.

[52] See W. M. Reisman, Note, (2000) 94 AJIL p. 721 at p. 729, and, for a more detailed analysis, N. S. M. Antunes, 'The second stage of the Eritrea–Yemen arbitration and the development of international law', (2001) 50 ICLQ p. 299 at pp. 301–16.

of the *Rainbow Warrior* case, and, on the other hand, arbitration according to law in, say, the *Channel* arbitration? It has often been pointed out that adjudication is never simply a mechanical process of applying rules, but always involves an element of legislation. Conversely, in cases where the arbitrator is deliberately given freedom, he legislates not in a vacuum, but against the background of the parties' legal rights. Arbitration according to law and arbitration *ex aequo et bono* should be seen, then, as points on a continuum rather than as fundamentally different operations, and the question is not so much whether law is relevant in a given arbitration, as how far the arbitrator is authorised to base his decision on other grounds.

But, if the distinction between arbitration according to law and arbitration *ex aequo et bono* should not be exaggerated, it should not be minimised either. Arbitration of the *Free Zones* type calls for the decision-maker to review a broader and more diverse range of evidence than a conventional legal arbitration, and therefore imposes a different and perhaps more oner-ous task. This clearly has implications for the composition of the tribunal and the organisation of its work. If technical issues of a non-legal nature are to be a prominent feature of the parties' submissions, the tribunal is likely to require the services of an expert, or, as in the *Free Zones* case, may itself be made up of non-lawyers with the appropriate skills. Here, there is an obvious parallel between arbitration and the processes of inquiry and con-ciliation which, as we have just seen, the *Rainbow Warrior* case has served to underline.

A more fundamental point is that the parties' directive to the tribunal normally defines the limits of its authority and must always be respected. A request for a decision according to law, for a decision *ex aequo et bono*, or for something in between, reflects the parties' wish that the tribunal settle their dispute on a narrower or a broader basis. If it turns out that the framework prescribed by the parties has not in fact guided the tribunal's approach to the case, this may, as we shall see, be grounds for setting aside the decision.

Effect of the award

An arbitral award is binding, but not necessarily final. For it may be open to the parties to take further proceedings to interpret, revise, rectify, appeal or nullify the decision. Whether such steps are permissible, and, if so, whether the new case can be heard by the original tribunal, or must be brought before another body such as the International Court, depends partly on general international law, but mainly on the terms of the arbitration agreement.

The power to interpret an award, or to appeal against it, must normally be the subject of an express grant. Since the object of the parties in going to arbitration is to end the dispute, provision for appeal is relatively rare. Interpretation, on the other hand, which concerns the clarification of the award, not its correctness, is easier to justify and more commonly allowed.

Thus, in the *Taba* case, the *compromis* provided that any dispute between the parties 'as to the interpretation of the award or its implementation' could be referred to the tribunal for clarification at the request of either party, within thirty days of the rendering of the award. Similarly, the agreement in the *Channel* arbitration allowed disputes 'as to the meaning and scope of the decision' to be referred back within a period of three months. In the second case, the arrangements for interpretation were to prove important because a serious disagreement arose relating to two parts of the award. This was resolved only after further proceedings in which the scope of the power of the court of arbitration to review its award became a crucial issue.

The *Channel* arbitration demonstrates that, when a tribunal is asked to revisit a decision, it must be careful not to exceed its authority. The same point emerges from the rejection by the Eritrea–Ethiopia Boundary Commission of a 'Request for Interpretation, Correction and Consultation' from Ethiopia on the ground that what was sought went beyond the Commission's powers of interpretation or revision, and as such was inadmissible.[53] On the other hand, the tribunal in the *Iron Rhine Railway* case, having made a minor correction at the request of Belgium, went on to issue an interpretation of its award,[54] answering a number of questions from the same state relating to its scope and implications. While it is true that 'judicial and arbitral practice on the exercise of the power of interpretation is somewhat limited',[55] these cases reflect the varying situations that can arise, and show how practice on interpretation is accumulating.

One of the many unusual features of the *Rainbow Warrior* case was that the question of disputes relating to implementation, instead of being dealt with in the initial agreement, was addressed in the award itself. New Zealand was anxious to ensure that the agreements which would be necessary to implement the Secretary-General's ruling would be subject to compulsory arbitration in the event of a dispute arising as to their interpretation or application. Observing that France was not averse to this, the Secretary-General decided that such a procedure should be created. This reinforces the point already made, that the ruling was concerned to create a framework for regulating the parties' relations in the future, as well as the suggestion outlined above to the effect that some of the elements of arbitration were here displaced by factors reminiscent of conciliation. It is also of interest that, in outlining the arrangements for the arbitration of future disputes, the Secretary-General gave himself the power to designate both the neutral member and the national members of the three-member tribunal if the parties failed to do so. Like the other parts of the ruling, these arrangements

---

[53] Eritrea–Ethiopia Boundary Commission, Decision on Interpretation of 24 June 2002, www.pca-cpa.org.

[54] *Iron Rhine Railway*, Award on Interpretation of 20 September 2005, www.pca-cpa.org.

[55] C. Brown, *A Common Law of International Adjudication*, Oxford, 2007, p. 173.

were subsequently incorporated in an agreement between the parties,[56] and their value was soon to be demonstrated.

The dispute which prompted the *Rainbow Warrior II* arbitration[57] arose because, having sent the two agents to the island of Hao in accordance with the Secretary-General's ruling, the French government returned them both to metropolitan France before the expiry of the stipulated three-year period of isolation. When New Zealand protested and maintained that this unilateral action was a violation of France's obligations, the issue was referred to arbitration in accordance with the parties' earlier agreement. A three-member tribunal was established to decide the case on the basis of the *lex specialis* established in the agreement and 'the applicable rules and principles of international law'. Unlike the original arbitration, the tribunal's award, which was handed down in 1990, was fully reasoned, containing important rulings on the law relating to state responsibility, remedies and various other matters. Although the tribunal upheld most of New Zealand's arguments, it decided for technical reasons not to award damages, making instead a declaration of illegality, and, in an unusual further step, recommended the creation of a joint fund to promote friendly relations between the two states to which France agreed to make an initial contribution equivalent to US$2 million. If the French government had carried out its original obligations in good faith, the Secretary-General's decision in the first arbitration would have concluded the matter. When regrettably it did not, New Zealand's foresight at least meant that there was a forum which could finally lay the dispute to rest.

Without an express grant, there is no general power to revise an award in order to take account of new facts. There is, however, nothing to prevent the parties from including a provision to this effect, if they think that it could be useful. So, for example, the agreement under which Guinea and Guinea-Bissau referred the *Maritime Delimitation* case to arbitration included both a provision permitting further proceedings in the event of dispute concerning the implementation and interpretation of the award and a provision allowing for the possibility of revision. The latter laid down that it was open to either party to request revision of the award 'if any new element has been discovered which could have decisively influenced the award, provided that before the delivery of the award this new element was unknown to the Tribunal and to the Party which requests the revision, and there is no fault on the part of this Party'. The wording of this article was modelled on Article 61 of the Statute of the International Court of Justice, and its inclusion is perhaps explained by the difficulty which the

---

[56] See 74 ILR p. 276.

[57] *Rainbow Warrior (New Zealand v. France)* (1990), 82 ILR p. 499. For analysis and commentary, see J. S. Davidson, 'The Rainbow Warrior arbitration concerning the treatment of the French agents Mafart and Prieur', (1991) 40 ICLQ p. 446.

absence of such a provision caused for the United Kingdom in the *Channel* arbitration.

In this connection, it should also be noted that a decision which contains an error in expression or calculation can probably be corrected, at least until the award has been executed, and, since this is an inherent power, no express authorisation is required. This point was made in the *Channel* arbitration, and, at the second stage of the proceedings in the case of *BP v. Libya*, the claimant went so far as to argue that a tribunal which is not *functus officio* also has an inherent power to reopen an award, if it has made a fundamental error of law, and if the earlier decision was not intended to be final. The arbitrator in that case found that it was unnecessary to decide the point, but the fact that, in the *Trail Smelter* case and a number of others, a limited power to reopen appears to have been recognised suggests that the argument may be well founded.

States take a case to arbitration with the intention of obtaining a decision which both parties will be bound to carry out and which will put an end to the dispute. But a decision is only binding in international law if the tribunal has been properly constituted, has carried out its instructions and has produced an adequate award. It is therefore possible for a party to deny that an award is effective by invoking the doctrine of nullity.[58]

An arbitrator clearly has no jurisdiction to make an award if the instrument from which he claims to derive his authority is invalid, not yet in force, or has terminated. In the *Arbitral Award* case[59] (1960), this was one of the grounds on which Nicaragua challenged a boundary award made in 1906 by the King of Spain. Nicaragua argued that the Gamez-Bonilla treaty under which the King had been appointed, and which had been signed with Honduras in 1894, had lapsed before he had agreed to act as arbitrator. The International Court, however, held that, because the treaty had not come into force until the exchange of ratifications in 1896, it was in force at the crucial time and so provided the necessary basis for the King's appointment.

Since an arbitrator's authority derives from the parties' agreement, it may be possible to dispute an award on the ground that the arbitrator's appointment was not in accordance with the agreement. This, of course, is why it was necessary to seek an advisory opinion as to the propriety of appointing a neutral arbitrator in the *Peace Treaties* case, and the same issue provided the basis for Nicaragua's other main argument in the *Arbitral Award* case.

The Gamez-Bonilla Treaty provided for the appointment of the King of Spain only after various other possibilities had been exhausted. Nicaragua

---

[58] For a comprehensive review of the issue of nullity, see W. M. Reisman, *Nullity and Revision*, New Haven, CT, 1971.

[59] *Arbitral Award Made by the King of Spain on December 23, 1906*, Judgment, [1960] ICJ Rep. p. 192. For commentary and analysis, see D. H. N. Johnson, Note, (1961) 10 ICLQ p. 328.

maintained that this requirement had not been observed, with the result that the appointment of the King was invalid. However, the Court again disagreed and held that Nicaragua had failed to show that the treaty had not been complied with. With regard to both this and the earlier issue, the Court noted that Nicaragua had clearly approved the appointment of the King as arbitrator at the time and had raised no objection until 1911. In these circumstances, said the Court, whatever the effect of the treaty, Nicaragua was in no position to challenge the setting up of the arbitration.

Cases in which the legality of the arbitrator's appointment is in question are rather rare. More commonly, the issue is whether an arbitrator has exceeded his authority by failing to follow instructions. A clear case of excess of jurisdiction will arise if an arbitrator fails to obey the parties' directive as to the law to be applied, which explains the caution of tribunals like that in the *OSPAR (Article 9)* case. Likewise, an award can be challenged if the arbitrator, asked to choose between two alternatives, devises a third solution, or if the award fails to answer the questions referred, or deals with others which were not presented. In another *Arbitral Award* case[60] in 1991, Guinea-Bissau asked the International Court to declare that the award in the 1989 *Maritime Delimitation* case was a nullity on the ground that the tribunal had failed to answer the second of two questions in the *compromis* and consequently had failed to settle its dispute with Senegal. The Court, however, rejected the argument, finding that the agreement between the two states made an answer to the second question conditional on a negative answer to the first. Accordingly, the tribunal, which had given a positive answer to the first question, had done what it was asked to do.[61]

Guinea-Bissau also argued that the award, which had been made by two votes to one, was a nullity because it lacked a true majority. This was because the president of the arbitral tribunal, though voting for the decision, had made a declaration in which he appeared to support the views of the dissenting arbitrator. The Court, however, rejected this argument also, finding that the voting was clear and the president's declaration reflected a preference rather than a contradiction. The conclusion to be drawn is that, while it is perhaps unwise for an arbitrator to display too much enthusiasm for conclusions he has rejected, if the decision itself is clear, indiscipline alone is not a ground for nullification.[62]

---

[60] *Arbitral Award of 31 July 1989*, Judgment, [1991] ICJ Rep. p. 53. For analysis, see F. Beveridge, Note, (1992) 41 ICLQ p. 891; and C. A. Hartzenbusch, Note, (1992) 86 AJIL p. 553.

[61] If the tribunal had interpreted its task more broadly, it could, as its president suggested, have answered both questions. However, while the availability of an alternative line of argument would have been relevant to an appeal from the decision, the ICJ held that it had no bearing on the issue of nullity. The case thus provides a clear illustration of the difference between appellate and nullification proceedings, especially the more limited scope of the latter.

[62] See further S. Schwebel, 'The majority vote of an international arbitral tribunal', in Schwebel, *Justice in International Law*, Cambridge, 1994, p. 213.

An award will be a nullity if in its handling of the case the tribunal has transgressed a basic rule of judicial procedure. The principle that no one may be a judge in his own cause prohibits the members of an arbitral tribunal from identifying with, or taking instructions from, either of the parties. The common practice of appointing 'national' arbitrators is not inconsistent with this principle, since national arbitrators, though nominated by the parties, are still required to act judicially. But, if there are grounds for believing that an arbitrator has rehearsed with a witness the evidence the latter is about to give, as in the *Buraimi* arbitration,[63] the award could be set aside.

The principle that both sides must be given a fair opportunity to present their case is likewise of fundamental importance. A party which refuses to appear cannot, of course, claim that an award is a nullity because its arguments have not been heard. It may be different, however, if a tribunal bases its decision on considerations which were never put to the parties. That is why it was a risk for the tribunal to introduce Islamic law at the second stage of the *Eritrea/Yemen* arbitration and was actually one of the grounds on which the claimant sought to reopen the proceedings in *BP* v. *Libya*.[64] Though the application in that case was dismissed on other grounds, there seems no reason in principle why such a judicial bolt from the blue should not have the effect of nullifying the award in an appropriate case.

Failure to give reasons for a decision can be another ground for nullifying an award. As already mentioned, unreasoned awards, particularly from sovereign arbitrators, were common in the early part of the last century, but were displaced by reasoned awards as the distinction between legal and political means of settlement became clearer. As late as 1899, however, the tribunal in the *Venezuela–British Guiana Boundary* case issued an unreasoned decision, the validity of which on this, and other grounds, must be considered doubtful.[65] Reasoned awards are important because, unless the parties are interested only in the result, they are entitled to know the tribunal's response to their argument and, more fundamentally, because a reasoned award is the best way of ensuring that the tribunal resists the temptation to simply 'split the difference' and bases its decision on the merits of the case.

---

[63] A useful collection of materials relating to the *Buraimi* arbitration will be found in Wetter, *The International Arbitral Process*, vol. III, pp. 357–87.

[64] *BP* v. *Libya: Competence to Re-open First Stage of Proceedings*, Award (1974), 53 ILR p. 375.

[65] *Venezuela–British Guiana Boundary Arbitration (Venezuela v. Great Britain)* (1899), *British and Foreign State Papers*, vol. 92, 1899–1900, p. 160. Also in Wetter, *The International Arbitral Process*, vol. III, p. 81, together with valuable ancillary documentation. For further discussion, see A. O. Cukwurah, *The Settlement of Boundary Disputes in International Law*, Manchester, 1967, pp. 161–2 and 214–16.

In the *Abyei* arbitration,[66] a tribunal set up by the Government of Sudan and the Sudanese People's Liberation Movement (SPLM) was asked to decide whether a Committee of Experts assigned to establish the boundaries of the Abyei Area had 'exceeded their mandate'. It decided that in certain respects they had, on account of a failure to support some of their decisions with adequate reasons. The focus of argument in this case was on the scope for subsequent review when a decision is challenged, not by way of appeal, but on the more limited ground of an 'excess of mandate'. The award therefore contains a wealth of material on this rather technical issue, including a discussion of the subtle relationship between the mandate in a given case and the general principles of judicial review, in which the tribunal's treatment of the obligation to provide a reasoned decision is particularly interesting.

Other grounds for nullifying an award are fraud, which includes deceit in the presentation of a case to the tribunal or corruption of one of its members, and 'essential error', of which it has been said 'the ramification of the views of writers . . . demonstrates the looseness, vagueness and lack of legal exactness of the term'.[67] It has, nonetheless, often been advanced – sometimes it must be said in desperation – as a ground for challenging a decision. Some cases can be more precisely classified under one of the headings already considered. In others, the plea is no more than a transparent attempt to challenge the merits of the decision, grounds for an appeal perhaps, but nothing more. The 'imbalance in the evaluation of the argumentation and evidence submitted by each party' and 'interpretation defects'[68] which Argentina claimed to detect in the *Beagle Channel* award clearly fall into this category. When a similar argument was advanced in the *Arbitral Award* case, the Court simply observed: 'The instances of "essential error" that Nicaragua has brought to the notice of the Court amount to no more than evaluation of documents and of other evidence submitted to the arbitrator. The appraisal of the probative value of documents and evidence appertained to the discretionary power of the arbitrator and is not open to question.'[69] Clearly, then, it is not enough to have lost; if essential error is a ground for nullifying awards at all, the decision must be wrong in some vital and obvious respect.

Private international arbitration

The type of arbitration discussed above, set up by states to decide a case or a series of cases between them, must be distinguished from another type

---

[66] *Abyei Arbitration (Sudan/Sudan People's Liberation Movement)* (2009), www.pca-cpa.org.

[67] K. S. Carlston, *The Process of International Arbitration*, New York, 1946, pp. 191–2.

[68] The Argentine Government's Declaration of Nullity may be found in (1978) 17 ILM p. 738; text also in Wetter, *The International Arbitral Process*, vol. I, p. 380.

[69] [1960] ICJ Rep. pp. 215–16.

which deals with disputes in which individuals or corporations are involved as parties. This kind of arbitration, briefly mentioned earlier, is known as private (as opposed to public) international arbitration, or international commercial arbitration. Arbitration is, of course, a recognised procedure under many municipal systems of law and offers advantages over litigation by enabling disputes to be resolved relatively quickly and cheaply without the need to go to court. International commercial arbitration represents the extension of this procedure to private disputes with an international element. As the need for a way of resolving such disputes outside traditional institutions has increased, the new procedure has grown and developed, so that at the present time several varieties of private arbitration are available.

A comparison between private and inter-state arbitration reveals a similarity in the sense that each creates its own internal legal world, covering such matters as the law to be applied, and resting on the agreement between the parties. As we have seen, this is a key element in encouraging inter-state arbitration because it enables the parties to exercise close control over the process. Where the two forms of arbitration differ sharply, however, is in the *lex arbitri* which governs the arbitration in its external aspects, that is, such matters as the validity and enforceability of awards. Whereas private arbitration is normally anchored in municipal law, the *lex arbitri* of inter-state arbitration is international law. This has important consequences in terms of the parties' power to modify the external framework, where international law provides the parties with much greater latitude, and, more significantly, in relation to the effectiveness of the two processes. For the parties to a private arbitration will expect to have access to a municipal legal system if any dispute as to the validity of an award arises. Likewise, if there is any difficulty over enforcement, they will probably be able to use the worldwide arrangements which exist for enforcing arbitral awards through municipal courts. States, on the other hand, find it much more difficult either to challenge an inter-state award or to enforce it, because in international law, although rules relating to validity and implementation exist, there is a lack of compulsory procedures to make them effective.

The distinction between inter-state and private arbitration is clear enough when we compare the traditional procedure for resolving disputes between states on the one hand, with the newer way of using arbitration to settle disputes between private individuals or corporations on the other. It becomes somewhat blurred, however, when the procedures employed to resolve a further type of dispute are considered, namely, disputes between a private party and a state. For, in such 'mixed arbitrations', we find processes which combine features of both public and private international arbitration, or which, less happily, shift uncertainly between the two.

The International Centre for the Settlement of Investment Disputes (ICSID) is an institution which has been created for the specific purpose of handling disputes of this kind.[70] Set up by multilateral treaty, the Centre conducts its arbitrations in accordance with rules laid down in its constituent instrument. Unlike normal commercial arbitration, municipal courts have no jurisdiction over disputes relating to the validity of awards and indeed are expressly prohibited from dealing with such issues. The only area in which they are utilised is in enforcement. Under the ICSID treaty, both states and private parties have a direct right to enforce awards in the municipal courts of contracting states. Thus, the ICSID system, while preserving some of the autonomy traditionally associated with arbitration involving states, in the crucial area of enforcement borrows from private arbitration to strengthen the effectiveness of its arrangements.

A similar arrangement is to be found in Chapter 11 of the 1992 North American Free Trade Agreement (NAFTA), under which investors from one of the states parties can refer disputes relating to the treatment of their investments by another state party to arbitration in accordance with NAFTA. Arbitrations under NAFTA apply the terms of NAFTA, together with 'applicable rules of international law', and from the investor's point of view have the advantage that the state concerned has already consented to arbitration by becoming a party to NAFTA, while any award is enforceable through municipal courts under the ICSID treaty and similar conventions. The facilities for mixed arbitration afforded by NAFTA are extensively used and, though still open to improvement in various respects, provide a regional procedure for dealing with economic disputes complementary to the system of the World Trade Organization, described in Chapter 9 below.

The value and flexibility of mixed arbitration is further evident from its use in two recent cases. In the *Bank for International Settlements* case[71] (2002–3), an international tribunal decided that private shareholders in the Bank had been lawfully dispossessed and also established the level of compensation to which they were entitled. Here, the respondent was an international institution and, in addition to important substantive points, the case raised numerous procedural issues. In the *Eurotunnel* case[72] (2007), on the other hand, the respondents were the British and French governments being sued by two companies alleging breach of the concession agreement under which they had built and were operating the Channel Tunnel. This,

---

[70] See A. Broches, 'The Convention on the Settlement of Investment Disputes between States and Nationals of Other States', (1972) 136 *Hague Recueil des Cours*, p. 331; and M. Hirsch, *The Arbitration Mechanism of the International Centre for the Settlement of Investment Disputes*, Dordrecht, 1993.

[71] *Bank for International Settlements Arbitration* (2002/3), www.pca-cpa.org; and see D. J. Bederman, 'The unique legal status of the Bank for International Settlements comes into focus', (2003) 16 Leiden JIL p. 787.

[72] *Eurotunnel Arbitration (The Channel Tunnel Group Ltd and France-Manche SA v. United Kingdom and France)* (2007), www.pca-cpa.org; and see M. Audit, Note, (2008) 57 ICLQ p. 724.

too, was a complex case, involving factual as well as legal issues, and exemplifying the use of internationalised contracts for major projects and the value of arbitration in enabling disputes over the meaning of such contracts to be resolved.

When arbitration involving a state takes place outside the ICSID framework, difficulties can arise in deciding how the proceedings should be classified. Although the internal law of the arbitration is normally set out in the contract, if a question arises as to the *lex arbitri*, the answer will depend on the arbitrator's views on transactions of this sort, along with the parties' presumed intentions. In the *ARAMCO* case,[73] for example, the tribunal considered that it was unlikely that Saudi Arabia had intended to subject itself to the Swiss legal system, and decided that the case should be treated as an inter-state arbitration. In the *Sapphire* case,[74] on the other hand, the arbitrator reached the opposite conclusion, and this was also the result in *BP* v. *Libya*, where the arbitrator specifically mentioned the effectiveness of the award as a factor in his decision. However, on rather similar facts, the arbitrator in the *TOPCO* case[75] reached the same result as in *ARAMCO*, whereas in the *AMINOIL* case,[76] where the evidence of intent was rather clearer, the court was able to conclude that the arbitration was subject to the French legal system.

A somewhat similar problem has arisen with regard to the Iran–US Claims Tribunal. As already mentioned, the Tribunal was established in 1981, after the diplomatic hostages crisis, to deal with a large number of claims arising out of the Islamic Revolution of 1979. It has jurisdiction over three types of case. It can hear 'national claims', that is, 'claims of nationals of the United States against Iran and claims of nationals of Iran against the United States'. It also has jurisdiction over 'official claims' of Iran and the United States against each other arising out of certain contractual arrangements between them. Finally, the Tribunal can hear 'interpretative disputes', that is, disputes between the two states relating to the interpretation or application of the two Declarations concerned with the Tribunal and its work. Of the three branches of its work, the first, the adjudication of national claims, is by far the most important.[77] The question therefore arises as to what sort of arbitral

---

[73] *Saudi Arabia* v. *Arabian American Oil Co. (ARAMCO)* (1958), 27 ILR p. 117.

[74] *Sapphire International Petroleums* v. *National Iranian Oil Co.*, 35 ILR p. 136; and see D. Suratgar, 'The Sapphire Arbitration Award, the procedural aspects: A report and a critique', (1964) 3 Colum. J. Transnat. L. p. 152.

[75] *Texaco Overseas Petroleum and California Asiatic Oil Co.* v. *Libya (TOPCO)* (1977), 53 ILR p. 389. For discussion of this case, *BP* v. *Libya* and a third case involving Libya, the *LIAMCO* case, see C. Greenwood, 'State contracts in international law – The Libyan oil arbitrations', (1982) 53 BYBIL p. 27.

[76] *Kuwait and American Independent Oil Co. (AMINOIL)* (1982), 66 ILR p. 518; and see A. Redfern, 'The arbitration between the Government of Kuwait and AMINOIL', (1984) 55 BYBIL p. 65.

[77] Of nearly 4,000 claims before the Tribunal, more than 97 per cent were national claims.

process the Tribunal is performing. Is it, as the creation of the Tribunal by international agreement might imply, a traditional inter-state arbitration? Or is it, as the bulk of its work seems to suggest, an unusual type of private arbitration? The answer is not entirely clear, but a persuasive case can be made out for avoiding a rigid classification and recognising that the Tribunal is actually a hybrid arrangement with features of both.[78] Consequently, as in cases like *AMINOIL*, what we have here is an example of the institutions of municipal law being used to underpin arbitral proceedings in which one of the parties is a state.

The development of procedures for resolving disputes between states and private bodies highlights the way in which supply can be adapted to meet demand in the field of dispute settlement.[79] Moreover, it shows how the emergence of new procedures affects the field of operation of existing institutions. Throughout the nineteenth and the early twentieth century, a dispute between a foreign investor and a host state would, when local remedies had been exhausted, normally have been handled as a case of diplomatic protection and transformed into a dispute between the host state and the national state of the investor. There was, of course, no guarantee that the national state would take up the claim and, if it did, the matter would generally be resolved through negotiation or diplomatic pressure rather than by litigation. The fact remains, however, that what was in essence a dispute between a state and a private body became at the international level a dispute between two states. Today, this is no longer so. Although the institution of diplomatic protection exists, and can still be used in commercial disputes, the development of private arbitration and the creation of ICSID have provided investors and states alike with alternative procedures which they have not been slow to use. The impact of these new forms of arbitration has consequently been to displace a whole class of disputes from the inter-state arena.

It is also significant that this change has occurred through the exploitation of the strengths of the institutions and procedures of municipal law in order to compensate for the weaknesses of international law. As with the move away from diplomatic protection, this tendency should not be exaggerated. In many commercial arbitrations, the substantive principles to be applied continue to be those of international law; arbitrations between a state and a private body are not invariably regarded as subject to municipal law; and, as we have seen, in ICSID proceedings the role of municipal law is carefully

---

[78] For an excellent review of this question, see D. D. Caron, 'The nature of the Iran–United States Claims Tribunal and the evolving structure of international dispute resolution', (1990) 84 AJIL p. 104. For a different view, see A. Avanessian, *Iran–United States Claims Tribunal in Action*, Dordrecht, 1993, pp. 272–91. And see further C. N. Brower, *The Iran–United States Claims Tribunal*, The Hague, 1998; M. Mohebi, *The International Law Character of the Iran–United States Claims Tribunal*, The Hague, 1999; and C. N. Brower, 'Review', (2000) 94 AJIL p. 813.

[79] Caron, 'The nature of the Iran–United States Claims Tribunal', p. 151.

circumscribed. But, if recourse to municipal law is a variable factor and its precise bearing is sometimes obscure, the general tendency is clear. This, it has been suggested,[80] is something which may well be relevant to the management of other types of international dispute such as those involving human rights or the environment. Like commercial disputes fifty years ago, these cannot be handled effectively by traditional procedures such as diplomatic protection. While distinct methods of dealing with these kinds of disputes are now emerging, especially in the field of human rights, there are lessons to be learned from the growth of private arbitration which it would be a pity to ignore.

The utility of arbitration

Arbitration as it has developed over the last 200 years provides the parties to a dispute with the opportunity to obtain a decision from a judge or judges of their own choice. This is important because, if governments are to be persuaded to refer disputes to third parties they must have confidence in those who are to give the decision. An arbitral tribunal, as we have seen, also has the subject matter of the dispute and the criteria for its decision laid down by the parties. Thus, another advantage of arbitration is that it can be used to produce a solution to a selected problem and on any agreed basis. Finally, arbitration, unlike inquiry and conciliation, results in a decision which is binding. Consequently, provided that no problems of interpretation, nullity, etc., arise, an arbitral award should dispose of the dispute.

In view of these advantages, it is not surprising that, in the period since 1945, states have continued to regard arbitration as an appropriate way of handling certain types of dispute. Of the various cases referred to *ad hoc* tribunals,[81] the majority have concerned territorial or quasi-territorial disputes in which the issues were primarily legal and the outcome of secondary importance. The *Palena* case, the *Lake Lanoux* case, the *Rann of Kutch* case, the *Channel* arbitration, the *St Pierre and Miquelon* case, the *Taba* dispute and the *Eritrea/Yemen* case all fall into this category, while in the *Brcko* case arbitration was used in an analogous way to deal with a territorial dispute between the Bosniac/Croat and Serb communities in Bosnia and Herzegovina. Of course, arbitration can also be used to dispose of a whole series of disputes. In 2000, for example, Eritrea and Ethiopia set up a Claims Commission[82] to deal with a variety of disputes stemming from their recent

---

80   *Ibid.*, p. 155. See also H. Fox, 'States and the undertaking to arbitrate', (1988) 37 ICLQ p. 1.
81   For a useful summary, see Gray and Kingsbury, 'Developments in dispute settlement', pp. 99–109; and, for an earlier survey, see D. H. N. Johnson, 'International arbitration back in favour?', (1980) 34 Yearbook of WA p. 305.
82   For a description of the Commission's work, see J. R. Weeramantry, Notes, in (2005) 99 AJIL p. 465, (2006) 100 AJIL p. 201 and (2007) 101 AJIL p. 616.

war, and its decisions, like those in single cases, show the value of arbitration as a means of removing obstacles to friendly relations.

Arbitration has also retained an important place in international treaty practice and, sometimes in combination with conciliation, is to be found in the dispute provisions of multilateral and bilateral conventions on a wide variety of subjects. The 1999 International Convention for the Suppression of the Financing of Terrorism,[83] for example, provides for the reference of disputes relating to the Convention to arbitration, and the treaties which comprised the provisional post-war settlement with Germany provided for arbitration through a series of tribunals each with its own jurisdiction. Thus, the Arbitral Tribunal for the Agreement on German External Debts on several occasions decided disputes between governments over the interpretation of the Agreement,[84] and the Arbitral Commission on Property Rights and Interests in Germany dealt with property and property-related claims from both states and private individuals.[85] The *OSPAR (Article 9)* case, as already noted, was referred to arbitration on the basis of Article 32 of the 1992 OSPAR Convention, the *Rhine Chlorides* case[86] was referred under the 1993 Protocol to the 1976 Convention on the Protection of the Rhine against Pollution by Chlorides, and the earlier *Heathrow Airport* case was one of a series in which the United States has been involved in the arbitration of disputes arising out of bilateral international air services agreements.[87] More recently, as we shall see in Chapter 8, there have been several arbitrations under the dispute settlement provisions of the 1982 Law of the Sea Convention. In this connection, it is also worth remembering that the value of arrangements for dispute settlement is not to be judged solely by the cases decided under those arrangements: a provision for compulsory arbitration, by its very existence, can discourage unreasonable behaviour, and so may be useful even if it is never invoked.

In addition to conventions with provision for compulsory arbitration, there are many in which it is included as an optional procedure. Since it is always open to states to arbitrate a dispute by creating an *ad hoc* tribunal, treaties of the latter type may seem at first sight to add little to the current position. In the sense that they encourage the use of arbitration, without requiring it, it is true that they are less significant than treaties with mandatory provisions. It should be noted, however, that, in many cases, such

---

[83] Text in (2000) 39 ILM p. 270. However, although Article 24(1) provides for compulsory arbitration, Article 24(2) permits reservations to this provision.

[84] See, for example, the *Young Loan Arbitration* (1980), 59 ILR p. 494.

[85] For example, the six cases reported in 42 ILR pp. 348, 380, 383, 387, 401 and 488.

[86] *Rhine Chlorides Case (Netherlands/France)* (2004), www.pca-cpa.org.

[87] See *Air Transport Services Agreement Arbitration (United States v. France)* (1963), 38 ILR p. 182; *Italy–United States Air Transport Arbitration* (1965), 45 ILR p. 393; *Case Concerning the Air Services Agreement of 27 March 1946* (1978), 54 ILR p. 304. For discussion of the last case, see L. F. Damrosch, 'Retaliation or arbitration – or both? The 1978 United States–France aviation dispute', (1980) 74 AJIL p. 785.

treaties not only specify how the parties may accept arbitration in advance, which is useful in itself, but go on to prescribe how such proceedings should be organised. This is true, for example, of a number of recent conventions concerned with the environment,[88] as well as the more general 1992 Stockholm Convention on Conciliation and Arbitration within the CSCE.[89] The latter sets out arrangements which the parties can either employ *ad hoc* when a dispute arises, or accept in advance by making a general declaration. Accordingly, while arbitration is not obligatory *per se* under any of these conventions, they are drafted in terms which facilitate its use.

Arbitration, then, is an important means of handling international disputes. It must be recognised, however, to have significant limitations. As we shall see in the next chapter, states are reluctant to make a general commitment to judicial settlement, and for much the same reasons resist the idea of arbitration. For an individual dispute, on the other hand, negotiation or another diplomatic means may be preferred. Consequently, as we shall see later, the 1982 Convention on the Law of the Sea, which contains extensive provisions on arbitration, also makes use of conciliation and a variety of other techniques of peaceful settlement.

The availability of other means of dealing with disputes and the high value which states attach to retaining flexibility mean that, even when arbitration is specified in the provisions of a treaty, to see whether it can be used in practice may require the arbitrators to examine the relation between arbitration and other means of settlement. In the *Southern Bluefin Tuna* case,[90] for example, as we shall see in Chapter 8, an attempt by Australia and New Zealand to have a dispute with Japan dealt with by arbitration under Annex VII to the Law of the Sea Convention failed when the tribunal ruled that its jurisdiction was barred by Article 281. In the *MOX Plant* case,[91] on the other hand, another Annex VII tribunal decided in 2003 that considerations of judicial comity required suspension of the proceedings pending clarification of the position of the European Court of Justice which might also be dealing with this case.[92] Such jurisdictional constraints are plainly not peculiar to arbitration, but something all courts and tribunals must work with as the legal world becomes more complex. They do, however,

---

[88] See, for example, three environmental conventions concluded in 1992: the Convention on Biological Diversity, the Convention on the Protection and Use of Transboundary Watercourses and Lakes, and the Convention on the Transboundary Effects of Industrial Accidents, texts in (1992) 31 ILM pp. 818, 1312 and 1333.

[89] Text in (1993) 32 ILM p. 557.

[90] *Southern Bluefin Tuna Case (Australia and New Zealand* v. *Japan)*, Award on Jurisdiction and Admissibility (2000), text in (2000) 39 ILM p. 1359.

[91] See *The MOX Plant Case (Ireland* v. *United Kingdom)*, Order No. 3, text in (2003) 42 ILM p. 1187.

[92] See R. R. Churchill and J. Scott, 'The MOX Plant litigation: The first half-life', (2004) 53 ICLQ p. 643 at p. 652. As noted in Chapter 8, following the decision of the ECJ, the proceedings were discontinued.

underline the point that, useful though arbitration can be, it must always be seen in the context of other techniques and procedures.

Another limitation concerns enforcement. Although arbitration produces a binding decision, there is usually no guarantee that the unsuccessful party will carry out its obligation to recognise the award. This does not mean that arbitral decisions are widely disregarded. On the contrary, since states often prefer to end a dispute rather than incur the political costs which would follow from refusing to accept a decision, arbitral awards are usually implemented. This is another parallel with judicial settlement. In the International Court, the major difficulty is usually persuading the states concerned to accept the jurisdiction of the Court. Once that hurdle has been surmounted, the question of enforcement will normally not arise. But, if there are practical reasons for carrying out unfavourable decisions, in some circumstances the factors arguing against performance predominate, and in these situations the lack of a procedure for enforcement is certainly a conspicuous limitation.

There are several ways in which the problem of enforcing arbitral awards may be overcome. The best, but also the rarest, is to devise a procedure which makes it difficult for the unsuccessful party to go back on its obligations. The awards of the Iran–US Claims Tribunal, for example, are paid out of a fund which was established by the original agreement and which Iran is required to replenish whenever it falls below US$500 million. Of course, even an arrangement like this depends ultimately on performance of the underpinning obligation and, when the scope of Iran's commitment itself became a matter of dispute in 1992, the issue had to be referred to the Tribunal for a ruling.[93] Clearly, then, no scheme of this kind is entirely without risk, but, as a consequence of its funding arrangements, American claimants who are successful before the Tribunal have enjoyed a good deal more security than their less fortunate counterparts elsewhere.[94]

Another approach is to try to make rejection unlikely by framing the tribunal's decision in a way which is acceptable to both parties. This used to be thought of as one of the features which distinguished arbitration from judicial settlement, and we have seen that the Secretary-General approached his task in the *Rainbow Warrior* case very much in this spirit. However, there are clearly limits on how far a tribunal can go in this direction while respecting the boundaries of its jurisdiction. States which request a decision on the basis of international law, for example, and argue a case in these terms, are unlikely to be satisfied by a decision which is merely conciliatory and which says more about the arbitrator's fondness for compromise than

---

[93] See *United States* v. *Iran*, Dec. No. 130-A28 FT, 19 December 2000, noted in (2001) 95 AJIL p. 414.

[94] It should be noted that successful Iranian claimants are in a different position. See M. Aghahosseini, 'The enforcement mechanism provided for the awards of the Iran–United States Claims Tribunal', (2003) 3 Global Community YBILJ p. 3.

about their legal rights. It is therefore doubtful if the *Rainbow Warrior* approach, though appropriate in the unusual circumstances of that case, is of more than limited application.

A final possibility, which would be of real value in improving compliance with awards and increasing the attractiveness of arbitration generally, would be to improve the arrangements for dealing with allegations of nullity. As noted earlier, it is an unfortunate fact that, at the present time, disputes over the validity of international arbitral awards can rarely be settled by judicial means. Thus, the *Venezuela–British Guiana Boundary* case, decided in 1899, of doubtful validity, yet never the subject of authoritative review, is typical; whereas the 1960 *Arbitral Award* case, in which the issue of nullity was laid to rest by the parties' reference of the matter to the International Court, is exceptional. This situation, accurately described by the International Law Commission as 'anarchic', means that nullity claims are handled diplomatically. This is a serious practical weakness of arbitration. On the one hand, if a state is unable to challenge a dubious or unsatisfactory award, submission to arbitration is made more hazardous and less attractive than it ought to be. The *Venezuela–British Guiana Boundary* award is an object lesson here. On the other hand, if it is open to a state to challenge the validity of an award on grounds which are legally worthless, but cannot be tested, the 'binding' effect of an arbitral award is emptied of most of its meaning. Argentina's implausible repudiation of the award in the *Beagle Channel* case demonstrates this side of the problem.

We have already seen that the advantages of using the institutions and procedures of municipal law to deal with the enforcement and validity of arbitral awards in commercial cases have led to the development of new forms of arbitration for these kinds of dispute. This trend, exemplified by the creation of the Iran–US Claims Tribunal, with its many unique features, is no doubt likely to continue. Aware of the deficiencies of traditional arbitration, as far as the review of awards is concerned, some have suggested that the answer is for the issue of nullity always to be subject to compulsory adjudication.

There is no doubt that compulsory adjudication would avoid many problems. However, at present, it appears to have little prospect of being adopted. Of course, states with a genuine desire to see a dispute settled do not repudiate arbitral awards on flimsy pretexts, while those that are prepared to take such action might not be discouraged by having their cynicism exposed in further litigation. The real answer, then, as regards the specific issue of nullity and the more general issue of compliance, lies with the parties. Arbitration, like other means of settling disputes in a world of sovereign states, depends for its effectiveness on responsible behaviour from the governments concerned.

6

The International Court I: organisation and procedure

Judicial settlement involves the reference of disputes to permanent tribunals for a legally binding decision. It developed from arbitration, which accounts for the close similarity between the two, and in various forms is now available through a number of courts of general or specialised jurisdiction. Examples of the latter will be considered when we examine the Law of the Sea Convention in a later chapter, but the advantages and limitations of tribunals of specialised jurisdiction will be more readily appreciated if we first consider the International Court.

The term 'International Court' embraces two courts, the Permanent Court of International Justice, set up as part of the 1919 peace settlement, and its successor, the International Court of Justice (ICJ), founded in 1945 as the principal judicial organ of the United Nations. Interest in both Courts has generated a literature of high quality, dealing with all aspects of their activity in considerable detail.[1] The focus of this chapter will be on features of the organisation and procedure of the Court with a particular bearing on its role in the settlement of disputes.

Contentious jurisdiction

The Court's powers to decide disputes are defined in its Statute and are known as its contentious jurisdiction. According to the Statute, only states may be parties to contentious proceedings and the Court's authority in such cases depends on the consent of the states concerned. The principle of consensuality is as fundamental to adjudication by the Court as to arbitration and means that, unless all the states involved in a particular dispute have given their consent, there is no jurisdiction to give a decision.

---

[1] For an excellent introduction, see A. Eyffinger, *The International Court of Justice 1946–1996*, The Hague, 1996. The standard work on the Court is S. Rosenne, *The Law and Practice of the International Court*, 4th edn, Leiden, 2006. Also A. Zimmermann, C. Tomuschat and K. Oellers-Frahm (eds.). *The Statute of the International Court of Justice. A Commentary*, Oxford, 2006. Essays on particular aspects of the Court's work, some of which are referred to below, may be found in: L. Gross (ed.), *The Future of the International Court of Justice*, New York, 1976; L. F. Damrosch (ed.), *The International Court of Justice at a Crossroads*, New York, 1987; V. Lowe and M. Fitzmaurice (eds.), *Fifty Years of the International Court of Justice*, Cambridge, 1996; A. S. Muller, D. Raic and J. M. Thuranszky (eds.), *The International Court of Justice*, The Hague, 1997; and C. Peck and R. S. Lee (eds.), *Increasing the Effectiveness of the International Court of Justice*, The Hague, 1997.

A state's consent can be given in a number of different ways. Consent can be given before the dispute arises by means of a compromissory clause in a treaty, or a declaration under Article 36(2) of the Court's Statute. Alternatively, consent can be given after a dispute has arisen by means of a special agreement between the parties, or in response to the unilateral reference of a dispute to the Court. Once a legal act indicating consent has been performed, jurisdiction may be established, even if the state is unwilling to litigate when an actual case arises. There is thus no contradiction between the consensual basis of the Court's jurisdiction and the fact that the Court is regularly called upon to consider – and frequently rejects as ill-founded – objections to its jurisdiction from unwilling respondents.

Treaties providing in advance for the reference of disputes to the Court are of two types. A number of multilateral instruments have been concluded with the general aim of promoting peaceful settlement. These treaties, which include the General Act (1928), the Pact of Bogotá (1948) and the European Convention for the Peaceful Settlement of Disputes (1957), constitute general acceptances of judicial settlement with far-reaching implications for the states concerned. For this reason, they have usually been either not widely supported, or accepted only with substantial reservations. Multilateral arrangements of this kind have therefore proved rather unsatisfactory. More successful has been the attempt to ensure that treaties on particular subjects include an article providing that disputes as to the interpretation or application of the agreement can be referred to the Court. Treaties of this second type have been concluded in considerable numbers, as reference to any recent volume of the Court's *Yearbook* will show, and have provided a basis for the Court's jurisdiction in several cases. In 2004, for example, the Court was able to decide a dispute over duties with regard to Mexicans on 'death row' in the United States because both Mexico and the United States were parties to the Protocol concerning the Compulsory Settlement of Disputes attached to the Vienna Convention on Consular Relations of 1963.[2]

The other method of submitting to the Court's jurisdiction in advance is by a declaration under Article 36(2) of the Court's Statute, known as the 'optional clause'. An optional clause declaration denotes a state's acceptance of judicial settlement on certain terms and conditions, and, when both parties have made declarations which cover the dispute, as in the *Arrest Warrant* case,[3] the Court's jurisdiction is established. Declarations are unilateral acts and thus have the advantage that a state can accept the Court's jurisdiction, and demonstrate its support for the principle of judicial settlement, without

---

[2] *Avena and Other Mexican Nationals (Mexico v. United States)*, Judgment, [2004] ICJ Rep.; and see D. L. Shelton, Note, (2004) 98 AJIL p. 559.

[3] *Arrest Warrant of 11 April 2000 (Democratic Republic of the Congo v. Belgium)*, Judgment, [2002] ICJ Rep. p. 3; and see C. Wickremasinghe, Note, (2003) 52 ICLQ p. 775.

the need for the agreement of other states. On the other hand, since declarations function in much the same way as agreements, their effectiveness in practice depends on how many states are prepared to participate in the optional clause system and the terms on which they are willing to do so. Here there is certainly room for improvement. Only about one-third of the members of the United Nations have made declarations under Article 36(2), and of those declarations in force many are emasculated by reservations.[4] The optional clause provides a potentially important source of jurisdiction, but its possibilities, as yet, are far from realisation.

The most commonly used method of consenting to the exercise of the Court's jurisdiction after a dispute has arisen is the negotiation of a special agreement. Such an agreement is similar to an arbitral *compromis* in that it provides the parties with an opportunity to define the issues in dispute and, subject to the provisions of the Statute, to indicate the basis on which the Court should give its decision. This flexibility makes special agreements attractive to states as a way of utilising the Court, and as a result they are employed quite regularly. In 2008, for example, the Court was able to decide the *Sovereignty over Pedra Branca* case[5] following a special agreement between Singapore and Malaysia, having also recently decided the *Kasikili/Sedudu Island* case[6] between Botswana and Namibia, and the *Gabcikovo-Nagymaros* case[7] between Hungary and Slovakia on a similar basis.

It has been clear since the time of the Permanent Court that, once jurisdiction is established through the optional clause or on some other basis, the parties may widen its scope by an informal indication of consent in the course of the proceedings. Subsequently, the principle was extended to allow jurisdiction to be based on a unilateral application, followed by an acceptance from the respondent state, something which occurred in 2003 when France informed the Court that it consented to proceedings against it initiated by the Republic of the Congo a few months earlier.[8] This doctrine, known as *forum prorogatum*, avoids the need to conclude a special

---

[4] For a fuller account of this problem, see J. G. Merrills, 'Does the optional clause still matter?', in K. H. Kaikobad and M. Bohlander (eds.), *International Law and Power. Perspectives on Legal Order and Justice*, Leiden, 2009, p. 431, and, earlier, 'The optional clause revisited', (1993) 64 BYBIL p. 197. For sample declarations, see document F in the appendix below.

[5] *Sovereignty over Pedra Branca/Pulau Batu Puteh, Middle Rocks and South Ledge (Malaysia/Singapore)*, Judgment, [2008] ICJ Rep.; and see C. G. Lathrop, Note, (2008) 102 AJIL p. 828.

[6] *Kasikili/Sedudu Island (Botswana/Namibia)*, Judgment, [1999] ICJ Rep. p. 1045; and see M. N. Shaw, Note, (2000) 49 ICLQ p. 964.

[7] *Gabcikovo-Nagymaros Project (Hungary/Slovakia)*, Judgment, [1997] ICJ Rep. p. 7; and see P. N. Okowa, Note, (1998) 47 ICLQ p. 688.

[8] See ICJ Press Releases 2002/37 (9 December 2002) and 2003/14 (14 April 2003) relating to the *Certain Criminal Proceedings in France* case. On the origins of this doctrine, see H. Waldock, 'Forum prorogatum or acceptance of a unilateral summons to appear before the International Court', (1948) 2 ILQ p. 377.

agreement and so provides states with an alternative means of accepting the Court's jurisdiction in a current dispute. In the normal course of events, however, a state which is prepared to litigate will wish to negotiate a special agreement, while one which is not will be careful to avoid actions which might be construed as indications of consent.

Jurisdictional disputes

Since jurisdiction to decide a dispute is based on consent shown by a legal act, there is sometimes disagreement as to whether the states concerned have given the Court the necessary competence. In such a situation, the question of jurisdiction is resolved by the Court, acting under Article 36(6) of the Statute, which confers what is known as the *compétence de la compétence*. It is therefore possible for a state to raise objections to the Court's jurisdiction but, if these are unsound, to find that its arguments are rejected. In the *Right of Passage* case,[9] for example, India raised no less than six preliminary objections based on the terms of the parties' respective optional clause declarations, but the Court rejected them all and went on to decide the substantive issue. Even when an objection is accepted, its effect may sometimes be merely to restrict the Court's competence, not to remove it altogether. For example, in the *Nicaragua* case,[10] which was brought by Nicaragua against the United States in 1984, the Court accepted the respondent's argument that a reservation covering certain multilateral treaties was applicable, but held that it was still competent to decide the case on the basis of customary international law.

Disputes over jurisdiction must be dealt with at the beginning and often form a separate stage of the proceedings. Thus, in a case between Nicaragua and Honduras in 1988, the Court considered a number of issues of jurisdiction and admissibility before deciding that its competence had been established on the basis of Article 31 of the Pact of Bogotá.[11] Similarly, in the *Fisheries Jurisdiction* case,[12] where jurisdiction was based on an agreement between the United Kingdom and Iceland, the Court established its competence in 1973 by examining and rejecting various arguments concerned with the validity and scope of the treaty, before going on to decide the main dispute the following year.

---

[9] *Right of Passage over Indian Territory*, Preliminary Objections, Judgment, [1957] ICJ Rep. p. 125.

[10] *Military and Paramilitary Activities in and against Nicaragua*, Merits, Judgment, [1986] ICJ Rep. p. 14. This issue was held over from the earlier proceedings concerned with jurisdiction and admissibility.

[11] *Border and Transborder Armed Actions*, Jurisdiction and Admissibility, Judgment, [1988] ICJ Rep. p. 69. For further discussion, see Chapter 11.

[12] *Fisheries Jurisdiction (United Kingdom v. Iceland)*, Jurisdiction of the Court, Judgment, [1973] ICJ Rep. p. 3. Parallel proceedings were instituted by the Federal Republic of Germany.

The range of legal issues which can arise when the Court is examining the question of jurisdiction is very wide. Thus, in the *Maritime Delimitation and Territorial Questions* case,[13] the Court had to decide whether Qatar and Bahrain had made a legally binding agreement and then determine its precise scope and effect. In the *Oil Platforms* case,[14] on the other hand, which was brought by Iran against the United States, a treaty between the two states had certainly been concluded, but the respondent sought to argue that the dispute over acts involving the use of force lay outside its ambit. In further contrast, much wider issues, including questions of recognition and statehood, were involved in the *Genocide Convention* case[15] between Bosnia and Herzegovina and the Federal Republic of Yugoslavia. Because the case arose out of events following the break-up of Yugoslavia, the Court had to consider whether Bosnia had become a party to the 1948 Genocide Convention and, if so, when, the scope of the Court's jurisdiction *ratione temporis* and the relevance of a number of other alleged bases of jurisdiction, including *forum prorogatum*.

Optional clause declarations have proved a particularly fruitful source of jurisdictional problems. In the *Norwegian Loans* case,[16] for example, the Court decided that it had no jurisdiction to decide a case brought by France against Norway because the former had made a reservation excluding 'differences relating to matters which are essentially within the national jurisdiction as understood by the Government of the French Republic'. Although there was no such reservation in the Norwegian declaration, the Court followed its previous practice and held that Norway, as respondent, was entitled to invoke the reservation in the French declaration and remove the case from the Court's competence. Limitations on a state's acceptance of the Court's jurisdiction are thus a double-edged weapon. While they provide a state with protection in the sense that they stop certain claims from being brought against it, they also have a disabling effect because they may prevent the reserving state from taking disputes to the Court in which it could appear as plaintiff.

If a state wishes to avoid litigation, it will naturally try to take advantage of any reservations in its own or its opponent's declaration. In the *Aerial*

---

[13] *Maritime Delimitation and Territorial Questions between Qatar and Bahrain,* Jurisdiction and Admissibility, Judgments of 1 July 1994 and 15 February 1995, [1994] ICJ Rep. p. 112 and [1995] ICJ Rep. p. 6. For comment, see M. D. Evans, Note, (1995) 44 ICLQ p. 691.

[14] *Oil Platforms (Islamic Republic of Iran* v. *United States of America),* Preliminary Objection, Judgment, [1996] ICJ Rep. p. 803. For comment, see M. D. Evans, Note, (1997) 46 ICLQ p. 693; and P. H. F. Bekker, Note, (1997) 91 AJIL p. 518.

[15] *Application of the Convention on the Prevention and Punishment of the Crime of Genocide (Bosnia and Herzegovina* v. *Yugoslavia),* Preliminary Objections, Judgment, [1996] ICJ Rep. p. 595. For comment, see P. H. F. Bekker and P. C. Szasz, Note, (1997) 91 AJIL p. 121; and C. Gray, Note, (1997) 46 ICLQ p. 688.

[16] *Certain Norwegian Loans,* Judgment, [1957] ICJ Rep. p. 9.

Incident case,[17] Pakistan sought to limit this power by arguing that reservations not expressly authorised by the Statute are 'illicit' and may not be relied upon, but the Court ruled that there is no such restriction and upheld India's right to invoke a reservation in its declaration covering disputes with states which were, or had been, members of the British Commonwealth. Shortly before, in the *Fisheries Jurisdiction* case[18] between Spain and Canada, the Court had rejected another attempt to limit the impact of reservations. Spain had argued that reservations must be interpreted consistently with legality; in other words, that they cannot protect illegal acts. As the Court pointed out, however, the aim of a reservation may well be to prevent acts of dubious legality from being challenged. It could therefore defeat the purpose of a reservation to accept the Spanish argument.

An important point raised by the *Nicaragua* case was how a state can terminate a declaration. The United States declaration provided that it was terminable on six months' notice. The Nicaraguan declaration, on the other hand, contained no provision on termination and arguably could be terminated instantly. Anticipating that Nicaragua was about to bring a case against it, the United States terminated its declaration without giving six months' notice and made a new declaration containing a reservation which covered the Nicaraguan claim. When this manoeuvre was challenged as inconsistent with the requirement of notice in the original declaration, the United States reply was that, since Nicaragua could have terminated its declaration with immediate effect, reciprocity required that the United States should enjoy the same facility. The Court, however, rejected the argument and held that the new reservation was ineffective.[19]

The optional clause system, like other ways of accepting the Court's jurisdiction, was originally part of the Statute of the Permanent Court of International Justice and a significant number of declarations under Article 36(2) were made in the inter-war period. When the present Court was established in 1945, arrangements were made in Article 36(5) of the Statute to permit those declarations which were still in force to operate as acceptances of the new Court. The aim was to ensure that the new Court began with a nucleus of acceptances of its jurisdiction, and to maintain a sense of continuity with the old Court. All this was achieved, though at a cost, for the application of this provision, and Article 37(5) which contains

---

[17] *Aerial Incident of 10 August, 1999 (Pakistan v. India)*, Jurisdiction, Judgment, [2000] ICJ Rep. p. 12; and see J. G. Merrills, Note, (2001) 50 ICLQ p. 657.

[18] *Fisheries Jurisdiction (Spain v. Canada)*, Jurisdiction of the Court, Judgment, [1998] ICJ Rep. p. 432; and see L. de La Fayette, Note, (1999) 48 ICLQ p. 664.

[19] *Military and Paramilitary Activities in and against Nicaragua*, Jurisdiction and Admissibility, Judgment, [1984] ICJ Rep. p. 392. And see generally E. B. Weiss, 'Reciprocity and the optional clause', in Damrosch, *International Court of Justice*, p. 82. The main reason given by the Court was that the duration of an optional clause is governed by its own terms and not by reciprocity. A subsidiary reason was that declarations with no termination clause are not terminable instantly but only on reasonable notice.

a similar arrangement for treaty-based jurisdiction, have raised technical questions of surprising complexity.

The Court's transferred jurisdiction under Article 36(5) was another of the preliminary matters which had to be addressed in the *Nicaragua* case. Nicaragua made its declaration in 1929 but for reasons which were obscure never ratified the Protocol of Signature of the Statute of the Permanent Court. Recognising that, in these circumstances, it might be difficult to persuade the Court that its declaration was 'in force' in 1945 and could therefore be maintained by Article 36(5), Nicaragua argued that it had sufficiently manifested its intent to accept the Court's jurisdiction by allowing its declaration to be reproduced in successive volumes of the Court's *Yearbook* without any protest. Although this concept of 'jurisdiction by acquiescence' was not entirely novel,[20] the position was naturally less clear cut than if Nicaragua had unequivocally shown its consent by either making a new declaration or ratifying the Protocol. A majority of the Court nevertheless accepted the argument and amid considerable controversy held that the combined effect of Nicaragua's resuscitated declaration and a declaration which the United States had failed to extinguish was enough to give it jurisdiction over the dispute.

Transferred jurisdiction under Article 37(5) was in issue in the *Aerial Incident* case where, as an alternative to its optional clause argument, Pakistan claimed that the Court had jurisdiction on the basis of the 1928 General Act. India rejected this conclusion on various grounds, arguing that the General Act was no longer in force and that, even if it was, neither state had succeeded to it when they became independent in 1947. In ruling on the issue of jurisdiction, however, the Court avoided pronouncing on these questions, and instead decided the case on a narrower ground, holding that, even if the General Act was originally binding on both states, India had validly denounced it, and so ceased to be bound by the Act in 1979. It followed therefore that the General Act did not provide a basis of jurisdiction and Pakistan could not employ Article 37(5).

In the majority of cases in which the Court is required to decide whether its jurisdiction has been accepted, the question will arise because some deficiency is alleged in the instrument or procedure by which either or both of the states which are before the Court has ostensibly done so. However, this situation, which is exemplified by the complex issues in the optional clause cases, is not the only way in which the issue of consent can arise. The principle, it will be recalled, is that all the states involved in a given dispute must have indicated their consent, and from this it follows that it

---

[20] An analogous point was considered in *Temple of Preah Vihear*, Preliminary Objections, Judgment, [1961] ICJ Rep. p. 17. In addition to the reason mentioned in the text, the Court supported its conclusion that Nicaragua's declaration was still in force by holding that Article 36(5) had the effect of reviving valid declarations even if they were not previously in force. This, however, does not seem very convincing.

is not open to two states to bring a case directly concerning the rights of a third, unless the latter has also consented to the exercise of jurisdiction. A clear demonstration of this principle may be seen in the *Monetary Gold* case,[21] where the four states which had brought the case had all accepted the Court's jurisdiction, but the Court declined to adjudicate because Albania, whose property rights formed the subject matter of the case, had not.

The scope of the principle of consent was further clarified in the *Nicaragua* case. For there, in addition to the matters already considered, the United States argued that the Court should rule the application inadmissible because the dispute concerned the legal interests of Honduras, Costa Rica and El Salvador which were not parties to the case. The Court rejected the argument and held that the principle in the *Monetary Gold* case applied only to situations in which the legal interests of a non-party 'would not only be affected by a decision, but would form the very subject-matter of the decision'.[22] As this was not the situation here, the Court held that it was entitled to proceed. The same rationale was subsequently applied in the *Phosphate Lands in Nauru* case,[23] where the Court held that, although Australia, New Zealand and the United Kingdom constituted the Administering Authority for Nauru when the island was being administered as a trusteeship territory, this did not prevent Nauru from bringing proceedings concerning international responsibility against Australia alone. Shortly afterwards, however, in the *East Timor* case,[24] the Court relied on the *Monetary Gold* case to hold that it was not open to Portugal to bring a case against Australia arising out of the latter's dealings with Indonesia over East Timor, because Indonesia was not a party to the case.

In rejecting the idea of a broad 'indispensable parties' rule in the *Nicaragua* case, the Court adopted an approach which indicates that the consent of third states will usually be unnecessary. Thus, by denying the need for their presence save in exceptional circumstances like those of the *East Timor* case, the Court's approach removes a potential obstacle to the exercise of its jurisdiction. On the other hand, the political reality is that international disputes are not exclusively bilateral and, in situations like that in the *Phosphate Lands in Nauru* case, judgments which ignore the interests of third states are unlikely to be fully effective. An awareness of this point led to the inclusion in the Court's Statute of provisions permitting intervention. These are part of the Court's incidental jurisdiction which must now be examined.

---

[21] *Monetary Gold Removed from Rome in 1943*, Judgment, [1954] ICJ Rep. p. 19. For commentary, see D. H. N. Johnson, The case of the Monetary Gold Removed from Rome in 1943', (1955) 4 ICLQ p. 93.

[22] [1984] ICJ Rep. p. 431.

[23] *Certain Phosphate Lands in Nauru (Nauru v. Australia)*, Preliminary Objections, Judgment, [1992] ICJ Rep. p. 240. For summary, see A. Anghie, Note, (1993) 87 AJIL p. 282.

[24] *East Timor (Portugal v. Australia)*, Judgment, [1995] ICJ Rep. p. 90. For comment, see C. Chinkin, Note, (1996) 45 ICLQ p. 712; and P. F. Bekker, Note, (1996) 90 AJIL p. 94.

Incidental jurisdiction

In addition to its contentious jurisdiction, the Statute entitles the Court to exercise two further kinds of jurisdiction: an incidental jurisdiction and an advisory jurisdiction. By virtue of its incidental jurisdiction, the Court has the power to indicate interim measures of protection, to allow intervention and to interpret or revise a judgment. Because these powers are conferred by the Statute, their exercise by the Court does not require a further expression of consent on the part of states and in appropriate circumstances these and other incidental powers can make a constructive contribution to the settlement of disputes. In contrast, the advisory jurisdiction, which is chiefly concerned with the rights and duties of international organisations, is not as important in the present context, although, as we shall see shortly, its bearing on inter-state disputes is sometimes closer than might be assumed.

Interim measures of protection are governed by Article 41 of the Statute and, as the name indicates, are concerned with the preservation of the parties' rights while litigation is in progress.[25] Their justification stems from the elementary juridical principle that the judgment of a court should be effective and that to ensure this it may, while a case is before the Court, be essential to restrain either party, or both, from disrupting the situation, or attempting to present its adversary with a *fait accompli*. Arrangements to protect the legal rights of litigants are, of course, a familiar feature of municipal legal systems. At the international level, such procedures are particularly necessary because litigation is often protracted, especially if there are jurisdictional issues to determine, and also because, if a dispute has precipitated an international crisis, the parties may be acting in a way which threatens to destroy the possibility of a peaceful settlement.

In the *Frontier Dispute* case,[26] between Burkina Faso and Mali, for example, both states asked the Court to resolve a boundary question which less than ten years before had caused a war between them. However, before the Court could give its decision, the dispute flared up and fighting broke out again. A cease-fire was arranged and, in order that the eventual judgment should not be prejudiced, both sides asked the Court to indicate interim measures. After examining the parties' requests, which were in somewhat different terms, the Court decided that interim measures were required to

---

[25] For an excellent review of all aspects of this question, see J. Sztucki, *Interim Measures in the Hague Court*, Deventer, 1983; and, for a survey of more recent practice, see J. G. Merrills, 'Interim measures of protection in the recent jurisprudence of the International Court of Justice', (1995) 44 ICLQ p. 90.

[26] *Frontier Dispute*, Provisional Measures, Order of 10 January 1986, [1986] ICJ Rep. p. 3. For a more recent case involving a rather similar situation, see the *Land and Maritime Boundary between Cameroon and Nigeria*, Provisional Measures, Order of 15 March 1996, [1996] ICJ Rep. p. 13, summarised in J. G. Merrills, Note, (1997) 46 ICLQ p. 676.

prevent the possible destruction of evidence and, more generally, to prevent the extension or aggravation of the dispute. It therefore ordered the parties to respect the cease-fire, to withdraw their armed forces from the frontier, and to do nothing to change the administration of the disputed area, to intensify the dispute or to interfere with each other's rights.

The Court will not make an order for interim measures of protection unless there is some instrument which *prima facie* recognises its jurisdiction to decide the main dispute. This is unlikely to be a problem in a case referred by a special agreement, such as the *Frontier Dispute* case, but may be an obstacle where the basis is declarations under the optional clause or a treaty, the effect of which is contested. In the *Legality of Use of Force* cases,[27] for example, Yugoslavia brought claims against ten NATO states arising out of the bombing campaign over Kosovo in 1999, relying as regards six of the respondents on their declarations under the optional clause, and as regards all ten on the 1948 Genocide Convention. But, when Yugoslavia asked for interim measures of protection its request was rejected on the ground that the Court lacked *prima facie* jurisdiction. In relation to the Genocide Convention, this was because the Court's provisional view was that the acts complained of could not be said to qualify as genocide, and in relation to the optional clause on account of reservations and limitations in either the applicant's or the respondents' declarations which seemed to exclude jurisdiction.

If the requirement of *prima facie* jurisdiction is satisfied, the Court must then decide whether interim measures are needed. Here, it must take account of a range of factors, including any steps which the parties may already have taken to reduce the tension. Thus, in the *Aegean Sea Continental Shelf* case,[28] which concerned a dispute which had brought Greece and Turkey to the brink of war, the Court decided that it was unnecessary to consider an order prohibiting the use of force because the Security Council had already adopted a resolution, which both states had welcomed, calling upon them to resolve their dispute peacefully. In the *Nicaragua* case,[29] on the other hand, the United States failed to persuade the Court that it should refuse interim measures because these might affect the Contadora process. While these rulings reflect different assessments of whether interim measures were 'necessary', they also demonstrate a broader point which has been emphasised throughout this study – that methods of dispute settlement are interconnected.

---

[27] *Legality of Use of Force*, Provisional Measures, Order of 2 June 1999, [1999] ICJ Rep. p. 124 (Belgium); and see C. Gray, Note, (2000) 49 ICLQ p. 730.

[28] *Aegean Sea Continental Shelf*, Interim Protection, Order of 11 September 1976, [1976] ICJ Rep. p. 3.

[29] *Military and Paramilitary Activities in and against Nicaragua*, Provisional Measures, Order of 10 May 1984, [1984] ICJ Rep. p. 169.

The element of discretion involved in assessing requests for interim measures may also be seen from the *Pulp Mills on the River Uruguay* case,[30] where the situation was rather unusual. Argentina began proceedings against Uruguay alleging violations of the treaty governing the river that forms the boundary between them. Argentina complained that Uruguay authorised the construction of two pulp mills on the river without observing the notification and consultation procedure required by the treaty. In its request for interim protection, Argentina asked the Court to order Uruguay to suspend construction of the pulp mills and also to co-operate in measures to protect the aquatic environment. The Court, however ruled that the circumstances were not such as to require the exercise of its powers under Article 41. Although Argentina's request was rejected, the Court explained that it was at liberty to submit a future request based on new facts. But it was then Uruguay that returned to the Court by submitting its own request for interim measures. Uruguay's complaint was that 'organised groups of Argentine citizens' were blockading a bridge over the river and Uruguay requested that Argentina should be ordered to put an end to this. The Court, however, having considered all the circumstances, again decided that the measures requested were unnecessary.

Interim measures are legally binding,[31] and so, when the Court makes such an order, states are expected to carry it out. In practice, however, interim measures are likely to be most effective in situations, like that in the *Frontier Dispute* case, where both parties are prepared to recognise the value of judicial intervention. They are less useful in situations like that in the *Nicaragua* case, where one side rejects the whole idea of judicial settlement, for, like the judgment on the merits in such cases, they cannot effectively be enforced. As noted above, the Court will not make an order for interim measures of protection unless there is some instrument which *prima facie* recognises its jurisdiction to decide the main dispute. Thus, it is not open to a state to use the Court's power to indicate interim measures as a way of by-passing the principle of consensuality. On the other hand, as we saw earlier, consent and willingness may not coincide, and it is not unusual for a state which finds a case brought against it to attempt to repudiate its previous acceptance of the Court. It is precisely in these cases, where steps to restrain the unwilling state from disregarding the applicant's rights may well be needed, that interim measures are often least effective.

It should be noted, however, that the significance of Article 41 is not limited to cases in which the Court makes an order for interim protection which is then observed. While that is the ideal situation, a state whose request

---

[30] *Pulp Mills on the River Uruguay (Argentina v. Uruguay)*, Provisional Measures, Orders of 13 July 2006 and 23 January 2007, [2006] ICJ Rep. and [2007] ICJ Rep.

[31] See *LaGrand (Germany v. United States)*, Judgment, [2001] ICJ Rep. p. 466 at paras. 99–103; and see M. Menneke and C. J. Tams, Note, (2002) 51 ICLQ p. 449. Prior to this decision, the status of interim measures was a matter of uncertainty.

is granted obtains widespread exposure for its claims at an early stage and, notwithstanding the provisional character of the Court's assessment, can be thought of as having won the first round of the contest, and wrong-footed its opponent. Indeed, even a request which is rejected can sometimes prove beneficial. In the *Passage through the Great Belt* case,[32] for example, Finland challenged Denmark's right to build a bridge across one of the exits from the Baltic. Finland made a request for interim protection, and in the course of the proceedings under Article 41 Denmark undertook not to complete the bridge before the hearing on the merits, while the Court for its part decided to accelerate the proceedings. These represented gains for Finland, despite the Court's ruling that interim protection was unnecessary.[33]

The powers of the Court to allow a state to intervene in a case are set out in Articles 62 and 63 of the Statute.[34] The latter entitles a state to intervene as of right when a case involves the interpretation of a treaty to which it is a party. Article 62, on the other hand, authorises a state to make a request to intervene if it considers that it has 'an interest of a legal nature which may be affected by the decision in the case'. Neither provision has been much used, but Article 62, which makes intervention a matter for the Court's discretion, has already posed a number of problems.

It is clearly undesirable for the Court, whose jurisdiction is consensual, to deal with the interests of states that are not present; hence the need to provide such states with an opportunity to intervene. But, although the function of Article 62 is plain, difficulties have arisen over two related issues: the question of what constitutes 'an interest of a legal nature' and the question of the circumstances, if any, in which a state seeking to rely on Article 62 must be able to point to a jurisdictional link between itself and the main parties to the case.

Both questions were prominent in the *Tunisia–Libya Continental Shelf* case, where the third state was Malta, seeking to intervene when the two North African states asked the Court to indicate the rules and principles of international law applicable to the delimitation of their respective areas of continental shelf in the central Mediterranean. There was no jurisdictional link between Malta and the main parties, but what led the Court to reject the request was that, while Malta sought permission to submit its views

---

[32] *Passage through the Great Belt (Finland v. Denmark)*, Provisional Measures, Order of 29 July 1991, [1991] ICJ Rep. p. 12. For commentary, see C. Gray, Note, (1993) 42 ICLQ p. 705.

[33] Moreover, the Court indicated that a decision on the merits in favour of Finland might not merely require the payment of compensation, but could result in Denmark's having to abandon the bridge project altogether. This may well have strengthened Finland's bargaining position in the subsequent negotiations between the two states. See further Merrills, 'Interim measures of protection', pp. 112–13 and 140–1.

[34] For a review of the issues raised by these provisions, see C. M. Chinkin, 'Third party intervention before the International Court of Justice', (1986) 80 AJIL p. 495; and J. M. Ruda, 'Intervention before the International Court of Justice', in Lowe and Fitzmaurice, *Fifty Years of the International Court*, p. 487.

with respect to the law concerning a large area, it attached to its request an express reservation that its intervention was not to have the effect of putting in issue its own claims *vis-à-vis* Tunisia and Libya. This qualification the Court found to be unacceptable, concluding that 'the very character of the intervention for which Malta seeks permission shows . . . that the interest of a legal nature invoked by Malta cannot be considered to be one "which may be affected by the decision in the case" within the meaning of Article 62 of the Statute'.[35]

The effect of this decision was that, in 1982, the *Tunisia–Libya* case was decided on the merits without Malta's participation. Malta and Libya then referred their delimitation dispute to the Court. This, in turn, prompted an application to intervene from Italy which, like Malta in the earlier case, found its request opposed by the main parties. The basis of Italy's case was that the continental shelf area which Libya and Malta had referred to the Court included areas over which Italy considered that it had rights. Italy therefore maintained that it had 'an interest of a legal nature' within the meaning of Article 62. To meet the objection which had proved fatal to Malta in 1981, Italy also made it clear that, if permitted to intervene, it would submit to whatever decision the Court might make with regard to its own asserted rights.

The Italian case looked strong but had one weakness. There was no jurisdictional link between Italy and Libya. Was this important? In its decision in 1984, the Court held that it was.[36] Holding that, if Italy were permitted to intervene, the Court would find itself deciding disputes between Italy and the main parties in circumstances in which its jurisdiction had not been established, it concluded that Italy's application must be dismissed. The decision, said the Court, could be justified in one of two ways. Either it could be said that a state which seeks to bring an independent dispute to the Court via Article 62 must demonstrate a jurisdictional link with the other parties in order to supply the requisite element of consensuality, or it could be said that such a state may never intervene under Article 62, and, whatever the jurisdictional position, can have its day in court only by instituting fresh proceedings. Since on either view the Italian claim failed, the Court held that it was unnecessary for it to decide which approach to Article 62 was correct.

The way the Court construed the Italian request in the *Libya–Malta* case meant that it did not need to decide whether a jurisdictional link is always required before a state can intervene under Article 62, and it is clear from the individual opinions that this was a point on which the judges

---

35 *Continental Shelf (Tunisia/Libyan Arab Jamahiriya)*, Application by Malta for Permission to Intervene, Judgment, [1981] ICJ Rep. p. 3 at p. 19.

36 *Continental Shelf (Libyan Arab Jamahiriya/Malta)*, Application by Italy for Permission to Intervene, Judgment, [1984] ICJ Rep. p. 3. For discussion, see G. P. McGinley, 'Intervention in the International Court: The Libya/Malta Continental Shelf Case', (1985) 34 ICLQ p. 671.

were divided. However, in the *Land, Island and Maritime Frontier* case[37] in 1990, a ruling on the issue of jurisdiction could not be avoided when a chamber of the Court decided that Nicaragua had shown the existence of 'an interest of a legal nature' in the regime of the waters of the Gulf of Fonseca, one of the matters in contention between Honduras and El Salvador. The chamber decided that it was unnecessary to demonstrate a jurisdictional link between Nicaragua and the litigating states on the ground that, when a state intervenes as a 'non-party', the Court's competence with regard to intervention derives not from the consent of the parties to the case, but from their consent to the Court's exercise of its powers under the Statute. This approach has been endorsed by the full Court in later cases[38] and is clearly correct. For it not only treats intervention in the same way as interim measures and other aspects of the Court's incidental jurisdiction, which has the merit of consistency, but also makes intervention possible whenever a state can show the requisite interest, thus enabling Article 62 to achieve its purpose.

In another way, too, the decision in the *Land, Island and Maritime Frontier* case seems likely to facilitate intervention. From the two earlier cases, it appeared that, if, to prove that it had an 'interest of a legal nature', a state specified rights which might be infringed, it could be accused of submitting a dispute to the Court. But if, on the other hand, it refrained from doing this, it could find, as Malta did, that it was held to have no 'interest of a legal nature'. In the *Land, Island and Maritime Frontier* case, however, the chamber provided a way out of this dilemma by examining Nicaragua's alleged legal interest in a balanced and constructive manner and upholding part of its claim. It is important to note that a general interest in the relevant rules of international law is not sufficient to ground an intervention under Article 62, and a number of Nicaragua's other claims were rejected on this basis. Nevertheless, by accepting Nicaragua's claim to intervene in relation to the status of the waters of the Gulf of Fonseca, the first case in which a request to intervene under Article 62 was accepted, the chamber set an important and encouraging precedent.

It would be wrong to leave this topic without pointing out that, for a would-be intervenor, the opportunity to invoke Article 62 may in itself be quite valuable. For example, when dismissing Italy's application in the *Libya–Malta* case, the Court, after emphasising that under Article 59 of the

---

[37] *Land, Island and Maritime Frontier Dispute (El Salvador/Honduras)*, Application to Intervene, Judgment, [1990] ICJ Rep. p. 92. This judgment was given by a chamber in accordance with the Court's Order of 28 February 1990. For comment on the Order and subsequent Judgment, see M. D. Evans, Note, (1992) 41 ICLQ p. 896.

[38] See J. G. Merrills, Note, (2000) 49 ICLQ p. 720, describing Equatorial Guinea's successful application to intervene in the *Land and Maritime Boundary* case between Cameroon and Nigeria (1999); and note also the subsequent endorsement of this approach to jurisdiction in the *Ligitan and Sipadan* case cited in note 40 below.

Statute its decisions bind only the parties to the case, explained that in its treatment of the merits it would take account of the interests of other states in the region. On the last point, Italy had, of course, provided the Court with a great deal of information in support of its application, and this clearly had a significant influence when the case was finally decided in 1985.[39] In the *Ligitan and Sipadan* case,[40] similarly, the Philippines attempted to intervene in a dispute between Indonesia and Malaysia in order to protect its claim to North Borneo, but the application was rejected on the ground that it had failed to show the necessary 'interest of a legal nature'. However, the Court assured the Philippines that the parties' submissions had no bearing on its territorial claim and also indicated that, despite the Court's rejection of the application to intervene, it remained 'cognizant of the positions stated before it by Indonesia, Malaysia and the Philippines in the present proceedings'.[41] There is thus a parallel here between Article 62 and Article 41 since, as we saw earlier, even requests for interim protection which are denied may have certain benefits.

The power to revise a judgment is contained in Article 61 of the Statute and can only be exercised if new facts come to light and these would have had a decisive effect on the decision. Interpretation of a judgment, in contrast, is a broader power and according to Article 60 can be performed at the request of any party. Like the provisions on intervention, these powers have been little used, but in the right situation can be employed to make judicial settlement more effective. Thus, in the final stage of the proceedings in the *Tunisia–Libya* case,[42] the Court refused a request by Tunisia that it should revise its 1982 judgment on the ground that the new facts could have been discovered earlier and because in any event they were not sufficiently important. It did, however, respond positively to a subsidiary request that it should interpret the previous judgment. There was considerable argument in this case over whether Tunisia's request for 'interpretation' was simply another attempt to secure a revision of the judgment, and the Court, though acceding to the request, was careful to emphasise the distinction between the two.

A rather similar point was made in the *Land and Maritime Boundary* case when, in an unusual move, Nigeria requested an interpretation of the Court's judgment on jurisdiction and admissibility, while the proceedings

---

[39] See *Continental Shelf (Libyan Arab Jamahiriya/Malta)*, Judgment, [1985] ICJ Rep. p. 13, paras. 20–3.

[40] *Sovereignty over Pulau Ligitan and Pulau Sipadan (Indonesia/Malaysia)*, Application to Intervene, Judgment, [2001] ICJ Rep. p. 575; and see J. G. Merrills, Note, (2002) 51 ICLQ p. 718.

[41] Judgment, para. 94.

[42] *Application for Revision and Interpretation of the Judgment of 24 February 1982 in the Case concerning the Continental Shelf (Tunisia/Libyan Arab Jamahiriya)*, [1985] ICJ Rep. p. 192.

on the merits were still pending.[43] There had been no previous requests of this kind, but the Court accepted that the language of Article 60 is sufficiently general to allow for interpretation of judgments on preliminary objections, as well as of those on the merits. It pointed out, however, that, by laying down that judgments are 'final and without appeal', Article 60 reflects a fundamental principle, that of *res judicata*, which must always be respected. As regards the particular point in issue, the Court explained that in its earlier judgment it had rejected the pertinent objection of Nigeria in terms which could not be reconciled with its current request. The Court would therefore not be able to 'interpret' that judgment without transgressing the principle of *res judicata*, from which it followed that Nigeria's request was inadmissible.

Requests to revise a judgment, like requests for interpretation, can relate either to a previous judgment on the merits, or to one on admissibility and jurisdiction. Thus, in the *Genocide Convention* case, Yugoslavia requested a revision of the Court's 1996 judgment on admissibility and jurisdiction, claiming that the earlier judgment rested on a mistaken view of Yugoslavia's legal status;[44] while in the *Land, Island and Maritime Frontier* case a chamber of the Court had to deal with a request from El Salvador calling for a revision of its earlier judgment on the merits on the basis of new documentary evidence.[45] Significantly, however, both requests were rejected: Yugoslavia's on the ground that its claim was not based on facts in existence at the time of the original judgment; and El Salvador's because its new facts were not of a decisive nature. While both decisions were justified, they confirm the impression from the *Tunisia–Libya* case that so compelling is the presumption of finality that the circumstances must be exceptional for a claim based on Article 61 to succeed.

In addition to the matters already described, which are all covered in the Statute, the Court has a further incidental power, to consider counterclaims, which are provided for in its Rules. Under Article 80 of the Rules, the conditions under which a counter-claim may be entertained are that it 'comes within the jurisdiction of the Court and is directly connected with the subject matter of the claim of the other party'. It follows that, when a

---

[43] See *Request for Interpretation of the Judgment of 11 June 1998 in the Case concerning the Land and Maritime Boundary between Cameroon and Nigeria (Cameroon v. Nigeria) Preliminary Objections (Nigeria v. Cameroon)*, Judgment, [1999] ICJ Rep. p. 31.

[44] See *Application for Revision of the Judgment of 11 July 1996 in the Case concerning Application of the Convention on the Prevention and Punishment of the Crime of Genocide (Bosnia and Herzegovina v. Yugoslavia) Preliminary Objections (Yugoslavia v. Bosnia and Herzegovina)*, Judgment, [2003] ICJ Rep.; and see N. Tsagourias, Note, (2004) 53 ICLQ p. 731.

[45] *Application for Revision of the Judgment of 11 September 1992 in the Case concerning the Land, Island and Maritime Frontier Dispute (El Salvador/Honduras: Nicaragua intervening) (El Salvador v. Honduras)*, Judgment, [2003] ICJ Rep.; and see M. N. Shaw, Note, (2005) 54 ICLQ p. 1013.

dispute is referred to the Court by application,[46] the Court is not limited to dealing with the claims of the state initiating proceedings, but can also address various related issues, should they be raised by its opponent. A respondent cannot, of course, use a counter-claim as a way of bringing a separate dispute before the Court, nor can it be used as a device to expand the basis of the Court's jurisdiction in the case. Counter-claims may, however, enable a complex dispute to be dealt with more fully than might otherwise be possible, and as such may help to promote international justice.

Although the facility to present counter-claims goes back to the days of the Permanent Court, until recently it had been little used. However, in the *Genocide Convention* case in 1997, the Court had to consider a counter-claim by Yugoslavia concerning alleged acts of genocide committed by Bosnia and Herzegovina, and shortly afterwards was presented by counter-claims from the United States, relating to the use of force by Iran, in the *Oil Platforms* case. As the admissibility of the counter-claims was contested in both cases, the Court carefully examined the requirements of Article 80 before deciding they were admissible.[47] In the event, however, the counter-claim in the *Genocide Convention* case was later withdrawn, while that in the *Oil Platforms* case was rejected when the Court gave its judgment on the merits in 2003.[48] In the *Land and Maritime Boundary* case, likewise, counter-claims, here relating to frontier incidents, were put forward by Nigeria and found to be admissible, but then proved relatively insignificant when the case was eventually decided on the merits.[49] In the *Armed Activities on the Territory of the Congo* case,[50] similarly, three counter-claims were raised by Uganda, but produced mixed results. One was ruled inadmissible; one rejected for lack of evidence, while a third, concerned with attacks on Ugandan diplomats, was upheld.

Advisory jurisdiction

The purpose of the Court's advisory jurisdiction is to enable it to give legal opinions at the request of international organisations. Although the details

---

[46] When a case is brought by special agreement, the claims of each party will normally be contained in the agreement and so no question of a counter-claim will arise: see H. Thirlway, 'The law and procedure of the International Court of Justice 1960–1989 (part twelve)', (2001) 72 BYBIL p. 37 at p. 175.

[47] See the Court's Orders of 17 December 1997 (*Genocide Convention* case), [1997] ICJ Rep. p. 243, and 19 March 1998 (*Oil Platforms* case), [1998] ICJ Rep. p. 190, discussed by P. H. F. Bekker, Note, (1998) 92 AJIL p. 508; and Thirlway, 'The law and procedure', p. 174.

[48] *Oil Platforms (Iran v. United States)*, Judgment, [2003] ICJ Rep.; and see P. H. F. Bekker, Note, (2004) 98 AJIL p. 550.

[49] *Land and Maritime Boundary between Cameroon and Nigeria (Cameroon v. Nigeria: Equatorial Guinea intervening)*, Merits, Judgment, [2002] ICJ Rep.; and see J. G. Merrills, Note, (2003) 52 ICLQ p. 788.

[50] *Armed Activities on the Territory of the Congo (Democratic Republic of the Congo v. Uganda)*, Judgment, [2005] ICJ Rep.; and see J. T. Gathii, Note, (2007) 101 AJIL p. 142.

and functioning of the advisory jurisdiction are outside the scope of this work, two points are worth mentioning, one relating to the contentious jurisdiction, the other of a more general nature.

As the principal judicial organ of the United Nations, the Court may find itself asked by the General Assembly, or some other body, for an advisory opinion on a legal dispute between states. Bearing in mind that the Court's contentious jurisdiction is consensual, how should it respond to such a request? This issue, which is linked with the question of *ad hoc* judges in advisory proceedings to be considered shortly, has been examined by the Court on several occasions. In the *Western Sahara* case,[51] the Court developed its earlier reasoning in the *Peace Treaties* opinion[52] and held that, the issue being the propriety of the Court's giving an opinion, rather than its jurisdiction to do so, the factors to be taken into account include the object and purpose of the request, the origin and nature of the dispute and the adequacy of the available evidence. The practice of the Court indicates that in assessing these factors there is a weighty presumption in favour of taking the case, a reflection perhaps of the United Nations background of many of the Court's members, and of the fact that disputes over human rights, decolonisation and a number of other issues are no longer simply affairs between states, but a proper concern of international organisations.

The general point is simply that even advisory opinions which do not relate to legal disputes between states in the strict sense are usually concerned directly or indirectly with matters of inter-state controversy. The advisory opinion in the *WHO Regional Headquarters* case,[53] for example, though ostensibly concerned with the circumstances in which a specialised agency could move its seat, in reality arose out of animosity between Egypt and its Arab neighbours. Similarly, the advisory opinion in the *Nuclear Weapons* case,[54] although concerned with the abstract question of whether the threat or use of nuclear weapons is permitted by international law, addressed an issue on which the members of the United Nations are deeply divided. In holding here, and in previous cases, that political circumstances are no bar to complying with a request for an advisory opinion, the Court has demonstrated that the clashes of states' interests which occur within international institutions can, when presented in legal form, be a proper object of judicial attention.

---

[51] *Western Sahara*, Advisory Opinion, [1975] ICJ Rep. p. 12. For commentary, see P. V. Lalonde, 'The death of the Eastern Carelia doctrine', (1979) 37 U. Toronto Fac. L. Rev. p. 80.

[52] *Interpretation of Peace Treaties with Bulgaria, Hungary and Rumania*, First Phase, Advisory Opinion, [1950] ICJ Rep. p. 65.

[53] *Interpretation of the Agreement of 25 March 1951 between the WHO and Egypt*, Advisory Opinion, [1980] ICJ Rep. p. 73. For commentary, see C. Gray, 'The International Court's advisory opinion on the WHO–Egypt Agreement of 1951', (1983) 32 ICLQ p. 534.

[54] *Legality of the Threat or Use of Nuclear Weapons*, Advisory Opinion, [1996] ICJ Rep. p. 66. For comment, see N. Grief, Note, (1997) 46 ICLQ p. 681; and M. J. Matheson, 'The opinions of the International Court of Justice on the threat or use of nuclear weapons', (1997) 91 AJIL p. 417.

The relation between advisory opinions and dispute settlement was confirmed in the *Construction of a Wall* case[55] which arose out of a request from the General Assembly for the Court's assessment of the legal consequences of the security wall being built by Israel in the Occupied Palestinian Territory. After confirming that it was competent to deal with the request, and that there was no reason to decline to exercise its jurisdiction, the Court examined the legal issues in considerable detail, concluding both that the wall was illegal and that this had serious consequences for Israel and for other states. Notable features of the opinion are the Court's assertion of its competence, despite the political aspects of the question and its obviously contentious character, and the near unanimity of the judges. Also interesting, though in no way surprising, is that, in the final part of its opinion, and to put the matter in context, the Court emphasised to the General Assembly the need to encourage efforts to achieve a negotiated settlement and the establishment of a Palestinian state with peace and security for all in the region.

Membership of the Court

The Court is composed of fifteen judges, elected for a nine-year term by the Security Council and General Assembly of the United Nations. At the end of this term, a judge is eligible to stand for re-election, and elections are staggered in such a way that five judges – one-third of the Court – are elected every three years. According to the Statute (Article 9), the election of judges is to be carried out in such a way that 'in the body as a whole the representation of the main forms of civilization and of the principal legal systems of the world should be assured'. The importance of this requirement can hardly be over-emphasised. Unless the distribution of seats on the Court is seen to reflect the balance and diversity of the international community as a whole, it is likely that states which consider their culture to be inadequately represented will not regard the Court as an appropriate body to handle their legal disputes. Moreover, in such circumstances, the Court's authority, perhaps even competence, to interpret and apply law for the world must be considered doubtful. Article 9, then, is directly concerned with the political underpinnings of adjudication and international law.

Elections to the International Court have always been the prerogative of political institutions, first the League and then the United Nations. Consequently, the changes which have taken place in the composition of the Court since 1919 reflect the shifting balance of institutional power over the same

---

[55] *Legal Consequences of the Construction of a Wall in the Occupied Palestinian Territory*, Advisory Opinion, [2004] ICJ Rep. p. 136; and see S. C. Breau, Note, (2005) 54 ICLQ p. 1003.

period.[56] African and Asian representation, for example, has risen from two in the colonial era (1922) to six at the present time, while European representation in the same period has fallen from ten to six, including France, the United Kingdom and the Russian Federation. As Permanent Members of the Security Council, the states just mentioned, together with the United States and China, are regarded as entitled to have a judge of their nationality on the Court. It now seems also to be agreed that the ten remaining seats on the Court should follow the pattern of 'equitable geographical distribution' agreed for the Security Council after its enlargement in 1965. With this arrangement, the present distribution of seats on the Court would appear sufficiently in conformity with Article 9 for enlargement of the Court, suggested at one time as a route to the same goal, to be unnecessary.

To establish and maintain its authority to handle disputes and complex questions of international law, the members of the Court must be demonstrably competent as individuals to decide the cases which come before them. Article 2 of the Statute requires that the judges shall be 'persons of high moral character, who possess the qualifications required in their respective countries for appointment to the highest judicial offices, or are jurisconsults of recognised competence in international law'. With the distribution of seats on the Court a matter of broad agreement, the fulfilment of Article 2 is a matter of nominations, rather than elections. In theory, nominations are the prerogative of independent national groups, but in practice governments exercise a major influence. Although disquiet has been expressed at the relative lack of experience of some members of the Court, and the nominating process could certainly be improved, the judges in general can hardly be described as insufficiently qualified.

Since it is vital that the judges are not only qualified in a general sense, but also capable of dealing impartially with the particular case, two provisions of the Statute, Articles 17 and 24, provide respectively for disqualification if a judge has been previously involved in a case in another capacity, and that he or she should stand down for other special reasons. Although the purpose of these provisions is obvious, a tendency to elect former legal advisers, members of the International Law Commission and career diplomats to the Court has made decisions as to whether individual judges should be disqualified from sitting in a particular case increasingly difficult. In the *Namibia* case, for example, the eligibility of three members of the Court was challenged on the ground of previous involvement in the dispute in another capacity, and, more recently, in the *Construction of a Wall* case, Israel challenged the eligibility of the Egyptian judge, a former diplomat,

---

[56] For a lucid examination of this and other aspects of the Court's composition, see S. Rosenne, 'The composition of the Court', in Gross, *Future of the Court*, p. 377.

on similar grounds. All the challenges were rejected by the Court,[57] though in one case only by a majority of ten votes to four, and it seems clear that, in this respect at least, the previous experience of members of the Court may continue to raise problems.

In a contentious case, if neither party has a judge of its nationality currently on the Court, both sides may appoint an *ad hoc* judge who becomes a member of the Court for that case only. In the *Maritime Delimitation in the Black Sea* case,[58] for example, between Romania and Ukraine, both states appointed a judge *ad hoc*. Similarly, if one party currently has a national on the Court and the other has not, the unrepresented party may also appoint a judge *ad hoc*. Thus, in the *CERD* case,[59] where the respondent was Russia, the applicant, Georgia, appointed an *ad hoc* judge. However, members of the Court sit as individuals, not as representatives of their national states. In view of this, and of the predictable tendency of *ad hoc* judges to accept the submissions of the state appointing them, the legitimacy of what one commentator has termed this 'concession to diplomatic susceptibilities'[60] has been seriously questioned.

In light of municipal judicial practice, the institution of the *ad hoc* judge certainly appears anomalous. But is the comparison really relevant? Municipal courts are composed of individuals from a single legal culture, draw on that culture to justify their decisions and enjoy compulsory jurisdiction. None of this is true in the international field. Thus, for a government to refer a dispute to the International Court calls for something of an act of faith. The vote of the *ad hoc* judge, like that of the 'national' member of a court of arbitration, is never likely to change the result of a case, but his presence provides an important link between the parties and the Court. Accordingly, it has been suggested that, while *ad hoc* judges have a duty to be impartial, they also have a responsibility to ensure that the factual and legal arguments of the state that has appointed them are fully understood and considered by the other judges.[61] In these circumstances, the institution of the *ad hoc* judge is perhaps still too useful to be dispensed with.

A question which has exercised the Court on several occasions concerns the circumstances in which *ad hoc* judges may be appointed in advisory

---

[57] See, for the *Namibia* case, [1971] ICJ pp. 3, 6 and 9; and, for the *Construction of a Wall* case, ICJ Press Release 2004/4 (3 February 2004). See also Thirlway, 'The law and procedure', pp. 42–6.

[58] *Maritime Delimitation in the Black Sea (Romania v. Ukraine)*, Judgment, [2009] ICJ Rep. See C. G. Lathrop, Note, (2009) 103 AJIL p. 543.

[59] *Application of the International Convention on the Elimination of All Forms of Racial Discrimination (Georgia v. Russian Federation)*, Provisional Measures Order of 15 October 2008, [2008] ICJ Rep. See S. Ghandhi, Note, (2009) 58 ICLQ p. 713.

[60] Rosenne, 'Composition of the Court', p. 407. For another critical view, see D. D. Nsereko, 'The International Court, impartiality and judges ad hoc', (1973) 13 Ind. J. Int. L. p. 207.

[61] See the separate opinion of Judge *ad hoc* Lauterpacht in the *Genocide Convention* case, [1993] ICJ Rep. pp. 408–9. See also S. M. Schwebel, 'National judges and judges ad hoc of the International Court of Justice', (1999) 48 ICLQ p. 889.

proceedings. The question arises because advisory opinions, which can only be requested by international organisations, sometimes relate to disputes between states, which if they were the subject of contentious proceedings would justify the appointment of a judge *ad hoc*. Recognising that the purpose of appointing such a judge is the same in both cases, the Court has sought to assimilate its advisory and contentious jurisdiction. Although in the *Namibia* case it held (controversially) that South Africa was not entitled to a judge *ad hoc* and that the Court had no residual discretion to authorise such an appointment,[62] in the later *Western Sahara* case,[63] it held on more convincing grounds that a similar application from Morocco should be allowed.

Chambers

Cases in the International Court are normally heard by the full Court. However, Articles 26–29 of the Statute provide for the creation of chambers composed of fewer judges for particular categories of cases, for the speedy dispatch of business, or to deal with an individual case. For many years, these procedures were hardly used, but their potential to enhance the Court's activity is now being realised. In 1972, as part of an effort to encourage greater use of its facilities, the Court revised its Rules so as to promote the use of *ad hoc* chambers and enable prospective litigants to influence the composition as well as the size of the bench. Similarly, in 1993, the Court decided to establish a chamber of seven judges to deal with disputes concerning international environmental law. The environmental chamber was never used and so was discontinued in 2006. However, *ad hoc* chambers have been employed in six cases to date from which certain conclusions may be drawn.[64]

The procedure for *ad hoc* chambers was used for the first time in the *Gulf of Maine* case, brought to the Court by Canada and the United States in 1981. The new Rules provide that the parties must be consulted about the composition of a chamber, although the question is finally determined by the Court after a secret ballot. To avoid the possibility that the ballot might produce the 'wrong' result, Canada and the United States made it clear that, unless their wishes as to the composition of the Court were carried out,

---

[62] See [1971] ICJ Rep. p. 12. For discussion, see M. Pomerance, 'The admission of judges ad hoc in advisory proceedings: Some reflections in the light of the Namibia case', (1973) 67 AJIL p. 446.

[63] See [1975] ICJ Rep. p. 6. For discussion, see I. R. Suh, 'National judges in advisory proceedings of the International Court', (1979) 19 Ind. J. Int. L. p. 20.

[64] For discussion of the chambers procedure, elaborating many of the points made in the text, see S. M. Schwebel, 'Ad hoc chambers of the International Court of Justice', (1987) 81 AJIL p. 831; R. Ostrihansky, 'Chambers of the International Court of Justice', (1988) 37 ICLQ p. 30; and E. Valencia-Ospina, 'The use of chambers of the International Court of Justice', in Lowe and Fitzmaurice, *Fifty Years of the International Court*, p. 503. See also Thirlway, 'The law and procedure', pp. 46–57.

they would withdraw the case and refer the dispute to arbitration. In these circumstances, the Court, over the protest of two of its members, elected the chamber requested by the parties.[65]

It is unlikely that, in normal circumstances, the Court will ignore the parties' wishes, for, as this case made plain, they are at liberty to go elsewhere, if dissatisfied. Consequently, though the Court retains the ultimate control over its composition, the secret ballot will usually be something of a formality. However, the situation here is the natural and not unexpected consequence of the effort to encourage the use of chambers. Not surprisingly, therefore, in subsequent cases in which the Court has been asked to create an *ad hoc* chamber, it has followed its approach in the *Gulf of Maine* case and elected the bench requested by the parties.[66]

There is currently no provision which establishes the minimum size for a chamber, and in theory it would be possible to set up a chamber consisting of a single judge. Likewise, no maximum is laid down, but, since a quorum of the full Court is nine, a chamber of more than seven judges appears unlikely. In the *Gulf of Maine* case and in subsequent cases in which a chamber has been formed, the Court has consisted of five judges, and this number, which is frequently used for courts of arbitration, now seems to have become standard. The judges selected for a chamber must normally be current members of the Court, but it is important to note that *ad hoc* judges may also be appointed, just as for conventional cases. Thus, in the *Gulf of Maine* case, Canada appointed a judge to act in this capacity,[67] while, in the *Land, Island and Maritime Frontier* case,[68] both states nominated judges, when the original chamber was set up in 1989 and again in 2002 when El Salvador requested revision of the judgment. As a result, the chambers in these proceedings contained three regular and two *ad hoc* judges.

The attraction of the chambers procedure is that it provides states with a method of resolving disputes which combines a major advantage of arbitration, namely, control over the size and composition of the court, with an acknowledged advantage of the International Court of Justice, which is that it comes equipped with a panel of available judges, a court building and the facilities needed for international litigation, all of which are paid for by the United Nations. The parties have to pay the costs of preparing and presenting their case in the normal way, but this is significantly cheaper than

---

[65] *Delimitation of the Maritime Boundary in the Gulf of Maine Area*, Constitution of Chamber, Order of 20 January 1982, [1982] ICJ Rep. p. 3. For discussion, see R. H. Brauer, 'International conflict resolution: The ICJ chambers and the Gulf of Maine dispute', (1982–3) 23 Va JIL p. 463.

[66] This is not expressly stated in the Orders in the various cases but may be inferred from the academic writings of Judges Oda and Schwebel, as well as from circumstantial evidence.

[67] Judge Ruda, who had been originally elected to the chamber, stood down in order that this might happen.

[68] *Land, Island and Maritime Frontier Dispute (El Salvador/Honduras)*, Composition of Chamber, Order of 13 December 1989, [1989] ICJ Rep. p. 162.

arranging and financing an arbitration. The Court also has its constitution, in the form of the Statute, and its established rules of procedure. These also relieve the parties of certain responsibilities, though they also, of course, place limitations on what the Court can do. Consequently, although the chambers procedure offers considerable flexibility, it remains distinct from arbitration.

The cases referred to chambers, though not very numerous, already suggest when the procedure is likely to be used. It might be thought that chambers are particularly suited to the resolution of relatively straightforward disputes where use of the time and resources of the full Court would not be justified. This may well be so, but it has to be said that, of the cases decided so far, only El Salvador's request for revision really falls into this category. The *Gulf of Maine* case[69] raised extremely complex issues relating to continental shelf delimitation and as a result the chamber's judgment is actually longer than either of the full Court's previous decisions in this field. The *Frontier Dispute* cases[70] between Burkina Faso and Mali (1986) and Benin and Niger (2005) both required their chambers to unravel tangled skeins of historical and geographical evidence typical of territorial disputes. In the *ELSI* case,[71] which involved a dispute between the United States and Italy, the evidence related to corporate financing and again was abstruse and voluminous. Finally, in the original *Land, Island and Maritime Frontier* case,[72] the chamber again delivered a long judgment in which it dealt with a mass of detailed evidence and addressed important questions concerning both the acquisition of land territory and the law of the sea.

The above cases suggest that, whatever its merits as a way of disposing of straightforward cases, states also see the chambers procedure as a way of having cases which raise highly technical issues heard by small tribunals selected for their expertise. This, it will be recalled, has traditionally been regarded as an important advantage of arbitration. Thus, recourse to chambers to decide cases of this type is further evidence of how the two procedures are drawing together. It is perhaps worth adding that, on account of its complexity, the *Gulf of Maine* litigation is estimated to have cost the United States and Canada about US$14 million.[73] The cheapness of litigation before a chamber is therefore very much a relative notion. On the other hand, if the dispute had been arbitrated, the parties would also have

---

[69] *Delimitation of the Maritime Boundary in the Gulf of Maine Area*, Judgment, [1984] ICJ Rep. p. 246.

[70] *Frontier Dispute*, Judgment, [1986] ICJ Rep. p. 554; and *Frontier Dispute (Benin/Niger)*, Judgment, [2005] ICJ Rep. And see S. Allen, 'Case concerning the Frontier Dispute (Benin/Niger)', (2006) 55 ICLQ p. 729.

[71] *Case concerning Elettronica Sicula SpA (ELSI)*, Judgment, [1989] ICJ Rep. p. 15.

[72] *Land, Island and Maritime Frontier Dispute (El Salvador/Honduras: Nicaragua intervening)*, Judgment, [1992] ICJ Rep. p. 351. For comment, see M. Shaw, Note, (1993) 42 ICLQ p. 929.

[73] See D. R. Robinson, D. A. Colson and B. C. Rashkow, 'Some perspectives on adjudicating before the World Court: The Gulf of Maine case', (1985) 79 AJIL p. 578 at p. 588.

had to pay for the tribunal, rendering litigation which was never going to be cheap even more expensive. The saving which comes from using the Court may therefore be particularly attractive in complicated disputes where the parties are already committed to substantial expenditure.

Before states began to use the chambers procedure, the fear was sometimes expressed that to allow the parties to influence the composition of the Court would encourage the formation of chambers with a particular ideological orientation, and that this in turn would affect both the quality and the authority of their decisions. Unlike the position with regard to the full Court, there is no requirement that a chamber should represent 'the main forms of civilization' and 'the principal legal systems of the world', and in practice, as we have seen, the composition of a chamber is determined by the parties. The chambers appointed so far, as might be expected, do reflect certain preferences. The judges for the *Gulf of Maine* case were drawn exclusively from North America and Western Europe. The chamber for the 1986 *Frontier Dispute* case, on the other hand, included no judge from these regions, while the judges for the *ELSI* case, which concerned an alleged expropriation, all came from industrialised states. Chambers, however, consistently make use of a range of judicial expertise. The risk of parochialism is therefore one that should not be exaggerated.

As far as the composition of chambers is concerned, then, practice does not suggest an undue narrowness of outlook, and this is confirmed if we consider the other matters of concern, the quality and authority of the decisions. The judgment in the *Gulf of Maine* case, far from reflecting an Anglo-European view of the law, closely followed the full Court's approach in the *Tunisia–Libya* case.[74] Similarly, the judgments in both *Frontier Dispute* cases, though largely taken up with analysis of the particular facts, applied well-established principles relating to the acquisition of territory; while the reasoning in the *ELSI* case again follows conventional lines. In the *Land, Island and Maritime Frontier* case, the chamber concluded that the waters of the Gulf of Fonseca were governed by a special historical regime rather than by the general law. On the other hand, in its treatment of the various territorial issues, it gave careful attention to the scope and application of *uti possidetis juris* and other recognised principles, and the subsequent decision to reject the request to revise the judgment, as noted earlier, was adequately explained. It is idle to speculate on whether the full Court would have made an identical decision in each of these cases, but, if its application of the law might sometimes have varied, it is improbable that its treatment of basic principles would have been very different. As regards their weight as precedents, if, as just suggested, their legal analysis is sound, one would expect to see these cases regularly cited and relied on. The fact that the

---

[74] See J. Schneider, 'The Gulf of Maine case: The nature of an equitable result', (1985) 79 AJIL p. 539.

decision in the *Gulf of Maine* case was extensively referred to when the full Court addressed similar issues in the *Libya–Malta Continental Shelf* case, and that there have been several references to the decisions of chambers in later cases, bears out this view.[75]

When the new rules were first put forward, fears were expressed in some quarters that the chambers procedure might prove so popular that states would no longer wish to use the full Court. As only a handful of cases have been referred to chambers, it now seems that such fears were groundless. But, if states generally prefer to use the full Court, the attempt to encourage the use of chambers can still be regarded as worthwhile. States have recognised that the new rules provide an opportunity to combine the convenience of the Court with several of the advantages of arbitration. The cases which have been referred suggest that chambers are seen as particularly useful for disputes which involve complex evidence, and perhaps also issues with a strong regional dimension. The decisions themselves, though inevitably lacking some of the weight which attaches to judgments of the full Court, can certainly stand comparison with those judgments and are far from the blinkered pronouncements which might have been feared.

In making an assessment of the value of the chambers procedure, two further points should be borne in mind. The first is that, although use of the chambers procedure has not been extensive, preferences in dispute settlement can change and the alternative procedure is now available if states wish to use it. The other point is that, in each of the cases to date, the chamber's decision settled the dispute, something which unfortunately cannot be said of every decision of the full Court. The background of the members of the Court is now so diverse and the subject matter of certain disputes so specialised, that the preference of states for a smaller and more select bench for certain cases is readily understandable. Like the issue of *ad hoc* judges, disqualification and the other matters considered earlier, the current revitalisation of the chambers procedure demonstrates that the question 'who decides?' is as relevant to judicial settlement as to arbitration.

---

[75] See M. Shahabuddeen, *Precedent in the World Court*, Cambridge, 1996, pp. 171–7. As indicated earlier, the full Court has now endorsed the approach to Article 62 taken by the chamber in the *Land, Island and Maritime Frontier* case.

The International Court II: the work of the Court

The institutional features of the International Court, as we have just seen, exercise a major influence on both the readiness of states to employ international adjudication and the ability of the Court to respond to their requests. However, the judgments which the Court hands down show how it deals with disputes when given the opportunity, and are no less important. This is not the place to describe the Court's jurisprudence in detail, nor to consider its contribution to the development of international law. What is needed therefore is not a survey of the Court's case law, but rather an indication of what its day-to-day work reveals about the relation between the settlement of disputes and adjudication. The decision itself is a good place to start.

The Court's decision

Establishing the facts

Proving a case at the international level is primarily a matter of finding and presenting suitable documentary evidence. This material, which is relevant to both fact and law, includes treaty texts, official records of international organisations and national parliaments, diplomatic correspondence, archive material, maps, films, photographs and affidavits. The quantity of such evidence may be extremely large and as there are virtually no exclusionary rules, states can and do bring forward everything which might assist their case. Although the facility is little used, documentary evidence may be augmented by the oral testimony of witnesses and experts, or even by the Court itself visiting the scene. In the *Gabcikovo-Nagymaros* case, for example, which concerned the construction of a barrage system on a boundary river between Hungary and Slovakia, the Court decided in 1997 to visit the relevant area at the parties' request.[1]

Evaluating the evidence is a task for the Court and, since the factual matrix is always the key to the application of the law, this can be a long and elaborate process. In some cases, much of the parties' material can be dismissed as inconclusive or irrelevant to the issues to be decided. In

---

[1] See the *Gabcikovo-Nagymaros Project*, Order of 5 February 1997, [1997] ICJ Rep. p. 3. The visit, which took place in April 1997, was the first to be made by the ICJ. See P. Tomka and S. S. Wordsworth, 'The first site visit of the International Court of Justice in fulfilment of its judicial function', (1998) 92 AJIL p. 133.

disputes over maritime delimitation, for example, the Court has tended to ignore elaborate evidence relating to ecology or geomorphology in favour of less contentious material relating to geography. In some disputes, however, narrowing the focus in this way is impossible and there is no alternative to grappling with the facts. Thus, in the *Nicaragua* case,[2] where the legal issues concerned border-crossing and the use of force in Central America, the Court had to evaluate a huge amount of confusing material and its findings of fact alone occupy fifty-five pages of the judgment.

The Court's difficulties in the *Nicaragua* case were compounded by the fact that, after its controversial ruling on the issue of jurisdiction, the United States decided to take no further part in the proceedings. Although this did not prevent the Court from deciding the case, it meant that, without evidence from one side, the Court was deprived of the interplay of argument which is a vital feature of the judicial process. In this case, as in others where a respondent has failed to appear, the Court made extensive use of admissions, inferences, judicial notice of matters of public knowledge and circumstantial evidence to establish the facts, and when drafting the judgment took unusual care to avoid any impression of bias.[3] It is clear, nonetheless, that by refusing to present its side of the case the United States put itself at an irretrievable disadvantage. However conscientious the Court may be, there is no way in which it can ensure that, if a state is absent, important points in its case will not be lost by default.

In the *Maritime Delimitation and Territorial Questions* case,[4] an unusual situation occurred when a significant quantity of documentary evidence which Qatar had put forward to support its case was challenged as fraudulent by Bahrain. Following exchanges between the parties, Qatar announced that it would not rely on the documents, with the result that the Court was never called upon to examine the documents' authenticity. Normally, of course, evaluating the evidence is not concerned with investigating fraud, but a matter of deciding and then applying the appropriate standard of proof, something on which the Court, like other international tribunals, is not always very explicit. In the *Oil Platforms* case,[5] for example, the Court was not persuaded by evidence from the United States seeking to establish Iran's responsibility for attacks on shipping, but failed to explain why more evidence was needed. This was unfortunate for, as a critic of the decision

---

[2] *Military and Paramilitary Activities in and against Nicaragua*, Merits, Judgment, [1986] ICJ Rep. p. 14.

[3] See K. Highet, 'Evidence, the Court and the *Nicaragua* case', [1987] 81 AJIL p. 1. These problems were anticipated in the same author's 'Litigation implications of the US withdrawal from the *Nicaragua* case', (1985) 79 AJIL p. 992.

[4] *Maritime Delimitation and Territorial Questions between Qatar and Bahrain*, Judgment, [2001] ICJ Rep. p. 40. For discussion of the contested documents, see M. Mendelson, 'The curious case of *Qatar v. Bahrain* in the International Court of Justice', (2001) 72 BYBIL p. 183 at pp. 197–201.

[5] *Oil Platforms (Iran v. United States)*, Merits, Judgment, [2003] ICJ Rep.

pointed out, a 'lack of clear standards and reasoned explanations for crucial factual decisions can easily become a target of suspicion and criticism for the losing party'.[6]

The problems that fact-finding can present may be seen in two recent cases where the Court was faced with exceptionally complex situations. In the *Armed Activities on the Territory of the Congo* case,[7] the Democratic Republic of the Congo (DRC) complained that Uganda had engaged in armed aggression against it, committed numerous violations of human rights law and international humanitarian law and illegally exploited its natural resources. As these allegations related to activities during a lengthy civil war involving at least seven other states, as well as numerous rebel groups, establishing the facts and deciding Uganda's responsibility proved a very demanding task. In the *Genocide Convention* case,[8] similarly, the question was whether Serbia had committed genocide in Bosnia and Herzegovina during the conflict in the Balkans which followed the violent break-up of Yugoslavia. As in the previous case, this inquiry called for the Court to examine a mass of evidence relating to both the atrocities themselves and official policies on the matter. However, since some of these issues had already been investigated by the International Criminal Tribunal for the Former Yugoslavia, the Court was able to make use of some of the Tribunal's findings of fact, describing them as 'highly persuasive'.

The Statute and Rules contain a number of provisions designed to enable the Court to supplement the parties' evidence with its own investigations. It is entitled to request the parties to call witnesses or experts and may call for the production of any other evidence on points of fact in regard to which the parties are not in agreement. Article 30(2) of the Statute permits the Court to appoint assessors to sit with it during the proceedings and is intended to ensure that the decision takes account of the latest scientific knowledge and contains no technical errors. Under Article 50 of the Statute, the Court is empowered to commission an inquiry or expert opinion. Although this power has rarely been used, its value was demonstrated in the *Corfu Channel* case.[9]

After hearing the conflicting evidence of the parties' witnesses and expert witnesses, the Court appointed a committee of experts, composed of senior officers of the Dutch, Norwegian and Swedish navies, which submitted two reports concerning the mining of the channel. After the second report,

---

[6] See J. R. Crook, 'The 2003 judicial activity of the International Court of Justice', (2004) 98 AJIL p. 309 at p. 311.

[7] *Armed Activities on the Territory of the Congo (Democratic Republic of the Congo v. Uganda)*, [2005] ICJ Rep. And see P. N. Okowa, Note, (2006) 55 ICLQ p. 742.

[8] *Application of the Convention on the Prevention and Punishment of the Crime of Genocide (Bosnia and Herzegovina v. Serbia and Montenegro)*, Merits, Judgment, [2007] ICJ Rep.; and see S. Sivakumaran, Note, (2007) 56 ICLQ p. 695.

[9] See [1949] ICJ Rep. pp. 142, 152 and 258.

which resulted from a visit to the scene, the Court was satisfied that Albania's responsibility had been established. This raised the question of compensation and further technical issues. The Court therefore appointed another committee of experts, consisting of two senior officers of the Dutch navy. Their conclusion, that the British claim represented a fair and accurate estimate of the damage sustained, was accepted by the Court and formed the basis of its final judgment.

Because international litigation is complex and the Court is now very busy, various measures to speed up the handling of cases have been introduced in recent years. These include several changes to the Court's Rules, and some important Practice Directions, as well as a series of other measures designed to simplify its procedures.[10] Steps with a particular bearing on the presentation of evidence include a requirement that documents annexed to a party's written pleadings should be strictly selected, a restriction on the production of new documents after the closure of the written proceedings and an encouragement to the parties to focus their oral statements on the issues which divide them. Other measures are intended to limit the number of rounds of written pleadings. In adopting these measures, the Court is seeking to promote efficiency without unduly constraining a party's ability to make its case, a policy requiring a balancing act of some delicacy.

Identifying the law

The sources of law which the Court is to utilise are set out in Article 38(1) of the Statute, and it is clear that the way in which these are applied is likely to exercise a major influence on states' attitudes towards judicial settlement. In the work of the Court, as in that of municipal courts, the essential problem is to reconcile continuity with innovation. Internationally, however, the problem is complicated by three factors: the lack of a single legal culture, the relatively undeveloped state of international law and the tensions of a period of radical changes in international society.

The cultural dimension is well illustrated by the *Western Sahara* case.[11] There, Spain argued that whether the territory was *terra nullius* at the time of colonisation must be determined by the criteria of classical international law, while Algeria and Mauritania argued that the Court should acknowledge the existence of an Arab–Islamic civilisation, outside the traditional legal framework, of which the Western Sahara formed an integral part. In its advisory opinion, the Court preferred Spain's argument on this point and rejected the more radical view. However, when the Court turned to the

---

[10] See R. Higgins, 'Respecting sovereign states and running a tight courtroom', (2001) 50 ICLQ p. 121, and the Notes by S. Rosenne in (2002) 2 Global Community YBILJ p. 207 and J. G. Merrills in (2003) 3 Global Community YBILJ p. 277.

[11] Western Sahara, Advisory Opinion, [1975] ICJ Rep. p. 12. For discussion of this aspect of the case, see M. Shaw, 'The Western Sahara case', (1978) 40 BYBIL p. 118.

issue of 'legal ties' with the territory, it examined the special characteristics of the region in great detail and made the Arab–Islamic elements in the case the focal point of its opinion. From a bookish standpoint, it is easy to criticise this attempt to blend a traditional approach with the concepts of non-Western legal cultures. Yet it is inevitable that broadening the Court's membership should bring with it a widening of the basis of its decisions. Moreover, it is right that it should do so. For, if judicial decisions are to be an acceptable means of resolving disputes, the Court must recognise the diversity of its audience and frame its judgments in language which the bulk of the members of the international community can support and understand.

The President of the Court recently observed that its decisions 'must continue to provide that core of predictability that distinguishes law from politics', while doing so 'in a way that is responsive to the legitimate needs and aspirations of the international community'.[12]

This tension can be seen in the *Arrest Warrant* case,[13] where the Court decided that a foreign minister enjoys complete immunity from the jurisdiction of courts in other states, even with regard to allegations of war crimes and crimes against humanity. In the absence of a clear body of state practice on this issue, the Court based its conclusion on functional criteria and, while careful to distinguish immunity from impunity, rejected arguments based on international public policy. In this case, then, the Court proceeded cautiously. In contrast, in the *LaGrand* case,[14] a few months earlier, it had accepted that Article 36(1) of the 1963 Vienna Convention on Consular Relations confers rights on individuals, as well as on states, thereby endorsing the progressive view that in modern international law a convention does not have to be a human rights treaty in order to confer such rights.

Adjudicating in an era of social and legal change requires both a technique for resolving disputes when state practice provides no clear guidance, and, after things begin to settle down, a way of deciding when new trends in practice, as evidenced in non-binding declarations, codes, guidelines and other 'soft' materials, cross the threshold of normativity and merit recognition as law. In the *Gabcikovo-Nagymaros* case,[15] for example, the Court held that a treaty concluded by Hungary and Czechoslovakia in 1977 had to be interpreted and applied in light of subsequent developments in international law relating to the protection of the environment. That in itself was

---

[12] Speech by HE Judge Rosalyn Higgins at the sixtieth anniversary of the inaugural sitting of the Court, ICJ Press Release 2006/15 (12 April, 2006).

[13] *Arrest Warrant of 11 April 2000 (Democratic Republic of the Congo v. Belgium)*, Judgment, [2002] ICJ Rep. p. 3. For comment, see C. Wickremasinghe, Note, (2003) 52 ICLQ p. 775.

[14] *LaGrand Case (Germany v. United States)*, Judgment, [2001] ICJ Rep. p. 466. For comment, see M. Menneke and C. J. Tams, Note, (2002) 51 ICLQ p. 449.

[15] *Gabcikovo-Nagymaros Project (Hungary/Slovakia)*, Judgment, [1997] ICJ Rep. p. 7. For comment, see P. N. Okowa, Note, (1998) 47 ICLQ p. 688.

a ruling of some significance in the present context, but tantalisingly left open the question of which of the various instruments cited in argument qualified as 'law' for this purpose.

A situation in which practice was in a state of flux and provided no clear guidance had to be addressed by the Court in the *Fisheries Jurisdiction* case of 1974.[16] The questions on which the United Kingdom sought a decision were whether Iceland's claim to a fifty-mile exclusive fishery was contrary to international law, whether the claim was opposable to the United Kingdom and whether the conservation of fish stocks in the disputed area was a matter for unilateral regulation by Iceland. In the face of a wide diversity in state practice, however, the Court declined to address the question of customary international law and based its decision on the non-opposability of Iceland's regulations to the United Kingdom in view of the latter's historic rights.

Although the Court's approach was criticised, in the circumstances of the case it had much to recommend it. The Court was here being called upon to act at a sensitive time and avoided a 'legislative' decision by deciding the case on the narrowest possible ground. Indeed, the Court went out of its way to emphasise that, as a judicial tribunal, political and other movements which have yet to achieve the status of international law cannot provide a basis for its decisions. This, however, is rather deceptive. The Court was unable to recognise the emerging concept of the exclusive economic zone, but took into account Iceland's 'preferential rights', a concept for which the evidence of state practice was certainly less than compelling. The explanation is not hard to find. The Court was ensuring that the orientation of its decision corresponded to the trends at the Third United Nations Conference on the Law of the Sea (UNCLOS III), which was then in session. While denying its ability to revise the law and refusing to abandon established principles altogether, it nonetheless achieved a substantial measure of legal innovation.

Extension of the Court's function

The cases discussed so far indicate that the Court's obligation to apply the law has not in practice prevented it from broadening the basis of its decisions to take account of cultural diversity, from refining and elaborating the law and from taking account of changing circumstances. Enough has been said, however, to indicate that the demands of continuity impose certain limits which the Court could only ignore at the cost of ceasing to be a court of law. If, therefore, the parties regard the law as unsatisfactory or inadequate, then a decision must be sought on some other basis.

---

[16] *Fisheries Jurisdiction (United Kingdom v. Iceland)*, Merits, Judgment, [1974] ICJ Rep. p. 3. For a critical comment, see R. R. Churchill, 'The Fisheries Jurisdiction cases: The contribution of the International Court of Justice to the debate on coastal states' fisheries rights', (1975) 24 ICLQ p. 82.

When considering how the judicial function may be extended, a point to appreciate at the outset is that the Court must always respect both the limits of the jurisdiction conferred by the treaty or other instrument, and the scope of the dispute as defined in the parties' pleadings. In the *Kasikili/Sedudu Island* case,[17] for example, the special agreement asked for a ruling on the boundary between Botswana and Namibia and the status of the disputed island. In its judgment in the case, the Court answered these questions, but then rather surprisingly went on to hold that in the two channels around the island the vessels and nationals of both states were entitled to equal treatment. This was a broad view of the Court's function, but one which could be justified in light of an earlier undertaking by the parties dealing with co-operation, and which could be regarded as relevant to the interpretation of their special agreement. However, one member of the Court would have gone further and required the parties to negotiate a joint regulatory regime for the island and waterway as a means of environmental protection.[18] This, no doubt, was a laudable objective, but so expansive a view of the judicial role is hard to reconcile with what the parties had actually asked the Court to do and with the special agreement providing the basis for its jurisdiction.

Under Article 38(2) of the Statute, the Court may at the request of the parties give a decision *ex aequo et bono*. This has the merit of achieving complete flexibility, but at the price of complete uncertainty as to the criteria for decision. Perhaps for this reason the Court has never been asked to decide a case under this provision. A less drastic alternative is to refer a case to the Court for a decision on an agreed basis. This too is rare, though common enough in arbitration, as already noted. Directives of this kind also sometimes lead to disagreements as to what the parties really intended. Thus, in the *Kasikili/Sedudu Island* case, the special agreement requested a decision on the basis of a treaty concluded in 1890 and 'the rules and principles of international law'. Botswana argued that the Court was not permitted to take into account arguments which Namibia had put forward on prescription and acquiescence as these were not covered in the agreement. The Court, however, disagreed and held that in referring to 'the rules and principles of international law' the agreement authorised it not only to interpret the treaty in light of those rules and principles, but also to apply them independently.

An example of the Court being given a very specific directive may be seen in the special agreement in the 1986 *Frontier Dispute* case. This asked a chamber of the Court to define the frontier between Mali and Burkina Faso and expressed the parties' desire that the line should be 'based in particular on respect for the principle of the intangibility of frontiers inherited from

---

[17] *Kasikili/Sedudu Island (Botswana/Namibia)*, Judgment, [1999] ICJ Rep. p. 1045. For a summary, see M. N. Shaw, Note, (2000) 49 ICLQ p. 964.
[18] See the dissenting opinion of Judge Weeramantry, *ibid.*, paras. 114–16.

colonization'.[19] Although this reference to the principle of *uti possidetis* appeared in the preamble to the special agreement, not in the main text, the chamber held that the parties had expressly requested it to resolve their dispute on this basis, and proceeded to do so. As the chamber explained, the principle it was required to apply here was not so much a special rule, as a principle of general relevance to territorial issues in Africa, the countries of Spanish America and elsewhere. It is therefore probable that, even without the special agreement, the principle of *uti possidetis* would have featured in the decision. By drawing specific attention to it, however, the parties ensured that it received the attention they considered it merited, and effectively became the pivot of the case.

A less oblique directive is to be found in the special agreement in the *Tunisia–Libya Continental Shelf* case. This asked the Court to decide what principles and rules of international law were applicable to the delimitation of the continental shelf in the disputed area, and required it to take its decision 'according to equitable principles, and the relevant circumstances which characterize the area, *as well as the new accepted trends in the Third Conference on the Law of the Sea*'.[20]

It is evident that, by this directive, the Court was required to reconcile its role as a traditional court of law with a function devised for it by the parties – that of a forward-looking quasi-legislative instrument of dispute settlement. In discharging this burden, it achieved a not uncharacteristic compromise. While emphasising its role as a judicial organ, it acknowledged the directive in the *compromis* and was at pains to demonstrate the congruence between its premises and the proceedings at UNCLOS III. To complete the circle, however, it further justified its decision by reference to established principles. Although it would be wrong to assume that the inclusion of 'new accepted trends' in the Court's mandate had no effect on its decision, its concern for the existing law produces almost a mirror-image of the *Fisheries Jurisdiction* case considered earlier. There, current developments played a larger and more constructive part than the Court's emphasis on the *lex lata* might lead one to expect; in the *Tunisia–Libya* case, where the Court was authorised to cast its net more widely, with equal prudence it elected to buttress its decision with the established law.

In both the cases just mentioned, the parties were able to modify the Court's function by indicating the principles it should apply. It may be possible to achieve much the same thing by framing the question in such a way as to limit the range of permissible solutions. Thus, in the *Gulf of Maine*

---

[19] *Frontier Dispute*, Judgment, [1986] ICJ Rep. p. 554 at p. 557.

[20] See *Continental Shelf (Tunisia/Libyan Arab Jamahiriya)*, Judgment, [1982] ICJ Rep. p. 18 at p. 23 (emphasis added). For comments on this and other aspects of the case, see M. B. Feldman, 'The Tunisia–Libya Continental Shelf case: Geographic justice or judicial compromise?', (1983) 77 AJIL p. 219.

case,[21] the special agreement asked the chamber to decide the course of the 'single maritime boundary' between their respective continental shelves and fisheries zones, and specified the points between which the boundary should run. Commenting on these prescriptions, the chamber observed that neither was contrary to the requirements of international law, and went on to draw the boundary accordingly. Even so, had it been free to choose, the chamber might have held that different boundaries were needed for continental shelf and fisheries purposes, and similarly might well have selected different terminal points. By ruling out such possibilities, the parties directed the chamber's attention to what they considered important, while excluding solutions which would be unacceptable, a result very similar to specifying the applicable law.

Whether the Court has an inherent power to use equity and thereby to extend its function on its own initiative is a question which raises issues of some complexity.[22] On the one hand, the Court is a legal tribunal, and, without express authorisation, is not entitled to perform a general legislative function, whether under the guise of equity or on some other ground. The view that the Court should ignore the existing law, and boldly decide all its cases 'equitably' – assuming it still had any – therefore has nothing to be said for it. On the other hand, to demand that every decision be justified by reference to a specific pre-established rule is not only quite unrealistic, given the patchwork nature of the modern law, but ignores what all courts do in practice which, as we have already suggested, is certainly to innovate, albeit within rather ill-defined conventions.

One of the recognised methods of introducing flexibility into the law is the use of equity *infra legem*. In the *Frontier Dispute* case, the chamber described this as 'that form of equity which constitutes a method of interpretation of the law in force, and is one of its attributes'.[23] It can be seen therefore that what is involved here is not especially radical. Nevertheless, this form of equity can provide the Court with a useful extra resource, as the judgment in this case demonstrates. For, having found that there were no special circumstances pointing to a different solution, the chamber used equity as its justification for dividing a frontier pool between the parties equally.[24]

A limited recourse to equity in the way just described is unlikely to be controversial. It was pointed out in a previous chapter that courts of arbitration regularly employ equity *infra legem* and the International Court is no less entitled to seek sensible solutions. If, however, the Court goes further and relies on equitable considerations of a more general character, then questions about the role of adjudication are bound to arise. In the *Fisheries*

---

[21] *Delimitation of the Maritime Boundary in the Gulf of Maine Area*, Judgment, [1984] ICJ Rep. p. 246.

[22] For an excellent discussion of this issue, see M. B. Akehurst, 'Equity and general principles of law', (1976) 25 ICLQ p. 801.

[23] [1986] ICJ Rep. pp. 567–8.   [24] *Ibid.*, p. 633.

Jurisdiction case, for example, the Court decided that, according to customary international law, the states concerned were under a legal obligation to undertake negotiations in good faith for the 'equitable solution' of their differences concerning their respective fishing rights. This conclusion, which in the Court's view followed from its earlier ruling that Iceland enjoyed preferential, but not exclusive, rights in the area concerned, can be regarded as a constructive attempt to provide a legal answer to a difficult problem. Presumably, however, in the event of the parties failing to negotiate an equitable solution, they would be entitled to return to the Court and ask it to indicate the solution required. Would it be able as a court of law to do so? It is this which raises questions about the role of the adjudication.

Subsequent developments in the law of the sea, specifically the general recognition of the rights of states to an exclusive economic zone, meant that the Court was never asked to indicate an equitable solution in a fisheries dispute. However, in another part of the law of the sea, the application of this form of equity is very much a live issue. In the first case on continental shelf delimitation, the *North Sea Continental Shelf* cases of 1969,[25] the Court held that, under customary international law, states were obliged to negotiate their continental shelf boundaries 'in accordance with equitable principles'. However, in its judgment in the *Tunisia–Libya Continental Shelf* case of 1982, the Court, influenced as we have seen by UNCLOS III, modified the requirement to an obligation to seek an 'equitable result'. This was a controversial step, and, both here and in the subsequent *Gulf of Maine* case, where a chamber of the Court followed the same approach, strong criticism was expressed by one member of the Court.

The thrust of the argument advanced by Judge Gros was that, by emphasising the result, the Court had indulged in 'an equity beyond the law, detached from any established rules, based solely on whatever each group of judges seised of a case declares itself able and free to appreciate in accordance with its political or economic views of the moment'.[26] In light of this criticism, it is interesting to note that in recent cases on delimitation the Court has put less emphasis on achieving an equitable result and more on its methodology, first establishing a provisional boundary line based on equidistance, then, where appropriate, applying equity as a corrective.[27] While this approach does not remove the element of discretion in decisions on delimitation, it does tend to make the process more predictable and consequently seem less like court-sponsored conciliation. Since conciliation, as Judge Gros pointed out, is something which judges are not normally called

---

[25] *North Sea Continental Shelf,* Judgment, [1969] ICJ Rep. p. 3.   [26] [1984] ICJ Rep. p. 388.
[27] See, for example, *Maritime Delimitation in the Black Sea (Romania* v. *Ukraine),* [2009] ICJ Rep. And see C. G. Lathrop, Note, (2009) 103 AJIL p. 543. For a good account of this approach to delimitation, see Y. Tanaka, 'Reflections on maritime delimitation in the Cameroon/Nigeria case', (2004) 53 ICLQ p. 369.

upon to do, and may have no qualifications to undertake, this is a welcome development.

Another way in which the Court has extended its function is by using the opportunity presented by the proceedings to address recommendations to the parties, reminding them of their obligations under the general law in addition to any specific consequences of the Court's decision. Thus, in the *Armed Activities on the Territory of the Congo* case, the Court urged 'all those involved in the conflict to support the peace process in the Democratic Republic of the Congo and other peace processes in the Great Lakes area in order to ensure respect for human rights in the region,[28] and has made similar calls in other recent cases. Recommendations are not binding, and so are quite different from the findings of law or fact in judgments or orders of interim protection. If used judiciously, however, recommendations are a way of stressing the parties' wider responsibilities and putting their dispute in context with a view to encouraging a peaceful settlement. As such, they can be thought of as a modest, but legitimate, extension of the Court's function.

Legal and political disputes

At the beginning of 1985, the United States announced that it would take no further part in the case brought against it by Nicaragua in the Court. This action, which we have noted had important procedural consequences, was stated to be justified by two reasons: first, that the Court had erred in finding that it had jurisdiction to decide the case; and, secondly, that, quite apart from the issue of jurisdiction, the Court should have held the case to be inadmissible on the ground that it raised a political and therefore a non-justiciable issue. As the official explanation put it, in the view of the United States the decision that the case could be heard on the merits represented 'an overreaching of the Court's limits, a departure from its tradition of judicial restraint and a risky venture into political waters'.[29]

The *Nicaragua* case is not the first to raise the question of whether adjudication has any place in the resolution of political disputes, and is unlikely to be the last. For this is a key aspect of justiciability in both international and domestic law. At the international level, however, it raises issues which concern the very possibility of adjudication. For courts are legal institutions and normally have no authority to decide political questions. Yet states are political entities whose disputes invariably have a political dimension. The Court, with the responsibility of deciding disputes between states, is therefore in a particularly delicate position.

---

[28] [2005] ICJ Rep. para. 221. For a thoughtful survey, see J. d'Asprement, 'The recommendations made by the International Court of Justice', (2007) 56 ICLQ p. 185.

[29] See the State Department's background paper quoted in (1985) 79 AJIL p. 438 at p. 441.

When deciding whether the political aspect of a dispute has any bearing on its power to adjudicate, the Court has always sought to apply two principles. The first is that, if a question is referred to the Court which cannot be resolved by applying legal criteria, then, unless its competence has been extended by the parties, it must decline to adjudicate. This follows from the fact that the normal function of a court is to apply the law, and has the effect of preventing the Court from deciding disputes and issues of an exclusively political or non-legal type. As already noted, it was because he considered that the Court had lost sight of this principle that Judge Gros dissented in the *Gulf of Maine* case.

The second principle, which is a corollary of the first and no less funda-mental, is that, provided a case raises a question of international law, then to fulfil its function the Court must give a decision, whatever the background or political complications may be. This point was made by the Court in a number of early advisory opinions concerned with the interpretation of the United Nations Charter, and has been reiterated in a number of later cases.

In one of Turkey's communications to the Court in the *Aegean Sea Con-tinental Shelf* case, for example, the suggestion was made that the dispute between Greece and Turkey was 'of a highly political nature'. This led the Court to consider whether the case might be said to concern a political rather than a legal dispute. Explaining that 'a dispute involving two States in respect of the delimitation of their continental shelf can hardly fail to have some political element', the Court held that it was clear from the parties' arguments that the dispute between them involved a conflict as to their respective rights. Concluding that 'there are certain sovereign rights being claimed by both Greece and Turkey, one against the other and it is manifest that legal rights lie at the root of the dispute that divides the two States',[30] the Court decided that a legal dispute existed between them in respect of the continental shelf in the Aegean.

Similarly, in the *Diplomatic Staff in Tehran* case, Iran maintained that the Court was precluded from taking cognisance of the case by the fact that the proceedings would be confined to the issue of the hostages' detention. For, Iran stated,

> this question only represents a marginal and secondary aspect of an overall problem, one such that it cannot be studied separately, and which involves, *inter alia*, more than 25 years' continual interference by the United States in the internal affairs of Iran, the shameless exploitation of our country, and numerous crimes perpetrated against the Iranian people, contrary to and in conflict with all international and humanitarian norms.[31]

---

[30] *Aegean Sea Continental Shelf*, Judgment, [1978] ICJ Rep. p. 3 at p. 13.
[31] *United States Diplomatic and Consular Staff in Tehran*, Judgment, [1980] ICJ Rep. p. 3 at p. 19.

In its order of December 1979 relating to interim measures of protection, the Court made it clear that the seizure of the United States diplomatic premises and the detention of internationally protected persons could not be regarded as something 'secondary' or 'marginal' in view of the importance of the legal principles involved. It further pointed out that no provision of the Statute or Rules prevents the Court from taking cognisance of one aspect of a dispute merely because the dispute in question has other aspects, and concluded by reminding the Iranian government that, if it considered the alleged activities of the United States in Iran to have a close connection with the subject matter of the dispute, it could present its arguments concerning those activities either as a defence or by way of a counter-claim.

When, in 1980, the Court came to consider the question of its jurisdiction to decide the merits, it repeated its earlier comments, and then noted that, since the preliminary proceedings, Iran had taken no steps to submit evidence and arguments in support of its contentions. In these circumstances, the Court decided that it could not accept the Iranian argument. The Court proceeded from the assumption that its duty is to decide legal questions and that to regard political considerations as an obstacle would be to abrogate its function. In the Court's words:

> legal disputes between sovereign States by their very nature are likely to occur in political contexts and often form only one element in a wider and long-standing political dispute between the States concerned. Yet never has the view been put forward before that, because a legal dispute submitted to the Court is only one aspect of a political dispute, the Court should decline to resolve for the parties the legal questions at issue between them ... [I]f the Court were, contrary to its settled jurisprudence, to adopt such a view, it would impose a far-reaching and unwarranted restriction upon the role of the Court in the peaceful solution of international disputes.[32]

In the *Nicaragua* case, the Court took this point further. There, at the jurisdictional stage, the United States maintained that the case was non-justiciable, but, although the argument was put in various ways, the United States did not try to say that the Court should refuse to deal with the case on the broad ground that the whole matter was political. Instead, it took a more specific point and argued, *inter alia*, that adjudication was incompatible with the Contadora process, which was generally recognised as the appropriate means of dealing with the problems of Central America. The United States pointed out that Nicaragua was asking the Court to examine only certain issues involved in the Contadora process and that a judicial decision would therefore disrupt the balance of the negotiations, which should be allowed to continue as a comprehensive, integrated process, without interference from the Court.

---

[32] *Ibid.*, p. 20.

Not surprisingly, the Court rejected this argument, which it regarded as essentially similar to Iran's argument in the earlier case. In both cases, said the Court, the respondent was suggesting that it should refrain from deciding certain legal questions because the case raised larger issues. The Court's job, however, is to decide whatever legal issues a case raises without reference to its wider context. Since the use of force in the *Nicaragua* case raised a legal issue in the same way as the previous case raised an issue of diplomatic law, in both cases the Court was entitled to proceed.[33]

Because all international disputes have a political dimension of some kind, arguments like those which were advanced and rejected in these cases could in theory be raised whenever a dispute is taken to the Court. In most cases, however, the objection that a dispute is too political for the Court to decide is not put forward for the simple reason that, by electing to have their dispute adjudicated, the parties have already agreed that its legal and political aspects should be separated. In other words, what distinguishes the cases in which the Court has to address this aspect of justiciability is not that these kinds of disputes are political whereas others are not, rather that, though all international disputes are political, some can be depoliticised by the parties, whereas in others depoliticisation, that is, separation of the legal from the political aspects of the case, must be done by the Court.

The cases in which the Court's competence to handle politically charged disputes has been questioned have all been referred unilaterally and involved a basic disagreement as to how the dispute should be characterised. For the applicant, the legal aspect was paramount and the intention in taking the case to the Court was to vindicate a claim based on legal rights. For the respondent, on the other hand, the core of the issue was political, and so, though legal issues might be involved, the case was unsuitable for adjudication. Faced with this incomplete depoliticisation, the Court has taken the only position open to a legal tribunal and, having established that it has the right to decide the issue of characterisation, has ruled that, whatever the politics of a dispute may be, the applicant has the right to a decision, provided only that the case presents a legal issue.

The Court, then, is prepared to depoliticise a dispute if the parties are unable to do so. However, though it has been correct to assume this responsibility, the consequences may sometimes be unfortunate.

Separating the legal from the political aspects of disputes is bound to mean that there will be difficulties in securing acceptance of certain judicial decisions, and, as we shall see in a moment, this limits the contribution which adjudication can make to the solution of international disputes. 'The whole political dossier of the relations between Iran and the United States

---

[33] A similar point was raised in the *Construction of a Wall* case (2004), but this and other arguments against the Court's giving an advisory opinion were rejected. For the outcome, see Chapter 6; and, for the United States' position on justiciability, see (2004) 98 AJIL p. 361.

over the last 25 years', which Iran saw as the context of the *Diplomatic Staff in Tehran* case, or 'the complex of interrelated political, social, economic and security matters that confront the Central American region', which the United States saw as relevant in the *Nicaragua* case, are obviously not the kinds of matters that are justiciable in legal proceedings. Yet, these were the matters which concerned the respondent states. It follows, then, that, if the isolation of the legal element is to result in a decision which can be implemented, it is important to ensure that the respondent's interests are recognised elsewhere.

Thus, to appreciate the significance of cases in which highly political disputes have been held to be justiciable, it is necessary to keep in mind the many important matters which are not justiciable. If the Court, rightly, holds that it is entitled to decide a case on the ground that it presents legal issues, and at the same time, and no less rightly, takes the view that 'issues which no legal rules can be found to touch are not justiciable, irrespective of any sense of grievance a disputant may feel',[34] then, unless those grievances can be dealt with somewhere, the Court's decision is unlikely to be respected.

The effect of judgments

Decisions in contentious cases are legally binding. Does it follow that they are effective in settling disputes?

The first point to notice is that litigation can serve different functions. So, when states refer a case to the Court, they may not be seeking a definitive settlement but merely a decision which will narrow the differences between them, or in some other way move the dispute nearer to resolution. In the *Ambatielos* case,[35] for example, the sole question was whether the United Kingdom was under an obligation to refer a commercial dispute with Greece to arbitration. The Court decided that it was, and arbitration was then attempted. Similarly, in the *North Sea Continental Shelf* cases, instead of asking, as they might have done, for the Court to delimit their continental shelf boundaries in the North Sea, the parties asked only for an indication of the relevant 'principles and rules', leaving the delimitation itself to subsequent negotiation.[36] Step-by-step solutions of this kind are

---

[34] S. Roberts, *Order and Dispute: An Introduction to Legal Anthropology*, Harmondsworth, 1979, p. 21. For further discussion of this issue, see E. Gordon, 'Legal disputes under Article 36(2) of the Statute', in Damrosch, *International Court of Justice*, p. 183; and T. Sugihara, 'The judicial function of the International Court of Justice with respect to disputes involving highly political issues', in A. S. Muller, D. Raic and J. M. Thuránszky (eds.), *The International Court of Justice*, The Hague, 1997, p. 117.

[35] *Ambatielos*, Merits, Judgment, [1953] ICJ Rep. p. 10. For similar use of the Court's advisory jurisdiction, see *Applicability of the Obligation to Arbitrate under Section 21 of the United Nations Headquarters Agreement of 26 June 1947*, Advisory Opinion, [1988] ICJ Rep. p. 12.

[36] For a review of the Court's 'conciliatory' function in this and other cases, see C. F. Murphy, 'The World Court and the peaceful settlement of disputes', (1977) 7 Ga J. Int. & Comp. L. p. 551.

attractive to states which are willing to sacrifice a measure of control over their disputes, and so tend to produce few problems of implementation.

Although it is often clear that the parties are using adjudication as no more than a stage in the settlement of a dispute, there is sometimes room for argument as to their precise intentions. In such a case, which arises when there is a real or imagined ambiguity in the *compromis*, the Court's first task is to resolve the disagreement and establish the scope of its competence. Thus, Article 1 of the special agreement in the *Libya–Malta Continental Shelf* case asked the Court to decide what principles and rules of international law were applicable to their respective areas of continental shelf and also 'how in principle such principles and rules can be applied by the two Parties in this particular case in order that they may without difficulty delimit such areas', with this to be done by an agreement which was provided for in a later article.[37] Malta argued that, to perform its function, the Court would have to draw the boundary on a map, as in the *Tunisia–Libya* case. Libya, on the other hand, maintained that the situation was more like the *North Sea Continental Shelf* cases and that all that was needed was an indication of the relevant principles and rules. After hearing these arguments, the Court decided in the end that it was appropriate to draw a boundary line, though it did not accept Malta's argument in its entirety. Like other cases on the scope of jurisdictional instruments, this decision shows how, even when states have committed themselves to the Court in principle, the extent of their commitment may need to be clarified. In terms of achieving a prompt and accepted settlement, it is obviously better if such matters can be agreed at the outset, for, if they cannot, they prolong the argument and become caught up in the tactics of litigation.

Of course, in many cases, states go to court with the clear aim of securing a definitive settlement. Provided both parties are willing litigants – and this is an important qualification – the resulting decision will usually be all that is required to end the dispute. In the *Minquiers and Ecrehos* case,[38] for example, where France and the United Kingdom went to the Court on an issue of territorial sovereignty 'arm in arm', there was never any doubt that the decision (which went against France) would be implemented. There is nothing surprising about this. Litigation is not an intrinsically hostile

---

[37] See *Continental Shelf (Libyan Arab Jamahiriya/Malta)*, Judgment, [1985] ICJ Rep. p. 13 at p. 16. In a similar way, Cameroon's application in the *Land and Maritime Boundary* case asked the Court 'to specify definitively' the course of the land boundary which led to some argument between the parties as to the exact nature of its task. See J. G. Merrills, Note, (2003) 52 ICLQ p. 788 at p. 790.

[38] *Minquiers and Ecrehos*, Judgment, [1953] ICJ Rep. p. 47. For comment, see D. H. N. Johnson, 'The Minquiers and Ecrehos case', (1954) 3 ICLQ p. 189. 'Arm in arm' is from S. Rosenne, *The World Court*, 3rd edn, Deventer, 1974, p. 142. On the issue of compliance generally, see C. Paulson, 'Compliance with final judgments of the International Court of Justice since 1987', (2004) 98 AJIL p. 434. See also C. Schulte, *Compliance with Decisions of the International Court of Justice*, Oxford, 2004.

act, but a convenient way of depoliticising a dispute by submitting it to third-party decision. A state which is willing to litigate will therefore be most unlikely to repudiate a decision, since to do so, apart from its inherent costs, would simply return the dispute to the political arena and so defeat the object of the exercise.

In certain cases of this kind there may be difficulties of implementation attributable to technical factors. Boundary awards, for example, often require implementation through a subsequent process of demarcation. After the *Arbitral Award* case,[39] there were further negotiations between the parties concerning demarcation and a mixed commission was established by the Inter-American Peace Committee to settle certain outstanding problems. In the *Frontier Dispute* case, the issue of implementation was actually dealt with in the special agreement. Anticipating that, when the chamber made its award, they would need assistance in establishing the boundary on the ground, the parties agreed to demarcate the frontier within twelve months of the decision, and asked that, in its judgment, the chamber should nominate three experts to assist them in this work. In its decision in 1986, the chamber supported this arrangement in principle, but stated that, before nominating experts, it wished to ascertain the views of the parties 'particularly as regards the practical aspects of the exercise'.[40] Consequently, the three experts, a French lawyer, an Algerian cartographer and a Dutch geodetic consultant, were named by an order of the chamber in 1987.[41]

There are a number of other ways in which the parties can seek to minimise any problems of implementation. Thus, the special agreement in the *Gulf of Maine* case contained elaborate provisions on geographic co-ordinates, charts and other technical matters probably designed to avoid the problems of implementation encountered in the *Channel* arbitration.[42] Moreover, as a further safeguard, the agreement provided for the appointment of an expert to assist the chamber in technical matters and specifically in carrying out the parties' wishes as regarded the preparation and depiction of the maritime boundary. The expert who was appointed, a distinguished hydrographer, was supplied with copies of the parties' pleadings, and, besides being present at the oral proceedings, was available to the chamber throughout for consultation.

---

[39] *Arbitral Award Made by the King of Spain on 23 December 1906*, Judgment, [1960] ICJ Rep. p. 192. See also the 1994 Agreement between Libya and Chad providing for implementation of the Court's judgment in the *Territorial Dispute* case, [1994] ICJ Rep. p. 6. Text of the Agreement in (1994) 33 ILM p. 619.

[40] [1986] ICJ Rep. p. 648.

[41] *Frontier Dispute*, Nomination of Experts, Order of 9 April 1987, [1987] ICJ Rep. p. 7.

[42] For the text of the Special Agreement, see (1981) 20 ILM p. 1378. On the problems in the *Channel* arbitration, see J. G. Merrills, 'The United Kingdom–France Continental Shelf arbitration', (1980) 10 Calif. Western Int. LJ p. 314 at pp. 349–55.

Another feature of the agreement in this case was an article of the agreement which entitled either side to request negotiations concerning the further extension of the parties' maritime boundary, following the chamber's decision. It went on to provide that, if such negotiations were held and no agreement was reached within a specified time, then, unless the dispute was referred to some other form of binding third-party procedure, either state was at liberty to bring it to the chamber. This interesting arrangement was a way of building on the parties' current commitment so as to provide in advance for the resolution of a possible future dispute. In contrast, in the special agreement under which the *Gabcikovo-Nagymaros* case was referred to the Court, the parties agreed that, following the judgment, they would 'enter into negotiations on the modalities for its execution' and that, if they were unable to reach agreement within six months, either party could request the Court for an 'additional judgment' on this issue.[43] This turned out to be a wise precaution, because, when efforts to secure implementation of the judgment proved unsuccessful, Slovakia was able to return to the Court in 1998 to request a further judgment.

Another possibility is to include in the special agreement a provision allowing either party to return to the Court to seek clarification of its decision. In 2002, for example, Benin and Niger concluded a special agreement to take a boundary dispute to a chamber of the Court[44] which included a provision laying down that the parties would begin the work of demarcation within eighteen months of the judgment being handed down, and that, in case of difficulty over implementation, either party could refer the matter back. Article 3 of the agreement in the *Tunisia–Libya Continental Shelf* case was to the same effect. In the *Avena* case,[45] Mexico sought to use Article 60 of the Court's Statute in a similar way. It will be recalled that this provision deals with interpretation and forms part of the Court's incidental jurisdiction. Mexico's complaint was that the United States had failed to implement parts of the Court's 2004 judgment concerning review of the convictions and sentences of certain Mexican's convicted of murder in the United States. The Court, however, decided that Mexico's request related to matters that had not been decided in the earlier judgment, with the result that it could not be entertained under Article 60.

Suppose one of the states involved in the dispute is an unwilling party to the litigation. It has already been seen that unwillingness does not prevent the Court from deciding a case provided there is consent. Under Article 53 of the Statute, even the refusal of a party to appear is no obstacle, provided

---

[43] See Article 5 of the 1993 Special Agreement, text in (1993) 32 ILM p. 1293; and document E in the appendix below.

[44] See ICJ Press Release 2002/13 (3 May 2002).

[45] *Request for Interpretation of the Judgment of 31 March 2004 in the Case concerning Avena and Other Mexican Nationals (Mexico v. United States of America)*, Judgment, [2009] ICJ Rep.; and see (2009) 103 AJIL p. 362.

the Court has jurisdiction and is satisfied that the applicant's case is well founded in fact and in law.[46] Moreover, a state may be a most unwilling litigant and yet still carry out a decision. In the *Temple* case,[47] for example, Thailand strenuously contested the Court's jurisdiction, but accepted a decision assigning disputed territory to Cambodia. It is clear, however, that disputes in which states are brought to court against their will are those in which a settlement is least likely to be achieved by litigation.

There have unfortunately been several cases in which a decision against an unwilling state failed to settle a dispute. These include the *Fisheries Jurisdiction* cases (1974), the *Diplomatic Staff in Tehran* case (1980) and the *Nicaragua* case (1986). In the first, developments in the law of the sea soon made attempts at enforcement seem inappropriate; in the second case, any attempt to secure enforcement of the judgment through the Security Council could be blocked by a Soviet veto; while, in the *Nicaragua* case, the United States was in the same position. In all three cases, although there were legal issues which the Court could and did decide, these were bound up with wider issues which in the respondent's view made the case non-justiciable. Thus, in each of the cases, when the applicant made a unilateral attempt to depoliticise the dispute by referring it to the Court, the respondent refused to appear and the Court had to invoke Article 53.

The fact that willingness is often no less important than consent in achieving a judicial settlement does not, as is sometimes suggested, make independent recourse to the Court pointless. Apart from the obvious consideration that an unwilling respondent may be persuaded to change its policy, a state which is ready to litigate can use this fact to its advantage in a number of ways. When both sides have clearly accepted the Court's jurisdiction by treaty or in some other way, the initiation of litigation indicates that the applicant takes such arrangements seriously, as well as demonstrating its support for the principle that disputes about legal rights ought to be settled by adjudication. Britain's decision to take its dispute with Iceland to the Court achieved both these objectives. Because litigation is a way of depoliticising a dispute, a state which goes to the Court is also signalling its desire to reduce tension and pursue a peaceful settlement. This can be extremely important if feelings are running high, or both sides are engaged in warlike preparations, as was the case in the *Aegean Sea Continental Shelf*

---

[46] For analysis of the problems posed by Article 53, see Sir Gerald Fitzmaurice, 'The problem of the "non-appearing" defendant government', (1980) 51 BYBIL p. 89; I. Sinclair, 'Some procedural aspects of recent international litigation', (1981) 30 ICLQ p. 338; and J. I. Charney, 'Disputes implicating the institutional credibility of the Court', in Damrosch, *International Court of Justice*, p. 288.

[47] *Temple of Preah Vihear*, Merits, Judgment, [1962] ICJ Rep. p. 6. For commentary, see D. H. N. Johnson, 'International Court of Justice, judgments of May 26, 1961 and June 15, 1962', (1962) 11 ICLQ p. 1183.

case. Finally – and here both the *Diplomatic Staff in Tehran* case and the *Nicaragua* case are very much in point – a state which takes its case to the Court and wins, gains vindication for its position from an authoritative and disinterested source, which may be useful in securing the support of neutral opinion and consolidating that of allies.

The significance of the Court

Since it was established in 1945, the Court has heard an average of just over three contentious cases a year, including incidental proceedings and judgments on jurisdiction. Adding those advisory opinions which in substance concerned disputes between states does little to change the picture of a situation in which litigation is exceptional and the vast majority of disputes are handled by other means. It would be easy to conclude that the Court makes an insignificant contribution to dispute resolution. But that would be to underestimate its importance. The number of cases referred to the Court has risen considerably in recent years, and it is now not unusual for there to be ten or more cases on its list, denoting an unprecedented growth in popularity.[48] Many treaties provide for the reference of disputes to the Court, and the number of states with declarations of some kind under the optional clause is slowly rising. It was pointed out earlier that commitments of this kind tend to discourage disputes, and so this 'background' role of the Court should not be overlooked. Furthermore, in recent years, several disputes have been settled following reference of the matter to the Court, without requiring a decision.[49] Although cases which are settled out of court do not call for judgments, they are, of course, a further illustration of the contribution which the availability of adjudication makes to dispute resolution.

Notwithstanding the points which have just been made, it is clear that, by comparison with domestic courts, international courts and tribunals occupy a relatively insignificant position. Many explanations have been advanced for this situation, including the reluctance of states to surrender control over their disputes, particularly where important interests are involved, an unwillingness to trust the individuals who make up the Court and the feeling that international law supplies inadequate answers to current problems.

[48] Accounts of the recent work of the Court may be found in the surveys published annually in the AJIL and the Global Community YBILJ.

[49] See the *Passage through the Great Belt* case, Order of 10 September 1992, [1992] ICJ Rep. p. 348; (1993) 32 ILM p. 101; the *Phosphate Lands in Nauru* case, Order of 13 September 1993, [1993] ICJ Rep. p. 322; the *Maritime Delimitation* case, Order of 8 November 1995, [1995] ICJ p. 423; and the *Aerial Incident of 3 July 1988*, Order of 22 February 1996, [1996] ICJ Rep. p. 9; (1996) 90 AJIL p. 278. In 2003, Libya agreed to discontinue the two *Lockerbie* cases against the United States and the United Kingdom: see ICJ Press Release 2003/29 (10 September 2003).

Analysis of the cases which states are prepared to litigate, and, perhaps more significantly, those which they are not, suggests that there is a measure of truth in all of these explanations and over the years a major part of the literature concerning the Court has been devoted to considering how the present position can be improved.[50]

Various suggestions for encouraging use of the Court will be made in the final chapter, but one general point should perhaps be made here. It is that too much is sometimes expected of judicial settlement.[51] Even at the municipal level, litigation is the exception not the rule and most disputes are settled by other means. Therefore, while it is certainly worth considering what can be done to improve the Court, it is important not to become fixated with adjudication and overlook the contribution which can be made by other techniques such as conciliation. As we shall see shortly, both legal and non-legal methods of settlement are prominent features of the 1982 Law of the Sea Convention.

The fact that not all disputes are suitable for adjudication has been recognised by the Court itself, which on a number of occasions has made the point that judicial tribunals have no general mandate to decide all matters of international controversy, but occupy a specialised place in the machinery of dispute settlement. It is clear, for example, that, because the Court can only adjudicate in cases where there is a 'dispute', its competence in contentious cases is limited to situations in which the parties' disagreement has achieved a measure of concretisation – or, to put it in a slightly different way, the function of the Court, like that of other judicial bodies, is not to head off disagreements before they become serious, nor to alleviate situations of amorphous tension, but to intervene only when called upon to resolve a particular crisis in the parties' relations.

The way in which adjudication is circumscribed underlines the part which political institutions and non-judicial processes can play at an earlier stage. So, as we shall see in Chapter 10, under Article 34 of the United Nations Charter, the Security Council may investigate 'any dispute or any situation which might lead to international friction or give rise to a dispute', while consultation through bilateral arrangements or regional institutions provides a way of avoiding disputes which need never reach the judicial stage.

---

[50] See, for example, the essays in C. Peck and R. S. Lee (eds.), *Increasing the Effectiveness of the International Court of Justice*, The Hague, 1997; and earlier in L. Gross (ed.), *The Future of the International Court of Justice*, New York, 1976. See also M. N. Shaw, 'The International Court of Justice: A practical perspective', (1997) 46 ICLQ p. 831.

[51] See R. A. Falk, 'Realistic horizons for international adjudication', (1970–1) 11 Va JIL p. 314; R. B. Bilder, 'Some limitations of adjudication as a dispute settlement technique', (1982–3) 23 Va JIL p. 1, and 'International dispute settlement and the role of adjudication', in Damrosch, *International Court of Justice*, p. 155.

Another way in which the role of the Court is limited can be seen by recalling our earlier discussion of the justiciability of political disputes. There are actually two limitations demonstrated here. One is that, although the Court can establish its competence in a case like *Nicaragua* at the technical level, its decisions, though not to be entirely discounted, clearly cannot solve disputes which raise much wider issues. The other limitation, which is related to the first, is that many disputes lie outside the Court's formal competence altogether, because they do not raise legal issues. So, as we have seen, unless the Court has been authorised to give a decision *ex aequo et bono*, it will not deal with questions which call for, say, a political or economic assessment, rather than a decision on legal grounds. Thus, in the *Haya de la Torre* case,[52] the Court refused to specify the manner in which its judgment in the *Asylum* case should be executed, on the ground that the way in which an unlawful grant of political asylum should be terminated depends on considerations of practicality or political expediency, which it is not the Court's function to assess.

A related point was raised by one of the preliminary issues in the *Western Sahara* case. In its request for an advisory opinion, the General Assembly asked the Court two questions: was the Western Sahara at the time of Spanish colonisation a territory belonging to no one (*terra nullius*)? If not, what were the legal ties between the territory and the neighbouring territories of Morocco and Mauritania? Spain argued that, since its title to the Western Sahara was not in issue, questions concerning the status of the territory at the time of colonisation, almost 100 years before, were only of historical interest and on grounds of propriety should not be answered. In the view of the Court, however, the object of the request was not to disinter a dead issue, but to obtain an opinion which might be of assistance to the General Assembly in dealing with the decolonisation of the territory. As such, the issues raised were sufficiently relevant to overcome any objection on grounds of propriety. Here, and in the earlier *Northern Cameroons* case,[53] the Court was in effect deciding when legal history is no longer a matter for litigation. The crucial difference was that, in the *Western Sahara* case, decolonisation had just begun, so legal considerations had a contemporary relevance, whereas in the *Northern Cameroons* case, since the essential decision had already been taken, raking over the ashes could serve no useful purpose.

Events occurring while a case is before the Court may raise analogous issues and further emphasise the distinctive characteristics of adjudication. The parties are at liberty to discontinue proceedings at any time and will

---

[52] *Haya de la Torre*, Judgment, [1951] ICJ Rep. p. 71. For commentary, see A. E. Evans, 'The Colombian–Peruvian Asylum case: Termination of the judicial phase', (1951) 45 AJIL p. 755.

[53] *Northern Cameroons*, Judgment, [1963] ICJ Rep. p. 15. For analysis, see D. H. N. Johnson, 'The case concerning the Northern Cameroons', (1964) 13 ICLQ p. 1143.

normally do so when they have come to some arrangement outside the Court and further proceedings would serve no useful purpose. However, if a case is discontinued this is regarded as the parties' prerogative and the Court will respect their decision without asking why they have done so. Unlike the position in certain other tribunals, therefore, there is no question of the Court retaining a case against the wishes of the parties.[54] Sometimes, moreover, the Court itself decides that the object of bringing a case has been achieved and that further proceedings are unnecessary. This was the situation in the *Nuclear Tests* cases,[55] where attaching exaggerated significance to French actions outside the Court enabled it to rule that the case had become moot and to dispose of a particularly awkward dispute without having to address the merits.

The *Nuclear Tests* cases had a sequel which provides further evidence of how the Court regards its function. The original proceedings were dismissed when France gave what the Court viewed as an undertaking that no further atmospheric nuclear tests would be carried out in the Pacific. The Court also stated that, if 'the basis' of its judgment were to be affected by future events, it would be open to the applicants 'to request an examination of the situation in accordance with the provisions of the Statute'.[56] In 1995, France announced that it intended to carry out a series of underground nuclear tests in the Pacific, which prompted New Zealand, one of the original applicants, to refer the situation back to the Court in reliance on the passage quoted.[57]

In the 1995 proceedings (*Nuclear Tests II* case), there were essentially two questions: whether it was open to the Court (in effect) to reopen the 1974 proceedings; and, if so, whether the necessary conditions were fulfilled for it to do so. The Court's answers were 'yes' to the first question, but 'no' to the second. The negative answer was based on its ruling that underground nuclear testing could not affect the basis of a judgment concerned only with atmospheric tests. Thus, here, the Court rejected the arguments of those who favoured expanding its role.[58] On the other hand, in answering

---

54 For discussion of the position of the European Court of Human Rights on this issue, see J. G. Merrills, *The Development of International Law by the European Court of Human Rights*, 2nd edn, Manchester, 1993, pp. 60–3.

55 *Nuclear Tests*, Judgments, [1974] ICJ Rep. p. 253 and p. 457. For criticism of these decisions, see P. Lellouche, 'The Nuclear Tests cases: Judicial silence v. atomic blasts', (1975) 16 Harv. Int. LJ p. 614. In the *Arrest Warrant* case (2002), Belgium argued that events subsequent to the filing of the application had deprived the case of its object, but the Court rejected the argument: see para. 32 of the Judgment.

56 *Nuclear Tests (New Zealand* v. *France)*, Judgment, [1974] ICJ Rep. p. 457 at p. 477 (para. 63).

57 See *Request for an Examination of the Situation in accordance with Paragraph 63 of the Court's Judgment of 20 December 1974 in the Nuclear Tests (New Zealand* v. *France) Case*, Order of 22 September 1995, [1995] ICJ Rep. p. 288. For commentaries, see M. C. R. Craven, Note, (1996) 45 ICLQ p. 725; and P. H. F. Bekker, Note, (1996) 90 AJIL p. 280.

58 See the dissenting opinions of Judges Weeramantry, Koroma and Sir Geoffrey Palmer.

the first question positively, the Court showed that, if France had resumed atmospheric tests, New Zealand could have challenged its action without having to bring fresh proceedings. As there is nothing in the Statute which expressly permits a case to be resurrected in this way, this was a bold piece of judicial legislation and an unusual enhancement of the Court's powers.

That the scope of the judicial function is limited and that states are reluctant to refer disputes to the Court are findings which could have been anticipated from our earlier discussion of arbitration. What, then, in conclusion, are the advantages of having an international court?

The first, and the most clear cut, is that the existence of a standing court relieves states of the need to set up a new tribunal whenever a justiciable dispute arises. Besides saving the time and effort involved in creating such a tribunal (and the cost of financing its operation), the ability to refer a case to a tribunal with an established composition and procedure avoids the need to negotiate about the membership of the tribunal and related matters, and thereby avoids the problems which can arise with arbitration. Of course, the other side of the coin is that the flexibility of arbitration makes it the more attractive option when there are special requirements, a consideration which, as we have seen, has led the Court in recent cases to consider how it can adapt itself to the parties' wishes.

Secondly, to the extent that the avoidance and settlement of disputes are assisted by the development of international law, permanent courts, with their ability to develop a consistent jurisprudence, may be expected to contribute more to legal progress than occasional arbitrations. Whether they can do so in fact depends, as already noted, on a number of factors, not least on the provision of suitable opportunities and the judges' perception of their role, but the possibility that through litigation 'the law can find some concrete measure of clarification and development'[59] is undeniably improved.

A final advantage is that a permanent tribunal provides a constant reminder to states of the availability of litigation as a means of peaceful settlement. True, there are now other standing tribunals of various kinds, including the International Tribunal for the Law of the Sea, discussed in the next chapter, and the Appellate Body of the World Trade Organization, examined in Chapter 9. Accordingly, the emblematic significance of the International Court has been reduced. On the other hand, since the

---

[59] [1970] ICJ Rep. p. 65 (Judge Fitzmaurice). For discussion of this aspect of the Court's work, see M. Lachs, 'Some reflections on the contribution of the International Court of Justice to the development of international law', (1983) 10 Syr. J. Int. L. & Com. p. 239; and R. Y. Jennings, 'The judiciary, international and national, and the development of international law', (1996) 45 ICLQ p. 1. See also P. Kooijmans, 'The ICJ in the 21st century: Judicial restraint, judicial activism, or proactive judicial policy', (2007) 56 ICLQ p. 741.

newer courts and tribunals are all rather specialised, the International Court is still the only court with general competence in the sense that disputes relating to any aspect of international law may be brought before it. Thus, the fact of the Court's existence, together with a simple procedure for establishing its jurisdiction, continue to give a prominence to adjudication in the international field it would not otherwise enjoy.

8

The Law of the Sea Convention

The methods of settlement considered so far can be used in all types of disputes and are available to all states. Alongside these general methods are to be found specialised procedures created by particular groups of states for the resolution of disputes in a specific subject area. The machinery available for the settlement of disputes in special fields has been extensively considered elsewhere[1] and will not be described again here. However, to convey an idea of the problems involved in constructing such machinery, and the way in which accepted methods can be adapted and combined to provide solutions, the next chapter examines some recent developments in the area of international trade law, while this chapter provides an outline and review of the arrangements for dispute settlement to be found in the 1982 Law of the Sea Convention.

The Convention and its system

The 1982 Convention contains 307 articles and eleven annexes and was eight years in negotiation.[2] With an instrument of such length and complexity, dealing with matters in which virtually all states have an interest of some kind, certain issues naturally proved more difficult than others. Not surprisingly, dispute settlement was one of the most contentious issues and the provisions which now comprise Part XV of the Convention went through several versions before the text was finally agreed.

The Third United Nations Conference on the Law of the Sea (UNCLOS III) held its first substantive session at Caracas in 1974 and decided that the issue of dispute settlement should be dealt with by each Main Committee to the extent that the matter was relevant to its work. It soon became clear, however, that the three Main Committees were likely to be preoccupied with other issues and would be able to give little time to this question. An informal group was therefore established to consider the issue of dispute

---

[1] For surveys, see C. M. H. Waldock (ed.), *International Disputes: The Legal Aspects*, London, 1972, Chapter 4; and United Nations, *Handbook on the Peaceful Settlement of Disputes between States*, New York, 1992, Chapter 4.

[2] The evolution of the Convention can be conveniently traced through a series of articles published by J. R. Stevenson and B. H. Oxman in the *American Journal of International Law* between 1974 and 1982. For an excellent survey of the impact of the Conference, see R. R. Churchill and A. V. Lowe, *The Law of the Sea*, 3rd edn, Manchester, 1999.

settlement, and the working paper which it produced supplied a focus for the Conference's early discussions. At the third session in 1975, the group was reconstituted as the Settlement of Disputes Group, and at the end of that session the Informal Single Negotiating Text, prepared by the President of the Conference, included a set of draft provisions on the subject.

After discussion at the fourth session, the President's draft was revised, and was considered again at the fifth session in 1976. Further revisions were incorporated in the Revised Single Negotiating Text in 1977 and the Informal Composite Negotiating Text in 1978. The identification of certain particularly difficult questions led to further discussions at the eighth session in 1979 and more modifications at the ninth session in the following year. Even as late as the tenth session in 1981, changes in the arrangements for dispute settlement were still being introduced, and the articles in question assumed their final form only when the Convention as a whole was approved and opened for signature in 1982.[3]

The Convention proceeds from the basic principle that the states which are parties will settle any dispute between them concerning its interpretation or application by peaceful means in accordance with Article 2(3) of the United Nations Charter (Article 279). This has a double effect. It extends the obligation contained in the Charter to non-members of the United Nations if they become parties to the Convention; and, for all states, it confirms that disputes relating to the Convention must be settled in accordance with justice. The Convention goes on to provide that nothing in that Part of the Convention impairs the right of states to settle such a dispute by any peaceful means of their own choice (Article 280). This emphasis on the parties' autonomy is of course consistent with general practice and was not controversial. However, the principle of free choice of means is elaborated in later articles which underline its implications.

When a dispute arises, the parties are under an obligation to 'proceed expeditiously to an exchange of views' as to the means of settlement to be adopted (Article 283(1)). This important provision, on which there is now some significant case law,[4] is clearly designed to emphasise consultation and provide the obligation to use peaceful means with a procedural buttress. However, the obligation to consult also arises when a settlement has been reached and 'the circumstances require consultation regarding the manner of implementing the settlement' (Article 283(2)) and also when a procedure

---

[3] For analysis of the provisions of the Convention relating to dispute settlement and discussion of their evolution, see S. Rosenne and L. B. Sohn (eds.), *United Nations Convention on the Law of the Sea 1982: A Commentary*, vol. V, Dordrecht, 1988; and A. O. Adede, *The System for Settlement of Disputes under the United Nations Convention on the Law of the Sea*, Dordrecht, 1987. Also N. Klein, *Dispute Settlement in the UN Convention on the Law of the Sea*, Cambridge, 2005.

[4] See, for example, *Barbados/Trinidad and Tobago*, Award on Jurisdiction and Merits, (2006) 45 ILM p. 800. For an outline of earlier jurisprudence on Article 283, see Klein, *Dispute Settlement in the UN Convention*, pp. 62–4.

has been used unsuccessfully. In this last situation, as has been pointed out, the effect is to ensure that a move from one means of settlement to another is never automatic, which inevitably reduces the impact of the Convention's own arrangements.[5]

No less significant is the provision laying down that, when the parties have selected a particular means of peaceful settlement, the procedures laid down later in the Convention apply only if such means prove unsuccessful and the agreement between the parties does not exclude any further procedure (Article 281). Moreover, any agreement of a general, regional, bilateral or other nature providing for the submission of a dispute to a procedure involving a binding decision supplants the procedure laid down later in the Convention, unless the parties otherwise agree (Article 282). The effect of these articles is to enable the parties by agreement in advance to avoid the settlement machinery provided in the Convention.[6]

Thus, the Convention's first principle is peaceful settlement with free choice of means. But what happens if the parties cannot agree upon a means of settlement, or if they choose a means which proves unsuccessful? At this stage, after the exchange of views required by Article 283 has taken place, Section 2 of Part XV, entitled 'Compulsory Procedures Entailing Binding Decisions', comes into play.

The principle of compulsory settlement

Whether or not the Convention should incorporate articles providing for the compulsory settlement of disputes was a question which provoked considerable disagreement. The corresponding provisions of the 1958 Conventions on the Law of the Sea were merely an optional protocol to the Conventions, and one view was that the same approach should be adopted in the new Convention. However, many found this unacceptable on the ground that the interpretation and application of an instrument containing so many innovations was bound to generate disputes which could only be resolved by the use of a third-party procedure which was both obligatory, in the sense that it had to be used, and binding in its result. As noted earlier, the knowledge that recourse to such procedures is ultimately possible also discourages unreasonableness and so acts as a means of dispute avoidance, and this too was no doubt a salient consideration. It was therefore eventually decided that compulsory procedures of some kind should be incorporated.

The first problem in establishing a procedure for securing binding decisions in an instrument such as the Convention is to find a method which

---

[5] See A. O. Adede, 'The basic structure of the disputes settlement part of the Law of the Sea Convention', (1982) 11 Ocean Devel. & Int. L. p. 125 at p. 129.

[6] It should be noted, however, that disputes concerning the sea-bed are subject to the special provisions of Part XI, Section 5, described below. Interpretation of Article 281 was crucial in the *Southern Bluefin Tuna* arbitration (2000), described in the text accompanying note 31 below.

all the parties to the instrument can accept. The International Court, as has been seen, is not universally supported, yet may be preferred by some states to alternatives such as permanent tribunals with restricted jurisdiction, or *ad hoc* arbitration. At the Conference, it became clear that there was so much disagreement that it was unlikely that a single method could be nominated.[7] Whereas several states wished disputes to be referred to the International Court and pointed to the contribution which its decisions had already made to the development of the law of the sea, others considered that disputes relating to the 'new' law of the sea could be more appropriately handled by a new tribunal. A third group regarded any kind of standing court as too rigid and emphasised the flexibility of arbitration, while a fourth group considered that the technical issues raised by many law of the sea disputes called for a functional approach and the creation of specialised bodies. Faced with this wide divergence of views, the negotiators of the Convention took the only practicable course and resolved the problem by again invoking the principle of freedom of choice, this time in the form of a choice of methods of binding settlement.

The Convention provides for states to make a written declaration accepting that disputes may be referred to one or more of the following tribunals: a new 'International Tribunal for the Law of the Sea'; the International Court; or an arbitral tribunal, or a special arbitral tribunal, with both forms of arbitral tribunal to be constituted in accordance with the Convention. Where both parties to a dispute have accepted the same procedure, that procedure is to be used, unless the parties otherwise agree. Where, however, they have accepted different procedures (or one party has not accepted any procedure), then the dispute may be referred to arbitration.[8] These arrangements, which are set out in Article 287 of the Convention, represent a neat solution to the problem of choice of forum and, subject to a point considered below, can be said to establish a useful and flexible system of compulsory jurisdiction.

The articles which comprise the remainder of Section 2 of Part XV of the Convention deal with a number of matters relevant to the functioning of the system of obligatory settlement. The unique role of another new body, the 'Sea-Bed Disputes Chamber', is recognised in Article 287(2). The crucial question of jurisdiction *ratione materiae* is dealt with in Article 288, which provides for the reference of disputes concerning the interpretation or application of the Convention and any international agreement 'related to the purposes' of the Convention. Article 289 provides for the appointment of scientific or technical experts, with a role similar to that of assessors in the

---

[7] See Rosenne and Sohn, *Commentary*, pp. 41–5.

[8] Attempts to use the International Court of Justice or the new International Tribunal for the Law of the Sea for this purpose were abandoned in 1977; see A. O. Adede, 'Prolegomena to the dispute settlement part of the Law of the Sea Convention', (1977–8) 10 NYUJ Int. L. & Politics p. 253 at p. 340.

International Court. Another provision reminiscent of the Court's Statute, Article 290, authorises the prescribing of provisional measures of protection (though only at the request of a party to the dispute), while Article 292, which was difficult to negotiate, but has proved very important in practice, deals with the problem of securing the prompt release of vessels and crews detained by national authorities.

An unusual provision permits a court or tribunal exercising compulsory jurisdiction to determine whether a claim 'constitutes an abuse of legal process or whether *prima facie* it is well founded' (Article 294). If the claim is determined to be an abuse of legal process, or *prima facie* unfounded, the court or tribunal in question is to take no further action in the case. This provision was inserted at quite a late stage to meet the concern of certain coastal states that they might be hampered in exercising their rights within the exclusive economic zone by a proliferation of groundless applications. It resembles Article 35(3) of the European Convention on Human Rights[9] in that it provides a way of disposing of frivolous applications and should also have a tendency to discourage them. Another provision with a counterpart in the European Convention is Article 295, which confirms that exhaustion of local remedies is a condition of admissibility for certain claims.[10] However, this only applies when such exhaustion is 'required by international law'. The effect is therefore to preserve the requirement for those disputes where the existence of local remedies would normally be relevant, without imposing it in disputes involving the direct interests of states, or other situations, in which it has not traditionally been necessary.

The question of choice of law is dealt with by a directive to courts and tribunals having jurisdiction to apply 'this Convention and other rules of international law not incompatible with this Convention' (Article 293). The parties may agree to request a decision *ex aequo et bono*, but, unless they do so, the clear intention is that the Convention will prevail over other sources of obligation. In the earlier discussion of arbitration and judicial settlement, we saw that the basis of an international tribunal's decision is a matter to which states, for obvious reasons, attach very great importance. Bearing in mind the widely held view that the reluctance of 'new' states to use the International Court in the immediate post-colonial period stemmed from a distrust of traditional international law, it is not difficult to see why the

---

[9] Article 35(3) provides: 'The Court shall declare inadmissible any individual application submitted under Article 34 which it considers incompatible with the provisions of the Convention or the protocols thereto, manifestly ill-founded, or an abuse of the right of application.' In the original Convention, the corresponding provision was Article 27(2). For discussion of Article 294, see T. Treves, 'Preliminary proceedings in the settlement of disputes under the United Nations Law of the Sea Convention: Some observations', in N. Ando, E. McWhinney and R. Wolfrum (eds.), *Liber Amicorum Judge Shigeru Oda*, The Hague, 2002, p. 749.

[10] See Article 35(1), formerly Article 26, of the European Convention.

'new' law of the sea, reflecting as it does the influence of those states in many of its elements, should have been given such priority in the Convention.

Exceptions to the principle of compulsory settlement

The third and final Section of Part XV of the Convention is headed 'Limitations and Exceptions to the Applicability of Section 2' and concerns disputes which are not, or need not be, subject to the procedures just described, and in certain cases may be referred to another compulsory procedure instead. Thus, if the principle of Section 2 is that disputes which the parties have failed to settle by means of their own choice are, as a general rule, to be submitted to some form of legal tribunal, Section 3 proceeds on the assumption that certain disputes ought not to be subject to obligatory settlement at all, while others call for a procedure not involving adjudication.

The details of Section 3, which went through many forms during the negotiations, are complex and closely bound up with the substantive provisions of the Convention. Their significance, however, can be grasped without an exhaustive analysis of each provision. Article 297 reflects the view of coastal states that certain decisions relating to the exercise of sovereign rights or jurisdiction, especially those concerning the exercise of discretion, should not be subject to challenge in any form of adjudication. Thus, after providing that the procedures of Section 2 apply to disputes involving an abuse or infringement of traditional maritime freedoms, the Convention lays down that disputes involving coastal states' rights with respect to marine research and fisheries shall be submitted to conciliation.[11] The important point here is that, while the use of conciliation in the cases specified is obligatory, the Convention is careful to state that the coastal state's exercise of its discretion cannot be questioned, and the conciliation commission's report is in any event not binding on the parties.

In an early version of the dispute settlement provisions, the exclusion of the procedures of Section 2 depended in all cases on a declaration to that effect by the state concerned.[12] In disputes covered by Article 297, the system of opting out was subsequently replaced by the comprehensive exclusion just described. It survives, however, in Article 298, which deals with three types of disputes which states may exclude from any or all of the procedures of Section 2 by written declaration. These are disputes involving sea-boundary delimitations or historic bays or titles,[13] disputes

---

[11]   For comments on this approach, see S. Rosenne, 'Settlement of fisheries disputes in the exclusive economic zone', (1979) 73 AJIL p. 89; and J. P. A. Bernhardt, 'Compulsory dispute settlement in the law of the sea negotiations: A reassessment', (1978–9) 19 Va JIL p. 69.

[12]   See A. O. Adede, 'Settlement of disputes arising under the Law of the Sea Convention', (1975) 69 AJIL p. 798 at pp. 813–14. For the transition to the final version, see the same author's Note in (1977) 71 AJIL p. 305; and Rosenne and Sohn, *Commentary*, pp. 87–106.

[13]   For a comprehensive discussion of the controversy over delimitation, see A. O. Adede, 'Toward the formulation of the rule of delimitation of sea boundaries between states with opposite or

concerning military activities or law enforcement connected with Article 297,[14] and disputes in respect of which the United Nations Security Council is exercising its functions under the Charter.[15]

In the case of sea-boundary delimitations and other disputes in the first category, the Convention provides that a dispute which arises after the Convention has entered into force may be subject to compulsory conciliation and then, if this does not result in an agreement, to the procedures laid down in Section 2. However, this elaborate arrangement has no application to such a dispute if it also involves sovereignty or other rights over land territory, and there is no corresponding provision concerning disputes in the second and third categories. It should also be noted that declarations can be made or withdrawn at any time and are expressly stated to be reciprocal in their effect (Article 298(3)). In other words, a state which makes a declaration excluding disputes of a particular type from the procedures of Section 2 secures an immunity to the extent permitted by this provision, but also loses the right to bring a claim arising out of such a dispute against other states. While this is in accordance with the usual principle governing limitations on international jurisdiction, it indicates that, if states were to make extensive use of the opportunities offered by Article 298, the resulting erosion of the principle of compulsory settlement would be very significant. On the other hand, as relatively few declarations under Article 298 have been made,[16] the effect of this provision in practice has been less than might have been anticipated.

The intricate provisions of Section 3 are an attempt to balance the desire to be a judge in one's own cause against the principle of binding third-party settlement. The exclusion of certain types of disputes from the procedures of Section 2 in Article 297 and the opportunity to exclude others provided by Article 298 reflect both traditional sensitivities – territorial sovereignty and military activities, for example – and the special concerns of developing states, whose voting power at the Conference, as the so-called 'Group of 77',[17] secured the exclusions relating to fishing and research. It is arguable, of course, that, for certain disputes – over the exercise of discretion, for example – conciliation is a more appropriate means of settling disputes

adjacent coasts', (1978–9) 19 Va JIL p. 209; P. C. Irwin, 'Settlement of maritime boundary disputes: An analysis of the law of the sea negotiations', (1980) 8 Ocean Devel. & Int. L. p. 105; Rosenne and Sohn, *Commentary*, pp. 116–35; and P. Weil, *The Law of Maritime Delimitation – Reflections*, Cambridge, 1989.

[14] For analysis of this exception, see M. W. Janis, 'Dispute settlement in the Law of the Sea Convention: The military activities exception', (1977) 4 Ocean Devel. & Int. L. p. 51.

[15] Unless, of course, the Security Council calls upon the parties to employ the means of dispute settlement provided in the Convention.

[16] For details, see the website of the UN's Division for Oceans and the Law of the Sea, www.un. org/Depts/Ios/.

[17] On the influence of the Group of 77, see A. G. Friedman and C. A. Williams, 'The Group of 77 at the United Nations: An emergent force in the law of the sea', (1978–9) 16 San Diego L. Rev. p. 555; and G. A. Pierce, 'Dispute settlement mechanisms in the Draft Convention on the Law of the Sea', (1980–1) 10 Denver J. Int. L. & Pol. p. 331.

than adjudication. Be that as it may, it is clear that, without the limitations and exceptions provided for in Section 3, the adoption of machinery for the binding settlement of disputes as an integral part of the Convention would not have been generally accepted.

Although the effect of Section 3 is to cut down the scope for compulsory settlement of disputes under the Convention, two further points about these provisions should be noted which, in a non-technical sense, qualify these limitations. The first is that whether a state can rely on Articles 297 or 298 in a particular case is not a matter to be decided by the state unilaterally, but, as the Convention makes plain, is an issue for the court or tribunal whose jurisdiction is in question. This is another example of the Convention incorporating a recognised principle of international law, and does not, of course, prevent the various limitations and exceptions from being utilised in an appropriate case. What it does do, however, is to discourage the abuse of these provisions which would certainly follow if they were subject to self-serving interpretation.

The other point is that, while the intention behind Section 3 is to prevent certain disputes from falling under the Convention's compulsory procedures automatically, the Section's final provision, Article 299, permits the parties to use these procedures, even for a dispute in an excluded category, so long as they agree to do so. In other words, where Articles 297 and 298 apply, their effect is to prevent the unilateral reference of a dispute to the Convention's procedures, without prejudice to the parties' right to employ such procedures by agreement. This is therefore a further example of the Convention's fundamental principle of freedom of choice. As Sohn and Rosenne put it:

> The last article of Part XV thus concludes in the spirit of section 1, emphasizing that even in matters where dispute settlement is restricted, there is still the possibility, by agreement of the parties, to find a dispute settlement procedure which would enable the parties to resolve their dispute amicably and peacefully.[18]

Conciliation

Conciliation is the only method of third-party settlement specifically mentioned in Section 1 of Part XV, dealing with the settlement of disputes by any means chosen by the parties.[19] Moreover, as has been seen, conciliation is obligatory for certain types of disputes excluded from adjudication in Section 3. Conciliation can therefore be said to occupy a prominent place in the Convention and could, at least in theory, be used twice in relation to certain disputes, first as the procedure chosen by the parties and then, if

---

[18] Rosenne and Sohn, *Commentary*, p. 146.
[19] See Article 284. References in early drafts to arbitration and judicial settlement were subsequently deleted; see Adede, 'Prolegomena', p. 282.

the initial attempt was unsuccessful, as the compulsory arrangement under Section 3. The procedure to be followed in voluntary or mandatory conciliation is set out in Annex V to the Convention. In general, the provisions which make up Annex V follow those of other recent multilateral treaties, though they are more elaborate in certain respects and also differ in certain details.

Like its predecessors, the Convention provides for the submission of disputes to *ad hoc* commissions rather than to permanent bodies. Unless the parties agree to a different arrangement, a commission is established by each party appointing two members, who then appoint an additional member as chairman. Thus, a commission will normally contain five members. In the event of a failure to agree, the chairman may be appointed by the Secretary-General of the United Nations, who can also act should a party fail to appoint its own members. To facilitate the appointment of commissions, each party to the Convention is entitled to nominate four conciliators to a list to be compiled by the Secretary-General.[20] In setting up a commission, preference is to be given to candidates on the list, though only the Secretary-General is bound by it, and a state cannot select more than one of its own nationals. The qualification for nomination to the list is 'the highest reputation for fairness, competence and integrity' (Article 2). A conspicuous, but not unprecedented,[21] omission is the absence of any reference to legal qualifications.

In accordance with the usual practice, a commission normally determines its own procedure and takes decisions relating to its report, its recommendations and other matters by majority vote. With the consent of the parties to the dispute, it may invite any party to the Convention to submit its views orally or in writing and, if the parties agree, can presumably extend this facility to other states.[22] In the course of its proceedings, a commission may also draw attention to any measures which might facilitate an amicable settlement.

The functions of a commission are to 'hear the parties, examine their claims and objections and make proposals to the parties with a view to reaching an amicable settlement' (Article 6). This formula, which is taken from the 1969 Vienna Convention on the Law of Treaties,[23] was originally put forward to emphasise the point that, although conciliation is not arbitration, legal, as well as factual, issues may be examined. The directive that, if the dispute has not been settled, the commission's report shall record 'its

---

[20] Originally, the Registrar of the Law of the Sea Tribunal. See Adede, *ibid.*, p. 350.

[21] See Article 85 of the Vienna Convention on the Representation of States in Their Relations with International Organizations of a Universal Character, 1975. Text in (1975) 69 AJIL p. 730.

[22] See Rosenne and Sohn, *Commentary*, p. 319.

[23] Vienna Convention on the Law of Treaties, 1969, Annex, Article 5. Text in (1969) 63 AJIL p. 875. On the negotiation of the dispute settlement provisions of this convention, see R. D. Kearney and R. E. Dalton, 'The treaty on treaties', (1970) 64 AJIL p. 495 at p. 554.

conclusions on all questions of fact or law relevant to the matter in dispute'
is also reminiscent of the Vienna Convention and was similarly intended
to underline the judicial element in the commission's work by requiring
it to present its conclusions. The earlier Convention, however, envisaged
conciliation by 'qualified jurists'. Whether the conciliators appointed under
the new Convention will in practice be competent to draw conclusions on
questions of law remains to be seen.

The provisions just discussed incline towards what was termed in
Chapter 4 'quasi-arbitration'. However, there is no lack of emphasis on
conciliation as a distinctive process. In addition to the point already noted,
that in certain cases a state's discretion cannot be challenged, the commission's conclusions are only to be presented when the parties, despite the
commission's assistance, have failed to reach agreement. Thus, an important
part of its task is the attempt to secure a settlement of the dispute while the
proceedings are in progress. Moreover, any conclusions in its report must
be accompanied by 'such recommendations as the commission may deem
appropriate for an amicable settlement' (Article 7). And the commission's
report, including its conclusions and recommendations, is, of course, not
binding on the parties.

The fact that in some situations the Convention envisages conciliation
as a compulsory procedure is reflected both in the arrangements for filling vacancies on a commission and in provisions indicating that a state is
obliged to submit to such proceedings (Article 11) and cannot prevent them
by non-co-operation (Article 12). As might be expected, any disagreement
as to whether a commission has competence is to be decided by the commission (Article 13). No case has so far been referred to conciliation under the
Convention's arrangements. However, if the prospect of obligatory conciliation discourages unreasonableness, it will have done its job. In any case, as
an expression of matters unstated, though implicit, in earlier conventions,[24]
these affirmations of principle are a timely and positive development.

Arbitration

According to the Convention, law of the sea disputes may be referred to
arbitration in three different ways. Under Section 1 of Part XV, the parties
may by agreement select any peaceful means and so can decide to set up
an arbitral tribunal along traditional lines. Under Section 2, both parties
may make declarations nominating arbitration as a preferred means of
settlement, in which case arbitration will be governed by the provisions
of the Convention. Alternatively, if there is no common declaration under
Section 2, arbitration under the Convention will be deemed to have been
accepted as the relevant obligatory procedure. Since only about a quarter of

[24] For previous conventions utilising conciliation, see Chapter 4.

the parties to the Convention have made declarations nominating a means of settlement,[25] this fall-back arrangement is potentially very significant. It is arbitration under the Convention, the arrangements for which are set out in Annex VII to the Convention, with which we are here concerned.

The arrangements for constituting a tribunal resemble the provisions described earlier concerning conciliation. A list of arbitrators is to be drawn up by the Secretary-General, and each party to the Convention may make four nominations. The persons nominated are to be 'experienced in maritime affairs and enjoying the highest reputation for fairness, competence and integrity' (Article 2(1)). While these qualifications are clearly most desirable, the omission of any reference to the legal competence of prospective arbitrators is again disquieting.[26] Unless a dispute involves more than two parties, or the parties otherwise agree, a tribunal is to consist of five members, one nominated by each party and three, including the president, appointed by agreement. The 'neutral' element, it will be noticed, is larger here than in conciliation commissions and will normally consist of non-nationals. In constituting a tribunal, preference is to be given to arbitrators on the Secretary-General's list.

It was explained in Chapter 5 that the failure of a state to appoint its members of an arbitral tribunal, or disagreement between the parties as to the neutral element, are matters that must be expressly provided for, to guard against difficulties in getting an arbitration under way. The Convention deals with the problem by providing that unfilled places on the tribunal, and disagreement over the president, shall be resolved either by a person or third state chosen by the parties, or by the President of the International Tribunal for the Law of the Sea.[27] All such appointments are to be made from the Secretary-General's list and in consultation with the parties. In an obvious attempt to provide assurance on the crucial issue of neutrality, the Convention lays down that members of the tribunal appointed in this way must also be of different nationalities and may not be 'in the service of, ordinarily resident in the territory of, or nationals of, any of the parties to the dispute' (Article 3(3)).

The provisions dealing with procedure and related matters contain a number of points of interest. The tribunal is normally to decide its own procedure, 'assuring to each party a full opportunity to be heard and to present its case' (Article 5), and takes decisions by majority vote. Frustration of the proceedings by members of the tribunal is discouraged by an

---

[25] See note 16 above.

[26] According to Adede, 'it was observed in this connection that the problems of interpretation of the Convention did not require experts on the law of the sea *per se* and that the tribunal could be tailored to suit a particular dispute by including experts on various matters'. Adede, 'Prolegomena', p. 354.

[27] For the view that the Secretary-General of the United Nations would have been a better choice, see Bernhardt, 'Compulsory dispute settlement', p. 76; on other suggestions which were made, see Adede, 'Prolegomena', pp. 354–5.

unusual provision stating that 'the absence or abstention of less than half the members shall not constitute a bar to the tribunal reaching a decision' (Article 8). In accordance with the usual practice, the tribunal's expenses are normally borne by the parties. The parties to the dispute are also obliged to facilitate the work of the tribunal by providing it with documents, facilities and information, access to witnesses and experts, and the means to visit the localities to which the case relates. However, the Convention's directive here is qualified by a provision that such assistance shall be 'in accordance with their law and using all means at their disposal' (Article 6), a formula which permits a state to plead lack of resources and, more seriously, to set up its own law to restrict its obligations.

Failure to appear or to defend a case is dealt with in terms similar to those of Article 53 of the Statute of the International Court. While such default cannot prevent a decision, before making an award the tribunal must satisfy itself that it has jurisdiction and that the claim is well founded in fact and in law. The award, which is binding on the parties, must be reasoned and limited to the subject matter of the dispute and may include separate and dissenting opinions. As is generally the case with arbitration, the award is final and without appeal unless the parties otherwise agree.[28] However, it is surprising to find that, according to Article 12, disagreements relating to the interpretation or manner of implementation of an award may apparently be submitted by either party to the original tribunal at any time, or to another court or tribunal by agreement. Like several other parts of the Convention, the provisions of Annex VII apply *mutatis mutandis* to disputes involving international organisations.

The value of these arrangements, along with some of their limitations, may be seen from the use which has been made of arbitration since the Convention came into force. The *MV Saiga No. 2* case was initially referred to an Annex VII tribunal by St Vincent and the Grenadines, then, following an agreement with the respondent, Guinea, was transferred to the International Tribunal for the Law of the Sea (ITLOS), which decided the case in 1999.[29] Similarly, in the *Swordfish* case between Chile and the European Community, there was first a reference to an Annex VII tribunal by Chile, but then, after discussions between the parties, the case was transferred to a Special Chamber of ITLOS, appointed under Article 17(2) of the Tribunal's Statute.[30] The *Southern Bluefin Tuna* case, in which Australia and New Zealand claimed that Japan had failed to comply with certain conservation obligations, actually reached the arbitrators, but here the Annex VII tribunal, in a controversial decision, adopted a strained interpretation

---

[28] This does not, of course, exclude the possibility of annulment of an award in appropriate circumstances, in which connection the requirement of Article 10 that the award 'shall be confined to the subject-matter of the dispute' could be particularly important. See Rosenne and Sohn, *Commentary*, p. 435.

[29] See note 53 below.   [30] See note 57 below.

of Article 281 of the Convention and dismissed the case on jurisdictional grounds.[31]

In the *MOX Plant* case between Ireland and the United Kingdom, which concerned alleged threats to the marine environment, an Annex VII tribunal exercised its power to prescribe provisional measures of protection under Article 290(1) of the Convention, but also decided to suspend proceedings, pending clarification of certain jurisdictional issues by the European Court of Justice. Following the Court's ruling,[32] Ireland decided to discontinue the case. In other cases, however, Annex VII arbitration proved more fruitful. In the *Land Reclamation* case between Malaysia and Singapore, which concerned reclamation projects in the Straits of Johor, the dispute was settled through negotiations while the arbitration was in progress, and so the tribunal made an award on agreed terms.[33] In contrast, the *Barbados/Trinidad and Tobago* case[34] and the *Guyana/Suriname* case[35] were litigated to a conclusion. Both cases involved maritime boundaries, with the latter also raising a point concerning the unlawful threat of force. In different ways, therefore, the record to date shows that arbitration is available under the Convention for disputes on a variety of matters, although its functioning in practice must be seen in relation to other means of peaceful settlement.

Special arbitration

The maritime activities of states, like many aspects of the contemporary international scene, are so complex that disputes often involve technical issues which arbitrators with no specialist qualifications may find difficult to handle. A partial attempt to meet this problem was made in the third of the 1958 Conventions on the Law of the Sea, which provided for the appointment of experts to decide disputes relating to fishing and conservation. When such a dispute arose, the procedure laid down by that Convention envisaged a special commission of five members established by agreement

---

[31] *Southern Bluefin Tuna Case (Australia and New Zealand* v. *Japan)*, Award on Jurisdiction and Admissibility (2000), text in (2000) 39 ILM p. 1359; and see A. E. Boyle, Note, (2001) 50 ICLQ p. 447.

[32] See the *MOX Plant Case (Ireland* v. *United Kingdom)*, Order No. 3, Suspension of Proceedings on Jurisdiction and Merits and Request for Further Provisional Measures (June 2003), text in (2003) 42 ILM p. 1187. In Order No. 4 in November the suspension was extended, and in Order No. 6 in June 2008 the proceedings were terminated. For a review of the proceedings in this case and the related *OSPAR (Article 9)* arbitration, see R. R. Churchill and J. Scott, 'The MOX Plant litigation: The first half-life', (2004) 53 ICLQ p. 643.

[33] *Case concerning Land Reclamation by Singapore in and around the Straits of Johor*, Award on Agreed Terms (2005), www.pca-cpa.org. See also J. G. Merrills, 'New horizons for international adjudication', (2006) 6 Global Community YBILJ p. 47 at pp. 48–57.

[34] *Barbados/Trinidad and Tobago*, Award on Jurisdiction and Merits, (2006) 45 ILM p. 800. For comment, see B. Kwiatkowska, Note, (2007) 101 AJIL p. 149.

[35] *Guyana/Suriname*, Award (2007), (2008) 47 ILM p. 166. For comment, see S. Fietta, (2008) 102 AJIL p. 119.

between the parties. The members were to be drawn 'from amongst well-qualified persons being nationals of states not involved in the dispute and specializing in legal, administrative or scientific questions relating to fisheries, depending upon the nature of the dispute to be settled' (Article 9(2)). The decisions of special commissions were to be made in accordance with scientific and technical criteria set out in the Convention and were binding on the states concerned. This functional approach to dispute settlement is taken considerably further in Annex VIII to the new Convention concerning special arbitration.

Special arbitration is one of the binding methods of settlement which a party to the Convention can accept in advance by a declaration under Section 2 of Part XV of the Convention. It may therefore be initiated unilaterally whenever a dispute of the appropriate type arises and both parties have deposited a declaration in appropriate terms. The disputes for which special arbitration may be employed are those concerning the interpretation or application of the articles of the Convention relating to: fisheries; protection and preservation of the marine environment; marine scientific research; and navigation, including pollution from vessels and by dumping. Since a state is free to accept special arbitration for all or any of these categories, it is essential for jurisdictional purposes that both parties' declarations cover the type of dispute in question.

To assist states in setting up a tribunal, lists of experts in each of the four fields are to be maintained by, respectively, the Food and Agriculture Organization, the UN Environment Programme, the Inter-Governmental Oceanographic Commission and the International Maritime Organization. Each state party may nominate to each list two experts 'whose competence in the legal, scientific or technical aspects' of the field is established and 'who enjoy the highest reputation for fairness and integrity' (Article 3). The inclusion here of a reference to legal competence and the corresponding omission in the provisions on conciliation and arbitration perhaps suggest that law is regarded more as another type of useful expertise, than, as might be thought, a primary qualification for interpreting and applying a major international convention.

The arrangements for constituting a tribunal essentially follow the pattern of conciliation, rather than arbitration, in that each party selects two members, preferably from the appropriate list, and the president is chosen by agreement. Similarly, vacant places must be filled from the appropriate list by the Secretary-General, not the President of the International Tribunal for the Law of the Sea. However, as might be expected, the provisions concerning the disqualification of certain candidates follow those on arbitration, and, in exercising his powers of appointment, the Secretary-General must consult with both the parties and the relevant international organisation.

The job of a special arbitral tribunal, as the name implies, will normally be adjudication. However, the last provision of Annex VIII (Article 5) provides that, in certain circumstances, its functions can be broadened to include fact-finding and conciliation. By agreement, the parties may set up a special arbitral tribunal to carry out an inquiry into the facts of any dispute of a type amenable to special arbitration. An interesting point here is that, unless otherwise agreed, such a tribunal's findings of fact are conclusive as between the parties. Here, then, in contrast to the cases considered in Chapter 3, we have the phenomenon of 'binding inquiry'. Moreover, if the parties so request, such a tribunal may formulate non-binding recommendations to provide the basis for a review by the parties of the questions giving rise to the dispute. Thus, in a suitable case and with the parties' agreement, the machinery of special arbitration can be employed as an additional form of conciliation. The term 'special arbitration' hardly seems appropriate to describe either inquiry or inquiry with conciliation. However, as we saw when considering the *Red Crusader* and other cases discussed earlier,[36] considerable expertise may be necessary to unravel the circumstances of an incident at sea. These facilities can therefore be regarded as a useful adjunct to the Convention.

The International Tribunal for the Law of the Sea

Among the several new institutions created by the Law of the Sea Convention is a new court, the International Tribunal for the Law of the Sea (ITLOS).[37] The idea that disputes of a particular type are best handled by tribunals set up for the purpose is nothing new – the machinery of the European Convention on Human Rights is a well-established example – and the Convention's arrangements for special arbitration clearly reflect the same impulse. However, since the law of the sea can scarcely be said to be so specialised as to be beyond the competence of existing tribunals, the creation of ITLOS may be thought to indicate a certain lack of confidence in the International Court. In light of this, it is interesting to compare the new Tribunal's Statute, which contains forty articles and forms Annex VI to the Convention, with that of the International Court.

ITLOS, whose seat is in Hamburg, has twenty-one members, elected for a nine-year term. They are required to be 'persons enjoying the highest reputation for fairness and integrity and of recognised competence in the field of the law of the sea' (Article 2(1)). The vital matter of distribution of seats is dealt with by requiring that 'the representation of the principal legal systems of the world and equitable geographical distribution shall be assured' (Article 2(2)). To clarify this point it is provided that no two members of the Tribunal may be nationals of the same state and that 'there

---

[36] See Chapter 3.

[37] For a detailed description of the structure and working methods of the Tribunal, see G. Eiriksson, *The International Tribunal for the Law of the Sea*, The Hague, 2000.

shall be no fewer than three members from each geographical group as established by the General Assembly of the United Nations' (Article 3(2)). At the time of the Third UN Conference on the Law of the Sea, there were five such geographical groups, but, as no number is mentioned in Article 3, the Convention is flexible in this respect. Election is by a two-thirds majority of the parties to the Convention and from a list of candidates which they have nominated. This is of course a quite different arrangement from that governing elections to the International Court, and means that the Permanent Members of the Security Council have no guarantee of a seat on the new Tribunal.[38]

The provisions dealing with disqualification of a member in a particular case contain the usual reference to previous participation as agent, counsel, etc., and are modelled on Article 17 of the Statute of the International Court. The treatment of incompatible activities of members of the Tribunal, however, expands the earlier Statute's prohibition on political and administrative functions to include active association or financial interest 'in any of the operations of any enterprise concerned with the exploration for or exploitation of the resources of the sea or the sea-bed or other commercial use of the sea or the sea-bed' (Article 7). As with the International Court, a member of the Tribunal is not disqualified by being a national of one of the parties to a dispute, and an *ad hoc* member may be appointed by a party or parties currently unrepresented.[39]

In light of the International Court's successful effort to encourage the use of chambers, it is interesting to see that the new Tribunal's Statute provides for these in terms very similar to those of the earlier instrument. Chambers of three or more members may be formed for dealing with particular categories of case. A five-member chamber of summary procedure is to be formed for the 'speedy despatch of business' (Article 15(3)). And a chamber may be formed to deal with a particular dispute if the parties so request. In the last case, the Statute makes it clear that the composition of the chamber is to be determined by the Tribunal 'with the approval of the parties' (Article 15(2)), a provision which appears to meet the point which initially caused difficulty in the *Gulf of Maine* case.[40] The Statute also provides for a special Sea-Bed Disputes Chamber, which is further discussed below.

The competence of ITLOS raises a number of points of interest. As already noted, a dispute may be referred to the Tribunal when both

[38] On this and other aspects of the Tribunal, see Adede, 'Prolegomena', pp. 361–73. At the first election for the Tribunal in 1996, those elected included candidates from China, Russia and the United Kingdom, but not from France or the United States.
[39] Article 17. On the problem of determining the applicability of this provision if entities other than states parties claim the right to appoint *ad hoc* judges, see Rosenne and Sohn, *Commentary*, p. 368.
[40] See Chapter 6.

parties have made a declaration accepting its jurisdiction. It also has jurisdiction when any agreement so provides, or when all the parties to any treaty concerning the law of the sea already in force agree that disputes may be so referred. Unlike the International Court, the Tribunal is open to entities other than states, including international organisations in certain circumstances (Article 20(2)), and under the same provision may be used by states which are not parties to the Convention. ITLOS, like other courts and tribunals forming part of the Convention system, also has the power to prescribe provisional measures at the request of a party to a dispute, provided a *prima facie* case for jurisdiction can be made out (Article 25). Its choice of law, as we have seen, is governed largely by the Convention.

Procedural arrangements are straightforward and in general resemble those of the Statute of the International Court. Each party to a case normally bears its own costs, while the running expenses of the Tribunal are borne by the parties to the Convention and the International Sea-Bed Authority on terms to be agreed.[41] Article 31 allows a state which considers that it has an interest of a legal nature in the outcome of a case to request permission to intervene, and Article 32 gives parties to the Convention, or to other international agreements being considered, the right to intervene in proceedings before the Tribunal. These are both modelled on the Statute of the International Court. The Court, as we have seen, has been reluctant to allow intervention on the few occasions when it has been attempted; it remains to be seen whether the Tribunal's policy will be equally restrictive. The provision governing default (Article 28) is likewise very similar to the Statute and the Convention's own articles on arbitration. Decisions, for which a quorum is eleven elected members, are by majority vote and may include separate opinions. Like decisions of the International Court, the Tribunal's decisions are final, but may be interpreted by the Tribunal at the request of any party. Similarly, they are binding only as between the parties and in respect of the particular dispute.

The Sea-Bed Disputes Chamber

Disputes concerning the complex arrangements envisaged in the Convention for the exploration and exploitation of the deep sea-bed are dealt with in a series of provisions separate from those relating to other types of dispute. Indeed, it was originally suggested that, because sea-bed disputes raise a variety of special problems, they should be handled by a distinct tribunal with no connection to ITLOS. However, it was eventually decided that, though such disputes required a functional approach, the best arrangement would be to create a Sea-Bed Disputes Chamber (SBDC) of ITLOS with its

---

[41] On the thinking behind this arrangement, see Rosenne and Sohn, *Commentary*, p. 372.

own constitution and jurisdiction.[42] As a result of this change of policy, the provisions governing the SBDC are to be found in two places in the Convention, Part XI, Section 5, dealing with the administration of the International Sea-Bed Area, and Annex VI, setting up ITLOS.

The SBDC consists of eleven members chosen for a three-year term by the twenty-one elected members of ITLOS from among their number. In electing the Chamber, they are required to ensure that the principal legal systems of the world are represented and that equitable geographical distribution is achieved. Since the Tribunal may have as few as three members from a particular geographical group, the element of choice in the election will sometimes be quite limited.[43] At one time, it was proposed that elections should be in the hands of a political body, the Assembly of the International Sea-Bed Authority. However, it was eventually accepted that, since the members of the Tribunal are elected by the parties to the Convention, their involvement in the election of the members of the SBDC was unnecessary. The Assembly was therefore restricted to making recommendations of a general nature relating to representation and the distribution of seats, which are provided for in Article 35(2) of Annex VI.

A quorum in the SBDC is seven, but for certain purposes a smaller *ad hoc* chamber of three may be formed (Article 36). The composition of this 'chamber of a chamber' is to be determined by the SBDC with the approval of the parties. If they cannot agree, it is to be set up in the same way as an arbitral tribunal, with each party appointing one member and the third appointed by agreement or, if necessary, by the President of the SBDC. The possibility of creating *ad hoc* chambers may appear to be an unnecessary complication in an already elaborate set of provisions, but is explained by the need to compromise between states which wished disputes relating to Part XI of the Convention to be dealt with by the regular SBDC, and those which would have preferred arbitration. Allowing chambers to be created gave the latter a measure of control over the composition of the tribunal, which was what they wanted, while preserving the principle that the law relating to this new and important area would be developed by a single set of judges.[44]

The competence of the SBDC is bound up with the complex arrangements for the administration of the International Sea-Bed Area, details of which must be sought elsewhere.[45] It is relevant to note, however, that the SBDC's jurisdiction, which is set out in Article 187,[46] covers disputes between states; between a state and the International Sea-Bed Authority; between the

---

[42] On the integration of the system for settling sea-bed disputes into the general system of the Convention, see the Note by A. O. Adede in (1978) 72 AJIL p. 84.

[43] See Rosenne and Sohn, *Commentary*, p. 406.   [44] *Ibid.*, p. 409.

[45] See note 50 below; and Churchill and Lowe, *Law of the Sea*, Chapter 12.

[46] In addition to the jurisdiction conferred by Article 187, the SBDC is competent to prescribe provisional measures under Article 290.

International Sea-Bed Authority and a prospective contractor; and between the parties to a contract, including state enterprises and natural or juridical persons. Thus, although the privileges traditionally accorded to states are by no means ignored,[47] the Convention seeks to ensure that machinery for the settlement of disputes is available to all prospective participants in the International Sea-Bed Area.

The law to be applied by the SBDC corresponds to the nature of its jurisdiction. In addition to the provisions of Article 293, which, as noted earlier, all tribunals are to apply, the SBDC is to apply 'the rules, regulations and procedures of the Authority' adopted in accordance with the Convention, together with 'the terms of contracts concerning activities in the Area in matters relating to those contracts' (Annex VI, Article 38). While it can perhaps be argued that the scope of Article 293 is wide enough to make such particularisation unnecessary, the aim here was presumably 'to specify, with a view to greater clarity by means of emphasis, those parts of the law of the Convention itself which would be likely always to be relevant in proceedings before the Sea-Bed Disputes Chamber, but which would be less likely to be of significance in proceedings before the full Tribunal'.[48]

The SBDC, unlike ITLOS, has a jurisdiction which is automatically accepted by all parties to the Convention. In respect of certain disputes there are nevertheless alternative procedures available. Thus, the principle of freedom of choice, already encountered in the general provisions of the Convention, emerges again in the treatment of sea-bed disputes. As an alternative to the SBDC, a dispute between states concerning the sea-bed articles of the Convention may be referred to an ordinary chamber of ITLOS by agreement. As a further alternative, it may, at the request of any party to the dispute, be referred to the type of *ad hoc* chamber of the SBDC already described (Article 188(1)(b)). Similarly, unless the parties otherwise agree, disputes concerning the application or interpretation of a contract can be referred at the request of either party to binding commercial arbitration in accordance with the UNCITRAL Arbitration Rules. The arbitral tribunal, however, has no authority to interpret the Convention and any such issue must be referred to the SBDC for a ruling (Article 188(2)(a)). This unusual arrangement, which may give rise to difficulties in practice, is clearly an attempt to combine the established advantages of commercial arbitration with the need for a uniform interpretation of the Convention.

The exclusion of certain issues on the ground of non-justiciability provides another parallel between the general provisions of the Convention and those relating to the SBDC. Article 189 prohibits the latter from questioning the exercise by the International Sea-Bed Authority of its discretionary

---

[47] In proceedings involving natural or juridical persons, Article 190 gives a right of appearance and participation to sponsoring states.

[48] A. R. Carnegie, 'The Law of the Sea Tribunal', (1979) 28 ICLQ p. 669 at p. 680.

powers under the Convention. Moreover, unless the SBDC is asked for an advisory opinion on the point,[49] it may not 'pronounce itself on the question of whether any rules, regulations and procedures of the Authority are in conformity with this Convention, nor declare invalid any such rules, regulations and procedures'. Essentially, therefore, its jurisdiction is confined to questions concerning the application of the Convention and its associated legislation. Like the provisions on the discretion of coastal states considered earlier, these prohibitions are an uncompromising assertion of the controversial proposition that certain disputes concerning the exercise of legal powers are unsuitable for adjudication.

Within its allotted sphere, decisions of the SBDC are binding and the Convention provides that in the territories of the states parties such decisions shall be enforceable 'in the same manner as judgments or orders of the highest court of the State Party in whose territory the enforcement is sought' (Annex VI, Article 39). Usually, of course, there is no question of enforcing the decisions of international tribunals through municipal law. In the case of the SBDC, however, the commercial orientation of its work and the fact that effective decisions are essential to the whole sea-bed enterprise, explain this unusual provision. Unlike its parent Tribunal, the SBDC has yet to be used. This is not surprising, as commercial mining of the deep sea-bed has not yet begun.

Inaugurating ITLOS

The 1982 Law of the Sea Convention came into force in November 1994, twelve months after the date of deposit of the sixtieth instrument of ratification or accession in accordance with Article 308. A little earlier, in July, the UN General Assembly had adopted Resolution 48/263 with an annexed Agreement relating to the Implementation of Part XI of the 1982 Law of the Sea Convention,[50] the aim of which was to modify the provisions on the international sea-bed in order to make them acceptable to the industrialised states. The Agreement, which had been under negotiation for several years, does not affect the existing arrangements for dispute settlement, but, as a revision of the Convention, it must naturally be applied by ITLOS and other tribunals when exercising their jurisdiction. With the Agreement in place, the Convention looked set to achieve general acceptance, and so attention turned to the question of implementation.

---

[49] The duty of the SBDC to give advisory opinions at the request of the Assembly or the Council 'on legal questions arising within the scope of their activities' is laid down by Article 191.

[50] Text in (1994) 33 ILM p. 1309. For analysis of the Agreement and discussion of its significance, see B. H. Oxman, 'The 1994 Agreement and the Convention', (1994) 88 AJIL p. 687; and D. H. Anderson, 'Further efforts to ensure universal participation in the United Nations Convention on the Law of the Sea', (1994) 43 ICLQ p. 886.

At meetings of the states parties in 1994 and 1995, arrangements were made to hold the first election of the members of ITLOS, an Acting Registrar for the Tribunal was appointed, and English and French were designated as its official languages.[51] It was also decided that the remuneration of the members of the Tribunal should consist of three elements: an annual allowance, a special allowance for each day that a member is engaged in the work of the Tribunal, and a subsistence allowance for each day of attendance. This arrangement, which contrasts with the annual salary paid to members of the International Court, reflects the fact that all the judges, apart from the President, currently work on a part-time basis. Although ITLOS and its offshoot, the SBDC, are standing tribunals, demand for their services has been hard to predict. Consequently, to begin in a limited way, with capacity to expand if demand makes this necessary, is a prudent and economical approach.

The first election of members of the Tribunal took place in 1996. It will be recalled that Article 2(1) of the Statute requires of the members 'recognised competence in the field of the law of the sea' and, not surprisingly, several of those elected had taken part in UNCLOS III or the negotiation of the 1994 Agreement, as legal advisers, government representatives or academic experts. To enable a system of triennial elections to operate, lots were drawn after the election to determine which seven members would serve for three or six years and which for the full nine-year term. Those elected included five each from the African and Asian groups, four each from the Latin American and Caribbean group, and the Western European and others group, and three from the Eastern European states. This provided a representative Tribunal in accordance with Article 2(2) of the Statute, and is a composition which has been maintained in subsequent elections.

At their various meetings before the election, the states parties had wisely decided to refrain from trying to regulate the Tribunal's internal processes. This was therefore the first task for its newly elected members, and so at meetings in 1996 and 1997 they arranged to set up the SBDC, together with a Chamber for Fisheries Disputes and one for Marine Environment Disputes, and at the same time dealt with various other administrative and organisational matters. The latter included adopting the Tribunal's Rules, and also guidelines on the preparation and presentation of cases before the Tribunal and a resolution concerning its internal practice. In 2007, a further Chamber was created for Maritime Delimitation Disputes. While the Tribunal's treatment of these matters predictably drew on the experience of the International Court, several departures and adaptations reflect differences between the two bodies' jurisdictions, as well as an

---

[51] See S. Rosenne, 'Establishing the International Tribunal for the Law of the Sea', (1995) 89 AJIL p. 806.

effort to make the Tribunal's proceedings efficient, cost-effective and 'user-friendly'.[52]

When ITLOS was founded, doubts were expressed in some quarters that the new tribunal might not have enough business to justify its existence. The record to date shows why those doubts were entertained. In the *MV Saiga No. 2* case,[53] it decided that Guinea must pay compensation for arresting and detaining an oil tanker registered in St Vincent and the Grenadines because the actions in question could not be justified under the Convention. This case, in which both the law and the facts were contested, is the only case so far to have been decided on the merits. On the other hand, the special procedure under Article 292, by which the Tribunal can be asked to order the prompt release of a detained vessel, has been invoked on several occasions and use of this provision is becoming something of a regular occurrence.[54] Similarly, the Tribunal has made a number of orders under Article 290(5) in response to requests for provisional measures of protection, pending arbitration proceedings,[55] and made such an order under Article 290(1) prior to its own decision in the *MV Saiga No. 2* case.[56] These orders, like the judgments under Article 292, not only helped to resolve the particular disputes, but have also served to clarify the meaning of key provisions of the Convention.

Various other features of the Tribunal's record shed further light on its significance and its potential. In the *Swordfish* case, as mentioned earlier, Chile originally referred its dispute with the European Community to Annex VII arbitration, but then, after discussions between the parties, the case was transferred to ITLOS, a special chamber being set up under Article 17(2) of the Tribunal's Statute at the end of 2000 for this purpose.[57] Although proceedings were subsequently suspended, the case is notable as the first contentious case between a state and an organisation to be referred

---

[52] See D. Anderson, 'The International Tribunal for the Law of the Sea', in M. D. Evans (ed.), *Remedies in International Law: The Institutional Dilemma*, Oxford, 1998, p. 71; and T. Treves, Introductory Note, (2001) 1 Global Community YBILJ p. 269.

[53] *MV Saiga (No. 2) Case (Saint Vincent and the Grenadines v. Guinea)*, Judgment, (1999) 38 ILM p. 1323; and see L. de La Fayette, Note, (2000) 49 ICLQ p. 467.

[54] See, for example, the *Volga Case (Russian Federation v. Australia)*, Application for Prompt Release, Judgment, 2002, (2003) 42 ILM p. 159. For a general review of the jurisprudence on Article 292, see P. Gautier, 'Les affaires de "prompte mainlevée" devant le Tribunal International du Droit de la Mer', (2003) 3 Global Community YBILJ p. 79; and, for discussion of the Volga case specifically, R. H. van Dyke, *ibid.*, p. 245, and T. Treves, *ibid.*, p. 387.

[55] In the *Southern Bluefin Tuna* case, see the Tribunal's Order of 27 August 1999, reprinted in (1999) 38 ILM p. 1624, and see R. R. Churchill, Note, (2000) 49 ICLQ p. 979; for the *MOX Plant* case, see the Tribunal's Order of 3 December 2001, (2002) 41 ILM p. 405, and see T. L. McDorman, Note, (2001) 12 YBIEL p. 592; and, most recently in the *Land Reclamation* case, see the Tribunal's Order of 8 October 2003.

[56] See the Tribunal's Order of 11 March 1998, (1998) 37 ILM p. 1204; and A. V. Lowe, Note, (1999) 48 ICLQ p. 187 at pp. 196–9.

[57] See the Tribunal's Order of 20 December 2000. On this and the subsequent suspension of the proceedings, see A. Serdy, 'See you in port', (2002) 3 Melbourne JIL p. 79.

to an international court, as well as a demonstration of the flexibility of the Convention's procedures. It is also a reminder of the value of obligatory jurisdiction in encouraging accommodation, a point also apparent from the *Chaisiri Reefer 2* case,[58] another prompt-release application under Article 292, which was entered on the Tribunal's list in 2001, but was then discontinued following an agreement between the parties.

A perceptive observer has noted that '[t]he experience of most international courts is to start slowly and steadily build up their docket'.[59] This may well be the route that ITLOS will follow. A member of the Tribunal described its judicial policy as 'to administer justice diligently, thoroughly and fairly, in accordance with the applicable law, without any unnecessary expense or delay'.[60] The Tribunal's work to date has shown its commitment to these objectives – its speed in dealing with cases under Article 292 and the constructive use of its discretion in responding to requests for provisional measures of protection being particularly commendable. As its intention to develop 'user-friendly' procedures is also evident from current practice, the record of ITLOS so far, although relatively limited, is far from negligible and contains encouraging signs for the future.

The significance of the Convention

Although the 1982 Law of the Sea Convention has been ratified by more than 150 states, and there has been some practice under Part XV, there is much that has not yet been tested. Consequently, how well it will achieve its purpose still remains to be seen. But, if the record so far can provide only some pointers to the future, the treatment of dispute settlement in the Convention is in itself highly significant, for it shows the issues which arise in attempting to create a regulatory framework for a major area of state activity, and the means available for handling such issues in the contemporary world.

The first, and in many ways the most important, question is whether the provision of machinery for the settlement of disputes is to be an integral part of the treaty. One of the most encouraging features of the Convention is that this question is answered positively. It must be remembered, of course, that the arrangements set out in the Convention come into play

---

[58] On this case, brought by Panama against Yemen, see T. L. McDorman, Note, (2001) 12 YBIEL p. 592.

[59] See the speech of the President of the ICJ, Rosalyn Higgins, on the occasion of the tenth anniversary of ITLOS in 2006, quoted in T. Treves, 'The International Tribunal for the Law of the Sea in 2006', (2007) 7 Global Community YBILJ p. 231 at p. 232.

[60] See Anderson, 'The International Tribunal', p. 79. See also P. Chandrasekhara Rao, 'The International Tribunal for the Law of the Sea: An evaluation', in Ando, McWhinney and Wolfrum, *Liber Amicorum*, p. 667.

only when the parties have not made other arrangements and in that sense are essentially ancillary. Even so, the recognition that the Convention must contain provisions dealing with dispute settlement was a key step forward, contrasting sharply with previous conventions on the subject. With this basic issue resolved, the characteristics of the machinery to be provided are a matter of who, what, when and how.

The Convention, as we have seen, deals with the issue of 'who' by utilising all the traditional means of dispute settlement including negotiation, the International Court and commercial arbitration. It then adds (in effect) two new courts – ITLOS and its associated SBDC – and a variety of *ad hoc* bodies in the form of conciliation commissions and general and special tribunals of arbitration. To some extent, this proliferation of tribunals is accounted for by the variety and complexity of the Convention's provisions. There is, however, reason to believe that a feeling by the Group of 77 that new tribunals would more accurately reflect their views was also influential. With ITLOS starting work, some questioned whether a new court, dedicated to law of the sea disputes, was really necessary, especially as the International Court, which has dealt with many such cases, is currently enjoying something of a resurgence.[61] This raises wider issues about the proliferation of international tribunals generally which will be considered in Chapter 12. All that need be said here is that ITLOS was conceived to meet a demand which was real enough at the time and through its developing jurisprudence has an opportunity to answer its detractors.

The question 'what' is answered by the creation of an elaborate series of overlapping and exclusive jurisdictions, reflecting a desire to see technical disputes handled functionally, certain issues excluded from third-party review altogether and other issues dealt with by conciliation rather than adjudication. On the last two points, the influence of the Group of 77 is again apparent. As one would expect, several parties to the Convention, including a number of industrialised states, have taken advantage of the opportunity to opt out of the compulsory procedures which is offered by Article 298. However, whereas most have excepted all three categories of disputes specified therein, others have made exceptions which are more limited. A point of some importance with regard to both Article 298 and the scheme of the Convention generally, is that, where a dispute involves several issues, the Convention's 'salami-slicing' approach means that not all aspects of the dispute may be subject to compulsory and binding

---

[61] See S. Oda, 'Dispute settlement prospects in the law of the sea', (1995) 44 ICLQ p. 863; and earlier E. Lauterpacht, *Aspects of the Administration of International Justice*, Cambridge, 1991, pp. 19–22. For the contrary view, see J. I. Charney, 'The implications of expanding international dispute settlement systems: The 1982 Convention on the Law of the Sea', (1996) 90 AJIL p. 69; and A. E. Boyle, 'Dispute settlement and the Law of the Sea Convention: Problems of fragmentation and jurisdiction', (1997) 46 ICLQ p. 37.

settlement.[62] So, for example, if a dispute involves both high seas freedoms and a coastal state's rights in its exclusive economic zone, resolving the whole dispute through ITLOS or arbitration will require both parties' agreement.[63]

In answering the question 'when', the Convention places great emphasis on the parties' choice of means at all stages and, in respect of certain disputes, enables entities other than states to set the machinery in motion. It seems clear that, in relation to the provisions on obligatory settlement in particular, this element of choice was crucial to the acceptability of the Convention. The consequences of adopting what has been termed the 'cafeteria' approach to compulsory settlement[64] will only become fully apparent as practice under the Convention develops. However, it may be indicative that, in making their choices under Article 287, several states have nominated ITLOS, while a few have chosen the ICJ, and some, as they are entitled to do, have opted for different forums for different purposes. Many states, on the other hand, have expressed no preference as yet, which suggests that arbitration, as the residual procedure, will continue to be prominent. In spite of the limitations already noted, the Convention's arrangements for obtaining binding decisions are actually quite extensive. Given the notorious difficulty of securing agreement on such procedures, this is a considerable achievement.

The last issue, 'how', raises the question of choice of law and the object of proceedings. The former, as we have indicated, is dealt with by according a dominant role to the Convention. The importance of this guarantee that the 'new' law of the sea will be the framework for decisions has already been explained. It should not be forgotten, however, that in conciliation proceedings the object is not to apply rules but to promote an amicable settlement. As conciliation occupies an important place in both the optional and obligatory machinery of the Convention, the inference to be drawn from the resolution of the *Jan Mayen* conciliation[65] – that in the law of the sea there are many problems 'which are better solved other than on a basis of strict law, or, indeed, cannot by their nature be solved on such a basis'[66] – appears to have been fully recognised.

As already noted, Article 288 envisages use of the machinery of Part XV to deal with disputes involving other international agreements related to the 1982 Convention. The value of this provision and the wider potential of the Convention's arrangements for dispute settlement may be seen in a

---

[62] See Boyle, *ibid.*, pp. 41–7.

[63] For discussion of just such a dispute, see P. G. G. Davies, 'The EC/Canadian fisheries dispute in the North Atlantic', (1995) 44 ICLQ p. 927.

[64] See Boyle, 'Dispute settlement and the Law of the Sea Convention', pp. 40–1.

[65] See Chapter 4.

[66] *Settlement of Disputes* (Australian Paper), 21 March 1975, quoted by Adede, 'Settlement of disputes', p. 80, n. 10.

subsequent treaty intended to fill one of the gaps in the 1982 Convention, namely, the Straddling Stocks Agreement of 1995.[67] The Agreement provides in Article 30(1) that the provisions of Part XV of the 1982 Convention shall apply to all disputes concerning its interpretation or application, whether or not the states concerned are parties to the 1982 Convention. This in itself is significant, but Articles 30(2) and 30(5) of the Agreement add two new features to Part XV, widening its reach even further. The former extends its provisions to disputes concerning regional and other fisheries agreements, while the latter requires a court or tribunal having jurisdiction to apply not only the relevant provisions of the 1982 Convention and the 1995 Agreement, but also those of any regional or other fisheries agreement 'as well as generally accepted standards for the conservation and management of living marine resources'. By utilising Part XV and extending its scope, the Agreement is thus intended to encourage states which have assumed obligations with regard to straddling and migratory fish stocks to carry them out, whatever their legal origin.

For Article 30(2) of the Straddling Stocks Agreement to apply it is, of course, essential for the parties to a dispute to have ratified the Agreement, as well as the relevant regional treaty. It is therefore significant that a number of treaties establishing regional fisheries management organisations contain provisions similar to Article 30(1) of the Agreement, extending the dispute settlement machinery of the 1982 Convention to disputes arising from the regional treaty, whether or not the states concerned are also parties to the 1995 Agreement. For example, the 2006 Southern Indian Ocean Fisheries Agreement contains a provision of this kind.[68] In this way, then, the obligations of the 1982 Convention may be extended beyond parties to the 1982 Convention itself and the 1995 Agreement to all those accepting the particular regional treaty.

However, to avoid misunderstanding, it must also be pointed out that several fishery conventions contain dispute settlement arrangements weaker than those of the 1982 Convention which will apply when the state or states concerned are not parties to the 1995 Agreement. Likewise, the numerous conventions concerned with marine pollution generally contain their own

[67] Text in (1995) 34 ILM p. 1542. For analysis, see D. A. Balton, 'Strengthening the law of the sea: The new Agreement on Straddling Fish Stocks and Highly Migratory Fish Stocks', (1996) 27 Ocean Devel. & Int. L. p. 125; see also D. H. Anderson, 'The Straddling Stocks Agreement of 1995', (1996) 45 ICLQ p. 463; F. Orrego Vicuña, *The Changing International Law of High Seas Fisheries*, Cambridge, 1999. Chapter 10; and A. Boyle, 'Problems of compulsory jurisdiction and the settlement of disputes relating to straddling fish stocks', in O. S. Stokke (ed.), *Governing High Seas Fisheries*, Oxford, 2001, p. 91.

[68] See R. Churchill, 'Trends in dispute settlement in the law of the sea: Towards the increasing availability of compulsory means', in D. French, M. Saul and N. D. White (eds.), *International Law and Dispute Settlement: New Problems and Techniques*, Oxford, 2010, p. 143 at p. 158.

arrangements for dealing with disputes.[69] These, as noted earlier, will displace the machinery of the 1982 Convention by virtue of Articles 281 and 282 of the 1982 Convention, and there is also nothing to prevent states utilising the International Court, or traditional arbitration, to resolve their law of the sea disputes, if they so choose. The significance of the 1982 Convention is thus not that it aims to provide exclusive machinery for dealing with law of the sea disputes, but rather that it establishes a residual framework for treating such disputes seriously.

In an essay in 1975, a leading commentator suggested that the establishment of an effective system for the settlement of disputes arising out of the 1982 Convention should be regarded as 'one of the pillars of the new world order in the ocean space itself'.[70] The arrangements which were eventually negotiated are, as has been seen, both complex and less than ideal in certain respects. Regarded, however, as an exercise in the art of the possible, they represent a remarkable achievement, the influence of which on both the handling of disputes and the law of the sea itself has already been profound.

---

[69] See Churchill, 'Trends in dispute settlement', pp. 163–6.
[70] Adede, 'Settlement of disputes', p. 798.

9

International trade disputes

The development of special arrangements to deal with disputes involving international trade began in the middle of the last century and has now produced one of the most effective, as well as one of the most important, systems of international dispute settlement. Thus, in contrast to law of the sea disputes, which we have seen are subject to a system which came into force in 1994, trade disputes can be dealt with through arrangements which have been progressively refined, based on regional as well as general agreements. Since limitations of space preclude examining this complex network in detail, this chapter focuses on the central element and outlines the dispute settlement system of the World Trade Organization (WTO).

From GATT (1947) to the World Trade Organization

As the Second World War drew to a close, governments were forced to consider the shape of the post-war world. First among their considerations was the issue of international peace and security, which led to the creation of the United Nations. However, not far behind came financial and economic issues, including international trade, which also had institutional implications. The 1930s had been an anarchic period in every sense, and to avoid repeating the experience the leaders of the post-war era resolved to establish arrangements which would reflect the realities of economic interdependence. The institutions created in this period, which include the International Monetary Fund, the World Bank and the General Agreement on Tariffs and Trade (GATT), have provided the framework for international economic relations ever since, supplemented, of course, by numerous subsequent instruments and organisations, including regional arrangements, set up for particular purposes.[1]

The 1947 GATT was originally intended as a provisional agreement for the liberalisation of tariffs, pending the establishment of permanent arrangements through a new body to be known as the International Trade

---

[1] See J. H. Jackson, 'Reflections on problems of international economic relations', in M. K. Young and Y. Iwasawa, *Trilateral Perspectives on International Legal Issues*, Irvington on Hudson, NY, 1996, p. 263. See also D. L. M. Kennedy and J. D. Southwick (eds.), *The Political Economy of International Trade Law*, Cambridge, 2002.

Organization (ITO). However, the ITO was never formed owing to domestic opposition within the United States. As a result, the GATT became a permanent system of great complexity, evolving into an institution with organs and decision-making powers, and eventually including more than 200 multilateral trade agreements. The failure of the ITO left a gap which the evolution of the GATT went some way to fill, but numerous problems remained. In areas not covered by GATT law, such as international movements of services, persons and capital, protectionist practices re-emerged, and, even in areas which were covered, governments often failed to observe their obligations.[2] An attempt to address some of these problems was made at the Tokyo Round of trade negotiations between 1973 and 1979, but it was not until the subsequent Uruguay Round, which began in 1986, that they were tackled comprehensively.

After much hard bargaining, the Uruguay Round concluded in 1994 with the signing of the Final Act, which contains the Agreement Establishing the World Trade Organization.[3] The aim of the Agreement, which entered into force in January 1995, is ambitious, being nothing less than the creation of an integrated legal system for world trade, intended to reconstruct the foundations of the international economic order. To this end, the Agreement creates an entirely new international institution, the World Trade Organization, to provide structural coherence, and in comprehensive substantive provisions brings together into a single legal framework all previous GATT agreements and thirty new Uruguay Round agreements, covering matters such as trade in services which previously lacked regulation.[4] The vital issue of dispute settlement is addressed in a new Dispute Settlement Understanding (DSU)[5] annexed to the main Agreement.

The Dispute Settlement Understanding

If rules to promote fair trading are to be effective, they need to be accompanied by provisions for settling disputes, for only thus can self-serving interpretation be exposed and unilateralism discouraged. There is an obvious parallel here with the law of the sea where, as noted earlier, similar thinking led many governments to see the provisions of Part V as a vital

---

[2] See E.-U. Petersmann, *The GATT/WTO Dispute Settlement System*, Dordrecht, 1997, p. 90, and, earlier, the same author's 'The dispute settlement system of the World Trade Organization and the evolution of the GATT dispute settlement system since 1948', (1994) 31 Common Market L. Rev. p. 1157 at p. 1160.

[3] Text in (1994) 33 ILM p. 1125. For general reference, see M. Matsushita, T. J. Schoenbaum and P. C. Mavroidis, *The World Trade Organization: Law, Practice, and Policy*, Oxford, 2003.

[4] Petersmann, *The GATT/WTO System*, pp. 44–54. For the important issue of transitional arrangements, see P. M. Moore, 'The decisions bridging the GATT 1947 and the WTO Agreement', (1996) 90 AJIL p. 317.

[5] WTO Understanding on Rules and Procedures Governing the Settlement of Disputes, 15 April 1994, (1994) 33 ILM p. 1226.

component of the 1982 Law of the Sea Convention. In the trade context, such considerations had prompted the development within the GATT of a relatively sophisticated procedure for dealing with disputes even before the 1994 Agreement.[6] While the new Dispute Settlement Understanding develops the procedure in various ways, it is firmly rooted in established practice. To understand its content and to see what it adds, it is therefore necessary to say a few words about the earlier system.

The original GATT treaty of 1947 dealt only briefly with dispute settlement, although it did provide in Articles 22 and 23 for consultation, followed, if necessary, by the submission of issues to the GATT Contracting Parties. In the early years, disputes were often referred to working parties, consisting of the representatives of states and always including the parties to the dispute.[7] The working party's function was to examine the question and produce a report setting out the various views. This method of dealing with disputes was essentially a kind of mediation, since the aim of the process was to encourage the protagonists to resolve their differences by bringing the influence of outside states to bear. Before long, however, a more rule-oriented system was evolved and the practice developed of referring disputes to panels, composed of individuals rather than governmental representatives, whose findings and recommendations were passed to the GATT Council, representing the Contracting Parties.

Panels proved increasingly popular and eventually supplanted the working party procedure. As reports began to focus on the issue of treaty violations, the procedure became increasingly legalistic and acquired some of the characteristics of arbitration. It is important to appreciate, however, that, as the primary aim was still to achieve an agreement between the parties to the dispute, elements of conciliation were present throughout the process. Moreover, as the report of a panel required adoption by all the Contracting Parties, usually acting through the GATT Council, it did not in itself create binding obligations.

As well as panels and working groups, it was possible for Contracting Parties to make use of the good offices of the Director-General of GATT, to set up inquiries and to refer disputes to arbitration. Between 1947 and 1995, more than 150 disputes were referred to the Contracting Parties and most were settled through its procedures.[8] However, despite this generally successful record, a number of weaknesses in the system had become apparent and were the subject of attention during the Uruguay Round. An obvious weakness of the panel procedure was that, since both setting up a panel and

---

[6] See Petersmann, *The GATT/WTO System*, pp. 66–92; I. Van Bael, 'The GATT dispute settlement procedure', (1988) 22 (4) J. World Trade p. 67; and E. Canal-Forgues and R. Ostrihansky, 'New developments in the GATT dispute settlement procedures', (1990) 24 (2) J. World Trade p. 67.

[7] See Y. Iwasawa, 'Settlement of disputes concerning the WTO Agreement: Various means other than panel procedures', in Young and Iwasawa, *Trilateral Perspectives*, p. 377 at pp. 386–9.

[8] *Ibid.*, p. 377.

the adoption of its report required consensus in the GATT Council, it was possible for a state whose actions were challenged to block effective action. A second weakness was that arrangements for securing the implementation of decisions were weak or unclear. And a third was that, since the various GATT and Tokyo Round agreements contained different substantive rules and different arrangements for dispute settlement, both 'norm shopping' (seeking the most favourable rule) and 'forum shopping' (seeking the most favourable procedure) were possible.[9]

The Dispute Settlement Understanding, as we shall see, incorporates many features of the existing GATT procedures. However, to deal with the deficiencies identified above, a number of major innovations are also introduced.[10] To deal with norm and forum shopping, the DSU establishes a unified dispute settlement system for the whole GATT/WTO system, including the issues of services and intellectual property. To deal with implementation, new and clearer procedures are laid down. And, to deal with the problem of political interference, the role formerly carried out by the GATT Council is assigned to a new organ called the Dispute Settlement Body (DSB). Although still made up of states, the DSB can refuse to establish a panel, or decline to approve a report, only if there is a consensus; these actions therefore become virtually automatic. Since this change effectively removes the political check on panel procedures, an appellate procedure is included as a further innovation. The general effect of the Dispute Settlement Understanding is thus to consolidate existing procedures and at the same time bring them up to date. The main features of the DSU may now therefore be considered in a little more detail.

Consultations

The aim of the GATT procedures has always been to resolve disputes, whenever possible, through agreement between the parties, rather than by seeking to identify treaty violations. Accordingly, consultation, which it will be recalled is also a good way of avoiding disputes, has always been prominent in those procedures. Articles 22(1) and 23(1) of the GATT provide for bilateral consultations in general terms, and the new DSU, based substantially on provisions agreed in 1989,[11] spells out the implications in some detail.

---

[9] See Petersmann, *The GATT/WTO System*, p. 90.

[10] For a concise overview, see A. F. Lowenfeld, 'Remedies along with rights: Institutional reform in the new GATT', (1994) 88 AJIL p. 477; and P. T. B. Kohona, 'Dispute resolution under the World Trade Organization', (1994) 28 (2) J. World Trade p. 23. For a more detailed treatment, see D. Palmeter and P. C. Mavroidis, *Dispute Settlement in the World Trade Organization. Practice and Procedure*, 2nd edn, Cambridge, 2004.

[11] See Canal-Forgues and Ostrihansky, 'New developments', pp. 68–70.

Article 4(3) contains an obligation to enter into consultations in good faith on request, and Article 4(5) reflects a preference for this method by giving consultations priority over other procedures.

An obligation to consult, like an obligation to negotiate, can be used by an unscrupulous government to postpone resort to other procedures, perhaps indefinitely, unless the precise scope of the obligation is carefully defined. To remove the possibility of abuse, and also to imbue the parties with a sense of urgency, the DSU contains strict time-limits. The state to which a request for consultations is submitted has just ten days to respond and must enter into consultations within thirty days of the request (Article 4(3)). Consultations must also be concluded within sixty days of the request (Article 4(7)). Even stricter deadlines apply in urgent cases (Article 4(8)) and failure to meet any of the deadlines immediately entitles the complaining party to request the establishment of a panel.

When consultations take place they are confidential and without prejudice to the rights of the states concerned (Article 4(6)). However, it is important to appreciate that the reference to confidentiality here relates to the content of the discussions, not to the fact that they are taking place or to their outcome. Articles 4(4) and 3(6) make it clear that the occurrence and outcome must both be notified to the DSB and relevant bodies. Such notification was not required before 1989, and so this was an innovation. Incorporating this requirement into the DSU has the effect of placing bilateral consultations under the control of the WTO, so helping to integrate the dispute settlement system.

International trade disputes, like some of the disputes considered in earlier chapters, are not exclusively bilateral but often involve the interests of third parties. Because this is frequently the situation in trade relations, the DSU contains a number of provisions concerned with disputes of a multilateral character. As regards consultation, the relevant provision is Article 4(11), which allows a third state which considers that it has 'a substantial trade interest' in any consultations to indicate a desire to join them. It may then do so, provided the member to which the request was made agrees that the claim of substantial interest is well founded. A study in 1994 found more than twenty instances in which third-party joinder had been permitted under an earlier version of this provision,[12] and the facility has been extensively used since, indicating its practical value. If a request for joinder is refused, the applicant can, of course, seek separate bilateral consultations under Article 4(3).

The significance of consultation as a means of dealing with international trade disputes can be seen from the record, which shows that far more disputes have been settled by consultation than by panels, this being in

---

[12] See Iwasawa, 'Settlement of disputes', p. 381.

fact the method by which most disputes are resolved in practice.[13] The high success rate is no doubt partly because a round of consultation may sometimes be all that is needed to reach agreement. It is worth pointing out, however, that consultation can be a continuing process, since governments often maintain a dialogue while the panel procedure or other moves are in progress. Thus, the initial obligation to try consultation by no means exhausts its possibilities, for, as the situation and the parties' perceptions change, a solution may emerge at a later stage, even if the first contacts are unsuccessful.[14]

Good offices, conciliation and mediation

A system which has consistently emphasised the settlement of disputes through agreement might be expected to recognise the role of good offices and mediation, which are both informal ways of bringing the parties together, and also of conciliation, which, as noted in Chapter 4, is a more structured process. In various forms, good offices, conciliation and mediation have all featured in the GATT system and demonstrated their usefulness. As mentioned earlier, these 'diplomatic' methods cannot always be sharply distinguished from each other in practice and this has certainly been so in the present context. While the Dispute Settlement Understanding contains more detail on these methods than previous instruments,[15] it groups them together in a single article, which visibly highlights their interconnection.

Good offices, conciliation and mediation are voluntary procedures and require the parties' agreement (Article 5(1)). This immediately distinguishes them from consultation which, it will be recalled, is mandatory. They may, however, be requested by a state at any time and at any point in a dispute. They can also be terminated at any time and, once terminated, entitle the complaining party to request the establishment of a panel, provided the sixty-day consultation period has elapsed (Article 5(3) and (4)). Under some of the Tokyo Round agreements, certain disputes had to be referred to a conciliation commission of member states before a state could request a panel. But this requirement, which tended to polarise positions, has now been abandoned.[16] As with consultations, proceedings involving good offices,

---

[13] On the use of consultations, see M. L. Busch and E. Reinhardt, 'Testing international trade law: Empirical studies of GATT/WTO dispute settlement', in Kennedy and Southwick, *Political Economy*, p. 457 at pp. 467–70.

[14] Moreover, panels have been known to suggest further consultations as a means of avoiding difficult decisions: see Iwasawa, 'Settlement of disputes', pp. 380–1. It has been suggested, however, that a greater emphasis on consultations would be beneficial: see T. J. Schoenbaum, 'WTO dispute settlement: Praise and suggestions for reform', (1998) 47 ICLQ p. 647 at pp. 648–52.

[15] On the treatment of good offices, conciliation and mediation in the 1989 'Improvements', see Canal-Forgues and Ostrihansky, 'New developments', pp. 70–1.

[16] See Iwasawa, 'Settlement of disputes', p. 386.

conciliation and mediation are confidential and without prejudice to the parties' rights, and a further similarity is that, as might be expected, if the parties agree, these procedures can continue while panel proceedings are in progress (Article 5(5)).

Who performs good offices, conciliation and mediation? In theory, if states employ those processes, they can refer a trade dispute to any competent individual, group or organ. In practice, however, the choice is more limited. Unlike the 1982 Law of the Sea Convention and many other treaties, the DSU contains no arrangements for establishing conciliation commissions and similar bodies, apart from the provisions on panels which we shall come to shortly. As already mentioned, in early GATT practice, working parties, consisting of the representatives of member states, often acted as mediators, but these have rather gone out of favour. Thus, although working parties can still be established with the parties' agreement, they do not feature in recent practice and receive no mention in the DSU. Indeed, the only possibility which is specifically mentioned in this section is reference of a dispute to the Director-General of the WTO, who under Article 5(6) is authorised to offer good offices, conciliation or mediation, acting in an *ex officio* capacity.

References to the good offices of the Director-General of the GATT are to be found in earlier instruments, but initially the facility does not appear to have been much used. There are, however, now a number of cases which illustrate both the characteristics of this form of intervention and its value. In the *Copper* case[17] in 1987, the European Community (EC) and Japan jointly requested the good offices of the Director-General in their dispute over copper ores and concentrates. The Director-General appointed a distinguished expert to act on his behalf, and the latter, after hearing the parties' representations, produced an 'advisory opinion' at their request. This concluded that Japan had not violated any of its GATT obligations, but recommended that the parties should negotiate with a view to reducing Japanese tariffs. Here, and in the *Wet Salted Cod* case[18] between the EC and Canada the following year, the Director-General's intervention helped the parties to resolve their dispute.

In the above cases, the Director-General's involvement, though termed 'good offices', was really a kind of conciliation since the parties were offered a specific set of conclusions and recommendations as a basis for further action. But more significant than the question of classification is the point that cases of this type show the value of procedures which enable third parties to go beyond the question of whether the rules have been broken and to suggest a solution in situations where the action complained of may be lawful, but there is nevertheless a dispute needing resolution. As we saw in Chapter 4, one of the strengths of conciliation is that by encouraging

---

[17] For an outline of this case, see Iwasawa, 'Settlement of disputes', p. 385.   [18] *Ibid.*

flexibility it is a way forward in just such cases, an advantage which it will be recalled is also recognised in the Law of the Sea Convention.

Although good offices, conciliation and mediation are voluntary and not normally a prerequisite to the use of other procedures, there is a qualification, relating to the position of least developed countries, which should be mentioned. Article 24(2) of the DSU provides that, in a dispute involving a least developed country member which has not been resolved through consultations, the Director-General or the Chairman of the Dispute Settlement Body shall offer their good offices, conciliation or mediation on the request of the member concerned before a request for a panel is made. Of course, the exercise of these functions requires the consent of both parties; however, by identifying a role for such intervention in a specific group of cases, the DSU plainly encourages the use of good offices, conciliation and mediation before recourse to panel procedures, so further advertising their value.

Panel proceedings

Important though consultations and the various other means of encouraging agreement are, in order to be fully effective a dispute settlement system must include arrangements for resolving differences by obtaining an authoritative decision from an independent body. For such a procedure may not only settle disputes which prove impervious to negotiation; it also encourages the parties to negotiate more seriously, and, as we saw when considering the work of the International Court, can provide an incentive to continue the search for a negotiated solution, when litigation has begun. In the GATT/WTO system, the mechanism for obtaining independent decisions is through panel proceedings, practice on which was first codified in 1979 at the end of the Tokyo Round.[19] The DSU now incorporates various changes which were agreed in 1989,[20] together with several further refinements.

The purpose of panels is to assist the Dispute Settlement Body in discharging its responsibilities under the DSU. This means that when a case is referred to a panel it is required to make an objective assessment of the facts and the law and to 'make such other findings as will assist the DSB in making the recommendations or in giving the rulings provided for in the covered agreements' (Article 11). A panel is also required to 'consult regularly with the parties to the dispute and give them adequate opportunity to develop a mutually satisfactory solution' (*ibid.*). It is therefore evident that panel proceedings have a special character, including, on the one hand, many of the typical features of arbitration, and, on the other, an underlying emphasis on conciliation.

---

[19] See Van Bael, 'The GATT dispute settlement procedure', p. 68.
[20] See Canal-Forgues and Ostrihansky, 'New developments', pp. 71–8.

The establishment of a panel requires a decision from the DSB, but, as already mentioned, a request can now be refused only if there is consensus. This means that there is effectively a 'right to a panel' and the procedure can no longer be frustrated by a state with objections to the procedure. Likewise, there is a provision to ensure that, when a panel is requested, the necessary decision is made promptly (Article 6(1)). When a panel is established, its terms of reference are normally in standard form, along the lines just indicated (Article 7(1)), but it is open to the parties to vary them by agreement.[21]

In any procedure involving compulsory decisions, the composition of the authoritative organ is clearly a crucial matter. It is therefore no surprise to find elaborate attention to this issue in the WTO system. The qualifications of panel members, which include relevant governmental or non-governmental experience,[22] are laid down in Article 8(1), and it is the task of the Secretariat to maintain a list of suitably qualified persons, indicating their particular areas of expertise (Article 8(4)). Panels are normally composed of three members, but may be composed of five, if the parties agree (Article 8(5)). The selection of panels must be made 'with a view to ensuring the independence of the members, a sufficiently diverse background and a wide spectrum of experience' (Article 8(2)). In disputes between a developed and a developing country member, the panel shall, if the latter requests, include at least one panellist from a developing country member (Article 8(10)). However, nationals of the parties to a dispute are ineligible to serve, unless the parties otherwise agree, and the same restriction applies to the nationals of intervening third parties (Article 8(3)). Panellists are nominated by the Secretariat and may only be objected to for 'compelling reasons' (Article 8(6)). In the event of disagreement over the composition of a panel, the necessary appointments are made by the Director-General in consultation with the Chairman of the DSB and the parties (Article 8(7)).

Although the panel system is essentially an elaboration of the GATT arrangements, the selection of panels has run into a number of problems in practice.[23] Because the WTO procedures have proved very popular, there has been a great demand for panels, which has led to a shortage of well-qualified panellists. The situation has been exacerbated by the increasing burden placed on panellists, as cases have become more complex and taken longer, and are also liable to generate related proceedings. At the same time, parties to disputes have become more fastidious and now regularly object

[21] The provision for standard terms of reference, which was first introduced in 1989, is also intended to eliminate delays: see Kohona, 'Dispute resolution', p. 36.

[22] On the increasing emphasis on the value of non-governmental experience, which is symptomatic of the increasingly legalistic approach to dispute settlement in GATT practice, see Kohona, 'Dispute resolution', p. 36; and Canal-Forgues and Ostrihansky, 'New developments', p. 74.

[23] See W. J. Davey, 'A permanent body for WTO dispute settlement: Desirable or practical?', in Kennedy and Southwick, *Political Economy*, p. 496.

to nominees, with the result that the Director-General is frequently called upon to make the necessary appointments. A solution to these problems might be to replace the present system of *ad hoc* panellists with a permanent body from which panels could be formed when needed. Such a 'court of international trade'[24] would have many advantages and seems a logical development of the current architecture.

Although government officials are permitted to serve as panellists, the DSU emphasises that panellists serve in their individual capacities and not as representatives of states or organisations. The element of independence, which we have seen in previous chapters is vital to the work of international judicial bodies, is not only made explicit in the DSU but is also addressed in Rules of Conduct for those acting on behalf of the WTO which were adopted in 1996.[25] The Rules, which apply to panellists, to members of the Appellate Body, to arbitrators and to experts, are contained in detailed provisions designed to ensure independence and impartiality, and which also stress the obligation to maintain confidentiality. To further its objectives, the Rules require panellists and others to disclose information which could affect or give rise to doubts as to their independence or impartiality, including information relating to financial interests, professional interests, family interests and previous statements of opinion. Procedures are also provided for dealing with allegations of non-disclosure relating to panellists and others.

The point was made earlier that the kinds of dispute with which the WTO is concerned often involve more than two parties. In the DSU provisions relating to panels, the multilateral nature of many trade disputes is taken into account in two ways. First, where more than one member requests the establishment of a panel in relation to the same matter, a single panel is to be used where possible to examine the complaints, taking into account the rights of all the members concerned (Article 9(1)). Secondly, any member having a substantial interest in a matter before a panel must be given an opportunity to be heard by the panel and to make written submissions (Article 10(2)). Although not termed 'intervention' in the DSU, this facility resembles those to be found in the corresponding provisions of the Statutes of the International Court of Justice (Articles 62 and 63) and the International Tribunal for the Law of the Sea (Articles 31 and 32), although it will be noted that the conditions under which intervention is authorised are defined differently.[26]

---

[24] See A. Porges, 'Comment: Step by step to an international trade court', in Kennedy and Southwick, *Political Economy*, p. 528.

[25] WTO, Rules of Conduct for the Understanding on Rules and Procedures Concerning the Settlement of Disputes, adopted 3 December 1996. Text in (1997) 36 ILM p. 477. An extract from this document is reproduced in document G in the appendix below.

[26] The WTO provisions are used very frequently: see Y. Iwasawa, 'Third parties before international tribunals: The ICJ and the WTO', in N. Ando, E. McWhinney and R. Wolfrum (eds.), *Liber Amicorum Judge Shigeru Oda*, The Hague, 2002, p. 871.

In a detailed section on procedures, which is further elaborated in an appendix, the DSU provides for strict time-limits to be observed in panel proceedings and establishes arrangements to govern the parties' submissions resembling those of an arbitration. Thus, in normal circumstances, a final report is to be delivered within six months, or within three months in cases of urgency (Article 12(8)). However, the panel may suspend its work at any time at the request of a complaining party for a period not exceeding twelve months (Article 12(12)). The parties' initial submissions are normally made consecutively, to permit a response, but simultaneous submissions can be authorised (Article 12(6)). Subsequent written submissions are always simultaneous and, in keeping with the normal practice, the documents submitted and the deliberations of the panel are confidential.

Since trade disputes often involve highly technical questions, the DSU lays down that a panel has the right to seek information and specialist advice from any source[27] and provides specifically for it to request an advisory opinion from an expert review group (Article 13(2)). The formation and activities of such groups are regulated in an appendix to the DSU which restricts participation in such groups to 'persons of professional standing and experience in the field in question', requires their members to act independently and disqualifies nationals of the parties to the dispute under normal circumstances. It is interesting to note that, before submitting its final report, an expert review group is required to submit a draft report to the parties with a view to obtaining their comments, which it can then take into account. The final report of the expert review group is submitted to the panel and to the parties and is advisory only.[28]

The report of a panel is produced in three stages. First, after receiving the parties' written submissions and hearing oral argument, the panel submits the descriptive sections of its draft report (i.e. the section setting out the facts and the parties' arguments) to the parties for comment. Then the panel issues an interim report, including both the descriptive sections and the panel's findings and conclusions. The parties have an opportunity to comment on this and then the panel produces its final report (Article 15(2)). Where the matter has been settled, the report is limited to a brief description of the case and to recording that a solution has been reached (Article 12(7)). Otherwise, the report must be reasoned and, if the dispute involves a developing country member, it must explicitly indicate the form in which account has been taken of relevant provisions on differential and more favourable treatment for the developing country (Article 12(11)).

[27] On the controversy over the scope of this power, which has been in issue in a number of recent cases, see E. Baroncini, 'The WTO Appellate Body and *amicus curiae* briefs', (2002) 2 Global Community YBILJ p. 181: and J. Darling and D. Hardin, '*Amicus curiae* participation in WTO dispute settlement: Reflections on the past decade', in R. Yerxa and B. Wilson (eds.), *Key Issues in WTO Dispute Settlement*, Cambridge, 2005, p. 221.

[28] See further J. Pauwelyn, 'The use of experts in WTO dispute settlement', (2002) 51 ICLQ p. 325.

When a final report has been produced, it is issued to all members of the WTO and then considered by the DSB. Members may object to the report, giving written reasons, and, when the DSB considers the report, the parties to the dispute have the right to participate fully in its consideration. Thus, a party whose arguments have been rejected by a panel can reiterate its position. However, within sixty days of a panel report being issued to the members, the DSB must adopt the report, unless there is a consensus not to do so, or a party has notified its intention to appeal. Thus, a state which objects to a panel report can no longer prevent its adoption by refusing to accept it, but, if it wishes to pursue the matter, it must invoke the new procedure for appellate review.

Although panel reports can be, and frequently are, appealed, it would be a serious mistake to under-estimate their importance. Not only are appeals, as we shall see, confined to matters of law, which makes panels the final arbiters of all questions of fact, but it is always possible for a dispute to be settled on agreed terms during the course of panel proceedings. This happened, for example, in the *Japan – Laver* case,[29] which was settled after the descriptive part of the panel's report had been issued, but before circulation of the interim report. Finally, a number of important cases have been dealt with on the basis of panel reports alone without recourse to the appeal procedure. In *EC – Biotech*,[30] for example, which raised complex scientific and technical issues, a panel decided that certain restrictions on the import and marketing of genetically modified plants and products were inconsistent with the Agreement on the Application of Sanitary and Phytosanitary Measures (SPS Agreement). Likewise, in *China – Intellectual Property*,[31] a panel upheld one of three complaints against certain features of Chinese intellectual property law and practice, on the basis of the Agreement on Trade-Related Aspects of Intellectual Property Rights (TRIPS Agreement). Both clearly raised fundamental issues, but for reasons that can only be conjectured, neither case was appealed.

Appellate review

Under the GATT dispute settlement procedure, panel reports were submitted to the GATT Council, on which all the contracting parties were represented, and approved only if there was a consensus. In contrast, under

---

[29] *Japan – Import Quotas on Dried Laver and Seasoned Laver*, Panel Report, WT/DS 323 (2006). See also J. Gomula, Introductory Note, (2007) 7 Global Community YBILJ p. 241.

[30] *European Communities – Measures Affecting the Approval and Marketing of Biotech Products*. Panel Report, WT/DS 291/R, WT/DS 292/R and WT/DS 293/R (2006). See S. Lester, Note, (2007) 101 AJIL p. 453; and M. A. Young, 'The WTO's use of relevant rules of international law: An analysis of the *Biotech* case', (2007) 56 ICLQ p. 907.

[31] *China – Measures Affecting the Protection and Enforcement of Intellectual Property Rights*, Panel Report, WT/DS 362/R (2009). See D. Gervais, Note, (2009) 103 AJIL p. 549.

the WTO system, as we have seen, reports are adopted by the DSB unless there is a consensus not to do so. This makes adoption almost automatic and means that the parties to a dispute are no longer in a position to prevent adoption. With the significance of panel reports having increased so dramatically, and new procedures for their implementation (as described below), it is not surprising that a mechanism for appellate review was considered essential. The organ created to perform this function is called the Appellate Body.

The Appellate Body is a standing organ consisting of seven individuals, of whom three, selected in rotation, serve for each case. The persons concerned are appointed by the DSB for a four-year term and may be reappointed, but only once. They must be 'persons of recognised authority, with demonstrated expertise in law, international trade and the subject matter of the covered agreements generally' (Article 17(3)). They must also be independent and broadly representative of membership in the WTO. Although serving on the Appellate Body is not a full-time occupation, members must be 'available at all times and on short notice' (*ibid.*) and must stay abreast of relevant WTO activities. As one would expect, they may not adjudicate in any case where there would be a conflict of interest.

The Appellate Body's task is to hear appeals from panel cases. Only parties to the dispute may make such an appeal, but it will be recalled that, during panel proceedings, third parties can present submissions if they have notified the DSB of a substantial interest in the matter, and a similar right extends to appellate proceedings. Appeals are limited to 'issues of law covered in the panel report and legal interpretation developed by the panel' (Article 17(6)). Since panel reports often contain extensive findings of fact, this is an important restriction on the Appellate Body's functions. Its reports may 'uphold, modify or reverse the legal findings and conclusions of the panel' (Article 17(13)) and are subject to strict time-limits, the normal duration of proceedings being no more than sixty days from the notification of the intention to appeal and the maximum duration no more than ninety days (Article 17(5)).

The proceedings of the Appellate Body, like those of panels, are confidential, and, similarly, opinions expressed in its report are anonymous. Each appellate report is submitted to the DSB and unconditionally accepted by the parties to the dispute unless the DSB decides by consensus not to adopt it within thirty days of its being issued to the members (Article 17(14)). This emphasis on speedy decision-making is further reinforced in Article 20, laying down the overall time-frame for DSB decisions. This provides that, unless otherwise agreed by the parties to the dispute, the period from the establishment of a panel to the consideration of the report shall not normally exceed nine months where there is no appeal, or twelve months where the report is appealed.

Article 17(9) of the DSU requires the Appellate Body to draw up its working procedures in consultation with the Chairman of the DSB and the Director-General. Accordingly, in February 1996, before its first case was heard, the Appellate Body issued a wide-ranging set of Rules covering all aspects of its procedures.[32] Three aspects of the Rules demonstrate the new Body's conception of its function and are of particular interest. First, in setting time-limits and dealing with other procedural issues, the Rules reflect the need for due process in what are plainly judicial proceedings. Secondly, there is an emphasis in the Rules on the independence and impartiality of the members of the Appellate Body which confirms this conception. Thirdly, in establishing how decisions will be taken and by whom, the Rules implement the principle of rotation, but skilfully combine it with the principle of collegiality. Thus while a three-member division is selected for each case randomly, all members of the Appellate Body receive the documents on every case and have the opportunity to comment before the final decision (Rules 4.2 and 4.3). In this way, while the decision in a case remains the responsibility of the division assigned to it, and can be given by a majority vote if there is no consensus (Rule 3.2), consistency and coherence in decision-making, desirable in any rule-based system, are also strongly encouraged.

The Appellate Body gave its first decision in 1996 in the *Gasoline Standards* case which was also the first dispute to be referred to a panel under the new DSU. The dispute arose out of rules concerning the standards of cleanliness for gasoline which were adopted in the United States in 1993 and which, according to Venezuela, treated domestic refiners of gasoline more favourably than importers. After consultations with the United States had failed to settle the dispute, Venezuela requested a panel under Article 6 of the DSU. The panel was established in April 1995, and, in May, Brazil joined the complaint pursuant to Article 9.

In their submissions, Venezuela and Brazil maintained, *inter alia*, that the rules in question were contrary to the relevant provisions of GATT 1994 and could not be justified under the exception in Article XX concerning conservation. The United States took the opposite view, while the European Communities and Norway, intervening under Article 10(2) of the DSU, reserved their position. After hearing the parties' arguments, the panel issued an interim report and, following a request from the United States, held a further meeting with the parties in accordance with Article 15(2). It then issued its final report in January 1996, incorporating certain revisions. The report concluded that the gasoline rules were indeed contrary to GATT 1994 since they were discriminatory, and that the provisions of Article XX

---

[32] World Trade Organization Appellate Body: Working Procedures for Appellate Review, 15 February 1996, (1996) 35 ILM p. 495.

were inapplicable. The United States then notified the DSB of its intention to appeal under Article 16.

On receipt of the US request, a three-member division was selected from the full Appellate Body which had been appointed at the end of 1995. In March 1996, the United States, Venezuela and Brazil filed their written submissions, followed shortly afterwards by the European Communities and Norway as third parties. Oral hearings were conducted, and all seven Appellate Body members convened to exchange views in accordance with Rule 4(3) of the Working Procedures. In its submissions, the United States did not contest the panel's finding of discriminatory treatment, but confined its argument to the scope and application of the exception in Article XX. In its decision,[33] which was given in May 1996, the Appellate Body rejected the panel's conclusion that Article XX was not applicable, but decided that, in view of their character, the disputed rules could not be justified. The decision therefore did not change the result of the case, but reached the same conclusion by different reasoning.

The Appellate Body's report was adopted by the DSB later in the same month, and in June the United States informed the WTO of its intention to comply with the decision. This case, typical of many dealt with subsequently by the Appellate Body, is a clear demonstration of the value of the new procedure. For it is evident that the proceedings here were successful, not only in the sense that they resolved the dispute, but also because they clarified important legal issues relating here to the scope for environmental measures under current trading agreements. Indeed, although there is no doctrine of *stare decisis* in the WTO, a feature of the dispute settlement system is the way in which reports of the Appellate Body, along with adopted panel reports, are treated as part of the GATT *acquis* and as such provide an ever-expanding body of legal precedent.[34]

Recent cases which have had the effect of elucidating members' obligations generally include *US – Gambling*,[35] which was the first case to interpret some of the key provisions of the General Agreement on Trade in Services, *Brazil – Tyres*,[36] which concerned the scope of a state's power to

---

[33] *United States – Standards for Reformulated and Conventional Gasoline*, Appellate Body Report, (1996) 35 ILM p. 603. For comment, see Petersmann, *The GATT/WTO System*, pp. 106–17; also G. Nogueira, 'The first WTO Appellate Body review', (1996) 30 (6) J. World Trade, p. 5; and M. D. Shenk, Note, (1996) 90 AJIL p. 669.

[34] See D. Palmeter and P. C. Mavroidis, 'The WTO legal system: Sources of law', (1998) 92 AJIL p. 398; and J. Cameron and K. R. Gray, 'Principles of international law in the WTO Dispute Settlement Body', (2001) 50 ICLQ p. 248. Also P. C. Mavroidis, 'No outsourcing of law? WTO law as practiced by WTO courts', (2008) 102 AJIL p. 241.

[35] *United States – Measures Affecting the Cross-Border Supply of Gambling and Betting Services*, Appellate Body Report, WT/DS 285/AB/R (2005), also in (2005) 44 ILM p. 540. See J. P. Trachtman, Note, (2005) 99 AJIL p. 861.

[36] *Brazil – Measures Affecting Imports of Retreaded Tyres*, Appellate Body Report, WT/DS 332/AB/R (2007). See K. R. Gray, Note, (2008) 102 AJIL p. 610.

impose trade restrictions to protect human health, and *US – Stainless Steel (Mexico)*,[37] which reviewed 'zeroing', a method of calculating anti-dumping duties in domestic trade remedy proceedings, favoured by the United States but opposed by many other WTO members. In this last case, one of a series to examine the practice of zeroing, the Appellate Body found that the measures in question violated WTO rules, and clarified aspects of the Anti-Dumping Agreement, as well as making some important comments on the significance of precedent in the WTO system.

With regard to the significance of practice, it is notable too that, while the Appellate Body has as its primary function clarification of states' obligations under the covered agreements, a key ancillary role is resolving procedural issues relating to the scope and operation of the DSU itself.[38] Thus, cases in recent years have called for rulings on issues such as standing, burden of proof, jurisdiction of panels and admissibility of evidence, as well as substantive matters. In the *EC – Bananas* case,[39] for example, the Appellate Body held that a member can bring a complaint without having to demonstrate a 'legal interest' in the matter; while, in the *US – Shrimp* case,[40] it ruled that panels have a discretion to accept unsolicited *amicus curiae* briefs submitted by non-governmental organisations.

As we shall see shortly, the WTO system places considerable emphasis on procedures to ensure the effective implementation of its rulings. It is therefore not surprising that a good deal of the time of the Appellate Body is taken up with cases concerned in one way or another with issues of implementation. In *US – Continued Suspension*,[41] for example, it had to consider whether the European Communities (EC) had complied with the ruling in the *EC – Hormones* case[42] and thus whether the continued imposition of sanctions on the EC by the United States could be justified. In *US – Upland Cotton (Article 21.5)*,[43] on the other hand, the question was whether the United States had itself done enough to comply with an

---

[37] *United States – Final Anti-Dumping Measures on Stainless Steel from Mexico*, Appellate Body Report, WT/DS 344/AB/R (2008). See S. Lester, Note, (2008) 102 AJIL p. 834.

[38] See Cameron and Gray, 'Principles of international law in the WTO Dispute Settlement Body', pp. 272–92. See also D. P. Steger, 'The Appellate Body and its contribution to WTO dispute settlement', in Kennedy and Southwick, *Political Economy*, p. 482 at pp. 487–92.

[39] *European Communities – Bananas*, Appellate Body Report, WT/DS 27/AB/R (1997).

[40] *United States – Shrimp*, Appellate Body Report, WT/DS 58/AB/R (1998), also in (1999) 38 ILM p. 121. See A. H. Qureshi, 'Extraterritorial shrimps, NGOs and the WTO Appellate Body', (1999) 48 ICLQ p. 199, and note 27 above.

[41] *United States – Continued Suspension of Obligations in the EC-Hormones Dispute*, Appellate Body Report, WT/DS 320/AB/R (2008). See Sungjoon Choo, Note, (2009) 103 AJIL p. 299.

[42] *European Communities – Measures Concerning Meat and Meat Products (Hormones)*, Appellate Body Report, WT/DS 26/AB/R (1998). See D. A. Wirth, Note, (1998) 92 AJIL p. 755.

[43] *United States – Subsidies on Upland Cotton Recourse to Article 21.5 of the DSU by Brazil*, Appellate Body Report, WT/DS 267/AB/RW (2008). See K. H. Cross, Note, (2009) 103 AJIL p. 110.

earlier ruling. *Mexico – Taxes*[44] was yet another compliance case, although there Mexico sought to justify the imposition of taxes on certain soft drinks and beverages on the ground that the United States had refused to resolve a related dispute under a regional trade agreement. However, Mexico's attempt to use the WTO Agreement to justify counter-measures for breach of a separate international obligation was unsuccessful.

Since there is always a great deal at stake in trade disputes, and the right of appeal under the DSU is automatic, it was anticipated that cases would be referred from panels to the Appellate Body as a matter of routine and that the latter would accordingly be very busy. This duly happened, with the result that, in its first six years, the Appellate Body issued reports in forty-five cases, on thirty-three distinct matters. In the first two years, nearly all panel reports were appealed, but, as the system has matured, the proportion has fallen, partly no doubt because the possibilities and limitations of the appeal process are now better appreciated, and partly because the progressive clarification of the rules and principles of the WTO system through the jurisprudence of the Appellate Body, along with their implementation by panels, has reduced the scope for argument. Even so, currently more than half the cases referred to panels are appealed, indicating the value which states attach to this facility.

Although not all panel reports are appealed, the large number of cases being referred to the WTO has created a formidable workload for the Appellate Body, an effect compounded by the range and complexity of the cases, which, as has been seen, now sometimes involve claims under the new Uruguay Round agreements, as well as more traditional claims under the GATT. Proposals to expand the Appellate Body were considered, but not taken up, when the DSB reviewed the DSU in 1998 and 1999, and other proposals for modifying its workings have been made subsequently.[45] Since the speedy resolution of disputes is one of the main aims of the DSU, changes may well need to be made. In a relatively short time, however, the Appellate Body has established a record of solid competence and contributed significantly to the success of the whole system.

Implementation of rulings and recommendations

Article 19(1) of the DSU concerns the results of the panel process and provides that, where a panel or the Appellate Body concludes that a measure is inconsistent with a covered agreement, it must recommend that the member concerned bring the measure into conformity with the agreement. In

---

[44] *Mexico – Taxes on Soft Drinks and Other Beverages*, Appellate Body Report, WT/DS 308/AB/R (2006). See J. Gomula, Introductory Note (2007) 7 Global Community YBILJ p. 241 at p. 243.
[45] See Steger, 'The Appellate Body', pp. 485–6.

addition, the panel or Appellate Body may suggest ways in which the member could implement the recommendations. With adoption of the report of the panel or Appellate Body by the DSB now subject only to the negative consensus procedure, the question of implementation of recommendations and rulings received close attention during the negotiation of the DSU, and two quite detailed provisions finally emerged: Article 21, concerned with surveillance by the DSB, and Article 22, concerned with compensation and the suspension of concessions.

Article 21 is based on the principle that prompt compliance with recommendations or rulings of the DSB is essential for effective dispute resolution, and therefore specifies a strict time-frame. Within thirty days of the adoption of a panel or Appellate Body report, the member concerned must inform the DSB of its intentions with regard to implementation. If immediate compliance is impracticable, the member has a reasonable period in which to comply, but this shall not normally exceed fifteen months from the date of adoption of the report. In the event of a dispute over the period of time allowed, the matter is to be determined by binding arbitration (Article 21(3)(c)). If, on the other hand, there is a dispute over whether the necessary measures have been taken, it is to be resolved through the normal procedures of the DSU, using the original panel wherever possible (Article 21(5)). The DSB is required to keep the whole issue of implementation under surveillance and, when doing so, specifically to take into account the interests of developing states.

The principle of surveillance was first adopted in 1989, along with the concept of a reasonable time for compliance, and so neither is new. However, no means of determining what a reasonable time might be was laid down, and so in this respect the DSU represents a significant step forward. It must be appreciated, however, that implementation of dispute settlement rulings is not automatic, and, as a leading commentator has pointed out, in practice 'will continue to be influenced by the relative economic and political weight of the parties to the dispute'.[46] This lends particular significance to Article 22, concerned with the remedies available when recommendations and rulings are not implemented within a reasonable time.

The relevant remedies are compensation (i.e. trade concessions by the losing party) and suspension of concessions, the difference between them being that compensation requires an agreement between the states concerned and involves recompense, whereas suspension of concessions is essentially a penalty at the disposal of the state which brought the complaint, if compensation cannot be agreed.[47] Article 22(1) codifies existing GATT practice

---

[46] Petersmann, *The GATT/WTO System*, p. 192. For the record on implementation under GATT and the WTO, see Busch and Reinhardt, 'Testing international trade law', pp. 470–4.

[47] Whether the penalty's function is to induce compliance, or simply to restore the balance of trade benefits, is a question on which there are differing views. See, for example, A. Kotera, 'On

by laying down that both compensation and suspension of concessions are temporary measures and that full implementation, avoiding the need for either, is preferred. Although compensation is voluntary, a state which has failed to comply with a recommendation or ruling within a reasonable time must enter into negotiations with the complaining state, if requested 'with a view to developing mutually acceptable compensation' (Article 22(2)). If no satisfactory compensation has been agreed within twenty days of the expiry of the reasonable period of time, the complaining state may request the DSB to authorise the suspension of concessions or other obligations under the covered agreement in relation to the state in default.

Counter-measures, which is what suspension of concessions or other obligations are, can be an effective means of encouraging compliance with rulings and recommendations, but also have the potential to disrupt international trade very seriously, which plainly runs counter to the aims of the DSU. To keep retaliation within bounds and control its effects, the DSU first specifies the nature of the counter-measures permitted, then places such measures within a tight regulatory framework.[48] Thus, on the first point, Article 22(3) requires that, wherever possible, an injured member shall limit its retaliation to the same sector, and Article 22(4) that the level of suspension of concessions shall be equivalent to the level of transgression. Procedurally, members agree that retaliation must be authorised by the DSB (Article 23(2)(c)). It is true that authorisation of retaliation is subject to the negative consensus procedure and will therefore usually be automatic. However, to prevent abuse, a state which objects to the level of suspension proposed, or claims that inappropriate measures have been imposed, is entitled to have these matters determined by binding arbitration (Article 22(6) and (7)). As one would expect, any suspension of concessions applies only until the failure which made it necessary has been removed, or a mutually satisfactory solution has been agreed. The situation will in any case continue to be monitored by the DSB, since the surveillance obligation in Article 21(6) extends to cases where compensation has been provided or concessions have been suspended.

Experience with these arrangements has in practice revealed the not unexpected fact that, while the DSU is generally good at generating adopted reports, securing their implementation, particularly in sensitive or controversial cases, may be subject to considerable delay. One reason, as a

the legal character of retaliation in the Word Trade Organization system', in Ando, McWhinney and Wolfrum, *Liber Amicorum*, p. 911; and D. Palmeter and S. A. Alexandrov, '"Inducing compliance" in WTO dispute settlement', in Kennedy and Southwick, *Political Economy*, p. 646.

[48] See Kohona, 'Dispute resolution', pp. 42–3. For discussion of the operation of the counter-measures regime and possible alternatives, see J. Pauwelyn, 'Enforcement and countermeasures in the WTO', (2000) 94 AJIL p. 335; and S. Charnovitz, 'Rethinking WTO trade sanctions', (2001) 95 AJIL p. 792. See also S. Charnovitz, 'Should the teeth be pulled? An analysis of WTO sanctions', in Kennedy and Southwick, *Political Economy*, p. 602.

shrewd observer has pointed out, is that the system described above pro-vides cost-free opportunities for foot-dragging by the losing party.[49] In the *EC – Hormones* case,[50] for example, the report of the Appellate Body was adopted in February 1998, but the EC asked for arbitration to determine a reasonable time for compliance in accordance with Article 21(3)(c). In May 1998, this was set at fifteen months from the date of adoption of the report (February 1998), giving a deadline of May 1999. At that deadline, however, the EC had still not complied with the report and so the United States requested authorisation to suspend concessions. This in turn pro-duced a further request for arbitration from the EU under Article 22(6). It was therefore only when that arbitration had taken place, in July 1999, that the retaliatory tariffs, authorised by the WTO and intended to encourage compliance with a ruling some eighteen months earlier, finally came into effect.

The elaborate provisions of Articles 21 and 22 are further evidence of the shift towards a legalistic approach to dispute settlement in the WTO system. After 'legalising' panel procedures and creating the Appellate Body, it was a logical step to tighten the arrangements for implementation and address the issue of non-compliance. The option of avoiding retaliation by agreeing compensation is in keeping with the general emphasis in the DSU on encouraging the parties' agreement, while the regulation of counter-measures, and in particular the undertaking that such measures will not be taken outside the WTO system, is a significant advance. There is, as we have seen, also recognition that disputes over the application of these provisions are inevitable. It is in keeping with the general approach in the DSU that the procedure laid down for dealing with such disputes should include mandatory arbitration, resulting in a binding decision.

Arbitration

Arbitration has always been available as a means of dispute settlement which parties to the GATT could select, but until recently was rarely used in practice. This is no doubt because the need for a rule-based method of dealing with disputes was largely satisfied by the development of panel procedures, which, especially in their latest form, have much in common with arbitration. However, the two processes are still distinct, and the latter is the subject of a separate article in the DSU, which recognises that expeditious arbitration within the WTO 'can facilitate the solution of certain disputes' (Article 25(1)). This point is borne out by a number of disputes in which

---

[49] See G. N. Horlick, 'Problems with the compliance structure of the WTO dispute resolution process', in Kennedy and Southwick, *Political Economy*, p. 636.
[50] See note 42 above.

arbitration has been used successfully and its designation in the DSU as the mandatory procedure in the cases noted earlier.

In 1990, Canada and the EC agreed to use arbitration in a dispute over Article 28 of the GATT, known as the *Article XXVIII Rights* case. The dispute, which concerned negotiation rights with regard to wheat, was referred to a single arbitrator, who concluded that, in a bilateral agreement of 1962, Canada had retained certain rights under Article 28, but relinquished others. Nearly thirty years earlier, in 1962, a dispute between the EC and the United States over the value of poultry exports was referred for an 'advisory opinion' to a panel appointed by the GATT Council.[51] Despite appearances, this too was an arbitration, since the award, which involved issues of law as well as fact, was presented directly to the parties and treated by them as binding. These awards settled the disputes concerned, and, though exceptional, show that, in trade disputes, as elsewhere, arbitration can be useful.

As already mentioned, the two situations in which arbitration is mandatory both concern disputes which may arise at the implementation stage under Articles 21 and 22. With these exceptions, arbitration under the WTO system requires mutual agreement, and, since the DSU has no provisions at all on relevant procedures, it is for the parties to arrange the details, including the names of the arbitrators, the procedure to be followed and the applicable law. This makes WTO involvement more limited than in the panel process, a difference which is emphasised by the fact that arbitration awards are binding on the parties immediately and do not need adoption by the Dispute Settlement Body. By the same token, of course, arbitral awards are binding *only* on the parties and, unlike adopted panel reports, cannot create obligations for third parties. Consequently, whereas the DSU contains provisions to protect the interests of third parties in panel proceedings which have already been mentioned, it makes it clear that, when arbitration takes place, the normal rule applies and third states can only become a party to the proceedings with the agreement of the litigating states (Article 25(3)).

Although the DSU reflects the party autonomy that has traditionally been the hallmark of international arbitration, its provisions are designed to ensure that the arbitration of trade disputes does not become an exclusively bilateral affair, but is integrated into the WTO system. Thus, states proposing to employ arbitration must notify other members of their agreement before the process begins to give them an opportunity to apply to become a party (Article 25(2)). When the award is made, it must be notified to the DSB and to the council or committee of any relevant agreement, where any member may raise a point relating to it (Article 25(3)). This is likely to be particularly important if other states disagree with the arbitrators' conclusions, and provides an opportunity for the DSB as a whole to indicate any reservations.

---

[51] See Iwasawa, 'Settlement of disputes', pp. 390–1; and H. Walker, 'Dispute settlement: The chicken war', (1964) 58 AJIL p. 671.

Whether others agree or not, the award is always binding on the parties and Article 25(4) underlines this by providing that at the implementation stage, involving Articles 21 and 22, the role of the DSB with regard to arbitral awards and panel reports which have been adopted is identical.

The WTO system in context

The Agreement Establishing the World Trade Organization came into force in January 1995, together with the Dispute Settlement Understanding which is in Annex 2 to the WTO Agreement. Judged by the extent to which the DSU is actually used, it has been outstandingly successful. In its first ten years of operation, more than 300 requests for consultations were made, leading to eighty-three panel reports and fifty-six from the Appellate Body.[52] Despite more selective recourse in recent years, the WTO system is plainly one that the members of the WTO are prepared to use. There are, of course, other criteria to consider as well. An effective dispute settlement must do more than generate rulings – it must produce good, in the sense of prompt and adequately reasoned, decisions and also be an effective procedure for resolving disputes. The point has been made above that reports of the panels and the Appellate Body are generally of good quality, and, while compliance is an issue that often needs attention, given what is at stake in trade disputes, the record is in this respect a vast improvement on less structured arrangements. There is also the point that, as explained in earlier chapters, the existence of an arrangement for compulsory dispute settlement has in itself a significant, though immeasurable, effect in discouraging extreme claims and promoting moderation.

If practice, which is more fully examined in the specialist literature on the WTO, is one aspect of the DSU calling for consideration, it is also useful to make a more general assessment and place these developments in context, a task which is, of course, greatly assisted by the fact that, in many respects, the DSU constitutes a distillation of four decades of experience and has already been the subject of a good deal of analysis. When reviewing the corresponding provisions of the 1982 Law of the Sea Convention in the previous chapter, it was noted that, once the key decision has been taken to make arrangements for dispute settlement an integral part of a treaty, the characteristics of the particular system are a matter of who, what, when and how. Though styled an 'understanding', the DSU is an integral part of the WTO Agreement, and according to Article 2(2) is legally binding.[53] It will therefore be convenient to put the DSU in context by adopting the same analytical framework.

---

[52] For details, see Yerxa and Wilson, *Key Issues*, pp. 271–89.
[53] See Kohona, 'Dispute resolution', p. 45.

The DSU, as already noted, deals with the issue of 'who' by utilising the familiar processes of consultation, good offices/conciliation/mediation (which are not distinguished) and arbitration, together with the panel process, a distinctive but established GATT procedure, and a process of appellate review through the new Appellate Body. Behind all this stands another new organ, the Dispute Settlement Body, with the political responsibility for integrating the dispute settlement system and ensuring its effectiveness. Panel proceedings, which have always been *sui generis*, are brought closer to arbitration by the emphasis in the DSU and the 1996 Rules of Conduct on the independence and impartiality of panellists and by the new negative consensus procedure for the adoption of their reports. The latter in turn prompted the creation of the Appellate Body, whose conception of its juridical functions can be seen in the 1996 Working Procedures.

The question 'what' is answered in the provisions dealing with the coverage and application of the DSU which provide that it embraces all the covered agreements. This, as we have seen, reflects the objective of the WTO to bring together old and new agreements in a single instrument, with, as a corollary, a unified system of dispute settlement. Thus, in principle, the procedures laid down in the DSU are available in respect of all the relevant agreements and the jurisdiction of panels and the Appellate Body is not normally restricted as to subject matter. It should be noted, however, that certain covered agreements contain special or additional rules and procedures, and, as these prevail in case of conflict, some disputes are subject to different arrangements.[54] Moreover, wide though the WTO system is, it is limited to the covered agreements. Accordingly, disputes involving only bilateral treaties, or regional agreements such as the 1992 North American Free Trade Agreement (NAFTA),[55] lie outside the DSU and must be dealt with elsewhere.

In answering the question 'when', the DSU contains a number of features of interest. In the first place, the choice of means, which is such an important feature of Part XV of the Law of the Sea Convention, is almost wholly absent. Although states are encouraged to settle their disputes by agreement, if they fail to do so, the complaining party can request a panel. After the panel has reported, recourse to the Appellate Body is again a matter of right, and, when the 'litigation' stage is complete, the DSB takes over. It is true that there is no obligation to request a panel and that arbitration is mentioned as a possible alternative. This is nevertheless conceptually a 'one track' system.

In the same connection, it is relevant to note that, by subscribing to the WTO Agreement, states not only forgo the right to impose unilateral

---

[54] See Article 1(2) of the DSU; and Petersmann, *The GATT/WTO System*, pp. 223–32, examining the problems which this provision could give rise to.

[55] Text in (1993) 32 ILM p. 289 and p. 605. The dispute settlement provisions in Chapter 20 may be found at pp. 693–9.

sanctions, but also undertake to resolve pertinent disputes through the DSU exclusively. So, for example, if a dispute arises which could be resolved either through the DSU or through the procedures of an agreement such as NAFTA, the former should be employed.[56] A final point concerns the relation between the DSU and domestic litigation. The WTO Agreement includes numerous provisions designed to strengthen judicial and other procedures at the national level, because here, as elsewhere, effective domestic arrangements tend to minimise international disputes. On the other hand, under the WTO Agreement, as under the GATT, exhaustion of domestic remedies is not a condition for activating the DSU system. Thus, even if domestic litigation is in progress, because trade disputes involve treaty rights, a state is entitled to begin the DSU procedure immediately, without waiting for the outcome.[57]

The last issue, 'how', concerns the criteria for decision-making and the object of the proceedings. These are particularly significant aspects of the DSU system in view of the changes which emerged during the Uruguay Round in the way many of the participants approach trade disputes and want to see them handled. The primary goal of the DSU, as of the former arrangements, is to secure a mutually acceptable solution. However, whereas under the old system this 'political' approach predominated, under its successor, if accommodation proves impossible, juridical machinery of a somewhat inexorable character comes into play. This switch from what has been termed a 'power-oriented' approach to a 'rule-oriented' approach[58] is exemplified in the change from positive to negative consensus for decision-making in the DSB, in the increasing assimilation of panel proceedings to arbitration, in the creation of the Appellate Body, and in the stricter arrangements for supervising decisions. It is therefore no surprise to find the purpose of the DSU defined in Article 3(2) as 'to preserve the rights and obligations of Members under the covered agreements, and to clarify the existing provisions of those agreements in accordance with customary rules of interpretation of public international law'.[59]

The DSU, though relatively recent, has already provided its value and, while a developing system, can never be thought of as a finished product,

---

[56] See Iwasawa, 'Settlement of disputes', p. 400. For an outline of the NAFTA arrangements, which influenced the drafting of the DSU, see J. L. Siqueiros, 'NAFTA institutional arrangements and dispute settlement procedures', (1992/3) 23 Calif. Western Int. LJ p. 383.

[57] For discussion of the merits of this approach, see Petersmann, *The GATT/WTO System*, pp. 233–40.

[58] See M. M. T. A. Brus, *Third Party Dispute Settlement in an Interdependent World*, Dordrecht, 1995, p. 31; and J. H. Jackson, 'Perspectives on the jurisprudence of international trade: Costs and benefits of legal procedures in the United States', (1984) 82 Mich. L. Rev. p. 1570 at pp. 1571–2.

[59] See further J. Pauwelyn, 'The role of public international law in the WTO: How far can we go?', (2001) 95 AJIL p. 535; and the references in note 34 above. See also J. Pauwelyn, *Conflict of Norms in Public International Law*, Cambridge, 2003.

its impact to date has been very positive. When considering the future, however, two general points concerning the relevance of a rule-oriented approach to disputes in this field should be borne in mind. The first is that trade disputes are complex, often involve changing economic and political interests and are capable of arousing strong national passions. If this makes peaceful methods of resolving such disputes indispensable, it also means that methods which provide opportunities for accommodation and addressing new situations are at least as important as those which emphasise existing rules.[60] As already noted, this has not been lost sight of in the DSU. The other general point is that, in international trade law, as elsewhere, an insistence on established rules can only be effective if the rules in question are not only interpreted competently, but also regarded as appropriate, and as such command general acceptance. In the WTO system, interpretation is the responsibility of panels and the Appellate Body, but the rules they apply are made by states, which thus bear a legislative, as well as an executive, responsibility for the future of the Dispute Settlement Understanding.[61]

---

[60] In this connection it is significant that Article 3(7) of the DSU provides that: 'Before bringing a case, a Member shall exercise its judgment as to whether action under these procedures would be fruitful'; see, on this point, Kohona, 'Dispute resolution', p. 29.

[61] See N. Saiki, 'WTO procedures for the settlement of disputes – Their formation: A practitioner's view', in Young and Iwasawa, *Trilateral Perspectives*, p. 403 at p. 417. See also L. Bartels, 'The separation of powers in the WTO: How to avoid judicial activism', (2004) 53 ICLQ p. 861; and J. H. Jackson, *Sovereignty, the WTO and Changing Fundamentals of International Law*, Cambridge, 2006.

10

The United Nations

The reference of disputes to international political institutions has a history as long as that of arbitration. For present purposes, however, it is unnecessary to go further back than 1919, when, with the creation of the League of Nations as a reaction to the First World War, the first attempt was made to establish a universal organisation with broad responsibilities in this area. Following the failure of the League, or more accurately its member states, to take effective action to forestall a second bloodbath, a fresh effort to bring disputes within the field of operations of a world organisation was made with the creation of the United Nations Organization in 1945.[1]

The purposes of the United Nations, as set out in Article 1 of the Charter, are to maintain international peace and security, to develop friendly relations among nations, to achieve international co-operation in solving problems of an economic, social, cultural or humanitarian character and in promoting human rights, and to be a centre for harmonising the actions of states in attaining these ends. Of these interrelated purposes, the maintenance of international peace and security occupies the primary place. Here, according to the Charter, the Organization has two distinct responsibilities: to bring about cessation of armed conflict whenever it occurs, and to assist the parties to international disputes to settle their differences by peaceful means. The scope of the Organization's powers in this second area, the ways in which they are exercised in practice and the effectiveness of the United Nations' contribution are the subject of this chapter.

The machinery of the Organization

There are three organs of the United Nations with principal roles to play in the peaceful settlement of disputes: the Security Council, the General Assembly and the Secretariat.

---

[1] There is an enormous literature dealing with all aspects of the United Nations. In addition to the works cited below, the following studies contain particularly useful reviews of the activities of the Organization in the field of dispute settlement: K. V. Raman (ed.), *Dispute Settlement through the United Nations*, New York, 1977; UNITAR, *The United Nations and the Maintenance of International Peace and Security*, Dordrecht, 1987; A. Roberts and B. Kingsbury (eds.), *United Nations, Divided World*, 2nd edn, Oxford, 1993; N. D. White, *Keeping the Peace*, Manchester, 1993; and C. Peck, *The United Nations as a Dispute Settlement System*, The Hague, 1996. See also K. A. Mingst and M. P. Karns, *The United Nations in the Post Cold-War Era*, 2nd edn, Boulder, CO, 2000; and N. D. White, *The United Nations System*, Boulder, CO, 2002.

The Security Council's powers derive from Chapter VI of the Charter, which is wholly concerned with the pacific settlement of disputes. Apart from Article 38, which entitles the Council to make recommendations with a view to the settlement of any dispute if all the parties so request, its competence is limited to disputes 'the continuance of which is likely to endanger the maintenance of international peace and security'. It is therefore clear that, although Article 2(3) imposes a general obligation on member states to settle disputes by peaceful means, only the more serious disputes, or those which have become serious, are regarded as the Council's concern.

The specialised role of the Security Council receives further emphasis in Article 33(1), which provides that the parties to such a dispute shall 'first of all' seek a solution by negotiation or some other peaceful means of their own choice, and Article 52(2), which provides that members of regional arrangements or agencies 'shall make every effort to achieve pacific settlement of local disputes' through such arrangements or agencies before referring them to the Security Council. However, it is worth noting that, despite these priorities, the Council has the right to recommend appropriate procedures or methods of adjustment under Article 36(1) at any time. Furthermore, the effect of Articles 11(3), 35(1) and 99 is to enable the Council to consider a matter at the request of the General Assembly, a member state or the Secretary-General, whether or not the states involved consent to its doing so.[2]

Of course, it is for the Council to decide by vote whether to place a particular matter on its agenda, but the important point is that its authority to consider a dispute, unlike that of a conciliation commission or court of arbitration, does not depend on the consent of the states concerned. Moreover, in deciding whether it should take a matter up, the Council is free to adopt a broader conception of an international 'dispute' than might be acceptable in a judicial forum. When this is combined with the authority under Article 34 to act in 'any situation which might lead to international friction', as well as in disputes, it can be seen that the Council's jurisdiction can be extended to virtually all matters of international significance.

Finally, if the provisions of Chapter VII are read alongside those of Chapter VI, it is evident that a dispute or situation which leads to an actual 'threat to the peace, breach of the peace or act of aggression' activates the provisions of the Charter concerned with political and military sanctions. As a result, the Council's authority in the field of dispute settlement, unlike that of, say, the International Court, is complemented, at least on paper, by powers of

---

[2] For a more detailed account of these provisions, see C. M. H. Waldock (ed.), *International Disputes: The Legal Aspects*, London, 1972, Chapter 3 (D. W. Bowett). Bowett points out that, under Article 35(1) of the Charter, any member of the United Nations has a right of recourse to the Security Council, and, under Article 37(1), the parties to a dispute have a duty to refer it to the Council should they fail to settle it by negotiation etc.

enforcement in the very circumstances in which they are most likely to be needed.

The powers of the General Assembly are less elaborate and can be dealt with more briefly. Under Articles 10 to 14 of the Charter the Assembly is given broad powers of discussion and recommendation. Its powers of discussion cover any questions or matters within the scope of the Charter. This plainly includes the settlement of all disputes except those which are 'essentially within the domestic jurisdiction of any state' as provided by Article 2(7). However, this limitation, which applies to all United Nations organs, including the Security Council, is less significant than it may appear. In practice it has not prevented the General Assembly from discussing human rights, civil conflict and other highly sensitive 'domestic' issues.

The Assembly's powers of recommendation likewise cover the settlement of disputes and under Article 14 extend to the recommendation of 'measures for the peaceful adjustment of any situation, regardless of origin, which it deems likely to impair the general welfare or friendly relations among nations'. It is evident here that the Assembly's powers of recommendation are not confined to issues of peace and security and so are somewhat broader than those of the Security Council. It must be noted, however, that Article 14 is subject to Article 12(1) which provides that:

> While the Security Council is exercising in respect of any dispute or situation the functions assigned to it in the present Charter, the General Assembly shall not make any recommendation with regard to that dispute or situation unless the Security Council so requests.

This limitation also applies to the Assembly's broad powers of recommendation under Article 10, its competence in the field of international peace and security under Article 11(2) and its proceedings in respect of matters brought to its attention by a non-member state under Article 35(2). Thus although the role which the Charter assigns to the General Assembly in relation to disputes is by no means negligible, as regards issues of peace and security the intention was to preserve the primacy of the Security Council.

The powers of the Secretariat are contained in Articles 98 and 99 and will be considered later.

The Security Council and General Assembly in action

Both the Security Council and the General Assembly have made extensive use of their powers to make recommendations to states concerning the settlement of disputes. Under Article 33(2) of the Charter the Council may call upon the parties to settle a dispute by the peaceful means specified in Article 33(1), and under Article 36(1) it can recommend the specific means to be employed. Thus in 1976 the Council called upon Greece and Turkey 'to resume direct negotiations over their differences' with regard to the Aegean

Sea dispute and appealed to them 'to do everything within their power to ensure that this results in mutually acceptable solutions'.[3]

The General Assembly exercises similar powers, and, like the Security Council, when it acts under Articles 37(2) and 38, can go so far as to recommend possible terms of settlement. In 1948, for example, in a recommendation addressed to the incipient Arab–Israeli struggle, the General Assembly set out an elaborate plan for the future of Palestine. The recommendation, incidentally, like so many others on this intractable issue, did nothing to resolve the dispute, a reminder of the self-evident, but basic, point that recommendations, which are not binding on the members of the United Nations, are also highly variable in their effects.

Another activity in which the Security Council and the General Assembly have been extensively engaged is fact-finding, and on numerous occasions both bodies have exercised their powers to set up subsidiary organs for this purpose. In the Corfu Channel dispute, the Security Council established a fact-finding sub-committee to investigate evidence relating to the incident which had already been laid before the Council. Usually, however, the purpose of establishing such a body has been to conduct an on-the-spot investigation. Among examples of such bodies are the Commission of Investigation set up by the Security Council to investigate incidents on the Greek frontier in 1947, a purely fact-finding operation, and the Special Committee on the Balkans set up by the General Assembly later in the same year, which combined fact-finding activities in the area with elements of mediation and conciliation. More recently, the Security Council appointed an International Independent Investigation Commission to assist the Lebanese authorities with the investigation of the terrorist bombing that killed former Prime Minister Rafiq Hariri in 2005.[4]

Assisting the parties to a dispute with negotiation, for which mediation and conciliation, together with good offices, provide possible means, is the third and perhaps the most important step open to the Organization.[5] The existence of the United Nations itself facilitates diplomacy by bringing together ambassadors in a setting in which unobtrusive contacts are easily arranged and outside states can make an effort to encourage

---

[3] Security Council Resolution 395 (1976) referred to by the International Court in the *Aegean Sea Continental Shelf*, Interim Protection, Order of 11 September 1976, [1976] ICJ Rep. p. 3 at p. 12.

[4] Security Council Resolution 1595 (2005). The Commission's report to the Council's setting up a special tribunal, composed of Lebanese and international judges to try those accused of the crime. See N. D. White and M. Saul, 'Legal means of dispute settlement in the field of collective security: The quasi-judicial powers of the Security Council', in D. French, M. Saul and N. D. White (eds.), *International Law and Dispute Settlement: New Problems and Techniques*, Oxford, 2010, at p. 191 and p. 202.

[5] An excellent study of this form of assistance may be found in the editor's contribution to Raman (ed.), *Dispute Settlement*, pp. 367–517. For recent activities of this kind by the UN in Abkhazia, Croatia and El Salvador, see M. C. Greenberg, J. H. Barton and M. E. McGuinness, *Words over War*, Lanham, MD, 2000, at pp. 15, 76 and 161.

settlement behind the scenes, without the publicity and complications of formal intervention.

When quiet diplomacy is not enough, more open methods may be attempted. One such method, much favoured in the early years of the United Nations, is to establish a special committee to assist negotiations. In 1947, the Security Council set up a Committee of Good Offices, consisting of the representatives of Belgium, Australia and the United States, to promote the resumption of negotiations over the independence of Indonesia and to supervise the implementation of a cease-fire between Dutch and Indonesian forces. This was later reconstituted as the United Nations Commission for Indonesia, and supervised the transition to independence. Likewise, in 1950, the General Assembly set up (among other bodies) a Good Offices Committee, consisting of the President of the Assembly and the representatives of Sweden and Mexico, to explore the possibility of a settlement of the Korean War.

Although such committees can be useful, and in the first case mentioned certainly helped to produce the desired result, their tendency to reflect the political divisions of the parent organ and the slowness and indecision characteristic of committees everywhere have handicapped their operations and encouraged the search for alternatives.[6] From the earliest days of the United Nations, the exercise of good offices was sometimes entrusted to individuals rather than to the representatives of member states, and, while this in no sense guarantees success, its advantages have led to its being utilised on an increasing scale. Thus, in 1948, the General Assembly appointed Count Bernadotte United Nations Mediator for Palestine, with the task of arranging for the operation of essential common services, securing the protection of the holy places and promoting 'a peaceful adjustment of the future situation' in Palestine.[7] Similarly, in the dispute between India and Pakistan over Kashmir, the Security Council appointed a Canadian, General McNaughton, to act as 'informal mediator' on the question of demilitarisation of the area in 1949; an Australian, Sir Owen Dixon, as 'United Nations Representative' with a similar brief in 1950; an American, Dr Frank Graham, as his successor in 1951; and a Swede, Dr Gunnar Jarring, with essentially the same task in 1957.[8]

The reference of disputes to individual mediators received its most important boost with the election of Dag Hammarskjöld as Secretary-General in

---

[6] See M. W. Zacher, 'The Secretary-General and the United Nations' function of peaceful settlement', (1966) 20 Int. Org. p. 724.

[7] For an account of this mission and Bernadotte's previous work, see R. Hewins, *Count Folke Bernadotte – His Life and Work*, London, 1949. It will be recalled that Bernadotte's assassination precipitated the International Court's advisory opinion in the *Reparation for Injuries* case, [1949] ICJ Rep. p. 174.

[8] For further details, see E. Luard, *A History of the United Nations*, vol. I, London, 1982, Chapter 14.

1953. In 1954, he was instructed by the General Assembly to seek the release of eleven American airmen held by the Chinese since their aircraft had been shot down during the Korean War some twenty months before. Instructed to use 'the means most appropriate in his judgment', Hammarskjöld secured an invitation to Peking and, after discussion and some delay, the airmen were eventually returned. Not surprisingly, the success of this personal diplomacy led to further requests to act in this capacity and, as we shall see, to a more active role for the Secretariat generally.

Leaving aside the option of taking coercive measures under Chapter VII, which is the prerogative of the Security Council and discussed below, a final possibility open to the Security Council and the General Assembly is to refer a dispute to a regional organisation[9] or another body for settlement. Under Article 11(2) of the Charter, the General Assembly must refer questions relating to the maintenance of international peace and security on which action is necessary to the Security Council 'either before or after discussion'. Other questions may be referred at any time. Although there is no corresponding duty on the Council to refer disputes to the Assembly, a power to make such references may be presumed.

Besides referring disputes to each other, the Council and Assembly can refer disputes to other organs of the United Nations. This has occasionally been done by the Council and more rarely by the Assembly. Article 36(3) of the Charter lays down that, in making recommendations for settlement, the Security Council should take into consideration that legal disputes should 'as a general rule' be referred to the International Court. However, neither the Council nor the Assembly can really be said to have encouraged use of the Court. In 1947, the Council recommended that the parties to the Corfu Channel dispute refer the case to the Court, but, to date, this is the only contentious case where this has occurred.

Requests for advisory opinions have also been sparse. As we have seen in Chapter 6, there can be no question of using advisory proceedings to nullify the consensual basis of the Court's contentious jurisdiction. But the fact that the reference of the *Peace Treaties* case[10] by the Assembly in 1949 was the only occasion on which the legal aspects of a dispute were referred to the Court in the first twenty-five years of the United Nations indicates a clear preference for the use of political means of settlement. This is still the case, although the reference of the *Namibia* case[11] by the Council in 1970 and the *Western Sahara* case[12] by the Assembly in 1974 suggest a willingness to make use of the Court for disputes over decolonisation, which the forward-looking opinions handed down in those cases did nothing to discourage.

---

[9] The relation between regional organisations and the United Nations is discussed in the next chapter.

[10] [1950] ICJ Rep. p. 65 and p. 221. For discussion of this advisory opinion, see Chapters 5 and 6.

[11] [1971] ICJ Rep. p. 16.   [12] [1975] ICJ Rep. p. 12.

Other kinds of issues too have been referred on occasion. Thus, the *Nuclear Weapons* case[13] was decided in 1996, the *Construction of a Wall* case[14] in 2004, and the *Kosovo* case[15] in 2010, in each instance at the request of the General Assembly. These opinions would never have been asked for by the Security Council, where involving the International Court was opposed by Permanent Members. This clearly demonstrates the Assembly's independence. At the same time, however, the impact of an advisory opinion is always likely to be affected by how it was requested and so this too is a factor to be borne in mind.

The role of the Secretary-General

The work of the Secretary-General in the field of dispute settlement falls into two distinct parts. On the one hand, there are the functions delegated by the Security Council and General Assembly under Article 98; on the other hand, there are the various actions undertaken at the request of interested parties, or on the Secretary-General's own initiative by virtue of his powers under Article 99.

The authority to investigate the possibilities of settlement given to the Secretary-General by the General Assembly in 1954 in the dispute over the detained American airmen set a precedent which has been followed in many subsequent cases.[16] In its resolution on the crisis caused by the detention of the United States diplomatic and consular staff in Tehran, for example, the Security Council called on Iran to release the personnel of the embassy immediately and requested the Secretary-General to lend his good offices for the immediate implementation of the resolution. In pursuance of his mandate to take all appropriate measures to this end, Secretary-General Waldheim first visited Tehran, and then set up a commission to investigate the dispute. The Commission was unable to resolve the crisis, but at least maintained contact, demonstrating that, when called upon for his good offices, the Secretary-General enjoys a wide measure of discretion and may, if he thinks it necessary, establish subordinate bodies.

In January 1980, shortly after the Soviet invasion of Afghanistan, the General Assembly passed a resolution asking the Secretary-General to use his good offices with regard to the situation. This was the first of a number of resolutions on this question, which ultimately led the Secretary-General to appoint one of his subordinates, Diego Cordovez, to serve as his personal representative in negotiations between Pakistan, the Soviet Union and Afghanistan on the procedure for removing Soviet troops from the territory. Negotiations were conducted by shuttling between Kabul and Islamabad and between separate rooms allocated to the parties in the Geneva headquarters

---

[13] [1996] ICJ Rep. p. 66.   [14] [2004] ICJ Rep. p. 136.   [15] [2010] ICJ Rep.
[16] See T. M. Franck, *Fairness in International Law and Institutions*, Oxford, 1995, Chapter 6.

of the UN. Progress towards a settlement was slow and complicated by the absence from the negotiations of the Afghan resistance leaders. Eventually, however, a settlement was agreed and the withdrawal of the last Soviet troops took place in 1989.

In cases where armed conflict has broken out, the Secretary-General's mandate has generally included a request that he use his good offices in an attempt to secure a cease-fire. For example, when India and Pakistan went to war over Kashmir in 1965, the Security Council requested the Secretary-General to 'exert every possible effort' to achieve an end to the fighting. Similarly, after the outbreak of hostilities over the Falkland Islands, the Security Council in its resolution of May 1982 requested the Secretary-General to enter into contact immediately with Argentina and the United Kingdom 'with a view to negotiating mutually acceptable terms for a cease-fire'.[17] Subsequently, following Security Council Resolution 598 of July 1987, the Secretary-General visited Iran and Iraq to assist with the negotiation of the cease-fire in the Iran–Iraq war which took effect in August 1988.

In a situation of armed conflict, it may also be possible for the Secretary-General to take certain steps with a view to restraining parties and limiting the scope of the fighting. Thus, in the war with Iraq, Iran asked the Security Council to investigate the use of chemical weapons by the Iraqi forces. As we have seen in Chapter 3, this led the Secretary-General to appoint a group to inquire into this issue. The resulting studies confirmed that chemical weapons had been used and were the basis for the Security Council's condemnation of the use of such weapons in March 1986. During the same conflict, a public appeal by the Secretary-General succeeded in obtaining from the belligerents an undertaking not to attack each other's civilian population.[18] This was intended as part of an incremental solution to the conflict and as such was not immediately successful. It did, however, have the effect of restraining the parties' conduct of hostilities for a period and preventing further deterioration.

A third function often assigned to the Secretary-General has in practice been one of the most important, namely, the organisation and administration of United Nations peace-keeping operations of various kinds. Thus, the negotiations envisaged in the resolution on the Falklands were to include 'if necessary, arrangements for the dispatch of United Nations observers to monitor compliance with the terms of the cease-fire'. In this instance, the group in question was never formed, but, as we shall see later, peace-keeping operations and the supervision of a United Nations 'presence' have been a

---

[17] Security Council Resolution 505 (1982). For the full text, see (1982) 21 ILM p. 680. For an evaluation of the Security Council's role in the Falklands crisis, see J. F. Murphy, *The United Nations and the Control of International Violence*, Manchester, 1982, pp. 67–71.

[18] See D. Cordovez, 'Strengthening United Nations diplomacy for peace: The role of the Secretary-General', in UNITAR, *International Peace and Security*, p. 161 at p. 172.

prominent feature of the mandates of successive Secretaries-General over the years.

With the exception of peace-keeping operations, which always require a mandate, the Secretary-General's exercise of his powers under Article 99 has involved him in activities similar to those already described. Thus, in 1958, in an attempt to alleviate the border tension between Thailand and Cambodia, Secretary-General Hammarskjöld discussed the issue with the parties, consulted members of the Security Council, and at the parties' invitation sent Ambassador Johan Beck-Friis of Sweden to the area as his Special Representative. As a result of the latter's efforts, the parties eventually resumed diplomatic relations. Similarly, in the Cuban missile crisis of 1962, Secretary-General U Thant devoted his efforts first to the formulation of various proposals to reduce the immediate tension and gain time, and then to discussions with the government of Cuba over possible arrangements for a United Nations presence.[19]

In these disputes, the Secretary-General's primary objective was to discourage precipitate action which might make a difficult situation worse; in other words, by filling a dangerous political vacuum to create a breathing space and the opportunity for a settlement later. In other cases his actions have been more obviously directed towards procedural or substantive solutions. In the dispute between the United Kingdom and Iran over the status of Bahrain, for example, U Thant spent many months discussing the issue with the parties. Then, following a formal request that he should act as mediator and ascertain the wishes of the inhabitants of the area, he appointed a personal representative to conduct an inquiry. The latter's report, which favoured independence for Bahrain, was subsequently accepted by the Security Council and formed the basis of the final settlement.[20]

The Bahrain dispute not only drew attention to the possibility of combining mediation with fact-finding, but also showed the usefulness of the Secretary-General's position in a dispute in which non-recognition could have caused difficulties, because Bahrain was not recognised by Iran. At about the same time, U Thant was making strenuous efforts to promote peace in Vietnam, where non-recognition was again a problem. The Secretary-General's ability to by-pass such difficulties through the use of quiet diplomacy is an important feature of his role. However, as U Thant's refusal to become involved in the Nigerian civil war and the rejection by the United Kingdom of his offer to intercede in Northern Ireland demonstrate,

---

[19] U Thant, *View from the UN*, London, 1978, Chapter 8.

[20] See H. Al-Baharna, 'The fact-finding mission of the United Nations Secretary-General and the settlement of the Bahrain–Iran dispute', (1973) 22 ICLQ p. 541. In 1996, a proposal by Secretary-General Boutros-Ghali to send a fact-finding mission to investigate frontier incidents between Cameroon and Nigeria was supported by both the Security Council and the International Court. See *Land and Maritime Boundary between Cameroon and Nigeria*, Provisional Measures, Order of 15 March 1996, [1996] ICJ Rep. p. 13.

the exclusion of matters of domestic jurisdiction from the United Nations is a major limitation on his powers.

The good offices role of the Secretary-General can on occasion also exploit the possibilities of utilising legal procedures for the settlement of international disputes. The Secretary-General was evidently instrumental in persuading Libya and Malta to take their dispute over continental shelf delimitation to the International Court in 1985,[21] and, in the following year, the Secretary-General himself acted as arbitrator in the *Rainbow Warrior* case[22] between France and New Zealand. In the latter instance, as we have seen in Chapter 5, the parties had succeeded in resolving some of their differences by negotiation, but outstanding issues included the future of the French agents imprisoned in New Zealand, and the question of compensation. In his award, the Secretary-General resolved these and certain other matters to the parties' satisfaction, and the incident was declared closed. Although the procedure in this case differed in some respects from that of a conventional arbitration, it had many of the same advantages. The decision was accepted in advance, so minimising the problem of implementation, while the source of the decision, a third party of unimpeachable independence, had the effect of legitimising a result which would have been difficult, if not impossible, to arrive at in direct negotiations.

In exercising the initiatives described, the Secretary-General's activity has usually been closely related to that of the other organs of the United Nations. In the Cuban missile crisis, the dispute was before the Security Council throughout the period of the Secretary-General's involvement, and in both the Falklands and Kashmir disputes a period of active diplomacy by the Secretary-General preceded his Security Council mandate. Even in cases like the Thailand–Cambodia dispute, where the matter is never formally considered by the Council, its members will expect to be kept informed. If, however, it would be wrong to see the efforts of the Secretary-General in isolation, it is clear that his ability to take the initiative will often have the advantage of enabling a potentially significant influence to be brought to bear on a dispute at a very early stage.

Although the Secretary-General must be prepared to co-ordinate his activity with that of the Security Council and General Assembly, the strength of his position clearly lies in his independence. The preservation of his independence must therefore be a primary goal since without it little could be achieved. Its value is evident in many ways. It was, for example, the Secretary-General's independence which made his good offices acceptable to both sides in the diplomatic hostages crisis and the negotiations on Afghanistan. It was similarly his independent position which enabled him

---

[21] Cordovez, 'Role of the Secretary-General', p. 171.

[22] See *Ruling pertaining to the Differences between France and New Zealand arising from the Rainbow Warrior Affair* (1986). Text in 74 ILR p. 241 and document J in the appendix below.

to address his appeal to the parties in the Cuban missile crisis and the Iran–Iraq war, and which enabled him to arbitrate in the *Rainbow Warrior* case. On several occasions during the Afghanistan negotiations, the Secretary-General privately told the parties that he might discontinue his efforts on account of a lack of progress. This produced strenuous pleas for him to continue, and shows how the Secretary-General can sometimes exploit his position to move the parties forward.

To preserve the Secretary-General's independence, it is important not only that he acts without fear or favour, but also that he stays within his constitutional competence.[23] Action which brought him into conflict with the other organs would lead inevitably to accusations that he was taking sides and ultimately render his position untenable. In this respect, the issue of independence is concerned with more than the question of how he does his job, but poses the basic question of what precisely the job consists of. Faced with a situation in which the political organs are unable to act effectively, it is tempting to believe that the Secretary-General should always step into the breach. That, however, would be a mistake. The objections to such a policy are not only constitutional, they are also practical. For, as former Secretary-General Pérez de Cuéllar has written, 'the temptation to aggrandizement can discredit the institution of Secretary-General, and thus the organization as a whole, because it can lead the Secretary-General into courses of action which are not realistically sustainable'.[24]

This does not mean that it is necessary to take the opposite position and regard the Secretary-General as merely the chief administrative officer of the Organization with no peace-making function. On the contrary, 'situations can, and do, arise when the Secretary-General has to exercise his powers to the full, as the bearer of a sacred trust, and as the guardian of the principles of the Charter',[25] and, in practice, as we have seen, this is a view which successive holders of the office have taken, though with differences of emphasis. But it is worth bearing in mind that, while the Secretary-General's scope for initiative is extensive, the decision to invoke Article 99 is a matter for his discretion. Efforts to make intervention a duty, rather than a power, were resisted on the ground that the Secretary-General was the best judge of whether action was appropriate. The wisdom of this decision is now apparent. Since the timing of initiatives is often crucial in the settlement of disputes, and much of the Secretary-General's work is in any case 'quiet diplomacy', treating the Secretary-General's authority under Article 99 as another facet of his independence was much better than trying to impose it as a duty.

---

[23] See N. Elaraby, 'The office of the Secretary-General and the maintenance of international peace and security', in UNITAR, *International Peace and Security*, p. 177 at pp. 181–7.

[24] See J. Pérez de Cuéllar, 'The role of the UN Secretary-General', in Roberts and Kingsbury, *United Nations, Divided World*, p. 124 at p. 126.

[25] *Ibid.*

A final point concerns the responsibility of the members of the Security Council and, to a lesser extent, the members of the General Assembly. The possibility noted earlier of a Secretary-General seeking to usurp the role of the other organs cannot be said to be a real risk at the present time. Unfortunately, the same cannot be said of the converse situation, that is, one in which the members of the Security Council fail to discharge their obligations in the field of peace and security, and matters are left to the Secretary-General. A moment's reflection will demonstrate that this situation, which is likely to arise whenever the major states find themselves at loggerheads, cannot provide a sustainable basis for international peace-making. To demand that the other organs deal with every problem, always adopt the measures most likely to be effective and invariably provide the Secretary-General with precise instructions is, no doubt, quite unrealistic. What is vital, however, is the point which has already been made, that the functions of the Secretary-General should be treated as complementary to those of the other organs. This means that neither the Security Council nor the General Assembly can abrogate their political responsibility for peace and security and expect the Secretary-General to bear the burden.

The ability of the Secretary-General to take action to promote the set-tlement of disputes on his own initiative or under Article 98 does not, of course, bring with it any guarantee that such intervention will be suc-cessful. For example, following the invasion and occupation of Kuwait in 1990, Secretary-General Pérez de Cuéllar twice sought to engage Iraq in discussions designed to bring about its withdrawal. However, neither the contacts at the beginning of the crisis in August 1990, nor those on the eve of the conflict between Iraq and the US-led coalition in January 1991, were fruitful, owing to Iraq's intransigence on both occasions.[26] As ways of settling disputes, good offices, mediation, conciliation and fact-finding are subject to very much the same constraints whether they are carried out by the Secretary-General and his representatives or by an outside party. But, if the gap between the disputants must sometimes prove unbridgeable, it is not always so. Bearing in mind that the possibilities of a solution can only be identified if they are first explored, a Secretary-General willing and able to undertake that task must be regarded as a major asset to the United Nations system.[27]

---

[26] See L. Freedman and E. Karsh, *The Gulf Conflict 1990–1991*, London, 1993, pp. 160–1, 268–70 and 274.

[27] For further information on the work of the Secretary-General, see Zacher, 'The Secretary-General'; L. Gordenker, *The UN Secretary-General and the Maintenance of Peace*, New York, 1967; V. Pechota, 'The quiet approach', in Raman, *Dispute Settlement*, p. 577; and K. Skjelsbaek and G. Fermann, 'The UN Secretary-General and the mediation of international disputes', in J. Bercovitch (ed.), *Resolving International Conflict: The Theory and Practice of Mediation*, London, 1996, p. 75. Also S. Chesterman (ed.), *Secretary or General? The UN Secretary-General in World Politics*, Cambridge, 2007.

The political organs and the International Court

Action by the Secretary-General, the involvement of the Security Council or the adoption of measures by the General Assembly all represent ways of attempting to deal with international disputes at the political level. In addition to these procedures, which are essentially discretionary, it is of course possible for states to seek to employ arbitration or judicial settlement to obtain a decision based on international law. Since the distinctive features of legal means of settlement have been considered earlier, they need not be described again here. One point, however, does need to be examined because it is directly concerned with the subject matter of this chapter. It is the relation between the International Court, the 'principal judicial organ of the United Nations',[28] and the political organs. This question has two aspects. The first, examined here, is whether, as a matter of principle, the Court's competence is affected if a political organ is also dealing with a dispute. The second, considered later, is whether, when a case is properly before the Court, it may exercise judicial control by holding the action of one of the political organs to be unconstitutional.

How far recourse to the Court is compatible with simultaneous use of the political organs was a question which was raised by a number of the arguments put forward by the United States in the *Nicaragua* case.[29] For, in addition to various objections to the jurisdiction of the Court, which have been discussed in Chapter 6, the United States maintained that the case should be declared inadmissible on the ground that a ruling on the merits would transgress the boundaries of the judicial function and involve the Court in issues which are the prerogative of the Security Council. The argument was put in two ways. First, it was said that Nicaragua's claim required the Court to decide whether the United States had used unlawful force and that questions of this kind fall within the exclusive jurisdiction of the political organs. Secondly, and as a development of the first point, the United States maintained that, by bringing the case to the Court, Nicaragua was in effect seeking to appeal from an adverse ruling on its complaints by the Council. Since the Charter makes no provision for such an appeal, the Court, according to the United States, lacked 'subject-matter jurisdiction'[30] over the claim.

The Court rejected both arguments. On the first point, it explained that, while Article 24 of the Charter confers on the Council 'primary responsibility for the maintenance of international peace and security', this is different

---

[28] Article 1 of the Statute of the Court provides: 'The International Court of Justice established by the Charter of the United Nations as the principal judicial organ of the United Nations shall be constituted and shall function in accordance with the provisions of the present Statute.'

[29] *Military and Paramilitary Activities in and against Nicaragua*, Jurisdiction and Admissibility, Judgment, [1984] ICJ Rep. p. 392.

[30] *Ibid.*, para. 91.

from exclusive responsibility. As the Court and the Security Council have quite separate functions, neither the fact that a matter is under consideration by the Security Council, nor the fact that a case concerns the use of force, is legally any bar to judicial proceedings. As to the proceedings being an appeal from the Security Council, the Court rejected this argument on the facts. The Court pointed out that it was 'not asked to say that the Security Council is wrong in its decision, nor that there is anything inconsistent with law in the way in which the members of the Council employed their right to vote'. On the contrary, the Court said that it was 'asked to pass judgment on certain legal aspects of a situation which has also been considered by the Security Council, a procedure which is entirely consonant with its position as the principal judicial organ of the United Nations'.[31] This objection too was therefore rejected.

The Court's decision on these points was unanimous, and its ruling is clearly correct. Not only is the decision to treat the case as admissible in line with its previous jurisprudence, but it is only necessary to reflect on what was at stake here to appreciate that acceptance of either of the United States' arguments would produce grotesque results. If the Court had accepted that claims relating to the use of force are outside its competence, it would have disqualified itself from dealing with a wide range of important international disputes and relegated the rules of international law which govern these matters to a second-class status. If, on the other hand, it had accepted the jurisdictional point and agreed that, when a matter has been vetoed in the Security Council, litigation amounts to an appeal from 'the decision which the Security Council did not take',[32] it would have extended the veto of the Permanent Members from the political to the legal arena. While the Charter invests the Security Council, and consequently the Permanent Members, with major responsibilities in the area of peace and security, it also recognises a role for legal procedures which the Court, as the institution's legal organ, has a duty to protect.

In drawing its conclusions in the *Nicaragua* case, the Court placed a good deal of reliance on its decision in the *Diplomatic Hostages in Tehran* case[33] in 1980. In that case, the question which the Court had to consider was not specifically concerned with the articles of the Charter relating to the use of force, but with the more general issue of the relation between the Court and the political organs. In addition, because the Secretary-General had established a Special Commission to look into the dispute, the Court took the opportunity to examine how far this type of initiative, which, as we have seen, is not uncommon, is compatible with the pursuit of judicial remedies. Both the general question and the specific matter of the Commission touched on issues which had been considered before, but

---

[31] *Ibid.*, para. 98.   [32] *Ibid.*, para. 91, referring to the United States' argument on this point.
[33] *United States Diplomatic and Consular Staff in Tehran*, Judgment, [1980] ICJ Rep. p. 3.

which, like the questions of justiciability raised in the *Nicaragua* case, go to the root of the United Nations system.

The question of the Court's role *vis-à-vis* the political organs arose in this case because shortly before the United States made its application to the Court, the occupation of the embassy and the detention of the staff as hostages were referred to the Security Council by both the United States and the Secretary-General. Although the matter was actively being considered by the Council, and the Secretary-General had already been given a mandate to use his good offices in the matter, the Court decided, in December 1979, that it was competent to entertain a request from the United States for provisional measures of protection and went on to make such an order. Commenting on this in its judgment of May 1980, the Court made the following observation about its action and the scope of its authority:

> [I]t does not seem to have occurred to any member of the Council that there was or could be anything irregular in the simultaneous exercise of their respective functions by the Court and the Security Council. Nor is there in this any cause for surprise. Whereas Article 12 of the Charter expressly forbids the General Assembly to make any recommendation with regard to a dispute or situation while the Security Council is exercising its functions in respect of that dispute situation, no such restriction is placed on the functioning of the Court by any provision of either the Charter or the Statute of the Court. The reasons are clear. It is for the Court, the principal judicial organ of the United Nations, to resolve any legal questions that may be in issue between parties to a dispute; and the resolution of such legal questions by the Court may be an important, and sometimes decisive, factor in promoting the peaceful settlement of the dispute.[34]

Having made the point that the involvement of the Security Council was not in itself an obstacle to the exercise of its jurisdiction, the Court proceeded to examine in some detail the Special Commission which the Secretary-General had established with the authority of the Council and which had already begun its work. With reference to the circumstances in which the Commission was set up, the Court made the important point that its creation was evidently not intended to postpone consideration of the dispute by the Court. It would have been open to the parties to agree to use the Commission for this purpose, but the Court said that it could 'find no trace of any understanding on the part of either the United States or Iran that the establishment of the Commission might involve a postponement of all proceedings before the Court until the conclusion of the work of the Commission and of the Security Council's consideration of the matter'.[35]

As regards the actual function of the Commission, the Court found that it had not been set up to decide disputed matters of fact or law, but rather

---

[34] *Ibid.*, para. 40.   [35] *Ibid.*, para. 42.

to carry out mediation, conciliation or negotiation in an attempt to ease the tension between Iran and the United States. Its establishment could not therefore 'be considered in itself as in any way incompatible with the continuance of parallel proceedings before the Court'.[36] Here the Court was really saying two things. It was confirming a view that it had previously expressed that mediation, conciliation and negotiation are normally compatible with judicial settlement. Then, by implication, it was recognising that a body which was empowered to decide 'matters of fact or law in dispute between Iran and the United States' would displace the Court by virtue of the recognised principle of litispendence.[37] However, as there was no question of litispendence here, it held that neither the Secretary-General's mandate, nor the setting up of his Commission, could be regarded as an obstacle to the exercise of jurisdiction.

In the *Genocide Convention* case[38] in 1993, the Court again had to consider the relation between its power to order provisional measures under Article 41 of its Statute and the actions of the Security Council. The situation in the former Yugoslavia was taken to the United Nations in 1991 before the initiation of proceedings by Bosnia against the Federal Republic of Yugoslavia and was under review by the Security Council throughout the Court's consideration of the case. Moreover, the Security Council had taken decisions on the basis of Article 25 of the Charter, and, when imposing an arms embargo and taking various other measures, had indicated that it was acting under Chapter VII. As a result, when Bosnia made its first request for interim protection, Yugoslavia argued that, so long as the Council was acting under these provisions, 'it would be premature and inappropriate for the Court to indicate provisional measures, and certainly provisional measures of the type which have been requested'.[39]

The Court, however, rejected the argument and ordered certain provisional measures, recalling that, at the jurisdiction and admissibility stage of the *Nicaragua* case, it had made the point that, in the absence of any provision in the Charter giving the Security Council priority over the Court, both organs can 'perform their separate but complementary functions with respect to the same events'.[40] This was therefore a rejection of the view that the involvement of the Security Council, even in disputes falling under Chapter VII, is *per se* an obstacle to the consideration of a case under Article 41. The Court's view of its relationship to the Security Council was further demonstrated six months later when Bosnia made a further request for

---

[36] *Ibid.*

[37] For an exhaustive examination of this issue, see D. Ciobanu, 'Litispendence between the International Court of Justice and the political organs of the United Nations', in L. Gross (ed.), *The Future of the International Court of Justice*, New York, 1976, p. 209.

[38] *Application of the Convention on the Prevention and Punishment of the Crime of Genocide, Provisional Measures*, Order of 8 April 1993, [1993] ICJ Rep. p. 3.

[39] *Ibid.*, para. 33.   [40] *Ibid.* The words quoted are to be found in [1984] ICJ Rep. p. 435, para. 95.

interim protection, following further Security Council resolutions.[41] Deciding that what was needed was not additional measures but the immediate and effective implementation of those already ordered, it reaffirmed the measures in its previous order, showing again that Security Council action in itself is no bar to measures under Article 41.

In the *Construction of a Wall* case, the Court's relation to the political organs had to be considered in the context of its advisory jurisdiction and, more specifically, in a situation where the General Assembly and the Security Council were in disagreement. The issue of Israel's wall in the Occupied Palestinian Territory was taken up by the General Assembly when the Security Council was unable to adopt a resolution on the matter owing to the exercise of a United States veto. Addressing the question of its jurisdiction to give an advisory opinion, the Court held that the General Assembly's request was within the latter's competence and did not violate Article 12(1) of the Charter. Since the Court went on to find that the question presented was a 'legal question' for the purposes of Article 65(1) of its Statute and Article 96(1) of the Charter, it also concluded that it had jurisdiction to respond to the request.

To reach this conclusion, the Court had to consider the position of the General Assembly *vis-à-vis* the Security Council in some detail and by implication rejected any notion that a 'decision which the Security Council did not take' can restrict its competence to give advisory opinions at the request of the General Assembly. It is notable, too, that, when the Court went on to consider and reject various arguments to the effect that it should exercise its discretion and not give an advisory opinion, it pointed out that the value of its opinion to the General Assembly was a matter for the Assembly, and not the Court, to determine. This confirms that the role of advisory opinions is to provide the requesting organs with the information they seek, helping them in performing their functions, but without encroaching on their responsibilities.

These cases provide a clear and consistent picture of the relation between the jurisdiction of the International Court and the political organs of the UN, and indicate that in general the reference of a dispute to the Security Council is no bar to consideration of the same matter by the Court. Moreover, the *Diplomatic Hostages in Tehran* case shows that there is no inherent conflict between litigation and action by the Secretary-General. It may be recalled from Chapter 1 that, when called upon to consider the relation between negotiation and litigation in the *Aegean Sea* case, the Court rejected the view that the two were incompatible, and we shall see shortly that it has taken the same view of regional political procedures. As the Court itself has often said, legal and political means of settling disputes are complementary.

---

[41] See the Court's Order of 13 September 1993, [1993] ICJ Rep. p. 325.

Peace-keeping operations

United Nations peace-keeping has been the subject of many detailed studies.[42] Consequently, all that is needed here is an outline of the types of activity undertaken by the Organization and their contribution to the work of dispute settlement. A preliminary point to note is that classification of the various peace-keeping groups established by the United Nations is difficult. Some were, from the beginning, intended to fulfil more than one function, while others, whose operations have spanned a decade or more, have in several instances performed different functions at different times. Moreover, the functions themselves, as we shall see, tend to merge and overlap. At the cost of some simplification, then, the following forms of operation can be distinguished.

Observation involves the sending of a team of United Nations personnel to a disturbed area in the hope that their presence and the knowledge that they are reporting what they see may have the effect of preventing, or at least discouraging, the crossing of international boundaries or other unauthorised activities. Observation is often combined with other peace-keeping functions, but on occasion has provided either the sole or the main objective of a United Nations presence. For example, the UN Observer Group in the Lebanon (UNOGIL), set up by the Security Council in 1958 to monitor alleged Syrian infiltration, was exclusively concerned with observation, whereas the UN Special Committee on the Balkans (UNSCOB), established by the General Assembly in 1947, acted as an observer group on the Greek border, and, as noted earlier, performed a number of other functions.

To improve relations in a sensitive border area, something more than observation is needed. Attempts to have UNOGIL assume an extended role in the Lebanon were unsuccessful, but the assumption of a positive role can be seen in the practice of United Nations observer groups elsewhere in the Middle East and in Kashmir. The UN Truce Supervision Organization (UNTSO) developed from the arrangements devised by the Mediator for Palestine, whose work has already been mentioned. The group, which was steadily enlarged, had as its task the observation of the Arab–Israeli borders, together with the settlement of incidents and the negotiation of a cease-fire, should an outbreak of fighting occur. In less difficult circumstances, the UN Military Observer Group in India and Pakistan (UNMOGIP) has performed the same function in Kashmir from 1949 to the present day.

---

[42] Useful studies include A. James, *Peacekeeping in International Politics*, London, 1990; A. Parsons, *From Cold War to Hot Peace*, London, 1995; and D. Warner (ed.), *New Dimensions of Peacekeeping*, Dordrecht, 1995. An invaluable collection of primary material is the four-volume series by R. Higgins entitled *United Nations Peace-keeping Documents and Commentary*, Oxford, 1969–81. On the latest activities, see White, *The United Nations System*, pp. 161–97; and C. Gray, *International Law and the Use of Force*, 2nd edn, Oxford, 2004, Chapters 7 and 9.

The value of this type of force can be seen very clearly in the work of the UN Observer Group in Central America (ONUCA).[43] This was set up by the Security Council in 1989 at the request of the five states of Central America. Its task was to discourage any state from attacking its neighbours, to verify that rebel forces were not launching cross-border raids and to prevent broadcasting by insurrectionary forces. Intended as a highly mobile border patrol, the force was equipped with jeeps, helicopters and speedboats and manned by about 600 personnel from Latin America and elsewhere. At about the same time, the UN Observer Mission to Verify the Electoral Process in Nicaragua (ONUVEN) was established to supervise elections. We shall see in the next chapter that the creation of these observer forces was the culmination of a long peace process in which the Contadora Group, as well as other members of the Organization of American States, were involved. ONUCA operated until the beginning of 1992, when, having successfully performed its functions, its mandate was terminated.[44] As the first major peace-keeping force to be deployed in the western hemisphere, ONUCA provides a striking example of co-operation between the United Nations and a regional body.

In situations in which fighting has broken out, it will often be easier to negotiate a cease-fire if arrangements for the disengagement of forces can be supervised by a third party. Here, then, is another function which peace-keeping forces can perform. In 1963, for example, the Security Council authorised the creation of a UN Observer Group in the Yemen (UNYOM) with the task of supervising the withdrawal of Egyptian and Saudi Arabian troops which had intervened in the civil war there, and, two years later, following the three-week war between India and Pakistan over Kashmir, set up the UN India–Pakistan Observation Mission (UNIPOM) to supervise a cease-fire and troop withdrawals from the disputed area. In 1988, the UN Good Offices Mission in Afghanistan and Pakistan was set up to perform a similar function in Afghanistan.[45] Although it was able to report on the withdrawal of all Soviet troops in accordance with the 1988 Geneva Accords, in the face of violations by all sides of pledges of non-intervention it was unable to perform its monitoring function and was withdrawn in 1990.

Clearly, the creation and operation of an observer force depends on the parties' desire to make and implement an effective agreement. What can be achieved when these conditions are present may be seen in the activities of the UN Aouzou Strip Observer Group (UNASOG) in 1994.[46] This small

[43] See White, *Keeping the Peace*, pp. 226–7.

[44] When ONUCA was terminated, its equipment and personnel were transferred to the UN Observer Mission in El Salvador (ONUSAL) to continue the regional peace process. See White, *Keeping the Peace*, pp. 226–7.

[45] See White, *Keeping the Peace*, p. 223; and (1988) 27 ILM p. 577.

[46] For the text of the Secretary-General's Report proposing the creation of UNASOG and the text of Security Council Resolutions 910 and 915 relating to the Group, see (1994) 33 ILM p. 785 and p. 791. The text of Resolution 915 is also reproduced in document H in the appendix below.

observer group was set up by the Security Council at the request of Libya and Chad to supervise the withdrawal of Libyan forces from a disputed border area, following the decision of the International Court in the *Territorial Dispute* case.[47] With the parties' co-operation, it performed its function successfully, and provides an object lesson in the use of peace-keeping forces to assist in the implementation of a judicial decision. Situations in which the use of observer missions was considered as a way of heading off conflict include the Falklands crisis of 1982, where a withdrawal of the Argentine garrison under United Nations supervision could have provided an excellent face-saving arrangement; the Kuwait crisis of 1990–1 where similar proposals were put to Iraq by the Secretary-General; and the Cuban missile crisis where, when it appeared that verification might be an obstacle to agreement, a UN observer group to ensure that the missiles had been removed was one of the possibilities explored by the Secretary-General.

Following a disengagement, it may be necessary to ensure that the rival forces remain separated. Although the groups already described can help achieve this to some extent, the task involved extends beyond observation and supervision, which can often be performed by relatively small groups, and calls for the deployment of more substantial forces. The creation of a force comparable to national military forces is beyond the capacity of the United Nations, and in any case the consent of the parties in dispute (which is essential) would hardly be given to the deployment of such a force on national territory. Fortunately, no such arrangements are necessary. What is required here is not a force capable of large-scale fighting but a group large enough to occupy a sensitive frontier area and to act as a buffer between the parties.

Examples of the usefulness of such a group are provided by the UN Emergency Force in the Middle East (UNEF I) and the UN Force in Cyprus (UNFICYP). In the first case, a force whose initial task was to supervise the withdrawal of French and British forces from Egypt in 1956 patrolled the Egyptian–Israeli border until 1967. After the war of 1973, the same functions were performed by UNEF II and by the UN Disengagement Observer Force (UNDOF) on the Syrian–Israeli border. UNEF II was particularly significant because the presence of this force contributed to the climate of confidence in which a peace agreement between Egypt and Israel was negotiated in 1979. In the case of UNFICYP, the group occupies the border between the Greek and Turkish communities in Cyprus and, though limited in certain respects, appears to have contributed significantly to an easing of tension on the island.[48]

---

[47] *Territorial Dispute (Libyan Arab Jamahiriya/Chad)*, Judgment, [1994] ICJ Rep. p. 6. For discussion, see G. J. Naldi, Note, (1995) 44 ICLQ p. 683.

[48] See Higgins, *United Nations Peace-keeping*, vol. IV, Part 2. For later developments, see J. Theodorides, 'The United Nations Peace-keeping Force in Cyprus (UNFICYP)', (1982) 31 ICLQ p. 765.

Although it is no part of the United Nations' function to intervene in domestic affairs, there are situations in which a breakdown of order in a state may become a matter of international concern on account of the risk of foreign intervention. Similarly, there are circumstances in which the implementation of the terms of an international settlement could be threatened by internal disorder. In situations of this type, United Nations forces may be employed with another objective, that of restoring or maintaining order. The foremost example of an operation with this purpose is the UN Operation in the Congo (ONUC).[49] There, following a mutiny of local troops, Belgian forces had intervened and the dispatch of United Nations forces, though highly controversial at the time, played a valuable role in preventing a further deterioration of the situation.

From time to time suggestions have been made that this or that disputed territory should be handed over to the United Nations to become the object of international administration. Although permanent administration will generally be out of the question,[50] a transitional arrangement as part of the process of changing sovereignty over a disputed area may be a more promising possibility. In 1962, for example, the territory of West Irian was administered by the United Nations for seven months, pending its transfer to Indonesia.[51] The advantage of this arrangement was that the Dutch could leave the territory without the humiliation of handing over to the rival claimant. Of course, a solution was possible here only because the issue of ultimate sovereignty had already been settled and Indonesia was prepared to wait. When a similar solution was proposed at an early stage of the Falklands dispute, it soon became apparent that, even if the United Kingdom might be prepared to consider international administration as a way of handing over responsibility for the islands, Argentina's insistence on the ultimate satisfaction of its claim precluded the possibility of such an arrangement.[52]

In 1989, the United Nations established a force which combined elements of the two functions which have just been described. This was the UN Transitional Assistance Group (UNTAG) which was sent to Namibia. The plan for Namibian independence was conceived as early as 1978,[53] but

[49] See Higgins, *United Nations Peace-keeping*, vol. III; and G. Abi-Saab, *The United Nations Operation in the Congo 1960–1964*, Oxford, 1978.

[50] Although the Saar was administered by the League of Nations for fifteen years following the First World War, the failure of the United Nations to implement similar schemes in respect of Trieste and Jerusalem indicates the difficulty of obtaining and maintaining the degree of support necessary to carry such schemes through.

[51] See Higgins, *United Nations Peace-keeping*, vol. II, Part 2; and J. Leyser, 'Dispute and agreement on West New Guinea', (1962–3) 10 *Archiv des Völkerrechts* p. 257.

[52] See Murphy, *Control of International Violence*, p. 108; and L. Freedman and V. Gamba-Stonehouse, *Signals of War: The Falklands Conflict of 1982*, London, 1990, Chapter 18.

[53] See Security Council Resolution 435 (1978). For the text of this and subsequent documents on the Namibia issue, see (1989) 28 ILM p. 944.

could not be put into effect until the South African government decided that it was prepared to withdraw from the territory. Among the matters which then had to be settled was how the transition to independence was to be supervised; in particular how conditions conducive to free and fair elections could be created against a recent background of war and political repression. This was the purpose for which the 6,000-strong UNTAG force was created. During its time in Namibia, the force witnessed a resurgence of fighting between guerrilla and South African forces, but, when this crisis had been resolved, succeeded in restoring confidence and arranging an election which brought an independent and democratic government to power in 1990. Throughout the period before independence, Namibia continued to be administered by the South African authorities. This was therefore not a case in which a peace-keeping force was called upon to provide international administration in the fullest sense. It is clear, however, that UNTAG played a key role in Namibia's transition to independence, and the elections, which were generally acknowledged to have been free and fair, were a remarkable achievement in the circumstances.

A further extension of this type of peace-keeping operation took place in 1999 with the creation of the UN Interim Administration Mission in Kosovo (UNMIK) and the UN Transitional Administration in East Timor (UNTAET).[54] Both situations arose out of internal conflicts in which there had already been external intervention, and the function of the peace-keeping operations was to establish a provisional territorial administration and institutional framework, pending the creation of permanent arrangements. These operations were based on Security Council resolutions under Chapter VII of the Charter and, since they involved the insertion of UN administration fulfilling all the functions of a state, indicate a novel interpretation of the Council's powers. If the Namibia operation represents a 'second generation' of peace-keeping, going beyond military and humanitarian operations to establish effective government, UNMIK and UNTAET have been aptly described as representing a 'third generation', embodying still wider responsibilities.[55]

Operations like UNTAG, UNMIK and UNTAET reflect what has been termed the 'integrated and pacific' approach to peace-keeping,[56] in which the parties to a conflict are persuaded to accept a UN presence not just to stabilise the situation as in Kashmir, Cyprus and elsewhere, but to support proposals for a settlement which UN forces then help to implement.

---

[54] For discussion of these arrangements, see M. Ruffert, 'The administration of Kosovo and East Timor by the international community', (2001) 50 ICLQ p. 613; and R. Wilde, 'From Danzig to East Timor and beyond: The role of international territorial administration', (2001) 95 AJIL p. 583.

[55] See Gray, *Use of Force*, pp. 210–15.

[56] See N. D. White, 'UN peacekeeping: Development or destruction', (1994) 12 (1) Int. Rel. p. 129 at pp. 137–49, and *The Law of International Organizations*, Manchester, 1996, p. 184.

The West Irian operation was the precedent for this type of intervention, and, with the ending of the Cold War, such forward-looking initiatives have become increasingly common, other examples including ONUCA and ONUVEN, which has already been mentioned, and the subsequent operations in El Salvador (ONUSAL, 1991), Liberia (UNOMIL, 1993) and Angola (UNAVEN II and III, 1991 and 1995).[57] As one would expect, operations of this type are not always successful, but, as some are, they constitute an important development.

In contrast, the Congo operation and a number of recent operations which have not yet been mentioned represent a more dangerous line of development which has been termed the 'quasi-enforcement' approach to peace-keeping.[58] Here, there are elements of peace-keeping in the traditional sense, but the activities of the UN involve a use of force beyond that required in self-defence and, while not amounting to enforcement action under Chapter VII, are difficult to reconcile with the normal peace-keeping requirements of neutrality, co-operation and consent. This was the case, for example, in Bosnia, where the UN Protection Force (UNPROFOR) was given an ever-expanding mandate from 1992 onwards,[59] and in Somalia, where in 1992 and 1993 UNITAF and UNISOM II used force well beyond that available in traditional peace-keeping operations.[60] While ONUC in the Congo was a success, UNPROFOR and the operations in Somalia were not, confirming the view that of the two styles of peace-keeping the 'integrated and pacific approach' is probably to be preferred to the 'quasi-enforcement' approach.[61]

The forces mentioned above were all established by the Security Council or the General Assembly and were usually organised and administered by the Secretary-General.[62] More than fifty states have contributed personnel to forces which have varied in size from as few as fifteen (UNASOG) to as many as 20,000 (ONUC). The cost of the forces has varied with their size

---

[57] See S. Morphet, 'UN peacekeeping and election-monitoring', in Roberts and Kingsbury, *United Nations, Divided World*, p. 183; R. Dreyer, 'State building and democracy in second-generation peacekeeping operations', in Warner, *New Dimensions*, p. 147; and J. Lewis, 'Angola 1995: The road to peace', (1996) 13 Int. Rel. p. 81.

[58] See White, 'UN peacekeeping', pp. 149–58; and M. Bertrand, 'The confusion between peacemaking and peacekeeping', in Warner, *New Dimensions*, p. 163. See also White, *The United Nations System*, pp. 161–5; and Gray, *Use of Force*, pp. 217–27.

[59] See V. Y. Ghebali, 'UNPROFOR in the former Yugoslavia', in Warner, *New Dimensions*, p. 13.

[60] See S. Lalande, 'Somalia: Major issues for future UN peacekeeping', in Warner, *New Dimensions*, p. 69.

[61] For the continuing difficulties with this issue, and in particular the problems encountered by UNAMSIL in Sierra Leone and MONUC in the Democratic Republic of the Congo, see Gray, *Use of Force*, pp. 244–50.

[62] The first peace-keeping operations were developed in circumstances which encouraged an enlargement of the role of the General Assembly at the expense of that of the Security Council. However, since the financial and constitutional crisis of the 1960s, the central importance of the Security Council has been recognised and given further impetus by the ending of the Cold War.

and duration, and financing them has been a source of constant difficulty. Although the constitutional problems surrounding the creation and operation of UN forces are not a subject which it is possible to enter into here,[63] it should be noted that peace-keeping operations are quite distinct from the kind of collective security operation envisaged in Chapter VII of the Charter and discussed below. Rather, they represent improvised responses to particular situations with no very clear constitutional basis, and it is here that practical and theoretical difficulties have arisen.

The fact that operations are improvised and that peace-keeping forces also tend to be introduced in haste are significant limitations on their effectiveness.[64] The first invites disagreement about the scope of a particular operation, or even its legitimacy, while the second factor means that without the full support of the states where the force is operating, difficulties in maintaining the force in place, or ensuring that it can function, are likely to arise. Moreover, in the Cold War era, most peace-keeping operations had to be carried out in areas of the world where the Soviet Union and the United States considered that they had strategic interests. In this respect, the number of operations in the Middle East is particularly noticeable. It is good that peace-keeping was possible even in those difficult circumstances. At the same time, there is no doubt that this rivalry greatly hampered the United Nations effort and added to the difficulties already mentioned. UNITAG and ONUCA, on the other hand, show what can be achieved when the members of the Security Council are in harmony.

Action under Chapter VII

As already noted, Chapter VII of the Charter enables the Security Council to adopt economic sanctions and military measures where there is a 'threat to the peace, breach of the peace or act of aggression', thereby equipping it with enforcement powers in disputes or situations that are particularly serious. Since this book is concerned with peaceful methods of dispute settlement, analysis of the coercive potential of Chapter VII, and the concept of collective security generally, would be out of place.[65] However, something needs to be said about this part of the Charter, partly in order to appreciate

[63] See A. Cassese (ed.), *United Nations Peacekeeping Legal Essays*, Alphen aan den Rijn, 1978; and White, *Keeping the Peace*, Chapter 8.

[64] See H. Wiseman, 'The United Nations and international peacekeeping: A comparative analysis', in UNITAR, *International Peace and Security*, p. 263. For other limiting factors, see I. Pogany, 'The evaluation of United Nations peace-keeping operations', (1986) 57 BYBIL p. 357. The *Brahimi Report* (2000) made far-reaching proposals for reforming peace-keeping, which are being implemented. For the text of the report, see (2000) 39 ILM p. 1432, and, for further discussion of this issue, see Chapter 12 below.

[65] For good overviews, see White, *The Law of International Organizations*, Chapter 7; and A. Hurrell, 'Collective security and international order revisited', (1992) 11 Int. Rel. p. 37. See also White, *The United Nations System*, Chapter 6; and Gray, *Use of Force*, Chapters 7 and 8.

the role of Chapter VI, and partly because, since the ending of the Cold War, the provisions of Chapter VII have acquired a practical importance with far-reaching implications.

To bring Chapter VII into play, Article 39 lays down that it is for the Security Council to determine that the necessary conditions are present. The first question therefore is what qualifies as a 'threat to the peace, breach of the peace or act of aggression'.[66] The term 'threat to the peace' has been interpreted very flexibly and extended beyond the obvious case of one state threatening another, to cover situations within a state, such as civil wars, which have international repercussions. In 1961, for example, the Security Council characterised the civil war in the Congo in this way and subsequently made similar determinations in relation to the conflicts in Yugoslavia (1991) and Liberia (1992). The 'third generation' peace-keeping operations in Kosovo and East Timor (1999) were also authorised under Chapter VII on this basis. In contrast, the terms 'breach of peace' and 'act of aggression' have so far been confined to situations in which force has been used between states, as in, for example, the Argentine invasion of the Falkland Islands in 1982 and the Iraqi invasion of Kuwait in 1990.

A survey of how the Security Council has used Article 39 shows very clearly that whether it is prepared to activate Chapter VII depends on political rather than legal considerations. Thus, although there have been numerous international wars and other cases of force being used between states in the United Nations era, only a handful have been characterised by the Security Council as involving a breach of the peace. Conversely, in the activist period following the end of the Cold War, the concept of a threat to the peace has been extended beyond civil conflicts to cover support for terrorism in the case of Libya (1992) and the denial of democracy in the case of Haiti (1993). Accordingly, while the Charter invests the Security Council with sanctioning powers and purports to define the conditions for their use, there is nothing automatic about this process. Because any determination under Article 39 requires a political decision, the potential of Chapter VII may be neglected in some situations and exploited in others according to the particular circumstances.

Once a determination under Article 39 has been made, it is open to the Security Council to make recommendations, or to decide what measures shall be taken in accordance with Articles 41 and 42 to maintain or restore international peace and security. Article 41 permits the employment of measures 'not involving the use of armed force' and is primarily concerned with economic sanctions. Although the intention behind this provision was to enable mandatory sanctions to be imposed on a delinquent state, in practice lack of agreement has often compelled the Security Council to call only for voluntary (i.e. non-obligatory) measures. These, as might be

---

[66] See White, *The Law of International Organizations*, pp. 172–4.

expected, are usually ineffective and demonstrate that, even when a situation is being considered under Chapter VII, political factors govern the ultimate decision.

Mandatory economic sanctions have, however, been applied in a number of situations.[67] During the Cold War, there were only two such cases, Southern Rhodesia from 1968 to 1979, and South Africa from 1977 to 1994. However, as the Security Council has become more active, there have been several more, including Iraq, where sanctions were imposed in 1990 after the invasion of Kuwait, Yugoslavia, Libya and Liberia in 1992, and Haiti in 1993. The measures adopted varied considerably. Whereas Southern Rhodesia, Iraq and Yugoslavia were subject to a comprehensive regime, the measures taken against Libya and Haiti were more selective, while in relation to South Africa and Liberia UN sanctions were limited to an arms embargo. These variations naturally reflect differences between the respective situations, which influenced the assessment of what was appropriate in each case, but also the different degrees of support for economic sanctions within the Security Council.

Since economic sanctions are sometimes thought of as a relatively cheap way of putting a state under pressure, it is worth pointing out that neither the cheapness nor the pressure can be taken for granted. To the extent that a sanctions regime is effectively enforced, the cost is bound to fall unequally, affecting not only the delinquent state, but also its trading partners. Thus, arrangements to compensate the latter may be needed. The pressure exerted by sanctions depends on the content and enforceability of the sanctions regime, and also on the vulnerability of the target state. Unless a state is very weak, sanctions are unlikely to produce quick results, and, even when economic damage is harsh and immediate, the first victims may well be the civilian population and not the government of the delinquent. Unless therefore the Security Council is willing to starve a state into submission, other options such as 'targeted sanctions' may need to be considered.[68] In 1999, for example, the Security Council established such a regime against the Taliban/Al-Qaeda in Resolution 1267, which was then further developed in later resolutions.

The Security Council's power to impose military sanctions rests on Article 42 of the Charter, which authorises it to 'take such action by air, sea or land forces as may be necessary to maintain or restore international peace and security'. Article 43 goes on to provide for member states to conclude agreements with the UN under which their forces will be available for use when needed. This arrangement would, in effect, have provided the UN

---

[67] See *ibid.*, pp. 185–91 and N. D. White, 'Collective sanctions: An alternative to military coercion?', (1994) 12 (3) Int. Org. p. 75.

[68] Targeted sanctions restrict the activities of particular individuals and so avoid injuring the general population. See White and Saul, 'Legal means of dispute settlement', p. 204.

with a standing army. In the event, however, such agreements were never concluded on account of East–West tensions. As a result, instead of initiating military action with its own forces, the Security Council has been limited to recommending military action by member states and has been forced to rely on their voluntary provision of forces.

As in the case of economic sanctions, little use was made of military measures in the Cold War period, but since then practice has been very different. Whereas the US-led Korean operation in 1950 was the only collective security operation in the former period, since the reactivation of the Security Council Chapter VII has been employed to authorise military operations in a variety of situations, including Iraq (1990), Somalia (1992), Bosnia (1993) and Haiti (1994). The measures in question have ranged from the broad authorisations 'to use all necessary means' to liberate Kuwait[69] and 'to create the conditions for the restoration of democracy in Haiti'[70] to the more limited attempts to combine peace-keeping with enforcement which were mentioned earlier. As with Article 41, the range of measures involving the use of force is explained by differences between the various situations and the commitments Security Council members were willing to support.

What lessons should be drawn from this experience? The first is that military measures, like economic sanctions, are not an all-purpose remedy, but only work if the objective is clearly defined, the situation is susceptible to a military solution, and the appropriate forces are committed. When these conditions are present, the Kuwait operation shows the value of Chapter VII in enabling the Security Council to impose a solution and defeat an aggressor. When they are not, problems experienced in Bosnia and Somalia show what is likely to happen. A second lesson is that the more the Security Council uses Chapter VII the more its actions need to be scrutinised to ensure that they are legitimate.[71] This has implications for the composition of the Security Council and for the control of UN forces in the field, as well as for the issue of judicial review to be considered shortly.

The measures described so far were all taken in circumstances where, whatever the merits of the decision, there was clear Security Council authorisation under Chapter VII. Sometimes, however, states elect to take military action unilaterally, and then try to justify it on the basis of a quite implausible construction of previous resolutions. Thus, in 2003, the United States and the United Kingdom sought to justify invading Iraq on the basis of a sequence of resolutions going back to 1991, concerned with the cease-fire regime imposed after the liberation of Kuwait; and, in 1999, the same states, along with other members of NATO, relied on implied authorisation by the Security Council as part of the justification for bombing Yugoslavia to

---

[69] Security Council Resolution 678 (1990).   [70] Security Council Resolution 940 (1994).
[71] See D. D. Caron, 'The legitimacy of the collective authority of the Security Council', (1993) 87 AJIL p. 552.

protect Kosovo.[72] However, in both episodes, the key resolutions did not authorise the use of force and the Security Council was plainly split on the issue. Accordingly, the idea that the Security Council had somehow authorised the use of force by implication was a transparent fiction. A further, very practical, objection to such sophistry is that, if Western states persist in abusing collective decisions by making far-fetched claims of implied authorisation, they may find other members of the Security Council unwilling to vote for any resolutions at all under Chapter VII, thereby making this part of the Charter completely unusable.[73]

Since the Charter puts the Security Council at the centre of the collective security system, it was fitting that, following the invasion of Iraq, Secretary-General Kofi Annan established a High Level Panel to bring forward new ideas on collective security, including a re-evaluation of the role of the UN's principal organs. The Panel's report[74] adopted a radical approach, proposing, among other steps, that the Security Council should employ five criteria to guide its decisions on the use of force. In response, the Secretary-General produced his own report which largely endorsed the Panel's conclusions.[75] However, the UN World Summit in 2005, which also considered these issues, did not support the five criteria, although another of the Panel's proposals, the concept of a 'responsibility to protect', was accepted.

Before leaving the topic of Chapter VII, mention should be made of a practice which has developed of using this part of the Charter as a basis for various measures not involving the use of force or economic sanctions. Thus, in Resolution 827 in May 1993, the Security Council established an international tribunal to prosecute persons responsible for violations of international humanitarian law in the former Yugoslavia, and, in Resolution 955 in the following year, used a similar procedure to create an international criminal tribunal for Rwanda. Since these tribunals exercise criminal jurisdiction over individuals, their creation is relevant only indirectly to the UN's role in dispute settlement between states. In 1991, however, again acting under Chapter VII, the Security Council adopted Resolution 687 which, among other measures, provided for the demarcation of the boundary between Iraq and Kuwait by an international commission. In normal circumstances, as we have seen, the creation of arbitral tribunals,

---

[72] For discussion of these and other examples, see Gray, *Use of Force*, pp. 264–81.

[73] See further White, *The United Nations System*, pp. 143–9; and J. Lobel and M. Ratner, 'By-passing the Security Council: Ambiguous authorisations to use force, ceasefires and the Iraqi inspection regime', (1999) 93 AJIL p. 124.

[74] *A More Secure World: Our Shared Responsibility*, UN Doc. A/59/565. See also A.-M. Slaughter, 'Security, solidarity and sovereignty: The grand themes of UN reform', (2005) 99 AJIL p. 619.

[75] *In Larger Freedom: Towards Development, Security and Human Rights For All*, UN Doc. A/59/2005. See also C. Gray, 'A crisis of legitimacy for the UN collective security system?', (2007) 56 ICLQ p. 157.

demarcation commissions and the like is a matter for agreement between the states concerned. Here, however, Kuwait had been liberated by coalition forces acting under Chapter VII and the Security Council had decided to guarantee its boundary with Iraq. Since the boundary had not yet been demarcated, to set up a procedure for doing so with binding effect can be regarded as a legitimate, if unusual, exercise of the Security Council's responsibility for maintaining international peace and security.

Are decisions of the political organs open to legal challenge?

Whether decisions of the Security Council or the other political organs can be challenged before the International Court is a complex and sensitive question. For, although states have no right to bring proceedings against the UN or to challenge decisions directly, the issue of *ultra vires* is one which can arise in both advisory and contentious cases. In the *Lockerbie* cases, for example, a crucial issue was whether the Security Council had acted lawfully in adopting resolutions under Chapter VII of the Charter and whether the Court was competent to examine this question. The disputed resolutions were intended to compel Libya to surrender two terrorist suspects and the issue of legality was raised first in 1992, when Libya requested interim protection under Article 41 of the Statute, and then again in 1998, when the Court had to consider questions of admissibility and jurisdiction.

The background to these proceedings was rather unusual. When Libya refused to surrender two of its nationals who were suspected terrorists, the United States and the United Kingdom took the issue to the Security Council, which, in January 1992, adopted Resolution 731 urging Libya to co-operate. Libya then instituted proceedings in the International Court against the United States and the United Kingdom, seeking a declaration that it had complied with its obligations under the 1971 Montreal Convention and at the same time requesting interim protection. However, three days after the close of the hearings on the request, the Security Council adopted Resolution 748. This resolution, unlike Resolution 731, expressly invoked Chapter VII of the Charter, and, stating that Libya's failure to renounce terrorism constituted a threat to international peace and security, laid down that Libya must comply with the earlier resolution. Resolution 748 also imposed economic sanctions which were to apply until the Security Council decided that Libya had complied with this directive.

The Court decided that it had no option but to reject Libya's request for interim protection.[76] Under Article 25 of the Charter, member states are obliged to carry out decisions of the Security Council, and the Court

---

[76] *Questions of Interpretation and Application of the 1971 Montreal Convention Arising from the Aerial Incident at Lockerbie*, Provisional Measures, Orders of 14 April 1992, [1992] ICJ Rep. p. 3 and p. 114. See F. Beveridge, 'The Lockerbie affair', (1992) 41 ICLQ p. 907.

considered that *prima facie* this obligation extended to the decision contained in Resolution 748. Moreover, according to Article 103 of the Charter, this obligation prevailed over those in any other international agreement, including the Montreal Convention. The Court therefore concluded that 'the rights claimed by Libya under the Montreal Convention cannot now be regarded as appropriate for protection by the indication of provisional measures'.[77]

The Court's decision was unanimous on this point and appears unavoidable. Once the Security Council had taken action under Chapter VII, compliance with Libya's requests would have needed a ruling that Resolution 748 was unconstitutional. Whatever the Court's powers to deal with such questions, it is difficult to see how they could be properly addressed in incidental proceedings. The situation in the *Lockerbie* cases was therefore one in which there was a direct challenge to Security Council action and was thus quite different from that in earlier cases under Article 41. A year later, however, a parallel case occurred when, in its second request in the *Genocide Convention* case, Bosnia requested certain interim measures which would have been inconsistent with the arms embargo on the former Yugoslavia imposed by Security Council Resolution 713. On that occasion, the Court was able to avoid dealing with the point by ruling that this aspect of the request lay outside its jurisdiction as defined by the 1948 Genocide Convention.[78] Had it been necessary to address the issue directly, however, there can be little doubt that it would have dismissed Bosnia's request by relying on Article 103 of the Charter, exactly as it did in the *Lockerbie* cases.

In 1998, when the Court had to consider various issues of admissibility and jurisdiction in the *Lockerbie* cases, it found that it had jurisdiction, but by putting its decision on the narrowest grounds avoided having to examine the legality of the Security Council's actions.[79] This left open the possibility that the Court's powers of review would be considered when it finally decided the merits. In the event, however, the matter was never tested because an agreement was reached providing for trial of the two suspects before a Scottish criminal court sitting in the Netherlands. After one of the accused was convicted and imprisoned, Libya agreed to pay compensation for the atrocity, and in 2003 the cases in the International Court were discontinued.

The Court's refusal to question the Security Council's action in the truncated *Lockerbie* proceedings does not, of course, mean that there are no situations in which it can do so. Indeed, once it is recognised that the Security Council, like other international bodies, is bound by international law, questions as to the role of the Court arise quite naturally. Accordingly, it

[77] [1992] ICJ Rep. p. 15, para. 40.   [78] See [1993] ICJ Rep. pp. 344–5, para. 41.
[79] [1998] ICJ Rep. pp. 9 and 115. See P. H. F. Bekker, Note, (1998) 92 AJIL p. 503; and F. Beveridge, Note, (1999) 48 ICLQ p. 658.

is not surprising that, in both 1992 and 1998, a number of judges in the *Lockerbie* cases considered this matter in their individual opinions. Nor is this the first time it has been judicially discussed.[80] However, the issue here is complex, and to avoid confusion it is essential to separate three distinct questions: whether the Court possesses a power of judicial review; if so, what aspects of the decisions of the political organs are reviewable; and, finally, with regard to such decisions, what standard of review should be applied.[81]

As regards the first question, there is nothing in the United Nations Charter or the Statute of the Court which expressly confers a power to review the actions of the political organs. Equally, however, there is nothing which expressly prohibits such review. The answer therefore depends on whether this power is implied by the provisions of the Statute concerned with the Court's substantive jurisdiction. It will be recalled from Chapter 6 that the Court's contentious jurisdiction extends to any question of international law, while its advisory jurisdiction covers any legal question. If, as suggested above, it is accepted that the political organs are subject to international law, then questions about the validity of their decisions are clearly legal questions and accordingly subject to review, provided that the other requirements of the Statute are satisfied.

What aspects of the decisions of the political organs are reviewable, assuming that there is room in principle for judicial review, is a question on which little has yet been decided and different views have been expressed. In the *Lockerbie* and *Genocide Convention* cases, as we have seen, the issue was raised in relation to the exercise of the Security Council's powers under Chapter VII of the Charter, and, although other contexts can be imagined, this situation is particularly critical. The key, it is submitted, is to distinguish determinations calling for political appreciation from those involving legal standards. Accordingly, it has been persuasively argued that a decision by the Council under Article 39 that a situation constitutes a threat to the peace, breach of the peace or act of aggression is not reviewable and that the same is true of a decision as to whether a certain measure is likely or necessary to restore or maintain the peace.[82] On the other hand, while the Court cannot question these essentially political assessments, it can decide that the measure is not open to the Council because it transgresses basic principles of international law, or is otherwise beyond its powers.

---

[80] See, for example, the *Namibia* case, [1971] ICJ Rep. p. 16, and the *Expenses* case, [1962] ICJ Rep. p. 151, in which various aspects of this issue were considered by the Court and by individual judges.

[81] For a more detailed review of these questions, see D. Akande, 'The International Court of Justice and the Security Council: Is there room for judicial control of decisions of the political organs of the United Nations?', (1997) 46 ICLQ p. 309.

[82] *Ibid.*, pp. 336–41.

The standard of review, like the standard applicable in other courts engaged in review,[83] involves deciding how far the Court should defer to the political organ when assessing its actions. Here, there is some guidance from the case law which suggests, as might be expected, that there is a *prima facie* presumption in favour of validity.[84] This has the effect of putting the burden on the state which wishes to challenge the action in question, enables the Security Council to perform its functions without judicial sniping and avoids the risk of constant conflict. It does not prevent the Court from exercising its review function, nor in an appropriate case from finding a decision *ultra vires*. It should, however, mean that such cases will be exceptional.

It should be obvious from what has been said that the issue of judicial review poses difficult questions, and that at this stage any answers must necessarily be tentative.[85] Whereas it is clear that the Court is entitled to proceed with a case which is also being considered by the political organs and, as indicated earlier, it has made this point many times, its power to question decisions made by such organs raises constitutional issues going to the very heart of the international system which are still controversial. When dealing with the earlier point, it will be recalled that the Court observed that legal and political procedures are complementary. The approach to judicial review sketched in above, though not yet supported by a comparable weight of judicial authority, proceeds from the same assumption.

The effectiveness of the United Nations

To assess the effectiveness of the United Nations as a dispute-handling institution calls for an investigation of two quite separate questions: the extent to which the Organization is regularly involved in international disputes, and the degree to which, in cases in which the United Nations is involved, its participation is successful in the sense of achieving or encouraging a settlement.[86]

---

[83] For example, the application of the 'margin of appreciation' doctrine by the European Court of Human Rights, examined in J. G. Merrills, *The Development of International Law by the European Court of Human Rights*, 2nd edn, Manchester, 1993, Chapter 7.

[84] See Akande, 'The International Court of Justice and the Security Council', p. 341.

[85] For other views on this matter, see, for example, W. M. Reisman, 'The constitutional crisis in the United Nations', (1993) 87 AJIL p. 83; J. E. Alvarez, 'Judging the Security Council', (1996) 90 AJIL p. 1; and K. Skubiszewski, 'The International Court of Justice and the Security Council', in V. Lowe and M. Fitzmaurice (eds.), *Fifty Years of the International Court of Justice*, Cambridge, 1996, p. 606.

[86] For wide-ranging surveys showing the historical evolution, see F. S. Northedge and M. D. Donelan, *International Disputes: The Political Aspects*, London, 1971; J. G. Ruggie, 'Contingencies, constraints and collective security: Perspectives on UN involvement in international disputes', (1974) 28 Int. Org. p. 493; E. B. Haas, 'The collective management of international conflict, 1945–1984', in UNITAR, *International Peace and Security*, p. 1; and Parsons, *From Cold War to Hot Peace*.

Because the Secretary-General's power to bring a matter to the attention of the Security Council has been rarely used, most disputes which come to the United Nations are brought by the parties or by outside states. The reference may be by both parties; more commonly, however, one party will seek United Nations involvement and the other will resist it. Reference by an outside state may be on behalf of a party, where for example a dispute involves a non-member. Alternatively, raising the matter may simply reflect concern from outside states over a dispute which the parties themselves have no desire to see referred to the Organization. It follows that many disputes are never considered by the United Nations because no incentive to raise them is present, while, of those which are considered, the extent, and ultimately the effectiveness, of institutional action is likely to depend very much on the nature of the dispute and the circumstances in which the reference to the United Nations is made.

Confrontations involving the Permanent Members of the Security Council are the clearest example of disputes in which the United Nations is likely to play at best a marginal role. Mediation in such cases, whether by the Secretary-General or third states, is extremely difficult; measures proposed by the General Assembly cannot be effectively implemented, while all but limited action by the Security Council can be prevented by use of the veto. As a result, disputes of this kind either do not come before the United Nations at all, as with the dispute over Berlin between 1958 and 1961, or, if they do, as in the Cuban missile crisis of 1962, the Organization provides a sounding board for each side's claims, and an opportunity for third parties, including the Secretary-General, to exert what influence they can, but beyond this little by way of substantive contribution to any settlement.

Closely related to confrontations, and no less impervious to intervention, are disputes in which major states consider that their interests are directly involved and unlikely to be furthered by United Nations action. This is the case, for example, with claims to act in a hegemonial capacity in a region of special strategic interest. Although the United Kingdom and France over Suez in 1956, and South Africa over Namibia, were unable to block United Nations measures, in the Cold War era the United States and the Soviet Union were politically in a much stronger position. Thus, while the Soviet interventions in Hungary in 1956 and in Czechoslovakia in 1968 were all raised in the United Nations, there was really no possibility of the Organization's becoming deeply involved in these issues. Relations between the United States and the countries of Latin America are not directly comparable, but here too efforts to bring disputes involving the dominant regional power before the United Nations have usually been strongly and effectively opposed.

Although hegemonial claims are the clearest case of disputes from which the United Nations has been excluded, they are by no means the only example. Indeed, the fact that for more than forty years the United States and the Soviet Union engaged in a worldwide struggle for power and influence led to a situation in which almost any dispute could be regarded as a matter of critical interest to be dealt with outside the world organisation. Thus, until fairly recently, the scope for United Nations action in the field of dispute settlement tended in practice to be restricted to situations in which either there was no such objection to the Organization's involvement, or, more rarely, the two states saw the Organization's involvement as positively advantageous.

What kinds of dispute does the United Nations deal with? Generalisation is difficult and the kinds of dispute with which the United Nations has been concerned have varied with the changing balance of political forces within the Organization. However, it is clear that, for many years, the cases of most active involvement tended to be those in which the central question was decolonisation or some related issue. So, taking peace-keeping operations as an example, Cyprus, the Congo, West Irian, Kashmir, the Yemen and Namibia all come under this heading, while the long involvement with Israel, which, it will be recalled, was created after the termination of the British mandate over Palestine, is essentially similar in origin.

Among cases which do not fall into the above category are the Soviet disengagement from Afghanistan, the crisis in Central America and the Iran–Iraq war. In all three, as we have seen, there was a significant degree of United Nations involvement, including in the first two situations the deployment of peace-keeping forces. These demonstrate that even during the Cold War the Organization could act in other types of situations, but the special features of these cases, and in particular the position of the superpowers, should be noted. In the case of Afghanistan, where the Soviet invasion caused a major international crisis, the General Assembly passed its first resolution in 1980, but it was not until the Soviet Union was prepared to contemplate withdrawal that exploration of the possibilities of a settlement became feasible. Similarly, the creation of ONUCA became possible only when the United States decided to abandon the cause of the Contra rebels in Nicaragua. In these cases, therefore, the involvement of the United Nations depended on a reassessment of interests by the hegemonial actor. The Iran–Iraq war was rather different because neither superpower was directly involved. There, however, there was no incentive for Security Council action until the conflict threatened to expand and engulf other states in the region. Since this would have drawn in the United States and possibly the Soviet Union, by 1987 both realised that they had an interest in trying to stop the war.

The ending of the Cold War had the effect of widening the field of UN involvement by removing the paralysing influence of East–West rivalry and also because with the end of Soviet hegemony in Eastern Europe and the break-up of the Soviet Union itself came a host of new problems requiring attention. The first of these effects was quickly apparent when the invasion of Kuwait in 1990 prompted an immediate response from the Security Council which would have been unthinkable a short time earlier, and both the continuing UN involvement with Iraq and the willingness to intervene in places such as Angola and Cambodia have a similar explanation. New problems are exemplified by the situation in the former Yugoslavia where civil conflict arising out of ethnic rivalry led to UN involvement in Bosnia, foreshadowing crises in parts of the former Soviet Union such as Georgia, which have also been taken up.[87]

Thus, the field of dispute settlement with which the United Nations has been concerned has been defined by the major political forces of the post-1945 period. One, the tension between the United States and the Soviet Union, excluded a major group of disputes from the Organization, while permitting or requiring its involvement in others; another, the process of decolonisation, changed the political complexion of the United Nations and provided its major area of concern; while a third, the ending of the Cold War, opened up new possibilities for co-operation, but at the same time has given rise to new matters of concern. If we add to these political factors a major institutional development, in the form of regional organisations to be considered in the next chapter, and a traditional constraint in the shape of domestic jurisdiction, the pattern of United Nations involvement in dispute settlement begins to fall into place.

To answer our second question, we must consider the successes, partial successes and failures of the Organization.

Tension between East and West effectively wrecked the United Nations as a collective security system. Thus, during the Cold War, in all but exceptional circumstances the sanctioning provisions of Chapter VII of the Charter proved to be a dead letter. At the same time, the disregard of Security Council resolutions in the diplomatic hostages crisis, the Iran–Iraq war, the Falklands dispute and other crises, showed that the force of collective opinion is hardly an adequate substitute. On some issues, moreover, dissension within the United Nations created a situation in which steps towards the settlement of a dispute had to be taken outside the Organization. The Camp David Agreements, for example, were concluded by Israel, Egypt and the United States without any reference to the Security Council. Moreover, in 1982, in a development of considerable significance, these Agreements led to the creation of a 3,500-strong peace-keeping force, the Multinational Force and Observers (MFO), again outside the United Nations.[88]

The reactivation of Chapter VII, although only one aspect of the UN's activity in relation to disputes, means that, for the first time, the use of

---

[87] See M. Webber, 'Coping with anarchy: Ethnic conflict and international organisations in the former Soviet Union', (1996) 13 (1) Int. Rel. p. 1.

[88] For the protocol between Egypt and Israel establishing the MFO, see (1981) 20 ILM p. 1190. For discussion, see R. W. Nelson, 'Peacekeeping aspects of the Egyptian–Israeli Peace Treaty and consequences for United Nations peacekeeping', (1980) 10 Denver J. Int. L. & Pol. p. 113.

economic and military coercion has become a real option. Both were used effectively when Iraq invaded Kuwait, although the limitations of these methods are also evident, and in view of their complex ramifications it would be wrong to see either as anything but a last resort. Also significant in terms of the UN's effectiveness in this context has been the recent tendency to combine its efforts with those of regional organisations. Thus, in Haiti, economic sanctions were imposed by the Security Council following earlier action by the Organization of American States; in Bosnia, NATO was used to supply military support while diplomatic efforts were conducted jointly with the EC; and, in Central America, both ONUCA and ONUSAL originated in regional initiatives.[89] As we shall see in the next chapter, the co-ordination of regional and United Nations action is a subject on which much remains to be done, but has already contributed something to the Organization's effectiveness.

If the reactivation of Chapter VII continues to provide opportunities for constructive action, as the creation of interim administrations for Kosovo and East Timor demonstrated, the other side of the picture is that, when members of the Security Council are divided on an issue, action through the Organization will not be possible. In such circumstances, one of two things will happen. Either nothing at all will be done, or individual members will act unilaterally, perhaps, as we have seen, citing previous expressions of Security Council concern as a disingenuous justification. Thus, NATO intervened in Kosovo in 1999 when it became clear that measures against Yugoslavia under Chapter VII would be limited to censure, and the military actions against Iraq taken by the United States and the United Kingdom, which culminated in the invasion of 2003, reflected an impatience with the supervision of Iraq's disarmament by the Security Council, together with a desire to achieve regime change. That Kosovo and Iraq had both been the subject of Security Council resolutions enabled the attackers to put forward specious arguments about implied authority, but cannot conceal the fact that, looked at objectively, these were enforcement actions undertaken without Security Council authorisation and as such contrary to the Charter.

Where does this leave the balance sheet? It was noted at the beginning of this chapter that the responsibilities of the United Nations in the field of peace and security were to terminate armed conflict and to assist the parties to international disputes to settle their differences by peaceful means. While no observer of international affairs since 1945 could conclude that the United Nations has been successful in terminating conflict whenever it has occurred, it would be difficult to deny that, through peace-keeping

---

[89] For these and other cases of inter-organisational co-operation, see A. K. Henrikson, 'The growth of regional organisations and the role of the United Nations', in L. Fawcett and A. Hurrell, *Regionalism in World Politics*, Oxford, 1995, p. 122 at pp. 142–59. See also Gray, *Use of Force*, Chapter 9.

operations and in other ways, it has sometimes made a significant contribution to that end. As far as aiding the settlement of disputes is concerned, all three major organs have had successes and, when reckoning the score, it is important to understand that the quiet diplomacy of the Secretary-General, by its very nature, will often leave no mark on the diplomatic record. But, if success has sometimes been achieved, it is only necessary to recall the cases mentioned earlier and the perennial issues – the Arab–Israeli dispute, Kashmir, Cyprus and the Lebanon – to see disputes on which the Organization has apparently had little impact.

In *An Agenda for Peace*,[90] his 1992 report to the Security Council, Secretary-General Boutros-Ghali examined the potential of the United Nations in the fields of preventive diplomacy, peace-keeping, peace-making and post-conflict peace-building. It is clear from the record that efforts so far have been mainly directed to the first two activities, which are also where most has been achieved. Thus, the fact that the United Nations has often been more successful in arranging truces and supervising periods of relative calm than in dealing with underlying problems has often been noted, and, as we have seen, peace-keeping operations, until quite recently, have certainly been less concerned with dispute settlement than with the prevention of violence. Such 'prophylactic' operations are valuable, of course, and may provide a vital foundation for a final settlement. On the other hand, this is by no means guaranteed, and though much better than nothing, operations which are interminable or repetitious may become in effect a substitute for a settlement, a perpetual treatment of symptoms rather than causes. As already noted, attempts to advance from this position by grafting enforcement capabilities onto peace-keeping forces have not been very successful. The 'integrated and pacific' approach, on the other hand, shows more promise, but, like all peace-making initiatives, depends very much on local conditions.

To see why all this is so is to begin to understand the nature and limitations of the United Nations system. The Organization is a reflection of the social and political relations of states. Largely as a result of the efforts of the Secretariat, the whole is now a little greater than the sum of the parts and the institution has acquired a degree of authority in dispute situations. However, effective action by the United Nations is possible only in so far as states are prepared to relinquish attempts to control disputes by the use of their own power. When things become sufficiently serious, a United Nations presence or other initiative may be acceptable, but, unless what is wanted is simply a face-saving arrangement, settling the basic issue is likely to be much more difficult. In cases like those which have been mentioned, prophylactic measures may be all that is politically possible, yet the fact that

---

[90] SC Doc. S/24111, 17 June 1992. Text in (1992) 31 ILM p. 953. See also *Supplement to Agenda for Peace*, S/1995/1.

a festering dispute remains on the agenda will be accounted another failure of the Organization.

In a trenchant observation, U Thant explained the true position:

> Great problems usually come to the United Nations because governments have been unable to think of anything else to do about them. The United Nations is a last-ditch, last-resort affair, and it is not surprising that the Organization should often be blamed for failing to solve problems that have already been found to be insoluble by governments. More often than not, the United Nations is criticised for failing to resolve a crisis or to enforce an action. It is not generally realised that the failure of the United Nations is the failure of the international community, and the failure to enforce an action is due to the refusal of the party or parties concerned to comply with the Organization's decisions.[91]

The United Nations, then, is in no sense a world government, but a diplomatic forum in which persuasion, argument, negotiation and a search for consensus are the means available for handling international disputes. Like any human institution, its organisation and procedures are imperfect and could be improved.[92] At root, however, its activities – successes as well as failures – are less a matter of institutional arrangements than a reflection of the statesmanship, or otherwise, of those responsible for the direction of affairs.

[91] U Thant, *View from the UN*, p. 32.
[92] For some suggestions as to how this might be done, see Chapter 12 below.

11

Regional organisations

The growth and development of the United Nations as the major universal organisation has been accompanied by a no less dramatic increase in the number and range of organisations with membership drawn from the states of a particular region. Such regional organisations frequently become involved in the resolution of disputes.[1] Sometimes this is because dispute settlement has been defined as a goal of the organisation. Article 4(e) of the Constitutive Act of the African Union, for example, lays down as one of its aims the peaceful resolution of conflicts between member states, and similar provisions can be found in the constitutions of other organisations. But even organisations whose primary concern is with matters of no present relevance may find themselves involved in some form of settlement activity. For bringing states together in an institutional setting provides the parties to a dispute with an opportunity to settle their differences and regional neighbours with the chance to add their encouragement, assistance and pressure as an incentive.

The range of regional organisations

The role played by a particular regional organisation depends very much on the characteristics of the organisation concerned: where it is located, how it is structured and what resources it commands. For this reason, though detailed treatment must be sought elsewhere,[2] a glance at some of the leading regional organisations may be useful. Europe, which contains an exceptional number and variety of organisations, is an instructive place to begin.

The Council of Europe was founded in 1949 for the discussion of matters of common interest, to promote conventions on such matters and with the

---

[1] On the role of regional organisations, see L. Fawcett and A. Hurrell (eds.), *Regionalism in World Politics*, Oxford, 1995; F. S. Northedge and M. D. Donelan, *International Disputes: The Political Aspects*, London, 1971, Chapter 11; E. Luard, *The International Regulation of Frontier Disputes*, London, 1970, Chapter 4; L. B. Sohn, 'The role of international institutions as conflict-adjusting agencies', (1960–1) 28 U. Chi. L. Rev. p. 205. See also C. Peck, *Sustainable Peace*, Lanham, MD, 1998; and C. Gray, *International Law and the Use of Force*, 2nd edn, Oxford, 2004, Chapter 9. On particular organisations, see the works cited below.

[2] For general surveys, see N. D. White, *The Law of International Organizations*, Manchester, 1996; and P. Sands and P. Klein, *Bowett's Law of International Institutions*, 5th edn, London, 2001.

specific aim of promoting and protecting human rights. The Council is in no sense a supranational organisation, but has achieved a great deal by way of consultation and co-operation. In the field of dispute settlement, the Council's major achievement has been the European Convention on Human Rights, an agreement by the states of democratic Europe to respect the rights defined in the Convention and to submit disputes concerning its application and interpretation to international supervisory machinery.

The European Community (EC) represents a radically different approach. In 1952, the European Coal and Steel Community was created as an instrument of economic integration and later expanded with the addition of the European Economic Community and the European Atomic Energy Community in 1957. Subsequent developments, notably the Single European Act (1986) and the Treaty of Maastricht (1992), furthered the process of integration, introducing political objectives and the concept of the European Union (EU) and consolidating institutional arrangements which already included majority voting and executive powers. Further evolution took place through the Treaty of Amsterdam (1997) and the Lisbon Treaty which came into force in 2009. Under the current arrangements, the settlement of disputes is the responsibility of the European Court of Justice and its Court of First Instance, with an extensive jurisdiction covering member states, Community organs and natural and legal persons.

Turning from economic to military integration, the North Atlantic Treaty Organization (NATO), founded in 1949 as a regional security organisation, includes in its membership the United States, Canada and Iceland, as well as many European states. Although primarily an alliance against external aggression, NATO is also concerned with promoting co-operation in the non-military field and the settlement of disputes between its members. In 1956, NATO's supreme organ, the North Atlantic Council, made this commitment quite explicit when it resolved that, with certain exceptions, disputes which cannot be settled by direct negotiation should be submitted to a good offices procedure within NATO before resort to any other organisation.[3] The same resolution recognised that the Secretary-General and each member have both a right and a duty to draw the Council's attention to matters capable of threatening the solidarity or effectiveness of the alliance. Moreover, the Secretary-General was authorised to offer his good offices to the parties to a dispute at any time, and with their consent to facilitate procedures of inquiry, mediation, conciliation or arbitration.

The Eastern European equivalent of NATO was the Warsaw Treaty Organization, a military alliance founded by the Soviet Union and covering most of Eastern Europe. The corresponding economic organisation was the

---

[3] C. M. H. Waldock (ed.), *International Disputes: The Legal Aspects*, London, 1972, p. 256. Also F. L. Kirgis, 'NATO consultations as a component of national decision-making', (1979) 73 AJIL p. 372.

Council for Mutual Economic Aid, established in 1949 as an instrument of economic co-operation but, like the Warsaw Pact, with apparently no formal machinery for the settlement of disputes. Between 1949 and 1989, Europe was sharply divided between East and West, with the rival military and economic organisations in static and seemingly permanent confrontation. However, when the Soviet Union at last withdrew support from its clients in Eastern Europe, the way was clear for non-communist governments to emerge. With the ending of the Cold War, the basis for the Warsaw Pact and its economic counterpart disappeared and both arrangements collapsed, along with the Soviet Union itself, and was replaced in 1991 by a new regional body, the Commonwealth of Independent States (CIS),[4] led by the Russian Federation.

These momentous changes had important effects on Europe's other institutions. In 1994, the Conference on Security and Co-operation in Europe (CSCE), a series of meetings which since 1975 had dealt with East–West affairs, was renamed the Organization for Security and Co-operation in Europe (OSCE) in recognition of its transformation from a loose arrangement of conferences to a fully fledged organisation with permanent arrangements concerning human rights, security, dispute settlement and other matters.[5] With a membership of more than fifty states, including the United States and Canada, the OSCE is now the largest European organisation. The three organisations mentioned earlier have also been profoundly affected. Thus, membership of the Council of Europe has been extended to many of the former communist states, including Russia itself. And, in 1997, decisions were taken to expand both the EC and NATO by inviting a number of Eastern European states to join, which took place soon afterwards.[6] These organisations have therefore all recently increased their membership significantly and may well expand further in the future.

On the other side of the Atlantic, the main regional organisation is the Organization of American States (OAS). Founded in 1948 in order to place earlier arrangements for inter-American co-operation on a firmer and broader constitutional basis, the OAS and its predecessors have been concerned with a wide range of matters of common interest, including, on numerous occasions, the settlement of disputes between member states.

The legal framework for the OAS is provided by three treaties. The Inter-American Treaty of Reciprocal Assistance (Rio Treaty, 1947) creates a defensive alliance comparable in some ways to NATO, in which the parties undertake to exercise their collective right of self-defence under Article 51 of

---

[4] For the texts of the 1993 Commonwealth of Independent States Charter and the CIS Treaty on Creation of Economic Union, see (1995) 34 ILM p. 1279 and p. 1298.

[5] See M. Sapiro, 'Changing the CSCE into the OSCE: Legal aspects of a political transformation', (1995) 89 AJIL p. 631.

[6] For the significance of these developments, see J. Woodliffe, 'The evolution of a new NATO for a new Europe', (1998) 47 ICLQ p. 174.

the United Nations Charter and to use the institutional machinery of the OAS for consultation. That machinery is largely contained in the Charter of Bogotá (1948), which lays down the principles of the Organization and defines its institutional arrangements. Significant changes to the Charter, including provisions to consolidate democracy, were introduced in the 1992 Protocol of Washington,[7] which came into force in 1997. The third treaty, the American Treaty on Pacific Settlement (Pact of Bogotá, 1948) is exclusively concerned with the settlement of disputes and contains elaborate arrangements for mediation, inquiry, conciliation and judicial settlement. The treaty has provided the basis on which a number of cases have been taken to the International Court, but in other respects has had only limited use. Consequently, OAS activity in the field of dispute settlement has usually been channelled through the various organs created by the Charter.[8]

There are five organs of the OAS of interest for present purposes. The supreme organ is the Inter-American Conference, or General Assembly. It 'decides the general action and policy of the Organization and determines the structure and function of its Organs, and has the authority to consider any matter relating to friendly relations among the American States'.[9] Its brief therefore includes the settlement of disputes, but the fact that the Conference's regular meetings are scheduled to take place at five-yearly intervals greatly restricts its significance in practice.

The Meeting of Consultation of Ministers of Foreign Affairs is much more important. It acts as the organ of consultation on matters of peace and security under the Rio Treaty. It can also meet at any time to consider urgent matters of common interest to the American states and in practice therefore tends to act as the supreme organ of the institution. Requests to convene a Meeting of Consultation may be made by any member and are addressed to the Permanent Council. The Council, as the standing political organ of the OAS, is permanently in session in Washington. Subordinate to the Council is the Inter-American Committee on Peaceful Settlement, consisting of five member states, elected by the Council. Created in 1970 to replace the earlier Inter-American Peace Committee,[10] the new Committee has the function of assisting in the resolution of disputes through inquiry, mediation and recommendations on appropriate means of settlement.

The other body that needs to be mentioned is the Secretariat. Under Article 116 of the OAS Charter, the Secretary-General participated 'with

---

[7] Text in (1994) 33 ILM p. 1005 and see E. Lagos and T. D. Rudy, 'The Third Summit of the Americas and the thirty-first session of the OAS General Assembly', (2002) 96 AJIL p. 173.

[8] For a useful account of the contrast between the theory and practice of the OAS system, see L. R. Scheman and J. W. Ford, 'The Organization of American States as mediator', in S. Touval and I. W. Zartman (eds.), *International Mediation in Theory and Practice*, Boulder, CO, 1985, p. 197.

[9] Charter of Bogotá, 1948, Article 33.

[10] See C. Sepulveda, 'The reform of the Charter of American States', (1972) 137 *Hague Recueil des Cours*, p. 83; and J. C. Drier, 'New wine and old bottles: The changing inter-American system', (1968) 22 Int. Org. p. 477.

voice but without vote in all meetings of the Organization'. This offered a more limited scope for initiative than Article 99 of the United Nations Charter, but in 1985 was amended to allow the Secretary-General, like his UN counterpart, to bring to the attention of the Assembly or Council 'any matter which in his opinion might threaten the peace and security of the hemisphere or the development of the Member States'.[11] This indicates an intention on the part of the member states to see the Secretary-General playing a more active role in the settlement of disputes, an impression which was confirmed soon afterwards when he was entrusted with a mandate relating to the situation in Central America and, together with the UN Secretary-General, gave assistance to the Contadora Group.[12]

No regional organisation in Africa or Asia is as structurally complex as the OAS, but two, the African Union (AU), formerly the Organization of African Unity (OAU), and the Arab League, have dispute settlement as a major objective. The OAU was founded in 1963 with the aim of encouraging and co-ordinating the activities of African states on matters of common interest, including the peaceful settlement of disputes and defence against external aggression.[13] Despite the similarity between these objectives and those of the OAS, the OAU was a much looser type of regional organisation with an emphasis on moral rather than legal obligations and on respect for the members' sovereignty. This difference was clearly evident in the main organs of the OAU which were four in number.

The supreme organ both in theory and in fact was the Assembly of Heads of State and Government, which met annually or sometimes in extraordinary session. It could discuss and pass resolutions on any matter, but only as recommendations, and there was no power to enforce decisions, or expel members for non-compliance. The Council of Ministers, which normally met twice a year, was made up of the foreign ministers of member states and had the task of implementing the Assembly's decisions, while a third organ, the General Secretariat, was run by an 'administrative secretary-general' whose functions, as the name implies, were intended to be more limited than those performed by the Secretary-General in the United Nations and other international organisations.

The specific issue of dispute settlement was originally intended to be the responsibility of a fourth major organ, the Commission of Mediation, Conciliation and Arbitration.[14] The Protocol setting up the Commission in 1964 contained elaborate provisions for the creation of boards of mediation,

---

[11] Protocol of Cartagena de Indias, 1985, Article 116.
[12] See H. Caminos and R. Lavalle, 'New departures in the exercise of inherent powers by the UN and OAS Secretaries-General: The Central American situation', (1989) 83 AJIL p. 395.
[13] See T. O. Elias, 'The Charter of the Organization of African Unity', (1965) 59 AJIL p. 243.
[14] See T. O. Elias, 'The Commission of Mediation, Conciliation and Arbitration of the Organization of African Unity', (1964) 40 BYBIL p. 336; and H. A. Amankwah, 'International law, dispute settlement and regional organisations in an African setting', (1981) 21 Ind. J. Int. L. p. 352.

conciliation or arbitration from a panel elected by the Assembly. However, the Commission, whose jurisdiction rested on the consent of the parties to a dispute, never became operational.[15] As a result the institutions of the OAU, including the administrative secretary-general, were more actively involved in dispute settlement than might have been anticipated. Recognising the ineffectiveness of the Commission, the Assembly established a 'Mechanism for Conflict Prevention, Management and Resolution' in 1993.[16] This was intended to put conflict management and dispute avoidance on a formal basis, using both the influence of the member states and contributions from the Secretary-General and seems to have been quite useful.

In 2001, the Constitutive Act of the African Union came into force, setting up a new regional organisation which is expected eventually to have, among other organs, its own Parliament, Court of Justice and Central Bank.[17] This major development, which was foreshadowed in the 1991 Treaty Establishing the African Economic Community, represents, at least potentially, a huge stride in institutional arrangements in Africa. In a further development, the AU Assembly adopted a Protocol in 2008 with the aim of establishing a new African Court of Justice and Human Rights.[18] In terms of the implications for dispute settlement in the region, the most significant features of the Union are that it has been created to replace the OAU and that the Constitutive Act, unlike the OAU Charter, both recognises the need for and encourages a collective response to internal conflict in certain circumstances. However, the Act also reaffirms the principles of domestic sovereignty and non-intervention. Accordingly, much will depend on how the powers of the AU are interpreted in practice, a matter in the hands of its supreme decision-making organ, the Assembly of Heads of State and Government, as in the OAU.

A number of members of the OAU are also members of the Arab League.[19] This was founded in 1945 to co-ordinate the members' activities in economic

---

[15] See T. Maluwa, 'The peaceful settlement of disputes among African states, 1963–1983: Some conceptual issues and practical trends', (1989) 38 ICLQ p. 299; and W. J. Foltz, 'The Organization of African Unity and the resolution of Africa's conflicts', in F. M. Deng and I. W. Zartman (eds.), *Conflict Resolution in Africa*, Washington, 1991, p. 347. See also G. J. Naldi, *The Organization of African Unity*, 2nd edn, London, 1999, pp. 24–9.

[16] See Naldi, *ibid.*, pp. 32–3; and Peck, *Sustainable Peace*, pp. 162–7.

[17] See K. D. Magliveras and G. J. Naldi, 'The African Union – A new dawn for Africa?', (2002) 51 ICLQ p. 415; and C. A. A. Packer and D. Rukare, 'The new African Union and its Constitutive Act', (2002) 96 AJIL p. 365. Although the Act establishing the Union outlines its structure, details of its organs were left for later protocols.

[18] See G. J. Naldi, 'Aspects of the African Court of Justice and Human Rights', in D. French, M. Saul and N. D. White (eds.), *International Law and Dispute Settlement: New Problems and Techniques*, Oxford, 2010, p. 321.

[19] For discussion of the activities of the League, see B. Boutros-Ghali, 'The Arab League (1945–1970)', 25 Rev. Egypt. Droit Int. p. 67; and S. J. Al Kadhem, 'The role of the League of Arab States in settling inter-Arab disputes', (1976) 32 Rev. Egypt. Droit Int. p. 1. See also Sands and Klein, *Bowett's Law*, pp. 237–40.

and financial affairs, commercial relations and a variety of political and social matters. An even looser arrangement than the OAU, the League has as its supreme organ a Council, which takes decisions unanimously, each member having one vote. Although members have agreed to renounce force in the settlement of their disputes and to accept decisions of the Council as binding, they are under no obligation to take a dispute to the Council. In the absence of other machinery, the settlement of disputes is therefore entirely a matter for the parties, prompted by whatever informal assistance may be offered by the Secretariat of the League and the other members.[20]

An attempt to provide a more formal procedure for the resolution of disputes has been put forward by another institution with a membership drawn from more than one region, the Organization of the Islamic Conference (OIC).[21] The Charter of the Conference, which was agreed in 1972, provides for co-operation among Muslim states in accordance with the principle of Islamic solidarity and several agreements relating to economic co-operation have been concluded. At the Third Summit Conference of the OIC in 1981, it was decided to establish an Islamic Court of Justice, and, at the Fifth Conference in 1987, a Statute for the Court was adopted as an amendment to the Charter.[22] It is evidently intended that the new court will eventually provide a forum for the resolution of inter-Islamic disputes under Islamic law, and so provide Islamic states with an alternative to the International Court. There can be no objection in principle to the use of an institution based on religious affiliation as a forum for dispute settlement, although identifying relevant norms and harmonising them with states' rights and duties under international law may present difficulties. However, as the Court is not yet functioning, the value of this innovation remains to be seen.

In this brief survey, it has been impossible to mention, let alone examine, every regional organisation whose work may have a bearing on dispute settlement. Moreover, it is worth pointing out that, within regions, there are often to be found sub-regional organisations, whose contributions can also be important. Though space precludes discussion of these, of the numerous river commissions and of other organisations with specialised functions, as well as relative newcomers like ASEAN and CARICOM, enough has been said to demonstrate the variety of purposes for which states set up regional organisations and their very different institutional structures.

So much for theory. What have regional organisations been able to contribute to the resolution of disputes?

---

[20] However, in 1996, the League resolved to set up a 'Mechanism for the Prevention, Management and Resolution of Conflicts among Arab States' and also to create an Arab Court of Justice. For the text of this resolution, see (1996) 35 ILM p. 1289.

[21] For a comprehensive account of the structure and activities of the OIC, see H. Moinuddin, *The Charter of the Islamic Conference*, Oxford, 1987, Part II.

[22] Resolution 13/5 – P [IS] (1987); see F. E. Vogel, Review, (1989) 83 AJIL p. 228.

The role of regional organisations in disputes

One of the most useful functions of a regional organisation is to provide its members with a forum for consultation and negotiation in actual or potential dispute situations. The opportunities for informal contact which the meetings of an organisation provide can be particularly valuable where a dispute has caused normal diplomatic relations to be suspended. In both the dispute over the status of Cyprus, involving Britain, Greece and Turkey, and the various 'Cod Wars' between Britain and Iceland, the fact that all the states concerned were members of NATO ensured that lines of communication remained open, despite a degree of bitterness and hostility which on several occasions led to the use of force.

In 1961, Anglo-Icelandic contact through NATO helped to secure a negotiated settlement of the dispute over Iceland's twelve-mile fishing zone. Fifteen years later, when the issue was a 200-mile zone, NATO again played a constructive role. As in the previous disputes, Iceland's attempts to enforce its new limits had met with a forceful response from the Royal Navy and relations between Britain and Iceland were at a low ebb. However, through the good offices of the Norwegian Foreign Minister and the Secretary-General of NATO, the two sides were brought together during a meeting of the Foreign Ministers of the NATO countries in Oslo and shortly afterwards negotiated an agreement to end the dispute.[23]

An example of the provision of good offices over an extended period is provided by the OAU's handling of the border dispute between Algeria and Morocco in 1963.[24] The OAU established an *ad hoc* commission which held a number of meetings with the parties, and, with the aid of the commission's good offices, agreements were negotiated concerning the withdrawal of troops, the return of prisoners and the restoration of diplomatic relations.

No doubt one can exaggerate the part regional organisations played in securing a settlement in these and similar cases. In the Cod Wars, Britain, which made most of the concessions, badly needed a settlement, and resolution of the Algeria–Morocco dispute in 1970 was finally achieved by an agreement in which the OAU commission played no part. But, if the settlement of these disputes ultimately depended on the parties' willingness to agree, it is clear that their respective regional organisations provided them with an opportunity which would not otherwise have been available, and with encouragement and assistance in surmounting critical obstacles to negotiation.

It is a short step from good offices to mediation, and regional organisations, through their officials and member states, are often well placed to

---

[23]   See H. Jónsson, *Friends in Conflict*, London, 1982, pp. 179–81.
[24]   See P. B. Wild, 'The Organization of African Unity and the Algerian–Moroccan border conflict', (1966) 20 Int. Org. p. 18.

act in this capacity. In 1957, for example, the OAS intervened as mediator in the dispute between Honduras and Nicaragua over the arbitral award of the King of Spain.[25] Following complaints of aggression from both states, the Council of the OAS met in special session and appealed to the parties to refrain from provocative acts. It then appointed a committee, consisting of representatives of five member states, with the task of considering the dispute. The committee visited the two capitals and soon secured agreements providing for a cease-fire and mutual troop withdrawals. When the committee returned to Washington, its report was adopted by the Council, which then appointed the same members to an *ad hoc* committee with the task of devising an acceptable procedure for settling the dispute. Here, the committee's attempts at mediation proved unsuccessful, but, as a result of a further effort by the Council, the parties were eventually persuaded to resolve the dispute by referring it to adjudication.[26]

More recently, mediation has proved to be one of the most useful functions performed by the CSCE/OSCE. In 1993, for example, a CSCE mission was deployed in Moldova to assist negotiations on the status of the disputed Dneister region and on the withdrawal of Russian troops based in the area. In the following year, Moldova accepted a CSCE plan recommending autonomy for the Dneister and the withdrawal of Russian troops was agreed in principle. It is better, of course, if, instead of being called upon to resolve disputes, an organisation can act at an earlier stage with a view to avoiding them. As well as mediating, the OSCE therefore assigns long-duration missions to likely trouble spots as a form of preventive diplomacy. In 1994, for example, it had nine such missions in operation, all in the former Soviet Union or ex-Yugoslavia.[27]

The OAU was also often involved in mediation, sometimes in conjunction with other organisations. In 1998, for example, following an outbreak of fighting between Ethiopia and Eritrea, the OAU assisted the parties to negotiate a peace agreement which came info force in 2000. As part of the settlement, the two states agreed to establish both a boundary commission to delimit their disputed frontier, and a claims commission to resolve issues arising out of the war. The regional mediation effort here was greatly assisted by support from the United Nations which contributed a

---

[25] See C. G. Fenwick, 'The Honduras–Nicaragua boundary dispute', (1957) 51 AJIL p. 761. For further examples, see Touval and Zartman, *International Mediation*, p. 197.

[26] See *Arbitral Award Made by the King of Spain on 23 December 1906*, Judgment, [1960] ICJ Rep. p. 192. For discussion of the Court's decision, see Chapter 5. Mediation by the OAU played a part in persuading Libya and Chad to refer another long-standing dispute to the ICJ leading eventually to the judgment in the *Territorial Dispute* case, [1994] ICJ Rep. p. 6. See S. G. Amoo and I. W. Zartman, 'Mediation by regional organisations: The Organization for African Unity (OAU) in Chad', in J. Bercovitch and J. Z. Rubin (eds.), *Mediation in International Relations*, London, 1992, p. 131.

[27] See M. Webber, 'Coping with anarchy: Ethnic conflict and international organisations in the former Soviet Union', (1996) 13 (1) Int. Rel. p. 1.

peace-keeping force (UNMEE), as well as the services of the Cartographic Section of the UN Secretariat to help with mapping.[28]

Instead of providing mediation through its own officials or organs, a regional organisation may encourage settlement of a dispute by lending its authority to, and thereby legitimising, mediation from another source. In 1972, for example, a dispute occurred between Tanzania and Uganda when the latter was invaded by supporters of the recently deposed president, who had taken refuge in Tanzania.[29] Uganda responded by bombing Tanzanian border villages, and fighting involving both states' forces broke out. With the assistance of the administrative secretary-general of the OAU, the President of Somalia intervened as mediator and succeeded in persuading both sides to agree to a truce, negotiations and troop withdrawals, and to undertake to respect each other's sovereignty. An observer mission under a Somali general supervised the execution of these arrangements and, following the OAU summit meeting in 1973, relations between the two states were temporarily restored.

Inquiry and conciliation are relatively formal processes which regional organisations with the necessary resources and institutions can also use to good effect. The Chaco Commission, set up by the Conference of American States in 1929 to investigate a border dispute between Bolivia and Paraguay, has already been described.[30] It will be recalled that the Commission combined the functions of inquiry and conciliation, and by emphasising the latter succeeded in obtaining the parties' agreement to a settlement. In 1937, another Inter-American Commission of Inquiry and Conciliation was set up to consider a dispute between Haiti and the Dominican Republic. The dispute arose out of a border incident in which it was alleged that a number of Haitians had been killed by Dominican soldiers. The Commission found the case to be proved and proposed that the Dominican Republic should pay Haiti an indemnity as compensation, a solution which was accepted by both parties.

Conciliation also occupies a prominent place in the various arrangements set up by the OSCE. It will be recalled from Chapter 4 that the Valletta Procedure, agreed in 1991, is essentially a process of mandatory conciliation,

---

[28] See B. Simma and D.-E. Khan, 'Peaceful settlement of boundary disputes under the auspices of the Organization of African Unity and the United Nations: The case of the frontier dispute between Eritrea and Ethiopia', in N. Ando, E. McWhinney and R. Wolfrum (eds.), *Liber Amicorum Judge Shigeru Oda*, The Hague, 2002, p. 1179. Also J. G. Merrills, 'Reflections on dispute settlement in the light of recent arbitrations involving Eritrea', in A. Constantinides and N. Zaikos (eds.), *The Diversity of International Law*, Leiden, 2009, p. 109.

[29] See B. D. Meyers, 'Intraregional conflict management by the Organization of African Unity', (1974) 28 Int. Org. p. 345 at pp. 359–60. For subsequent developments, see M. Shaw, 'Dispute settlement in Africa', (1983) 37 Yearbook of WA p. 149 at pp. 156–7. For further examples, see M. Wolfers, 'The Organization of African Unity as mediator', in Touval and Zartman, *International Mediation*, p. 175.

[30] See Chapter 4.

with elements of mediation and inquiry, and in 1992 was complemented by the creation of formal arrangements for voluntary and directed conciliation. In addition, by subscribing to the 1992 Stockholm Convention, OSCE states can assume a legal commitment to employ conciliation or arbitration. While the Convention is binding only on the states which are parties to it, the other procedures represent a political commitment on the part of all the OSCE states. This is particularly significant because, apart from the UN, the OSCE is the only organisation that includes in its membership all the members of NATO and the former Warsaw Pact, together with the Soviet successor states. In so far as its procedures can be effectively employed in dispute situations, they therefore have a reach and legitimacy unique among European organisations.[31]

The value of an organisation's ability to deploy resources is well illustrated by two disputes between Costa Rica and Nicaragua which came before the OAS soon after its creation.[32] In the first, in 1948, the OAS set up an 'Information and Study Committee' to examine Costa Rican allegations that Nicaragua had supported an invasion of its territory. In light of its committee's investigation, the OAS decided that both sides were partly to blame, set up a commission to supervise the border and persuaded the parties to sign a Pact of Amity, pledging respect for each other's sovereignty. The second dispute, in 1955, followed a similar pattern. Again, Costa Rica complained of aggression and a committee was established to investigate the complaint. A more comprehensive system of border supervision, involving aerial surveillance and the creation of a demilitarised zone, was set up, and, in January 1956, a new agreement (which proved more durable than its predecessor) was signed by the two states.

Even more elaborate were the various initiatives in the same region which together made up the Contadora process.[33] In 1983, alarmed by the dangerous tension in Central America, the foreign ministers of Colombia, Mexico, Panama and Venezuela met on Contadora island, Panama, to consider the contribution which their countries could make to the resolution of the problems of the region. This was followed by a series of visits to Nicaragua, Honduras, Costa Rica, El Salvador and Guatemala which set in motion an elaborate multilateral negotiation. From 1985, the process was joined by the foreign ministers of Argentina, Brazil, Peru and Uruguay, who became known as the 'Support Group', and, in 1986, this phase of the process culminated in the Act of Contadora, a proposed regional agreement, which was unfortunately rejected by several of the protagonists. In 1987, however, the

---

[31] See Webber, 'Coping with anarchy', p. 8.

[32] On these disputes and the Haiti–Dominican Republic dispute, see P. Lyon, 'Regional organisations and frontier disputes', in Luard, *Frontier Disputes*, p. 109 at pp. 126–7.

[33] A detailed account of the Contadora process and its aftermath can be found in paragraphs 70–5 and 81–8 of the judgment of the International Court in the *Border and Transborder Armed Actions* case, [1988] ICJ Rep. p. 69. The Court's decision in this case is discussed below.

presidents of the five Central American states made a new agreement, known as the Esquipulas II Accord. This provided for free elections, the termination of hostilities and an end to assistance for irregular forces. The Contadora Group and the Support Group were enlisted to provide security, verification and control, and, as mentioned earlier, the OAS Secretary-General and the UN Secretary-General were also involved.

In 2000, the OAS undertook a similar constructive role in a long-standing dispute between Guatemala and Belize over their common boundary. Here, the OAS sponsored a 'Facilitation Process', in essence a type of conciliation which involved each side nominating a Facilitator, who would then be assisted by the Secretary-General of the OAS in proposing confidence-building measures, examining the substance of the dispute and recommending a solution. Subsequently, the two Facilitators were joined by a third, nominated by Honduras, to assist with discussions relating to maritime areas in the Gulf of Honduras. Initially, efforts were devoted to developing confidence-building measures in order to relieve tension in the border area, and a series of such measures was agreed, including the creation of a mixed commission to promote co-operation. The dispute has not yet been resolved, but with additional assistance from the OAS the parties have discussed further ways of improving relations.[34]

From the cases considered so far it is evident that much of the work of regional organisations in the field of dispute settlement is simply an application of familiar techniques in an institutional setting. In other words, it is often more accurate to speak of settlement *through* rather than *by* regional organisations. This is not the whole picture, however. Regional organisations can also make a contribution which is uniquely their own. Through collective action the members of a body like the OAU or OAS may be able to achieve something which would be difficult or impossible for any state acting alone.

In 1964, the OAU agreed by an overwhelming majority to respect the boundaries of each member as they existed on the achieving of national independence.[35] The endorsement of this principle was clearly intended to stabilise the *status quo* and thus to avoid disputes about African boundaries. It has had that effect by demonstrating to potential trouble-makers that challenges to the *status quo* would be costly, and, when this was not enough, by imposing some constraints on their actions.[36] The resolution has therefore been quite successful in practice and shows

---

[34] See J. G. Merrills, 'The Belize–Guatemala territorial dispute and the Legal Opinion of January 2002', (2002) 2 Global Community YBILJ p. 77 at pp. 81 and 93–4.

[35] See S. Touval, 'The Organization of African Unity and African borders', (1967) 21 Int. Org. p. 102; and A. O. Cukwurah, 'The Organization of African Unity and African territorial and boundary problems 1963–1973', (1973) 13 Ind. J. Int. L. p. 176.

[36] See I. W. Zartman, 'Conflict reduction: prevention, management and resolution', in Deng and Zartman, *Conflict Resolution in Africa*, p. 299 at p. 317.

how collective legitimisation, already noted as relevant to mediation, can operate at an earlier stage, and prevent, or at least discourage, disputes from arising.

For some types of disputes or situations, a collective declaration of non-intervention, for which a regional organisation supplies a convenient forum, can be a way of avoiding escalation. Individual declarations of non-intervention, in, for example, a civil war or a revolution, may be politically disadvantageous, or dismissed as misleading propaganda. Issued collectively, however, and buttressed by reciprocity, such declarations are both easier to make and harder to break and by reducing the danger of outside involvement can make a real contribution to peaceful settlement.

Collective action can also take a positive form. In 1960, the Meeting of Foreign Ministers of the OAS heard a complaint brought by Venezuela against the Dominican Republic in which acts of intervention were alleged to have culminated in an attempt on the life of Venezuela's Chief of State.[37] An OAS committee had earlier found the charges to be true, and, in light of this, it was decided, for the first time in the Organization's history, to apply sanctions under Articles 6 and 8 of the Rio Treaty. The Organ of Consultation decided to break diplomatic relations with the Dominican Republic and to suspend the sale of arms, a measure which was later extended to petrol and trucks.

Regional organisations have also taken part in peace-keeping operations of various kinds. Although established only in 1991, the CIS has already deployed forces in several parts of the former Soviet Union, including Georgia, where the collapse of civil order led to the sending of a force, following a cease-fire agreement in May 1994. A UN observer mission, UNOMIG, was already in the area, and Security Council resolutions in July 1994 and May 1995 welcomed the co-operation between UN and CIS forces.[38] In 1996, the CIS Council adopted a far-reaching policy statement related to the prevention and settlement of conflicts in the member states, indicating their intention to further develop peace-keeping and related activities (document K in the appendix below). Particularly interesting features of this statement are the emphasis on the possible role of the CIS in conflict prevention and the elaborate arrangements for co-operation with other international organisations, especially the UN and the OSCE. In a further decision at the same time, the Council adopted a statute on collective

[37] See R. St J. Macdonald, 'The Organization of American States in action', (1963–4) 15 U. Toronto LJ p. 359 at pp. 367–72.

[38] Webber, 'Coping with anarchy', p. 18. See also Gray, *Use of Force*, pp. 310–12, dealing also with the CIS operation in Tajikistan at pp. 309–10. More recently, however, in the lead-up to the conflict between Russia and Georgia in 2008, the presence of CIS forces was an aggravating factor. See C. Gray, 'The protection of nationals abroad: Russia's use of force in Georgia', in Constantinides and Zaikos, *The Diversity of International Law*, p. 133 at p. 141.

peace-keeping forces,[39] covering their legal basis, composition, functions, training and other matters, in considerable detail, confirming that more operations of this type are envisaged.

In recent years, a number of peace-keeping operations have been carried out in Africa under the auspices of regional or sub-regional organisations.[40] Between 1990 and 1997, for example, the Economic Community of West African States (ECOWAS) undertook a major operation in Liberia, and was involved there again in 2003. ECOWAS was also active in Sierra Leone in 1997 and in Ivory Coast in 2003, in all three cases receiving support from the UN Security Council. In 2002, the Communauté Econonomique et Monétaire de l'Afrique (CEMAC) began a peace-keeping operation in the Central African Republic, replacing a force established in 2001 by the Community of Sahel-Saharan States (CEN-SAD). In 2004, the African Union, in one of its first initiatives, agreed to send peace-keeping troops to Darfur in western Sudan to back up AU observers who were already in the country. These subsequently formed part of a hybrid operation with the United Nations, whose mandate was renewed by the Security Council in Resolution 1828 in 2008.

An earlier example of regional enterprise is provided by the actions of the Arab League over Kuwait.[41] When Kuwait achieved full independence in 1961, Iraq immediately laid claim to the territory. The Sheikh of Kuwait protested to the Arab League and asked for British troops to protect the territory. The troops were sent, but attempts to raise the matter in the Security Council were unsuccessful. The Arab League dispatched its Secretary-General on a mediation mission which also proved abortive, but subsequently decided first to admit Kuwait as a member, thereby acknowledging its claim to independence, and then to substitute Arab for British forces. An Arab defence force was created and replaced the British forces. Although Iraq boycotted the League and continued to press its claim, it was unable to improve its position and, in 1963, following a change of government, diplomatic relations with Kuwait were established.[42]

Less successful was the attempt to provide a regional peace-keeping force for the Lebanon.[43] In June 1976, the League created a 2,500-man 'Symbolic

---

[39] Text in (1996) 35 ILM p. 792; the text of the CIS 'Concept', which is reproduced as document K in the appendix below, can also be found at *ibid.*, p. 786.

[40] For analysis of the operations by ECOWAS, CEMAC and CEN-SAD mentioned in this paragraph, see Gray, *Use of Force*, pp. 302–22.

[41] See M. D. Donelan and M. J. Grieve, *International Disputes: Case Histories 1945–1970*, London, 1973, pp. 220–2.

[42] When Iraq invaded and occupied Kuwait in August 1990, the Arab League immediately condemned the action and called for withdrawal. At the same time, arrangements were made for the dispatch of Arab troops to Saudi Arabia as part of the multinational force confronting Iraq. See L. Freedman and E. Karsh, *The Gulf Conflict 1990–1991*, London, 1993, p. 99.

[43] For a detailed account, see I. Pogany, *The Arab League and Peacekeeping in the Lebanon*, Aldershot, 1987.

Arab Security Force' with a mandate to 'maintain security and stability' in Lebanon. Recognising the inadequacy of the force in a country which had been torn apart by civil war, in October the League transformed the force into an 'Arab Deterrent Force' (ADF) and expanded both its size and functions. Initially, the ADF was able to contribute to the restoration of peace and security, but was prevented from achieving any long-term success by the complexity of a situation in which Syrian and Israeli interests could not be reconciled, as well as by inherent weaknesses in the structure and command of the force. Peace-keeping forces can fulfil many functions, but, as a commentator has written, 'they cannot *impose* peace on unwilling states or on entire peoples'.[44] The force in the Lebanon, in addition to its other difficulties, found itself trying to do this. It is therefore not surprising that, at a summit conference in September 1982, the mission of the ADF was terminated with its purpose unachieved.

Limitations of regional organisations

That regional institutions have a useful part to play in the settlement of international disputes is clear from the examples of constructive involvement already mentioned. But it is important not to overstate the case, for neither the possibility nor the desirability of regional action can be taken for granted.

In all the disputes considered so far, the parties were states within a single region. Although this is to be expected, it underlines the point that both the authority of regional institutions and their capabilities are restricted geographically. Some types of disputes are almost always intra-regional – boundary disputes are an example – but to the solution of the multitude of inter-regional disputes that occur, including some territorial disputes, regional organisations generally have little to contribute. Indeed, by providing the antagonists with the diplomatic and material support necessary to continue the struggle, regional organisations may actually make accommodation more difficult. In the Falklands dispute, for example, Britain and Argentina saw their membership of the EEC and OAS as a way of mobilising support for military action and sought to exploit their respective regional alliances for that end. Although each organisation also tried to exercise a restraining influence on its member, they clearly lacked the capacity to act as peace-makers, with the result that the prospects of a non-military solution, as noted earlier, rested on the efforts of the United States and the United Nations.

External limitations on the influence of regional organisations are matched by an internal limitation of comparable importance – the inability

[44] *Ibid.*, p. 161.

to deal effectively with disputes *within* member states. Regional organisations are created to further co-operation *between* states, and only in special cases, such as the European human rights system or the European Community, are they given jurisdiction over internal affairs. In practice, this consideration does not altogether rule out regional intervention over matters of internal government if regional neighbours become sufficiently alarmed, and the OSCE and CIS, as we have seen, already have considerable experience in such situations. It will also be recalled that the Constitutive Act of the African Union indicates that traditional views on this issue are now being modified. Often, however, revolutions, civil wars and other disruptive events within states will so divide the membership as to make regional initiatives politically impossible.[45] With such obstacles to overcome, regional organisations seem likely to continue to show a marked disinclination to become involved in domestic affairs.

The next point concerns the significance of regional solidarity as a factor in dispute settlement. It is sometimes assumed that, except for situations involving domestic jurisdiction, the regional environment is peculiarly suited to the settlement of local disputes. That is to say, the members of a regional organisation have common interests and loyalties which provide them with an incentive to encourage the settlement of conflicts and increase the chances that, when such efforts are made, they will be successful. However, this assumption is open to question.

Expressions of regional loyalty and hemispheric solidarity have certainly been prominent in the inter-American system and are now to be found in all regional institutions. The significance of such sentiments for dispute settlement is difficult to assess, but the evidence suggests that they can sometimes prompt constructive interventions that would not otherwise occur, particularly when there is an established tradition of involvement, as in the OAS, or where the policy of a regional organisation is directly determined by heads of state, as in the African Union and its predecessor, the OAU.

From the point of view of the parties to a dispute, regional loyalties are perhaps mainly significant as a way of legitimising both the search for a peaceful settlement and the terms of the settlement itself. As explained earlier, the involvement of third parties as mediators, or in some other capacity, can make it easier for states to agree to arrangements which might be difficult to concede in direct negotiations. This tendency is no doubt encouraged when accommodation can also be presented as motivated by considerations of regional solidarity.

---

[45] On the early practice of the OAS, see Macdonald, 'Organization of American States'. On the OAU, see S. A. Tiewul, 'Relations between the United Nations Organization and the OAU in the settlement of secessionist conflicts', (1975) 16 Harv. Int. LJ p. 259.

Too much should not be expected of regional loyalties, however. Regions, after all, are large areas, made up of a variety of states. As a result, certain states may not be members of their local organisation, and others, which are members, may have more in common with states outside the region than with those within it.[46] Both are factors which can limit the possibility of concerted regional action very significantly. Thus, the fact that South Africa did not become a member of the OAU until 1994, though easily explained, greatly limited the scope of that organisation's influence, while in the Falklands dispute the English-speaking members of the OAS provided Britain with a useful source of support and helped to offset Argentina's influence in the Organization.

Even when special factors are not present, regional solidarity cannot be assumed, especially if substantial interests are at stake. All regional organisations are less united than their ceremonial rhetoric or constitutions might suggest, and disputes between the members can place institutions under great internal strain. In the Cod Wars, Iceland obtained a good deal of political leverage by threatening to leave NATO, hardly an inspiring example of regional loyalty, while a major reason for the relative ineffectiveness of the Arab League has been the deep division of opinion in the membership on major issues of policy. Sometimes, indeed, dissension may undermine the whole idea of regional solidarity and pose a threat to the very existence of the organisation. In 1982, for example, the split between the moderate and the radical members of the OAU was so serious that it proved impossible to hold the meeting of the Organization's Council, despite two attempts to do so.[47]

The fact that regional loyalties may on occasion be more apparent than real lends added significance to the existence of the sub-regional groups mentioned earlier. Here, relations will normally be closer than in the larger institution and intervention with a view to dispute settlement correspondingly easier. In 1964, for example, the Union Africaine et Malagache (UAM), comprising the French-speaking states of Africa, played a constructive role in the settlement of a territorial dispute between Dahomey (Benin) and Niger,[48] and, more recently, as we have seen, the Contadora Group was actively involved in efforts to avoid war in Central America. A particularly striking example of action by a sub-regional organisation is provided by the intervention of the Economic Community of West African States in the civil war in Liberia. In 1990, the Liberian government accepted a peace

---

[46] See C. Moneta, 'The Latin American Economic System as a mechanism to control conflicts', in M. A. Morris and V. Millán, *Controlling Latin American Conflicts*, Boulder, CO, 1983, p. 99 at p. 104.

[47] In August 1982, the issue was the admission of the Saharan Arab Democratic Republic, which caused Morocco to leave the organisation; in November, the issue was the representation of Chad. After considerable uncertainty, a meeting was finally held in June 1983.

[48] See Cukwurah, 'Territorial and boundary problems', pp. 191–3.

proposal put forward by ECOWAS as a result of which a 4,000-strong peace-keeping force, ECOMOG, arrived in the country and soon became involved in the fighting. In 1992, the Security Council took up the issue, and, when a peace agreement was concluded in 1993, created an observer mission to work alongside ECOMOG. As already noted, the first phase of ECOWAS involvement concluded in 1997, but was then followed by further operations in 2003.

A final point concerns resources. Regional organisations, it is worth remembering, are largely dependent on the willingness of member states to provide whatever may be necessary for a given operation. Thus, the provision of border surveillance in the Costa Rica/Nicaragua dispute and peace-keeping forces in Kuwait in 1961 depended on the members' readiness to make the appropriate resources available. Of course, all organisations have some resources of their own, but even something as simple as mediation may present difficulties for certain organisations as the combination of a small budget and limited personnel may restrict the activities which can be undertaken. In 1982, for example, a peace-keeping force which the OAU sent to Chad had to be withdrawn, having failed to achieve any improvement in the situation. Although logistic and financial difficulties were not the only reason for its failure, they do seem to have been a contributory factor.[49] Similarly, the fact that the Commission of Mediation, Conciliation and Arbitration never became operational was due in part to a lack of political support, and in part to the budgetary problems which were always a weakness of the Organization.[50]

The resource requirements of regional action, then, like the political factors with which they are linked, are an important element in the settlement of disputes. As a result, if interest in a dispute is lacking, or if the price of intervention is too high, or if a matter is highly controversial, attempts to secure a peaceful settlement from within a region are conceivably no more likely than attempts from outside.

Regional organisations and adjudication

Adjudication and regional organisations are linked in many different ways. A procedure for the reference of disputes to a judicial tribunal may be laid down in a regional agreement and a regional court created for this purpose. The European Court of Human Rights and the European Court of Justice

---

[49] See G. J. Naldi, 'Peace-keeping attempts by the Organization of African Unity', (1985) 34 ICLQ p. 593 at p. 595.

[50] See Maluwa, 'Conceptual issues and practical trends', p. 313. When the OAU celebrated its twenty-fifth anniversary in 1988, it had an annual budget of US$23 million. Of this sum, only US$5 million had been paid, and thirty-three states were behind in their contributions. Other arrears amounted to US$26 million; see *The Independent*, 25 May 1988, p. 12.

are regional tribunals of this kind, and the Inter-American Court of Human Rights and the projected Islamic Court of Justice are further examples. Alternatively, a regional treaty may provide for the reference of disputes to the International Court of Justice, or to arbitration. Thus, Article 31 of the Pact of Bogotá provides:

> In conformity with Article 36, paragraph 2, of the Statute of the International Court of Justice, the High Contracting Parties declare that they recognize, in relation to any other American State, the jurisdiction of the Court as compulsory *ipso facto*, without the necessity of any special agreement so long as the present Treaty is in force, in all disputes of a juridical nature that arise among them concerning:
>
> (a) The interpretation of a treaty;
> (b) Any question of international law;
> (c) The existence of any fact which, if established, would constitute the breach of an international obligation;
> (d) The nature or extent of the reparation to be made for the breach of an international obligation.

In addition to arrangements establishing legal obligations, regional organisations can also provide effective support for adjudication at the political level. When a dispute arises between states within a region, the pressure of other regional states can be a way of persuading the parties to settle it by adjudication. Similarly, when judgment has been given the members of a regional organisation may have a part to play in encouraging the parties to implement the decision, or helping them to do so. We have seen that, in the *Arbitral Award* case, the OAS performed both functions: first, persuading Honduras and Nicaragua to refer the dispute to the International Court; then, when the case was decided, assisting the parties with implementation of the judgment.[51]

The kind of mutually supportive relationship which existed in the *Arbitral Award* case cannot, of course, be guaranteed. In some situations the search for a political solution may be under way in a regional organisation, while at the same time, and quite independently, an attempt is being made to have the dispute adjudicated. This raises the question of whether the two processes are compatible and, if priorities have to be determined, how this is to be done. As the issue here is the respective areas of competence of political and judicial organs, this is a matter with a vital bearing on the role of regional organisations.

---

[51] For the OAS contribution before the reference to the Court, see the text accompanying note 25 above; for the post-adjudication phase, see the text accompanying note 39 in Chapter 7, and J. G. Merrills, 'The International Court of Justice and the adjudication of territorial and boundary disputes', (2000) 13 Leiden JIL p. 873 at p. 899, and C. Schulte, *Compliance with Decisions of the International Court of Justice*, Oxford, 2004, pp. 126–32.

In the *Nicaragua* case,[52] the United States sought to persuade the International Court that its competence was affected by the Contadora negotiations in which Nicaragua, the applicant in the case, was involved. Specifically, the United States argued that Nicaragua was obliged to exhaust the possibilities of a political settlement through the Contadora process, before submitting the legal aspects of its dispute with the United States to judicial settlement. The Court, however, rejected the argument. Relying on cases which have been mentioned earlier,[53] it held that, even if negotiations were currently in progress, this would be no bar to the Court's exercising its functions under the United Nations Charter. It therefore concluded that, in the present situation, there was no 'requirement of prior exhaustion of regional negotiating processes as a precondition to seising the Court'.[54] In other words, there was no incompatibility between participation in the Contadora process, a regional procedure of a political nature, and simultaneous recourse to the International Court.

At an earlier stage of the case, the Court had considered another aspect of this issue. When Nicaragua asked the Court to indicate interim measures of protection, the United States resisted the claim, putting forward, among other arguments, the point that interim measures might prejudice the Contadora process. The submission, which lacked plausibility, was summarily rejected.[55] In a different situation, however, an argument of this type might merit attention. At the corresponding stage of the *Aegean Sea* case, where the ruling was that interim measures were unnecessary, the Court appears to have been influenced by the fact that the Security Council was actively seised of the matter.[56] Thus, there seems no reason why, in an appropriate case, the fact that a dispute is being dealt with by a regional body should not also carry weight.

In the *Border and Transborder Armed Actions* case[57] in 1988, the relation between regional and judicial procedures was given further consideration. The case was referred to the International Court by Nicaragua, which alleged that Honduras was allowing armed bands to operate from its territory. The basis of jurisdiction relied on by Nicaragua was Article 31 of the Pact of Bogotá, which has already been quoted. Both states were parties to the Pact, but, before the Court could address the merits of the case, it had to deal with

---

[52] *Military and Paramilitary Activities in and against Nicaragua*, Jurisdiction and Admissibility, Judgment, [1984] ICJ Rep. p. 392.

[53] See Chapter 1.

[54] [1984] ICJ Rep. p. 440.

[55] *Military and Paramilitary Activities in and against Nicaragua*, Provisional Measures, Order of 10 May 1984, [1984] ICJ Rep. p. 169.

[56] See *Aegean Sea Continental Shelf*, Interim Protection, Order of 11 September 1976, [1976] ICJ Rep. p. 3.

[57] *Border and Transborder Armed Actions*, Jurisdiction and Admissibility, Judgment, [1988] ICJ Rep. p. 69. This case was subsequently withdrawn; see the Court's order of 27 May 1992, [1992] ICJ Rep. p. 222.

a number of preliminary objections raised by Honduras, some of which, like the United States objections in the *Nicaragua* case, concerned the relation between adjudication and other means of settlement.

As regards the issue of jurisdiction, the Court decided that, despite the similarity between Article 31 of the Pact and Article 36(2) of the Court's Statute, the Pact establishes an independent basis of jurisdiction. This was important because it meant that it was unnecessary for the Court to decide whether Honduras had validly modified its declaration under Article 36(2) in 1986, and in addition meant that any reservations in the latter were irrelevant to the obligations of Honduras under the Pact. The Court also decided that the jurisdiction which Article 31 invested in the Court was quite separate from the arrangements for conciliation and arbitration provided for in Article 32 and could therefore be invoked by Nicaragua before the latter had been attempted.

As regards the admissibility of the claim, the issues before the Court concerned various aspects of the Contadora process. Article 2 of the Pact provides for use of its procedures for disputes which 'in the opinion of the parties cannot be settled by direct negotiations through the usual diplomatic channels'. Honduras submitted that the present dispute failed to satisfy this requirement and cited the Contadora process as evidence that negotiations were in progress. The Court, however, rejected the argument. After examining the origin and character of the Contadora process, the Court concluded that, at the relevant time, it was 'primarily a mediation, in which third States, on their own initiative, endeavoured to bring together the viewpoints of the States concerned by making specific proposals to them'.[58] As such, the process was markedly different from 'direct negotiations through the usual diplomatic channels' and consequently fell outside Article 2.

Honduras next argued that the claim was barred by Article 4 of the Pact, which provides that, when any 'pacific procedure' has been initiated, no other procedure may be commenced until that procedure has been concluded. Honduras maintained that the Contadora process was a 'pacific procedure' and had not yet been concluded. The Court, however, again disagreed. Without deciding whether the original Contadora process of mediation could be regarded as a 'pacific procedure', the Court held that the process had ended in June 1986 when the states concerned put forward the unsuccessful Act of Contadora. What followed, 'the Contadora – Esquipulas II process', was, in the Court's view, 'an independent mechanism of multilateral negotiation'[59] and as such must be treated as a new procedure.

---

[58] [1988] ICJ Rep. p. 99.

[59] *Ibid.*, p. 105. Although 'the Contadora–Esquipulas II process' could also be argued to be a 'pacific procedure', Nicaragua had filed its application before this second regional procedure began. It was therefore irrelevant for the purposes of Article 4.

Since the original Contadora process had therefore been concluded, Article 4 did not have the effect of barring Nicaragua's claim.

A final argument was that, whatever the status of the Contadora process under the Pact, Nicaragua was barred by the principle of good faith from referring the case to the Court while the process continued. This submission, which was not unlike the argument put forward by the United States in the *Nicaragua* case, was also rejected. As on the previous point, the Court considered that it was significant that the original Contadora process had terminated, and pointed out that in any case there had never been any suggestion that the use of the Contadora process was intended to be exclusive.

The *Border and Transborder Armed Actions* case has been discussed here in some detail because it is a good illustration of the issues which can arise when adjudication and regional procedures are employed simultaneously. Of course, the precise questions which the Court had to answer stemmed from the language of the treaty under which the dispute had been referred. However, the analysis which was required of the nature and effect of the Contadora process at its various stages shows the sort of review which is called for when a treaty provides several procedures for the settlement of disputes and, as will usually be the case, is also intended to regulate the relation between them. Moreover, the decision confirms the point which was crucial in the *Nicaragua* case, that, where different procedures are being used simultaneously, diplomatic methods have priority over legal methods only in so far as this is provided for.

In the *Land and Maritime Boundary* case[60] between Cameroon and Nigeria, the Court again had to consider the role of regional procedures, on this occasion in a dispute over territory. One of the many issues in that case was the location of the frontier in the vicinity of Lake Chad where, according to Nigeria, a body called the Lake Chad Basin Commission had 'exclusive power in relation to issues of security and public order'.[61] Nigeria argued that this rendered Cameroon's reference of the boundary issue to the International Court inadmissible, but the Court disagreed. Ruling that the Commission was neither a judicial body intended to displace the Court, nor a regional organisation acknowledged under Chapter VIII of the UN Charter, it reiterated the point made in earlier cases, that in any event the mere existence of procedures for regional negotiation cannot prevent the Court from carrying out its functions.

It is clear that, if the parties to a dispute have agreed that a regional procedure, or some other means of settlement, shall be used exclusively, or in priority to adjudication, then they will be held to their agreement.

---

[60] *Land and Maritime Boundary between Cameroon and Nigeria*, Preliminary Objections, Judgment, [1998] ICJ Rep. p. 275.

[61] *Ibid.*, para. 66.

There are countless examples of governments agreeing either that judicial settlement must take second place to other procedures, or that some other means of settlement must be used instead. Governments are at liberty to make such arrangements, and they will be given effect. The point which the International Court was making in the cases above was not that judicial settlement has a privileged status, but simply that the overriding objective is a peaceful settlement, and so, in principle, unless they have made special arrangements, the parties to a legal dispute are free to employ any of the means set out in Article 33 of the Charter, including regional procedures, without prejudice to their juridical position.

Regional organisations and the United Nations

The place of regionalism within a universal political organisation was an issue which taxed the founders of the League of Nations after the First World War.[62] After some debate, the matter was eventually dealt with by Article 21 of the League of Nations Covenant, which provided that: 'Nothing in this Covenant shall be deemed to affect the validity of international engagements, such as treaties of arbitration or regional understandings like the Monroe Doctrine, for securing the maintenance of international peace.' A quarter of a century later, a more elaborate treatment of regional arrangements formed Chapter VIII of the United Nations Charter (Articles 52–54), while 'resort to regional agencies or arrangements' is one of the methods available for settling disputes whose continuation is likely to endanger the maintenance of international peace and security, under Article 33.

During the period of the Cold War, the relationship between regional organisations and the United Nations gave rise to controversy on a number of occasions. Disagreement, a reflection of political rivalry in the form of inter-organisational competition, centred on two issues: the limits of the authority of regional organisations in matters concerning international peace and security, and whether regional means of settlement must be exhausted before a dispute can be considered by the Security Council.[63] With the ending of the Cold War the debate about Chapter VIII has taken a more constructive turn and attention has been given to how regional organisations and the UN can work together.[64] The framework for such

---

[62] See R. A. Akindele, 'From the Covenant to the Charter: Constitutional relations between universal and regional organisations in the promotion of peace and security', (1973) 8 Israel L. Rev. p. 91.

[63] See R. St J. Macdonald, 'The developing relationship between superior and subordinate political bodies at the international level', (1964) 2 Can. Yearbook Int. L. p. 21.

[64] See, for example, B. Rivlin, 'Regional arrangements and the UN system for collective security and conflict resolution: A new road ahead?', (1992) 11 Int. Rel. p. 95; and A. K. Henrikson, 'The growth of regional organisations and the role of the United Nations', in Fawcett and Hurrell, *Regionalism in World Politics*, p. 122.

co-operation is, however, still based on the Charter. Accordingly, before we examine the latest developments, something should be said about the constitutional position.

The crucial limitation on the authority of regional organisations is contained in Article 53(1) of the Charter, which provides that 'no enforcement action shall be taken under regional arrangements or by regional agencies without the authorisation of the Security Council'. The question of what constitutes 'enforcement action' has been exhaustively considered elsewhere[65] and need not be investigated here. Two cases in which the question was raised will, however, indicate its importance.

In the Dominican case, mentioned earlier, the Soviet Union argued in the Security Council that the diplomatic and economic sanctions imposed on the Dominican Republic by the OAS constituted 'enforcement action', requiring the authorisation of the Council under Article 53(1). During the Cuban missile crisis of 1962, on the other hand, the United States proceeded on the assumption that no Security Council authorisation was required for the interdiction of Cuba by the US Navy and various other coercive measures approved by the OAS.

Neither interpretation of Article 53(1) is really very convincing. The Soviet view has the curious consequence that states are denied the right to do collectively what they would clearly be entitled to do individually, and deprives regional organisations of an opportunity to make a real contribution to dispute settlement by bringing political pressure to bear on a recalcitrant member. The United States view, on the other hand, allows a state to be the target of military coercion, perhaps directed by a dominant regional member, a situation in which the rest of the world has an overwhelming interest in preserving the requirement of Security Council authorisation.

Reconciling effective regional action with the interests of the international community is a major element in the other issue to be considered: the priority to be given to regional means of settlement. On several occasions a state has sought to bring a dispute to the Security Council before a regional organisation has had an opportunity of dealing with the matter. In the border dispute between Morocco and Algeria, for example, Morocco's initial instinct was to take the matter to the Security Council rather than the OAU, perhaps because it believed that the former might have more sympathy with its demand for frontier revision. In this type of situation, which is likely to occur whenever a state perceives an advantage in having its case considered in a wider forum, there is clearly a potential conflict of jurisdiction between the regional and universal organisation. In the Guatemala

---

[65] See M. Akehurst, 'Enforcement action by regional agencies with special reference to the Organization of American States', (1967) 42 BYBIL p. 175, with references to previous literature. See also Gray, *Use of Force*, Chapter 9.

case in 1954, the United States sought to argue that a case which was being handled by the OAS was beyond the competence of the Security Council, an assertion which was strongly challenged by the Soviet Union. Following the invasion of Czechoslovakia by Warsaw Pact forces in 1968, however, it was the Soviet Union that denied the Council's competence and the United States that called for United Nations action.[66] The self-serving character of these arguments is clear, and Security Council practice, though not always consistent, provides little support for these extreme versions of the regionalist approach.

The intention of those who drafted the Charter was to create a presumption in favour of the use of regional institutions and the view that regional procedures should be tried first has, as one would expect, been vigorously endorsed by the major regional organisations. It is, however, widely recognised that regional organisations cannot remove the Security Council's ultimate responsibility for the maintenance of international peace and security. States cannot therefore be deprived of the right to take a dispute or situation to the Security Council, if they consider it necessary to do so. Of course, it does not follow that the Council will necessarily wish to deal with the matter, nor that, if it decides to do so, it will be able to do anything effective, but the right to have the matter put before the Council is something which regional organisations, however insistent, can never take away.

In his 1992 report to the Security Council, entitled *An Agenda for Peace*, UN Secretary-General Boutros-Ghali observed that the Cold War 'impaired the proper use of Chapter VIII' and that in that era 'regional arrangements worked on occasion against resolving disputes in the manner foreseen in the Charter'.[67] There was, as we have seen, ample justification for that assessment, but, with the Cold War over, it has been possible to see the relation between the UN and regional organisations in a new light and to explore the possibilities for co-operation between them. In his report, the Secretary-General described what he saw as the contribution of regional organisations in this context, emphasising that a variety of bodies, including 'regional organisations for mutual security and defence' and 'groups created to deal with a specific political, economic or social issue', may all have a role to play.[68]

The thrust of the Secretary-General's argument, with which it is easy to agree, is that regional bodies plainly possess a potential which can be utilised in serving the functions identified in *An Agenda for Peace*. These, it will be recalled, are preventive diplomacy, peace-keeping, peace-making and post-conflict peace-building. As might be expected, the point is made

---

[66] See R. A. Akindele, 'The Warsaw Pact, the United Nations and the Soviet Union', (1971) 11 Ind. J. Int. L. p. 553.
[67] SC Doc. S/24111, 17 June 1992. Text in (1992) 31 ILM p. 953.   [68] *Ibid.*, para. 61.

that regional organisations must act in a manner consistent with the Charter and that the Security Council has primary responsibility for maintaining international peace and security. However, so long as these constitutional limitations are respected, regional action is valuable because 'as a matter of decentralisation, delegation and co-operation with United Nations efforts could not only lighten the burden of the Council but also contribute to a deeper sense of participation, consensus and democratisation in international affairs'.[69]

As the former Secretary-General has indicated, co-operation between regional organisations and the UN is particularly useful in situations which call for peace-keeping forces or related action, and a number of cases which have already been mentioned show how institutions can perform complementary functions when the political atmosphere is favourable. We have seen how in the complex situation in Central America the main diplomatic work was carried out through the Contadora process, but when security arrangements were needed a UN force (ONUCA) was established by the Security Council. In the Liberian crisis, local peace-keeping forces were supplied by ECOWAS and subsequently supported both politically and on the ground by the UN. In Georgia, on the other hand, a UN observer mission was already in place when CIS forces arrived, and co-ordination was then overseen by the Security Council.

Similarly, it will be recalled from Chapter 10 that the initial response to the coup in Haiti came from the OAS, but only became effective when backed up by the UN, while, in the complex and protracted crisis in Bosnia, the EC intervened with diplomatic and economic measures, but, when the Security Council became involved and military action was needed, NATO was utilised as the organisation with the necessary capabilities. Co-operation between the UN and regional organisations has therefore been extensive in recent years with many Security Council resolutions authorising or approving regional action of various kinds and a number of joint peace-keeping operations in different parts of the world. The record thus suggests that the potential of regional organisations in what *An Agenda for Peace* called 'this new era of opportunity'[70] is now being realised.

Assessing the role of regional organisations in relation to the United Nations comes down in the end to appreciating both the limitations and the advantages of delegation. As regards limitations, securing agreement within a regional organisation on peace-keeping or other measures may be no easier than within the United Nations, not least when it calls for resources which members of the organisation may be unable or unwilling to provide. Regional action, particularly when it involves the use of force,

---

[69] *Ibid.*, para. 64.
[70] B. Boutros-Ghali, *An Agenda for Peace*, SC Doc. S/24111, 17 June 1992, para. 63. Text in (1992) 31 ILM p. 953.

may well raise the issue of impartiality, and, when it is authorised by the Security Council, still needs to be properly controlled, which can present its own difficulties.[71] Finally, there is, of course, no guarantee that, when regional solutions are attempted, they will be successful. It is clear therefore that, on account of their various limitations, regional organisations are in no sense a panacea. On the other hand, although co-operation between the UN and regional organisations can be very valuable, when a body like the African Union or the OAS is seised of a dispute, Security Council involvement will only be needed if regional measures are inadequate. Regional organisations, as has been seen, can often make a constructive contribution to dispute settlement without outside help. Encouraging regional organisations to use their own resources enables the United Nations to reserve its efforts for inter-regional disputes and the more intractable intra-regional conflicts, and thereby achieves a useful division of labour. Insisting that the Security Council should always be involved, on the other hand, would tend to discourage regional organisations from taking responsibility, while perhaps introducing complications in the form of outside states' involvement, which treatment at the regional level may be able to avoid.

[71] See Gray, *Use of Force*, pp. 326–7.

12

Trends and prospects

Having reviewed the various ways of attempting to resolve international disputes individually, we are now in a position to consider what this survey as a whole demonstrates about the possibilities open to a state when confronted with a dispute, the factors which influence decisions on whether to use a particular procedure and the prospects for improving this situation in the future. To deal with these issues it will be necessary to consider separately some of the legal and political factors which form the context in which decisions relating to the conduct of disputes are taken, and then to suggest some ways of modifying or developing current methods of settlement with a view to making them more effective and easier to use. First, however, it may be useful to recall in brief outline what our study has revealed about the present situation.

Dispute settlement today

The idea that international disputes should be settled by peaceful means rather than by the use of force has a long history. From the survey in the preceding pages, however, it is clear that the attempt to devise techniques and institutions with this objective is a more recent phenomenon, much of what exists today having been created in a period of little more than 100 years. What has all the interest which states have shown in this subject succeeded in producing?

In one respect, at least, remarkably little. It was explained at the beginning of this book that the basic means of resolving disputes peacefully is still negotiation. Noteworthy developments here, however, are the increasing use of consultation and related techniques as a means of avoiding disputes and new forms of diplomacy associated with the growth of international organisations. All disputes are likely to involve negotiation at some stage, but as a method of settlement it is evidently subject to serious limitations. To some extent these can be overcome by good offices and mediation, yet these in turn are circumscribed in various ways and, like negotiation, wholly dependent on the readiness of the parties to agree.

With the introduction of inquiry and conciliation we find third-party assistance institutionalised, in the shape of permanent or *ad hoc* commissions, and objectified, in the sense that the necessary findings or recommendations are arrived at independently and passed to the parties for assimilation. Inquiry, as we have seen, has principally been employed when the disputed issue is one of fact. Conciliation, on the other hand, has often been used as a form of quasi-arbitration in cases concerned with present or future legal rights. The usefulness and flexibility of both procedures are shown by the variety of cases in which they have been used successfully. Thus, although both have features which make them unsuitable for certain types of dispute, each has a potential which ought to be, and in the case of conciliation is, coming to be more widely recognised.

From the perspective of the parties to a dispute, inquiry and conciliation offer the benefit of a third-party opinion with no commitment to accept the result. Although the non-binding character of these procedures is plainly an advantage to a party whose ultimate object is a negotiated settlement, a state which is prepared to relinquish such control can reap the additional advantages of judicial settlement or arbitration. It has been explained that these legal means offer the possibility of a binding decision for individual disputes or whole classes of disputes. Given the type of dispute which a judicial tribunal is capable of handling, the prerequisites here are a court which the parties are prepared to trust – thus the constitution and composition of the tribunal are of major importance – and agreement on terms of reference, an issue involving both the nature of the dispute and the adequacy of international law. To these should be added a willingness to carry out the decision. For on this the effectiveness of all binding methods of settlement actually depends.

The factors which determine the approach of states to the different methods of dispute settlement emerge with particular clarity in the provisions of the 1982 Law of the Sea Convention. Recognising that suitable arrangements must be an integral part of the Convention, states have here succeeded in combining the principle of free choice of means with exploitation of the full range of existing techniques and many novelties. The machinery of the Convention thus provides the framework for a flexible and useful system, the value of which is now being demonstrated. Though open to criticism in certain respects, the provisions of the Convention are also an indication of a positive attitude towards dispute settlement and the kind of results that a major effort can achieve.

The dispute settlement system of the World Trade Organization, though no less progressive, represents a quite different approach. Like the Law of the Sea Convention, the 1994 Dispute Settlement Understanding utilises established methods for dealing with disputes in its particular field, and also develops them. Thus, consultations and panel proceedings, which have been employed in trade disputes for several decades, are not only formalised in the DSU, but also supplemented by a system of appellate review and implementation. However, a key difference is that, whereas the Law of the Sea Convention, with its emphasis on choice of means, creates, as it were, a lateral system of competing methods, the DSU employs what is plainly intended as a vertical system with the various methods available successively, and in accordance with a strict timetable, until a solution is achieved. The difference may be accounted for by the capacity of unresolved trade disputes to inflict a great deal of damage quickly, which makes resolution a matter of urgency, and also perhaps by the fact that, while trade disputes are often complex, they tend to be less diverse than maritime disputes, making a uniform procedure for dealing with them easier to agree. Be that as it may, the extensive use now being made of the DSU reflects states' confidence in the new system.

Our final reflections concerned the United Nations and regional organisations. The former, it was noted, is not a world government, or an international policeman, but essentially a body through which pressure and influence can be brought to bear on states whose disputes come before the Organization. The ending of the Cold War, though enabling the Security Council to make significant use of its powers under Chapter VII, has not changed this basic situation. Consequently, although the Secretary-General exercises a role of considerable importance and peace-keeping operations can reduce international tensions, it is more accurate to speak of settlement through, rather than by, the United Nations. Of course, many disputes never reach the United Nations, while of those that do many remain unsettled. Regional organisations, however, can sometimes help by providing a forum for negotiation, or involving regional neighbours in the capacity of mediators or conciliators. There is also now the real possibility of combining regional action with action by the United Nations. Again, though, action in the form of legitimisation or sanctions is less important in practice than the use of regional machinery by the parties themselves. Organizations, then, like the other institutions we have considered, represent not so much a transformation of the international scene, as a new arena in which the sovereign state can exercise its traditional power to pursue (or not to pursue) a settlement of its disputes.

A political perspective

What has been said so far is enough to demonstrate that, although a great many different ways of handling disputes have been developed, there is often a considerable gap between what is possible in theory and what states are prepared to do in practice. Moreover, as we have frequently had occasion to note, even when a particular method of settlement is available and utilised, there is no guarantee that it will be effective in a given case. Before we consider what can be done to improve this state of affairs, it is worth considering just why international disputes are so difficult to deal with, beginning with some features of their political context.

From the political perspective, international disputes can be thought of as having three dimensions: the social, the material and the temporal. The social dimension is concerned with where a dispute occurs, and establishes who the protagonists are. The material dimension relates to what the dispute is about and identifies its subject matter. And the temporal dimension concerns when the dispute occurs, how long it lasts and when it is resolved. All three dimensions are present in every dispute and can exercise a crucial influence on the effectiveness of peaceful means of settlement.

The social element is important because the traditions, interests and attitudes of states are very different, as also is the power which each can bring to bear in a particular situation. In Western Europe, for example, there is now a high degree of political and economic integration, a readiness to lay aside historic animosity, a high level of economic prosperity and no dominant state. In these circumstances, it is not surprising that governments generally make every effort to avoid disputes and that, when disputes do occur, they are normally settled quite quickly, often through the use of regional procedures. In contrast, the situation in Africa and Latin America is much more volatile. Procedures for avoiding disputes are less developed, the states of these regions are more diverse and the potential for violence is ever-present. In Latin America, the situation is complicated by the hegemonial interests of the United States, and in Africa by the fact that the region's most powerful state, South Africa, was for many years regarded as an enemy. To be sure, these factors do not preclude the use of peaceful means of settlement, and many such cases have already been noted. They do, however, mean that approaches to international conduct which can be taken for granted in Europe cannot be regarded as universal and that whether a dispute is settled peacefully or by force – and indeed whether a disagreement becomes a dispute in the first place – may well depend on its location.

The greater the interaction between states, the more opportunity there is for disagreement. Consequently, the majority of international disputes involve states which are neighbours, and so the nature of the regional environment is extremely significant. However, some disputes cross regional boundaries, and here too the social factor is important. When states have a great deal in common, then, even if they happen to be separated geographically, the chances that they will be able to resolve their disputes peacefully are good. For example, it is difficult to imagine any dispute between the United States and the United Kingdom which would be comparable to the diplomatic hostages dispute between the United States and Iran. In the Anglo-American situation, both sides have an incentive to maintain good relations and to resolve any disputes peacefully; in the latter case, as we have seen, cultural, as well as historical and political, factors not only brought about the crisis, but also made resolution of it exceedingly difficult. In the same way, it is instructive to contrast the long-standing dispute between the United Kingdom and Spain over Gibraltar with the not dissimilar issues raised by the dispute with Argentina over the Falkland Islands. In the first case, though the dispute has not been resolved and must be regarded as an irritant in Anglo-Spanish relations, neither side is interested in provoking a crisis. In the case of the Falklands, on the other hand, while the British tended to assume that the situation was broadly similar, Argentina was in fact prepared to regard force as an available option, and, when negotiation proved unsuccessful, had no compunction in mounting an invasion.

The significance of the material dimension stems from the fact that, other things being equal, the difficulty of resolving a dispute depends on what is at stake. Thus, a dispute over a technical obligation under a treaty will usually be easier to dispose of than a disagreement over a major issue of policy. Similarly, a dispute concerning an isolated point is normally more straightforward than one which is bound up with larger aspects of the parties' relations. Thus, the diplomatic hostages crisis was exceptionally difficult because the particular dispute became a symbol for Iran of the repudiation of all things American in the period immediately after the Islamic Revolution. In the Falklands dispute, on the other hand, the issue itself was not bound up with larger questions, but raised issues of national sovereignty and self-determination on which all states, including the protagonists, are extremely sensitive.

The material element also has a bearing on which methods of peaceful settlement may be appropriate. As we saw when considering inquiry, for this procedure to be relevant it is essential for there to be a disputed issue of fact. Conciliation, on the other hand, addresses the issue of what should be done, rather than what happened, and so is more appropriate for accommodating differences of policy. Likewise, arbitration and judicial settlement are clearly most suitable for disputes involving legal questions. It is, of course, necessary to add that these are not inflexible prescriptions. Just as disputes themselves often combine issues of fact, law and policy in varying proportions, so it may be necessary for a particular method of settlement to perform more than one function. The differences are nevertheless important. Thus, conciliators should not be criticised for failing to apply the law, and, by the same token, judges should not normally be thought of as conciliators. The fact that states can, if they wish, modify the position and introduce elements of arbitration into conciliation, or conciliation into judicial settlement, does not alter this, but rather serves to emphasise the distinctions between these processes which exist under normal circumstances.

A further point is that the material element in a dispute is not a fixed quantity but depends on the parties' perceptions. The easiest disputes to resolve are those in which the states concerned agree about how the dispute is to be classified; the hardest are those where this is a matter of disagreement. Thus, the *Diplomatic Staff in Tehran* case[1] was not resolved by the International Court because only the United States was prepared to treat

---

[1]   *United States Diplomatic and Consular Staff in Tehran*, Judgment, [1980] ICJ Rep. p. 3.

it as a legal dispute. Similarly, the *KE 007* incident[2] was not amenable to inquiry because, despite appearances, the dispute was not about how a civilian aircraft came to be so far off course, but about the Soviet policy of shooting it down. It follows that, in the preliminary stages of a dispute, one of the main functions of negotiation is to establish an agreed classification of the dispute in order to decide the best way of handling it.

The final dimension which needs to be considered is time. Whether a disagreement becomes a dispute, which, if any, method of peaceful settlement is tried and whether, to the extent that such methods are used, they are successful, may all depend on when a dispute occurs. For example, if Argentina had invaded the Falkland Islands in 1983 instead of a year earlier, the United Kingdom would have been unable to respond militarily because the Royal Navy was being run down and would have reached the point where an amphibious assault to recover the territory was no longer feasible. Moreover, had Argentina been prepared to wait a little while longer, it might not have been necessary to invade at all, given that the British policy of relinquishing overseas commitments would in normal circumstances probably have produced a diplomatic settlement.

Argentina's miscalculations, like the British response, were partly attributable to internal political factors. The political significance of a dispute within a state is also related to its timing and is conditioned by the style and traditions of its political leadership. Some British governments might not have gone to war over the Falklands, just as most Argentine governments would not have taken the risk of invasion. Similarly, some British governments would have avoided a crisis altogether by either negotiating a settlement of the dispute at an earlier stage, or ensuring that the islands were properly defended, just as many leaders in General Galtieri's position would have accepted the terms which were on offer during the various attempts at mediation. That these alternatives can all be conceived without straining the imagination confirms that the war of 1982 was the result of a particular combination of unfavourable historical circumstances and thus underlines the significance of timing in determining the course of an international dispute.

If the timing of the Falklands crisis was unfortunate, time can sometimes have a beneficial effect by effectively removing the causes of a dispute. In 1973, for example, the United Kingdom challenged Iceland's extension of its exclusive fishing zone to fifty miles and took the dispute as far as the International Court. This was in line with a traditional policy of seeking to protect freedom of the seas which successive British governments had followed for many years. In 1975, however, when Iceland extended its claim to 200 miles, although there was an initial protest, the matter was not pursued. This was because an increasing number of states were now making

---

[2] See Chapter 3.

such claims and, rather than maintain a futile rearguard action, the United Kingdom, together with the other members of the EEC, elected to make its own 200-mile claim.[3] Here, then, developments in state practice had legitimated actions which would formerly have been unacceptable. Time had eliminated a possible source of dispute. The old saying, 'when rain falls, water disputes turn to bubbles', makes the same point.

Sometimes, the time element is not concerned with an individual dispute but with a whole class of disputes. A particularly clear illustration of this may be seen today in Eastern Europe and the former Soviet Union. At the end of the Second World War, Eastern Europe fell under the domination of the Soviet Union, with the result that normal political relations between the states of the region, including the promotion and defence of national interests, were effectively suspended. In 1989, however, as Soviet power retreated, these states were able to reassert their national sovereignty and rejoin the international political system. Similarly, with the break-up of the Soviet Union itself in 1991, an entirely new group of states with separate national interests came into being. These dramatic developments do not mean that, with so many new possibilities for public assertiveness, Eastern Europe and the Commonwealth of Independent States are bound to be torn apart by chauvinism and aggrandisement. But disputes, as we have seen, are a regular part of international politics. Consequently, in addition to many long-standing grievances which were masked by Soviet hegemony, these states must now deal with the differences with their neighbours and with other states which are a normal incident of independence.

A legal perspective

The relevance of law and legal institutions to the settlement of international disputes is a subject which has generated an abundant and varied literature. To some, the answer to all the world's problems is to be found in legal codes and international tribunals. To others, observing the disregard for legality which is a feature of most international crises, law at best has a marginal role in world affairs, and at worst is a pious illusion. Although it is unnecessary to pursue this controversy here, legal methods bulk large in any discussion of peaceful means of settlement, and three chapters have already been devoted to outlining the main features of arbitration and judicial settlement. It may therefore be appropriate to identify a number of general considerations with a bearing on our theme. These will also be useful later, when we consider how the present legal means of settlement might be improved.

The first point to make is that the role of law and the role of adjudication are two issues, not one. While it is difficult to imagine adjudication without

---

[3] For an account of events following the 1974 judgment of the International Court, see C. Schulte, *Compliance with Decisions of the International Court of Justice*, Oxford, 2004, pp. 151–5.

law, law without adjudication is actually the normal situation in international affairs. Even within states, this position is more common than is generally appreciated once the practical obstacles to litigation are taken into account. In international affairs, where even 'compulsory' jurisdiction is voluntary, law frequently stands alone, totally unsupported by institutional arrangements.

Is there any value in legal rules without procedures for adjudication? The answer is yes: first, because in practice where legal rules exist they are normally followed, and, secondly, because, although international disputes are generally resolved without adjudication, law will frequently play a significant part in defining the points in issue, and in providing a framework for negotiation, conciliation or the presentation of a state's case in a political forum. Law can, of course, also supply an acceptable vehicle for a settlement in the form of a treaty. To draw attention to the fact that international law is significant in practice is not to suggest that law is the key to international relations, nor that states live under the rule of law in the same sense as citizens within a state. Neither is it to imply that adjudication is irrelevant, or not worth improving. The point is simply that to appreciate the place of legal methods of settlement one must first be clear about the role of law.

Turning now to adjudication, the most fruitful approach is perhaps to consider the special features of legal methods of settlement and to see how these govern their usefulness. This is a matter which can be analysed in different ways,[4] but for our purposes the following characteristics are particularly relevant.

Probably the most striking feature of adjudication is that it is dispositive. Because the decisions of courts and tribunals are treated as binding, litigation is a good way of disposing of a troublesome issue when the resolution of a dispute is considered to be more important than the result. Conversely, when the result is all-important, adjudication is unlikely to be used because it is simply too risky. These attitudes are reinforced by the fact that adjudication is not merely dispositive, but tends to produce a winner-takes-all type of solution. This can obviously render an unfavourable outcome a catastrophe and so encourages states to choose other procedures for disputes which they cannot afford to lose.

Because adjudication is dispositive, the attitude of states towards compulsory jurisdiction is conspicuously ambivalent. On the one hand, there is a good deal of support for the principle of the optional clause and similar arrangements, since the idea of establishing a binding system to resolve international disputes is an attractive one. On the other hand, as soon as

---

[4] For excellent surveys of this issue, see R. B. Bilder, 'International dispute settlement and the role of adjudication', in L. F. Damrosch (ed.), *The International Court of Justice at a Crossroads*, New York, 1987, p. 155; and R. Y. Jennings, 'The proper work and purposes of the International Court of Justice', in A. S. Muller, D. Raic and J. M. Thuránszky (eds.), *The International Court of Justice*, The Hague, 1997, p. 33.

such arrangements are established, states become aware of the risks involved in a commitment to litigate disputes which cannot be foreseen and begin to have second thoughts. The result, as we have seen, is a reluctance to subscribe to the more general arrangements for compulsory jurisdiction and a preference for agreements concerned either with particular types of cases or individual disputes.

A second characteristic of adjudication is that the binding decision is given by judges who are impartial. Looking to individuals who are neutral for assistance in settling disputes is by no means unique to adjudication and is also to be found in other third-party methods such as conciliation. In relation to adjudication, however, impartiality is not only by tradition a definitive feature, but also assumes a crucial importance owing to the consequences of the decision. While bias on the part of conciliators is no doubt regrettable, on the part of a court empowered to make a binding decision it is far more serious. However, an impartial process also offers great advantages. Referring a dispute to a court which is demonstrably impartial can be very useful when a government is anxious to settle a dispute, but is under pressure not to make concessions. As the decision is not the government's responsibility, then, provided it has been arrived at fairly, a strong case can be made out for accepting it even if it is unfavourable.

Since international law is more controversial than domestic law, the international judge is more like a US Supreme Court justice, deciding a point of constitutional interpretation, than a domestic judge with a routine case. It follows that it may be better to ensure that a court as a whole represents a range of views rather than to expect each individual to be able to synthesise all approaches. Alternatively, states can seek to ensure that their cases are heard by judges whose general legal philosophy they accept. It will be recalled that both ways of dealing with the issue of impartiality are employed internationally: the first by the provision requiring the representation of 'the main forms of civilization' and 'the principal legal systems of the world' on the International Court, and the second by the control which states exercise over the composition of arbitral tribunals and the possibilities offered by chambers of the International Court.[5]

A further aspect of adjudication, bound up with the issue of impartiality and hinted at above, is that the resolution of disputes by legal means employs a special sort of justification. For the reference of a dispute to arbitration or to the International Court demonstrates more than a desire for an impartial decision. It also shows that the parties want a decision which can be justified in a particular way, in terms of rules or principles rather than expediency or the judges' whim. This requirement is the basis of many of the rules relating to the nullity of awards, including the rule that a judgment should

---

[5] See further T. M. Franck, *Fairness in International Law and Institutions*, Oxford, 1995, Chapter 10.

be reasoned and that an arbitrator must follow his instructions as regards the applicable law. Because it is founded on principles, adjudication supplies a way of settling disputes which is rational, orderly and authoritative. No doubt the rationality of the judicial process can be exaggerated, and no one who has ever been involved in litigation is likely to think of it as a bloodless procedure. It is nevertheless true that, as methods of dealing with serious and sensitive issues go, adjudication is as rational a process as fallible mortals can make it.

The orderly quality of adjudication has been well described as follows:

> The well-established structure of the adjudicative process provides a framework for the orderly presentation and development of the opposing arguments concerning the dispute. Where complex and difficult factual and technical questions are involved – as may be the case, for example, in land or maritime boundary disputes – the adjudicative process may facilitate a more orderly and thorough examination of the issues than might otherwise be the case. Adjudication also typically requires at least some contact and co-operation between the parties. At the least, this may lead to a more thorough examination of the issues by each party and a fairer disposition of the controversy. Conceivably, it may lead to a better understanding by the parties themselves of the respective merits of each other's positions concerning the issue in dispute, and to their own negotiation of a settlement.[6]

Adjudication is authoritative because the decision is reasoned and the jurisdiction of the tribunal has been accepted by the parties. It is therefore vital to ensure that these conditions are maintained. In the last analysis, authority depends on substantive, not formal, considerations, and so a decision which is not convincingly reasoned or is handed down in circumstances where there is reason to doubt whether jurisdiction has been accepted will lack authority in the eyes of the parties, whatever the status or reputation of the tribunal. In the same way, one of the advantages of adjudication is that the decision legitimates the successful party's claim in the view of the international community. However, this will only be achieved if the court pays scrupulous attention to the demands of its role. For it is not the fact of obtaining judgment which vindicates a claim, so much as the reasoning by which the decision is supported.

Judgments based on principles cannot avoid having an impact as precedents, and this feature of the judicial process has both advantages and disadvantages. The advantage is that it enables the settlement of individual disputes to make a contribution to the development of international law. This is especially significant on issues such as human rights, where abstract principles require concrete application, and the law relating to evidence, jurisdiction and procedure, where the formulation of principles by

---

[6] Bilder, 'International dispute settlement', p. 165.

tribunals is of direct assistance to adjudication. The disadvantage is that states are sometimes anxious for a dispute to be resolved in a way which will not prejudice their position in other disputes. In such a situation, they are likely to regard adjudication as much less attractive than methods such as negotiation or conciliation, where the precedential effect of the outcome can be minimised.

A further aspect of adjudication, related to its precedential significance, is that this method of resolving disputes tends to be conservative. This is because law itself is conservative, resting as it does on principles to be found in past practice and, in a broader way, because the purpose of adjudication is to decide disputes by reference to certain criteria which qualify as legal, while excluding others which, however much a part of the dispute, do not. The conservative element in law makes adjudication attractive in any situation where there is broad agreement about the relevant law and resolution of the dispute is a matter of establishing who has the better case. It is totally unsuitable for disputes in which there is fundamental disagreement about what the law is, or should be. That is why boundary disputes are litigated more frequently than disputes about foreign investments. The parties to a dispute can, of course, counteract the conservatism of the law by providing their own directive to the tribunal, and adjudication, as we have noted, is flexible enough to respond to such initiatives. Moreover, law itself is far from inflexible and is always being adapted to new situations. Adjudication, however, is not a free-ranging legislative operation and so is unlikely to be effective in settling disputes where the adequacy of the law is the central issue.

The same conclusion can be drawn where the parties classify a dispute in completely different ways. The question here is not whether a legal tribunal is competent, which will depend on technical considerations of admissibility and jurisdiction, but rather whether a legal decision can contribute anything to the solution of a dispute. In the *Diplomatic Staff in Tehran* case, as was mentioned earlier, the United States emphasised the legal aspects of the dispute, whereas Iran saw it as part of a wider political issue. In the *Nicaragua* case,[7] it was the United States which defined the dispute politically and Nicaragua which sought a legal judgment. In both cases, the International Court, having held that it had jurisdiction, proceeded to examine the case in the legal framework relied on by the applicant. As a legal tribunal it was right to do so. However, although the judgments in these cases were not without effect, no one expected them to resolve the underlying disputes and they did not do so. Adjudication by its nature is well suited to dealing with the legal aspect of disputes; for disputes which raise other issues, however, different methods are needed.

---

[7] *Military and Paramilitary Activities in and against Nicaragua*, Jurisdiction and Admissibility, Judgment, [1984] ICJ Rep. p. 392. For discussion, see Chapters 6 and 7.

The last feature of adjudication which merits attention was thrown into prominence in one of the cases which have just been mentioned. It will be recalled that one of the arguments of the United States in the *Nicaragua* case related to the absence from the proceedings of certain third parties whose presence was said to be indispensable. Similarly, it will be recalled that various cases have posed the question of when a third state can intervene in the Court, and, as noted in Chapter 6, in 1990 this question was raised in relation to proceedings before a chamber.[8] What these cases have in common is that, in different ways, they all present problems which concern the position of third parties in international litigation.

It is clear from the history of arbitration and judicial settlement that because international adjudication is consensual it works best for bilateral disputes and not so well for multilateral disputes. When a case involves the interests of a third state, there are two difficulties. The first, exemplified by the *Monetary Gold* case,[9] is the problem of the third state whose rights are in issue but which does not wish to litigate; the second, raised by the cases on intervention, is the third state which does wish to litigate, but whose presence is objected to by the main parties. In both situations, the root of the problem is that a bilateral procedure is being employed for what are effectively multilateral disputes and that reconciling the interests of the parties with those of the third state is a virtually impossible task.

In the first situation, too much protection for the third state will prevent the states which are present from obtaining a decision. This no doubt accounts for the Court's rejection of the American argument in the *Nicaragua* case. In the second situation, admitting the would-be intervenor may cause the original parties to withdraw the case, preferring to settle the matter outside the courtroom, rather than defend a flank against a third party. This probably explains the Court's restrictive stand on intervention. The treatment of both issues is open to criticism, but it is as well to recognise that no answer to this problem is wholly satisfactory because the real difficulty is with the attitudes of states. If all the states concerned are prepared to resolve a dispute by adjudication, the procedures exist for enabling them to do so. If, on the other hand, some of them are not, no amount of tinkering with rules can transcend the practical limitations of adjudication.

Improving the capacity of political methods

The Charter of the United Nations, as critics of the Organization never fail to point out, was intended to put the conduct of international relations on

---

[8] See *Land, Island and Maritime Frontier Dispute (El Salvador/Honduras)*, Application to Intervene, Order of 28 February 1990 and Judgment, [1990] ICJ Rep. pp. 3 and 92.

[9] *Monetary Gold Removed from Rome in 1943*, Judgment, [1954] ICJ Rep. p. 19. For discussion of this case and its subsequent interpretation, see Chapter 6. For a review of the general issue, see L. F. Damrosch, 'Multilateral disputes', in Damrosch, *International Court of Justice*, p. 376.

a new footing. It is therefore part of a tradition which includes the League Covenant and the various schemes for a new world order put forward by thinkers before 1945 and subsequently. Clearly, the UN has not worked, or, to be more accurate, it does not work in the way that a reading of the Charter suggests that it should. It is nevertheless by far the most important international political organisation and, as we have seen, is often in a position to contribute to the resolution of disputes. It is therefore an appropriate focus when thinking about improvements in political means of settlement.

The first suggestions for change relate to the Security Council. It will be recalled that under the Charter the Security Council has the primary responsibility for maintaining international peace and security and dealing with disputes, and for these purposes is equipped with extensive powers under Chapters VI and VII. In the Cold War era between 1946 and 1989, little use could be made of Chapter VII, and, although some initiatives were possible under Chapter VI, there too the scope for initiatives was severely constrained. In recent years, with greater co-operation among the Permanent Members, the situation has changed and the Security Council has been much more active. While there is still a tendency to neglect disputes until they become critical, and although preventive measures are rarely considered, cases which reach the Security Council now often receive a positive response. However, as the Security Council has become more active, especially in employing Chapter VII, questions have been raised about its authority which have yet to be satisfactorily answered.

An organ which acts on behalf of the international community, which can authorise the use of force, set up peace-keeping forces and take other far-reaching measures must, if its actions are to be regarded as legitimate, be adequately representative. When the United Nations was founded, it had about fifty members, and nine were represented on the Security Council. Since the membership is now nearly 200 and the Security Council is a mere fifteen, the problem here is plain. Moreover, of the five Permanent Members, only two, the United States and China, would retain that status on the criteria of wealth, size or world influence. Accordingly, there is a qualitative, as well as a quantitative, aspect to the issue of legitimacy. The composition of the Security Council is currently under discussion and the outcome remains to be seen. Enlarging the Council and making its membership more representative are, however, now urgent matters.[10]

---

[10] See further A. Parsons, 'The United Nations in the post-Cold War era', (1992) 11 Int. Rel. p. 189; P. Wilenski, 'The structure of the UN in the post-Cold War period', in A. Roberts and B. Kingsbury (eds.), *United Nations, Divided World*, 2nd edn, Oxford, 1993, p. 437; and C. L. Willson, 'Changing the Charter: The United Nations prepares for the twenty-first century', (1996) 90 AJIL p. 115. See also K. A. Mingst and M. P. Karns, *The United Nations in the Post-Cold War Era*, 2nd edn, Boulder, CO, 2000, pp. 202–5; and Y. Z. Blum, 'Proposals for UN Security Council reform', (2005) 99 AJIL p. 632.

No less important, and almost as controversial, would be a decision to adopt a set of principles to guide the Security Council when it is deciding whether to authorize the use of force. As noted in Chapter 10, a High Level Panel set up by Secretary-General Kofi Annan proposed that the Security Council should employ five criteria to guide such decisions and also that both the Council and the General Assembly should adopt resolutions setting out these criteria. Although the proposal was welcomed by the Secretary-General in his own report, as mentioned earlier the UN World Summit in 2005 did not support it. While there were a number of predictable objections, ranging from doubts as to whether such guidelines would be effective, to fears that they might merely provide an excuse for the UN failing to take action when it was needed, it seems a pity that the proposal was so swiftly rejected. In a situation then in which the need is for principled decision-making from the Security Council, the recommendation of the High Level Panel may be worth revisiting.

Changing the composition of the Security Council or redefining its powers would each be significant institutional developments, and are therefore difficult. There are, however, steps which could be taken now to enhance the Council's authority because the way it takes its decisions and the decisions themselves also have a bearing on the issue of legitimacy. As regards the decisions which are taken, while the merits of this or that resolution can be debated, the general point is that, if the Security Council is to be respected, it must be seen to act fairly.[11] As regards the way decisions are taken, the need is for the Council to operate with greater transparency and to consult more widely with the membership.[12] This is more than a matter of presentation, for, as Secretary-General Boutros-Ghali observed in 1992, 'agreement among the Permanent Members must have the deeper support of the other members of the Council, and the membership more widely, if the Council's decisions are to be effective and endure'.[13] Recognising this point, the Security Council has already introduced a number of changes in its working methods and procedure,[14] but further attention to these matters is needed.

Specific suggestions for reducing what has been called the Security Council's 'deliberative deficit' that are worth considering include ensuring: that when far-reaching measures are being debated consultations should be wide-ranging and at least involve all those likely to be affected by the decision; that all such decisions should be publicly justified as a means of

---

[11] See Franck, *Fairness in International Law*, Chapter 7.

[12] See F. L. Kirgis, 'The Security Council's first fifty years', (1995) 89 AJIL p. 506 at pp. 518–19; and C. Peck, *The United Nations as a Dispute Settlement System*, The Hague, 1996, p. 219.

[13] B. Boutros-Ghali, *An Agenda for Peace*, SC Doc. S/24111, 17 June 1992, para. 78. Text in (1992) 31 ILM p. 953.

[14] See M. C. Wood, 'Security Council working methods and procedure: Recent developments', (1996) 45 ICLQ p. 150.

promoting reasoned debate and discouraging irresponsible use of the veto; and that, where appropriate, as with the Council's measures directed against terrorism for example, the effect of its decisions should be subject to independent review. Of course, as has been pointed out, 'All this must occur within limits: the Council can tolerate only so much consultation, publicity, and review before it becomes hopelessly inefficient.'[15] Nevertheless, there is currently a good case for urging the Security Council to take further steps in this direction.

Another possible area for change is the Secretariat. Although reform of the Security Council is important, whatever changes are made there, the good offices work of the Secretary-General is likely to remain the United Nations' most practical contribution in many dispute situations. Secessionist conflicts, for example, or civil wars within states, have increased in recent years, but for various reasons the Security Council has often been slow to act. If, therefore, there is to be UN involvement at an early stage, the Secretary-General may have to provide the response. There are, however, a number of ways in which the potential of the office could be improved.[16] Some of the proposed changes are concerned with the resources which are available to do the job; others are related to the job itself.

Improving the Secretary-General's resources is partly a matter of ensuring that, when an opportunity occurs to promote the settlement of a dispute, lack of available funds is not a significant constraint. Resources, however, are not just a matter of money. If action is to be effective, there is a need for information and individuals who can process it and decide what should be done. Here, also, improvements can be suggested. A previous Secretary-General has drawn attention to the fact that the position of the UN is much inferior to that of its member states and indeed most transnational corporations.[17] In an attempt to improve the information flow and facilitate preventive diplomacy, various changes have been made in the internal organisation of the Secretariat. However, problems have been encountered in relation to two matters.[18] One is the need to integrate the work of those who gather and analyse information with the activities of those in the Secretariat who decide what action, if any, should be taken in response. The other is the difficulty of maintaining staffing and providing essential resources in the face of frequent cost-cutting and down-sizing. While the responsiveness

---

[15] I. Johnstone, 'Legislation and adjudication in the UN Security Council: Bringing down the deliberative deficit', (2008) 102 AJIL p. 275 at p. 303.

[16] See also Wilenski, 'The structure of the UN', pp. 449–56; and S. Chesterman (ed.), *Secretary or General? The UN Secretary-General in World Politics*, Cambridge, 2007, Part IV.

[17] J. Pérez de Cuéllar, 'The role of the UN Secretary-General', in Roberts and Kingsbury, *United Nations, Divided World*, p. 124 at p. 136.

[18] See C. Peck, *Sustainable Peace*, Lanham, MD, 1998, pp. 71–5. For earlier efforts, see B. G. Ramcharan, *The International Law and Practice of Early-Warning and Preventive Diplomacy: The Emerging Global Watch*, Dordrecht, 1991, Chapters 2 and 4; and Peck, *The United Nations*, Chapter 7.

problem is essentially organisational and bureaucratic, the resource issue is ultimately the responsibility of the member states, specifically the major contributors, who, if they wish the UN to have the capacity to provide early warning, must be prepared to pay for it.

Change could also be considered with regard to the period of office. At present, the Secretary-General is elected for a five-year term and can stand for re-election. If the term of office was increased and at the same time re-election was precluded, the results would probably be beneficial. A term of seven or eight years would be long enough for any Secretary-General to make a mark and, with no possibility of re-election, there would be less opportunity for governments to seek to influence the Secretary-General's decisions, especially towards the end of a term. Governments which are opposed to the Secretary-General exercising an independent role could be expected to oppose this change, just as they would also be against improving the Secretariat's resources. Independence, however, has rightly been described as 'the heart and soul of the office of the Secretary-General',[19] and modifying the present election arrangements would be a way for states which support this principle to show that they take it seriously.

Finally, it was pointed out in Chapter 10 that the Secretariat does not work in isolation, but as an integral part of the whole United Nations system. This is relevant to the issue of reform when the contribution of the Secretary-General to the prevention and settlement of disputes is seen in relation to the work of the Security Council. The latter, as we have noted, tends to find itself dealing with disputes late in the day and should be prepared to intervene earlier. It has to be said, however, that the Secretariat, which has generally been reluctant to exercise its power to bring issues to the Council under Article 99, cannot escape all responsibility for this state of affairs. The fact that the Secretary-General has been very active in performing his good offices function is, no doubt, some compensation for this deficiency, but the Secretariat could make an even greater contribution to the effectiveness of the Charter system by ensuring that the members of the Security Council are aware of potential disputes at an early stage and, where necessary, by placing the matter on its agenda.

Peace-keeping is a further aspect of the United Nations system where it is clear that improvements can be made. The *Brahimi Report*,[20] a review of peace-keeping presented to and endorsed by the Security Council in 2000, contained numerous practical proposals and has already had a major impact. Among its goals was to promote the rapid deployment of peace-keeping forces. This aim had been recognised earlier as best achieved by having states earmark units in advance for possible UN service, so that,

---

[19] Pérez de Cuéllar, 'UN Secretary-General', p. 135.

[20] Text in (2000) 39 ILM p. 1432. For discussion, see C. Gray, *International Law and the Use of Force*, 2nd edn, Oxford, 2004, pp. 239–51.

instead of having to make hasty *ad hoc* arrangements, the Secretary-General could draw on a roster of available units when a peace-keeping force was needed. The Secretary-General began reporting on this issue to the Security Council in 1994, and the effort to create standby forces has been quite successful, with more than eighty states now having such units designated.[21]

Less successful has been the attempt to ensure that peace-keeping troops are available in the numbers needed, a matter of particular concern in view of the number of UN operations currently being undertaken. When reviewing the steps needed to implement the *Brahimi Report*, the Secretary-General made the point that peace-keeping must be seen as the responsibility of all the member states and that for performance in this area to improve it is essential for those with the greatest capacity, notably the Permanent Members of the Security Council, to participate in such operations by contributing troops. So far, however, the response to this call has been unenthusiastic, as the Permanent Members, and the developed states in general, evidently prefer to provide only financial and logistical support, leaving the actual troops to be found from elsewhere. It is doubtful, however, if extensive UN peace-keeping can be sustained on this basis. A significant step forward would therefore be for the developed states to be more active.

Another issue raised by the *Brahimi Report* was the relationship between the Security Council, the Secretariat and troop-contributing countries, where improvements in consultation were seen as important both for running effective operations and for maintaining the necessary political commitments. This was accepted in principle by the Security Council,[22] but discussion of the issue revealed a difference of opinion between the Permanent Members, who emphasised the need for the Security Council to be in charge, and troop-contributing countries who wanted more say over how their forces are used. To the extent that the Permanent Members can themselves be persuaded to become troop-contributing countries, the question of consultation will become less critical. As things stand, however, defining the role of such countries is now a priority.

The final matter to mention is the question of peace-keeping mandates. We saw in Chapter 10 that peace-keeping operations can take many forms and that confusion over the nature of a mission, or the related phenomenon of 'mission-creep' (i.e. the expansion of a mission's mandate through force of circumstances after it has begun) are highly undesirable. The *Brahimi Report*, reflecting experience with peace-keeping in Somalia, Rwanda and the former Yugoslavia over the previous decade, emphasised the need for clear, credible and achievable mandates, and its recommendations to that

---

[21] See *ibid.*, p. 239.
[22] See Security Council Resolution 1327 (2000), text in (2001) 40 ILM p. 503; and see Gray, *Use of Force*, p. 241.

effect have been accepted by the Security Council.[23] For such a policy to be effective, however, it will be necessary either to develop a broader resource base for peace-keeping operations, or for the Security Council to limit its ambitions. Either way, ensuring that UN peace-keeping always has a clear, credible and achievable mandate is another way in which it can be improved.

Although the focus here has been on the United Nations system, this is not intended to suggest that the traditional diplomatic means for handling disputes cannot be improved, nor that the record of regional organisations is completely satisfactory. In relation to the latter, however, it is unnecessary to add to the general comments of the previous chapter, and proposals concerning specific organisations may be found elsewhere. As regards other political procedures, perhaps the point which emerges most clearly is the need to encourage consultation both as an informal practice and, where appropriate, in an institutional setting. This could be done by, for example, making its advantages more widely known and ensuring that states with little experience of its benefits are provided with examples of good practice and help in setting up their own arrangements. While the record demonstrates that states are reluctant to restrict their prerogatives, there are many situations where consultation, when once established, is an excellent way of promoting and protecting interests. This being so, it is reasonable to suppose that a wider dissemination of information, accompanied by practical assistance, might increase its use significantly.

Improving the capacity of legal methods

Reform of the legal methods for handling disputes has been a subject of concern to those with an interest in international affairs from the earliest days of arbitration. The creation of the Permanent Court in 1919 and its successor, the present International Court, far from propitiating the advocates of change, made adjudication the focus of even greater attention. As a result, everything done by international judges and arbitrators is now studied, analysed and criticised in minute detail and the would-be reformer is presented with an almost embarrassing wealth of suggestions.

This is, of course, excellent because it indicates that the ideals which animated the pioneers of adjudication are still alive, and, pragmatically, because informed criticism is indispensable if institutions are to retain their relevance or improve. On the other hand, though the reform of legal institutions is no less important than that of political institutions, here, as with the proposals we have just been considering, suggestions which ignore the constraints within which legal and political arrangements operate are not at all helpful. Into this category, for example, fall proposals for making adherence to the optional clause compulsory, or prohibiting reservations to

---

[23] In Resolution 1327 (2000); see note 22 above, and Gray, *Use of Force*, p. 243.

states' acceptances, because these treat problems which are a reflection of the political context of adjudication as though they were merely technical. What is needed is not prescriptions for an ideal world, but practical proposals. The following, though not exhaustive, are thought to fulfil this requirement.

The first improvement is already being implemented. It is to make litigation more attractive to states by reducing its cost. In 1989, the UN Secretary-General announced that he was setting up a Trust Fund to assist states in settling their disputes through the International Court.[24] Stating that he saw himself as having a special responsibility to promote judicial settlement, the Secretary-General indicated that the object of the Fund is to assist states which are prevented from using the Court by either lack of legal expertise or lack of money. Initially two categories of cases would be considered eligible for assistance: first, cases where there is a joint agreement to submit a dispute to the Court and consequently no question of disputed jurisdiction; secondly, cases where the parties are ready to implement a judgment which has already been given, but one or both are unable to do so on account of a lack of funds or expertise.

Administration of the Fund is the responsibility of a panel of experts whose task is to examine each application and make recommendations regarding the sums to be awarded and the expenses to be covered. The latter may include 'counsel fees, the costs of translation and interpretation, [and] expenses for producing cartographic materials', as well as costs relating to the execution of a judgment such as demarcation of boundaries. The panel to consider each application consists of three persons 'of the highest judicial and moral standing', who work in strict confidentiality and must 'be guided solely by the financial needs of the requesting State and the availability of the funds'. The Fund is not part of the regular UN budget but is financed by voluntary contributors who can include individuals, national and international organisations and corporations, as well as states. More than fifty states initially made significant contributions to the Fund, and others indicated that they would be prepared to offer support in response to particular applications.[25] The sums involved are not large, but it has been possible to provide assistance in several cases, an early beneficiary being Chad, which was given help in the *Territorial Dispute* case.[26]

---

[24] Text in (1989) 28 ILM p. 1584. For a contemporary reaction, see T. Bien-Aime, 'A pathway to The Hague and beyond: The United Nations Trust Fund proposal', (1991) 22 NYUJ Int. L. & Politics, p. 671.

[25] See P. H. F. Bekker, 'International legal aid in practice: The ICJ Trust Fund', (1993) 87 AJIL p. 659. See also A. Eyffinger, *The International Court of Justice 1946–1996*, The Hague, 1996, pp. 365–6.

[26] *Territorial Dispute (Libyan Arab Jamahiriya/Chad)*, Judgment, [1994] ICJ Rep. p. 6. During the oral proceedings, the Agent of Chad revealed that help had been received: see Bekker, 'International legal aid', p. 666, n. 45.

Following the above example, a number of other courts and tribunals have made arrangements to provide prospective litigants with financial assistance.[27] The Permanent Court of Arbitration has set up a Financial Assistance Fund for this purpose, and the Secretariat of the World Trade Organization has been authorised to provide technical and legal assistance to developing member states for cases being dealt with through the procedures described in Chapter 9. One of the latest organs to benefit from an arrangement of this kind is the International Tribunal for the Law of the Sea, for which the UN General Assembly established a Trust Fund by resolution in 2000.[28] The Fund is administered by the Secretary-General and is similar in many respects to that already available for the International Court. There are, however, also some significant differences; for example, there is no need for a special agreement between the litigants.[29] The creation of these new sources of assistance is an imaginative way of encouraging adjudication and as such is to be welcomed. What is required now is for those who approve of these measures in principle to continue supporting them financially.

The second measure is the further development of the chambers procedure. This is related to the Secretary-General's initiative in two ways. Like the Trust Fund, it is a way of encouraging judicial settlement by making it cheaper, in this instance by relieving the parties of some, though not all, of the costs of litigation. Moreover, though relatively new, it too is not a proposal but an established scheme. Indeed, as we saw in Chapter 6, there is now a significant amount of experience with the new procedure, and an interesting and varied 'chambers jurisprudence' is already emerging. It would be wrong to imply that chambers should always be seen as preferable to using the full Court, since both have their merits. But, without going so far, it would be worth ensuring that governments are regularly reminded of the positive record of chambers in settling disputes expeditiously (and relatively cheaply) and also that they are aware that they have the option of setting up a chamber if they wish to do so.

The next issue is more traditional. It is the contribution which can be made to the Court's efficacy by the quality of its judgments. Good judgments help to develop and maintain confidence in the Court by giving users of adjudication the kinds of results they are entitled to expect. Poor judgments have the opposite effect.[30] What constitutes a good judgment? The facts

---

[27] See D. Anderson, 'Trust funds in international litigation', in N. Ando, E. McWhinney and R. Wolfrum (eds.), *Liber Amicorum Judge Shigeru Oda*, The Hague, 2002, p. 793.

[28] See Document I in the appendix below.

[29] Similarly, although the main aim of the new Fund is to provide assistance for proceedings on the merits, where jurisdiction is not an issue, 'in exceptional circumstances' assistance can be provided for any phase of the proceedings. For further discussion, see Anderson, 'Trust funds in international litigation', pp. 801–3.

[30] For explanation and illustration of this point, see J. G. Merrills, *The Development of International Law by the European Court of Human Rights*, 2nd edn, Manchester, 1993, Chapter 2.

that a decision is criticised, or even that a state refuses to carry it out, are not in themselves reasons for regarding a judgment as defective. In a case of any complexity, it will usually be possible to justify more than one conclusion and so the critic can almost always find something to object to. Equally, there will always be bad losers, and consequently the rejection of a decision by a state may be no more than a sign that the Court has done what it is supposed to do and has applied the law without fear or favour. The criticisms which matter are those which question whether the Court is adequately discharging its function and here, it is suggested, there may be scope for improvement.

The series of cases in which the Court had to grapple with the legal consequences of the break-up of the former Yugoslavia, although unusually complex, highlight some of the dangers. In 1993, Bosnia and Herzegovina (Bosnia) began proceedings against Yugoslavia in respect of a number of alleged violations of the 1948 Genocide Convention. In 1996, the Court found that it had jurisdiction on the basis of the Convention.[31] Although the status of Yugoslavia between 1992 and 2000 was a matter of great uncertainty owing to the disintegration of the country, the question was not discussed in the 1996 judgment because at the time neither side saw an advantage in raising it. In 2001, however, Yugoslavia applied for a revision of the 1996 judgment, but this, as we saw in Chapter 6, was refused as incompatible with the Court's Statute, despite Yugoslavia's having been admitted to the United Nations as a new state in November 2000. Next, in the *Legality of Use of Force* cases[32] in 2004, the Court accepted that Serbia and Montenegro, as Yugoslavia was now styled, was not a party to the Statute in 1999 and so was not entitled to initiate judicial proceedings against eight NATO states.

In 2007, when the case brought by Bosnia was considered on the merits, Serbia argued that, if it could not bring a case, it could not be a respondent either. However, this apparently logical argument was rejected on the ground that the original 1996 judgment on jurisdiction was *res judicata*.[33] In the meantime, Croatia had begun proceedings against Serbia, again alleging violation of the Genocide Convention. When the issue of jurisdiction was considered in this case in 2008,[34] there was obviously no question of *res judicata*, but the Court, invoking the principle of 'judicial economy',

---

[31] *Application of the Convention on the Prevention and Punishment of the Crime of Genocide (Bosnia and Herzegovina v. Yugoslavia)*, Preliminary Objections, Judgment, [1996] ICJ Rep. p. 595.

[32] See, for example, *Legality of Use of Force (Serbia and Montenegro v. Belgium)*, Preliminary Objections, Judgment, [2004] ICJ Rep. p. 279. The judgments in respect of the other seven respondents were essentially similar.

[33] *Application of the Convention on the Prevention and Punishment of the Crime of Genocide (Bosnia and Herzegovina v. Serbia and Montenegro)*, Merits, Judgment, [2007] ICJ Rep.

[34] *Application of the Convention on the Prevention and Punishment of the Crime of Genocide (Croatia v. Serbia and Montenegro)*, Preliminary Objections, Judgment, [2008] ICJ Rep.

held that the key date was not July 1999, when the case was begun, but November 2000, when Serbia joined the United Nations. Accordingly, as in the case brought by Bosnia, the Court held that it had jurisdiction. The reasoning in this sequence of cases has been described as 'disquieting'[35] and 'problematic'[36] and both comments seem well-founded.

The essential purpose of adjudication is to resolve disputes by reference to law, or, where this is authorised, on some other basis. This requires a reasoned decision which addresses the arguments put forward by the parties and explains the Court's conclusion. It follows that judgments which are inconsistent, inadequately reasoned, based on points not raised in argument, or which evade crucial issues, are defective. These are all unfortunately criticisms which can be made of some recent international decisions including those just mentioned. Without under-estimating the difficulty which confronts any collegiate court in drafting a collective opinion on a controversial issue, the conclusion must be that there is room for progress here. The point is not that better judgments will increase the readiness of states to use adjudication, which seems unlikely, nor even that better judgments will mean that cases will have different results, though no doubt this will sometimes happen. The point is rather that, as a technique for dealing with international disputes, adjudication has properties which are uniquely valuable, but to survive requires practitioners both willing and able to preserve its integrity.

This leads to a related point concerning the multiplication of international tribunals and its consequences.[37] Far more judicial bodies exist today than was once the case, and the number is constantly increasing. Thus, as already noted, the last two decades have seen the creation of the International Criminal Tribunals for the Former Yugoslavia (1993) and for Rwanda (1994), the World Trade Organization's Appellate Body (1995) and the International Tribunal for the Law of the Sea (1996). This proliferation poses two problems, one procedural and one substantive. The procedural problem is to establish priorities, given that in some situations more than one tribunal may have jurisdiction and that views may differ as to how a dispute should be handled. The substantive problem is to ensure that, when different tribunals are dealing with similar legal issues, their decisions are consistent.

It cannot be said that either the procedural or the substantive problem has yet been properly addressed, but both have become increasingly pressing and, as mentioned in Chapter 8, have already led some to question the need

---

[35]   See C. Gray, Note, (2005) 54 ICLQ p. 787.

[36]   See S. Sivakumaran, Note, (2007) 56 ICLQ p. 695 at p. 697.

[37]   See E. Lauterpacht, *Aspects of the Administration of International Justice*, Cambridge, 1991, Chapter 2; and G. Guillaume, 'The future of international judicial institutions', (1995) 44 ICLQ p. 848. See also the essays by H. Caminos and others in Ando, McWhinney and Wolfrum, *Liber Amicorum*, pp. 569–667; and Y. Shany, *The Competing Jurisdictions of International Courts and Tribunals*, Oxford, 2003.

for new tribunals. It is not possible to deal fully with this complex matter here, but thinking about it will be easier if several distinct issues of legal policy are separated. The first of these is the factors to be taken into account when proposals are being considered to set up a new tribunal. It would be absurd to establish bodies to duplicate the work of existing tribunals, but it would be equally absurd to believe that our present range of tribunals can supply all that will ever be needed. It is only necessary to consider the four tribunals mentioned in the previous paragraph to appreciate that new bodies will always be required when there are demands which for one reason or another cannot be met by existing arrangements. A proliferation of tribunals in itself is therefore neither good nor bad. Everything depends on their justification.

A second issue of policy concerns the jurisdiction of the new courts and tribunals, more specifically how they interpret and apply their powers when these are challenged. The Law of the Sea Convention, the WTO Agreement and similar treaties, as we have seen, create elaborate systems of essentially compulsory jurisdiction over most disputes relating to their subject matter. When a dispute involving the treaty arises, it is therefore necessary to decide whether it is one falling within the system, if the point is contentious, as happened, for example, in the *Southern Bluefin Tuna* case,[38] where an Annex VII arbitral tribunal decided that it did not have jurisdiction over the case brought by Australia and New Zealand against Japan. How questions of this kind are resolved is plainly crucial if attempts to extend compulsory jurisdiction and make it effective in practice are to succeed. Accordingly, while the limits of states' commitments must be respected, it is also important for new courts and tribunals to avoid jurisdictional decisions that are too restrictive.[39]

A third issue of policy concerns the problem of priorities which may arise when more than one court or tribunal has jurisdiction over a dispute. This situation is unavoidable as networks of compulsory jurisdiction multiply, and there can be no objection in principle to separate aspects of a dispute being addressed by different tribunals.[40] However, matters become more complicated when different tribunals are asked to deal with similar questions, leading to the possibility of conflicting decisions.[41] Although in

---

[38] *Southern Bluefin Tuna Case (Australia and New Zealand v. Japan)*, Award on Jurisdiction and Admissibility (2000), text in (2000) 39 ILM p. 1359; and see A. E. Boyle, Note, (2001) 50 ICLQ p. 447.

[39] It is instructive to compare the restrictive approach adopted by the tribunal in the *Southern Bluefin Tuna* case with the broader view favoured by its counterpart in the *MOX Plant* case (2003). For discussion of this point, see R. R. Churchill and J. Scott, 'The MOX Plant litigation: The first half-life', (2004) 53 ICLQ p. 643 at pp. 652–7.

[40] In the MOX Plant dispute, for example, the question of access to information was dealt with by means of an arbitration in 2003 under the OSPAR Convention. On those proceedings, see Churchill and Scott, 'The MOX Plant litigation', pp. 645–7.

[41] For example, in the *Swordfish* case, mentioned in Chapter 8, the EC submitted elements of the dispute to WTO procedures, but Chile initially invoked Annex VII arbitration under the Law

one sense a procedural problem, this has substantive aspects since it may involve conflicting treaty obligations, for example where trade and environmental treaties relate to the same activities, as well as procedural concepts such as *res judicata* and litispendence. As there is no hierarchy of international courts, these questions are currently resolved in an *ad hoc* manner by the tribunals concerned,[42] and as there seems no prospect of establishing such a hierarchy, this will probably continue for the foreseeable future. It would, however, be useful if thought could be given to codifying the relevant rules and principles of international law in this area and perhaps developing them by reference to the treatment of similar questions in national law.

A fourth policy issue concerns the substantive question of ensuring that the decisions of the various international courts and tribunals are consistent. Here, there is a link with a topic already considered, since one of the theoretical objections raised to the International Court's revival of the chambers procedure was that chambers might decide cases differently from the full Court. It will be recalled from Chapter 6 that this does not seem to have happened, but the risk is undoubtedly present and is, of course, much greater where other tribunals are concerned. It would certainly be regrettable if, as a result of the proliferation of international courts, international law lost its character as a common reference point and became fragmented. Since there is no doctrine of precedent in international law, a way to reduce this risk is to ensure that those elected to international courts and tribunals not only possess whatever special knowledge may be required, but are also competent international lawyers. If this is combined with steps to eliminate conflicting obligations when these come to light, decisions congruent with those elsewhere should follow as a matter of course.[43]

When considering the proliferation of international courts and tribunals and thinking about the implications of this, a further point to bear in mind is that, while some of these developments concern arrangements for inter-state litigation of a traditional kind, others involve individuals, corporate persons or international organisations, all of which are now increasingly able to use similar procedures for disputes which they may have, whether or not a state is also a party.[44] The emergence of 'transnational' dispute resolution, as this broadening of the range of legal procedures has been termed,[45] has

---

of the Sea Convention. See A. Serdy, 'See you in port', (2002) 3 Melbourne JIL p. 79; and Churchill and Scott, 'The MOX Plant litigation', p. 654.

[42] See, for example, the tribunal's suspension of proceedings in the *MOX Plant* case in 2003, pending clarification of certain jurisdictional issues by the European Court of Justice. On this aspect of the case, see Churchill and Scott, 'The MOX Plant litigation', pp. 647–52.

[43] On this point, see R. Higgins, 'The ICJ, the ECJ and the integrity of international law', (2003) 52 ICLQ p. 1; and J. Pauwelyn, *Conflict of Norms in Public International Law*, Cambridge, 2003.

[44] See F. Orrego Vicuña, *International Dispute Settlement in an Evolving Global Society*, Cambridge, 2004. For an example of the process described in the text, see the *UNESCO–France* arbitration (2003), summarised in D. D. Reichert, Note, (2004) 98 AJIL p. 163.

[45] See R. O. Keohane, A. Moravcsik and A.-M. Slaughter, 'Legalized dispute resolution: Inter-state and transnational', (2000) 54 Int. Org. p. 457.

far-reaching consequences which the present work, focusing as it does on the settlement of inter-state disputes, does not claim to explore. No discussion of improvements in legal methods and the multiplication of judicial organs would, however, be complete without mentioning this innovation.

A final suggestion is directed not to judges and arbitrators but to the states which they exist to serve. Because adjudication is primarily a matter of applying rules to facts, the future of courts and tribunals is intimately linked with that of the law itself. As a leading commentator puts it: 'Settling disputes is not just about "settling disputes". It is also about how issues are addressed, regulated and engaged with. It is about *how* law is generated, about *what* law is generated and about the manner in which it is engaged with and responded to.'[46] To be sure, it is wrong to think of adjudication as a mechanical process, to deny the significance of judicial creativity or to ignore the functions which various non-legal criteria can perform. Nor is it true that the creation of new rules of international law is in itself a guarantee that they will be used to settle international disputes. All that having been said, however, adjudication needs a basis in law and the responsibility for developing new law lies not with judges but with states.

To the extent that states discharge their responsibility by taking the difficult political decisions which are needed to formulate new legal principles, they strengthen the process of adjudication by providing courts and tribunals with a legitimate basis for their decisions. On the other hand, if they avoid their responsibility, the task of the international judge becomes immeasurably more difficult and perhaps even impossible. This is not because adjudicators lack the skill to produce solutions to international problems, but because it is unreasonable to expect them to do so alone. If adjudication is to work, there must first be a substantial measure of agreement on the rules of decision. For it is this agreement which, if a judgment is also competent technically, makes a ruling legitimate. Thus, a commitment to the progressive development of international law offers both a way of bringing the conduct of international politics within a legal framework and real support for the process of adjudication.

Conclusion

The peaceful settlement of international disputes is the most critical issue of our time. Although human rights, the environment, and economic and financial issues, among other matters, present challenges which must be addressed if our planet is to have a future, the problems which these subjects pose are always going to generate an abundance of international disputes. However, the use of force in certain disputes could result in the destruction

[46] M. D. Evans, 'Foreword', in D. French, M. Saul and N. D. White (eds.), *International Law and Dispute Settlement. New Problems and Techniques*, Oxford, 2010, p. viii (emphasis in original).

of civilisation. Even without such nuclear nightmares, it is clear that the destructiveness of modern warfare is such as to inflict suffering on an unprecedented scale. And, leaving aside for a moment the terrible risks associated with force, for states, as for individuals, a persistent failure to resolve disputes leads only to wasted effort and antagonism. In this book, I have tried to show how the intelligence and resourcefulness that have produced contemporary weapons have also developed methods of dispute settlement that can make the use of force unnecessary. To suppose that a time will come when all international disputes are resolved by peaceful means is perhaps unrealistic. Yet the present situation can and must be improved. The tools are already to hand. Now, more than ever, it is the moral responsibility of leaders, advisers and citizens to see that they are used.

Appendices

A. Agreement between Argentina and the United Kingdom establishing an Interim Reciprocal Information and Consultation System, 1990

Both parties agree to establish an Interim Reciprocal Information and Consultation System for movements of units of their Armed Forces in areas of the South West Atlantic. The aims of this system are to increase confidence between Argentina and the United Kingdom and to contribute to achieving a more normal situation in the region without unnecessary delay. The system consists of the following provisions:

I. Direct Communication Link

A. A direct communication link will be established between the respective military authorities – under the supervision of both Foreign Ministries – in order to:
  - reduce the possibility of incidents and limit their consequences if they should occur;
  - increase common knowledge of activities in the South West Atlantic.
B. The respective military authorities will be:
  British Authority: Commander British Forces Falkland Islands (Malvinas).
  Argentine Naval Authority: Commandante del Area Naval Austral (Ushuaia).
  Argentine Air Authority: Jefe de la Novena Brigada Aérea (Comodoro Rivadavia).
C. It is agreed to establish a direct radio link between the respective authorities which will include voice and/or telex transmissions. The link will be manned on a 24 hour basis and will be tested at least once a week. Technical information relating to equipment, frequencies and modalities of use will be exchanged through diplomatic channels.
D. It is agreed to establish a communications plan for radio links between units and stations of the parties. Technical information will be exchanged through diplomatic channels.

II. Definition of Units

A. Ship:

Any ship belonging to the naval forces of the parties bearing the external marks distinguishing warships of its nationality, under the command of an officer duly commissioned by the governments and whose name appears in the naval list, and manned by a crew who are under regular naval discipline, and British Fleet Auxiliaries.

B. Aircraft:

Any aircraft belonging to the Armed Forces of the parties, manned by a military crew who are under regular Armed Forces discipline.

C. Combatant Units:

Any ship or aircraft equipped with weapons systems or means of offensive power or offensive projection capabilities (naval examples: aircraft carriers, cruisers, destroyers, frigates, corvettes, submarines, fast patrol boats, amphibious ships or ships carrying troops: aircraft examples: strike aircraft, fighters, bombers, missile or troop-carrying aircraft).

III. Reciprocal Information about Military Movements

1. Reciprocal written information will be provided through diplomatic channels, not less than 25 days in advance, about:
   A. Movements of naval forces involving four or more ships;
   B. Movements of aerial forces involving four or more aircraft;
   C. Exercises involving more than 1,000 men or more than 20 sorties by aircraft;
   D. Amphibious or airborne exercises involving more than 500 men or more than 20 sorties by aircraft.

The areas of application of this measure are:

For British Forces: the area south of parallel 40°S, west of meridian 20°W and north of 60°S.

For Argentine Forces: within rhumb lines joining the following geographical coordinates in the specified order: 46S 63W, 50S 63W, 50S 64W, 53S 64W, 53S 63W, 60S 63W, 60S 20W, 46S 20W, 46S 63W.

Each party will accept the presence of an observer ship from the other party in the vicinity of naval forces involving four or more ships engaged in manoeuvres within the relevant area of application.

2. Reciprocal notification of identity, intended track and purpose will be given, not less than 48 hours in advance, of a ship or an aircraft that intends to approach closer to coasts than 50 miles by sea or 70 miles by air.

When specific movements of the kind described in this paragraph are intended to be carried out by combatant units and might cause political difficulty to the Argentine Government or to the British Government, the notifying party will be informed immediately and mutual agreement will be necessary to proceed.

IV. Verification

Verification of compliance with the reciprocal information arrangements in provision III above will be by national means, by observer ships (as provided for in III. 1), and by consultations through the direct communication link. If disagreement should persist, the parties shall have recourse to the diplomatic channel.

V. Reciprocal Visits

Reciprocal visits to military bases and naval units may be agreed through the diplomatic channel on a case by case basis.

VI. Applicability of International Practice

In situations not specifically covered above, it is understood that normal international practice will be applied on a reciprocal basis.

VII. Duration

This system, including the reciprocal information measures, shall be reviewed at regular diplomatic–technical meetings. The first of these meetings shall take place within one year after the entry into force of the system and shall be convened at a date to be agreed through the diplomatic channel.

[*Source*: Falkland Islands Department, Foreign and Commonwealth Office, February 1990.]

B. Report of the Commission of Inquiry into the Red Crusader Incident, 1962 (extract)

1. Facts leading up to the arrest of the Red Crusader and circumstances of the arrest

. . . [T]he Commission finds:

(1) that no proof of fishing inside the blue line has been established, in spite of the fact that the trawl was in the water inside the blue line from about 21.00 hours until 21.14 hours on May 29, 1961;

(2) that the *Red Crusader* was with her gear not stowed inside the blue line from about 21.00 hours until 21.14 hours on May 29, 1961;

(3) that the first signal to stop was given by *Niels Ebbesen* at 21.39 hours and that this signal and the later stop-signals were all given outside the blue line.

2. Events between the arrest of the Red Crusader and the meeting with the British naval vessels

... [T]he Commission finds:

(1) The *Red Crusader* was arrested. This conclusion is established by Captain Sølling's declarations as well as by the evidence given by Skipper Wood. Even if the Skipper formally denied his guilt, his answers clearly implied that he considered at the time that he had been duly arrested for illegal fishing. Notes made in the Skipper's red pocket-book and the *Red Crusader's* log-book also leave no doubt on that point.

(2) Skipper Wood, after having obeyed for a certain time the order given him by Captain Sølling, changed his mind during the trip to Thorshavn and put into effect a plan, concerted with his crew, whereby he attempted to escape and to evade the jurisdiction of an authority which he had at first, rightly, accepted.

(3) During this attempt to escape, the Skipper of the *Red Crusader* took steps to seclude Lieutenant Bech and Corporal Kropp during a certain period and had the intention to take them to Aberdeen.

(4) In opening fire at 03.22 hours up to 03.53 hours, the Commanding Officer of the *Niels Ebbesen* exceeded legitimate use of armed force on two counts: (a) firing without warning of solid gun-shot: (b) creating danger to human life on board the *Red Crusader* without proved necessity, by the effective firing at the *Red Crusader* after 03.40 hours.

The escape of the *Red Crusader* in flagrant violation of the order received and obeyed, the seclusion on board the trawler of an officer and rating of the crew of *Neils Ebbesen*, and Skipper Wood's refusal to stop may explain some resentment on the part of Captain Sølling. Those circumstances, however, cannot justify such violent action.

The Commission is of the opinion that other means should have been attempted, which, if duly persisted in, might have finally persuaded Skipper Wood to stop and revert to the normal procedure which he himself had previously followed.

(5) The cost of the repair of the damage caused by firing at and hitting of the *Red Crusader* submitted by the British Government has been considered reasonable by the Danish Agent.

3. Events after the meeting with the British naval vessels.

. . . [T]he Commission finds:

that Commander Griffiths and the other officers of the British Royal Navy made every effort to avoid any recourse to violence between *Niels Ebbesen* and *Red Crusader*. Such an attitude and conduct were impeccable.

[*Source*: 35 ILR pp. 486–500.]

C. Conciliation Commission on the Continental Shelf Area between Iceland and Jan Mayen, May 1981

Summary of Recommendations

1. For the purposes of these recommendations the Commission proposes a specified area defined by the following coordinates: $70^{35°}$ N. Lat. $68°$ N. Lat. $10^{30°}$ W. Long. $6^{30°}$ W. Long.
2. Taking the demarcation line between the 200 mile economic zone and the Norwegian fisheries zone as a dividing line, the specified area has two parts: the part north of the demarcation line comprises some 32.750 km^2. The area south of this line comprises some 12.725 km^2.
3. The Commission proposes a joint cooperation arrangement for the area so defined.
4. In the pre-drilling stage, which includes a systematic geological mapping of the specified area mainly by seismic surveys, the Commission recommends that such surveys should be undertaken jointly by the Norwegian Petroleum Directorate and the equivalent government organisation of Iceland. These seismic surveys should be carried out by the Norwegian Petroleum Directorate according to plans elaborated by the two governments jointly. The costs of such surveys should be borne by Norway unless otherwise agreed by the parties. Icelandic and Norwegian experts should have the opportunity to participate in the seismic surveys on an equal footing. The results and evaluations of the surveys should be equally available to both parties.

   If any profits accrue from the sale of the seismic surveys to interested companies or organisations, such profits should be shared by the two countries on a basis to be negotiated.
5. If the surveys justify further exploration, drilling and possible exploitation activities, the Commission proposes that concession contracts with joint-venture arrangements between the two parties and oil companies be negotiated.

6. In the part of the specified area north of the Icelandic 200 mile economic zone Iceland should have the opportunity to acquire a 25 per cent interest in any joint venture arrangement. In negotiations with oil companies an effort should be made to assure that the costs of both Norwegian and Icelandic state participation are 'carried' by the oil companies up to the moment when a commercial find has been declared.

   Should the oil companies refuse to 'carry' the state participation wholly or in part, the Conciliation Commission refers to its proposals made for such event in the foregoing Section VI [*not reproduced here*].

   Norwegian legislation, oil policy and control, safety and environmental regulations and administration would apply to the activities in this part of the specified area.

7. In the part of the specified area south of the northern demarcation line of the Icelandic 200 mile economic zone, Norway should have an option to acquire a 25 per cent interest in any joint-venture arrangement. It should not be expected that Iceland will accommodate Norway with a carried-interest arrangement in the same manner and to the same extent proposed for the Norwegian part of the specified area. However, Norway should be allowed to participate in the negotiations with the oil companies.

   Icelandic legislation, oil policy control, safety and environmental regulations and administration would apply to the activities in this part of the specified area.

8. In the development phase in any part of the specified area it is understood that each of the two States parties would carry a share of the development costs proportional to its share of State participation.

9. The Commission at the end of Section VI has made certain recommendations for dealing with deposits on both sides of the 200 mile demarcation line or overlapping some part of the specified area boundary and refers to its proposals in this respect and considers them included among the present recommendations.

[*Source*: 62 ILR p. 134.]

D. Arbitration Agreement between the United Kingdom and France, July 1975

The Government of the United Kingdom of Great Britain and Northern Ireland and the Government of the French Republic . . . have agreed as follows:

Article 1

1. The Court of Arbitration (hereinafter called the Court) shall be composed of:

Sir Humphrey Waldock, nominated by the United Kingdom Government.
Messrs Paul Reuter, nominated by the French Government.
Herbert Briggs.
Erik Castren.
Endre Ustor.
The President of the Court shall be: Mr Erik Castren.

2. Should the President or any other Member of the Court be or become unable to act, the vacancy shall be filled by a new Member appointed by the Government which nominated the Member to be replaced in the case of the two Members nominated by the United Kingdom and French Governments, or by agreement between the two Governments in the case of the President or the remaining two Members.

Article 2

1. The Court is requested to decide, in accordance with the rules of international law applicable in the matter as between the Parties, the following question:

   What is the course of the boundary (or boundaries) between the portions of the continental shelf appertaining to the United Kingdom and the Channel Islands and to the French Republic, respectively, westward of 30 minutes west of the Greenwich Meridian as far as the 1,000 metre isobath?

2. The choice of the 1,000 metre isobath is without prejudice to the position of either Government concerning the outer limit of the continental shelf.

Article 3

1. The Court shall, subject to the provisions of this Agreement, determine its own procedure and all questions affecting the conduct of the arbitration.
2. In the absence of unanimity, the decisions of the Court on all questions, whether of substance or procedure, shall be given by a majority vote of its Members, including all questions relating to the competence of the Court, the interpretation of this Agreement, and the decision on the question specified in Article 2 hereof.

Article 4

1. The Parties shall, within 14 days of the signature of the present Agreement, each appoint an Agent for the purpose of the arbitration, and shall communicate the name and address of their respective Agents to each other and to the Court.

2. Each Agent so appointed shall be entitled to nominate an Assistant Agent to act for him as occasion may require. The name and address of an Assistant Agent so appointed shall be similarly communicated.

Article 5

The Court shall, after consultation with the two Agents, appoint a Registrar and establish its seat at a place fixed in agreement with the Parties. Until the seat has been determined the Court may meet at a place provisionally chosen by the President.

Article 6

1. The proceedings shall be written and oral.
2. Without prejudice to any question as to burden of proof, the Parties agree that the written proceedings should consist of:
   (a) a Memorial to be submitted by each Party not later than six months after signature of the present Agreement:
   (b) a Counter-Memorial to be submitted by each Party within a time-limit of six months after the exchange of Memorials:
   (c) any further pleading found by the Court to be necessary. The Court shall have power to extend the time-limits so fixed at the request of either Party.
3. The Registrar shall notify to the Parties an address for the filing of their written pleadings and other documents.
4. The oral hearing shall follow the written proceedings, and shall be held in private at such place and time as the Court, after consultation with the two Agents, may determine.
5. The Parties may be represented at the oral hearing by their Agents and by such Counsel and advisers as they may appoint.

Article 7

1. The pleadings, written and oral, shall be either in the English or in the French language; the decisions of the Court shall be in both languages.
2. The Court shall, as may be necessary, arrange for translations and interpretations and shall be entitled to engage secretarial and clerical staff, and to make arrangements in respect of accommodation and the purchase or hire of equipment.

Article 8

1. The remuneration of Members of the Court shall be borne equally by the two Governments.

2. The general expenses of the arbitration shall be borne equally by the two Governments, but each Government shall bear its own expenses incurred in or for the preparation and presentation of its case.

Article 9

1. When the proceedings before the Court have been completed, it shall transmit to the two Governments its decision on the question specified in Article 2 of the present Agreement. The decision shall include the drawing of the course of the boundary (or boundaries) on a chart. To this end, the Court shall be entitled to appoint a technical expert or experts to assist it in preparing the chart.
2. The decision shall be fully reasoned.
3. If the decision of the Court does not represent in whole or in part the unanimous opinion of the Members of the Court, any Member shall be entitled to deliver a separate opinion.
4. Any question of the subsequent publication of the proceedings shall be decided by agreement between the two Governments.

Article 10

1. The two Governments agree to accept as final and binding upon them the decision of the Court on the question specified in Article 2 of the present Agreement.
2. Either Party may, within three months of the rendering of the decision, refer to the Court any dispute between the Parties as to the meaning and scope of the decision.

Article 11

1. A Party wishing to carry out, at any time before the Court has rendered its decision on the question specified in Article 2, any activity in a portion of what it considers to be its continental shelf within the area submitted to arbitration shall, subject to the remaining provisions of this Article, obtain the prior consent of the other Party.
2. If such a request for consent is made by one Party the other Party may not withhold its consent for more than one month nor if it consents within this period, subject its consent to conditions, except on the ground that the proposed activity relates to an area which it intends to claim or might claim as part of its own continental shelf at any stage in the course of the arbitration.
3. The Party withholding consent or subjecting its consent to conditions shall, when notifying the Party making the request, briefly state the grounds upon which it justifies its position.

4. The Party making the request may, if dissatisfied with the justification provided, refer the issue to the Court for a ruling.
5. Without prejudice to paragraph 4, either Party may refer any dispute as to the interpretation or application of this Article to the Court for a ruling.
6. The Court shall give, as soon as possible, a ruling on any issue referred to it pursuant to paragraph 4 or 5, and may order such provisional measures as it considers desirable to protect the interests of either Party.

Article 12

The present Agreement shall enter into force on the date of signature.
[*Source*: 54 ILR p. 13.]

E. Special Agreement for Submission to the International Court of Justice of the Differences Between the Republic of Hungary and the Slovak Republic Concerning the Gabcikovo-Nagymaros Project (1993)

The Republic of Hungary and the Slovak Republic:

Considering that differences have arisen between the Czech and Slovak Federal Republic and the Republic of Hungary regarding the implementation and the termination of the Treaty on the Construction and Operation of the Gabcikovo-Nagymaros Barrage system signed in Budapest on 16 September 1977 and related instruments (hereinafter referred to as 'the Treaty'), and on the construction and operation of the 'provisional solution';

Bearing in mind that the Slovak Republic is one of the two successor States of the Czech and Slovak Federal Republic and the sole successor State in respect of rights and obligations relating to the Gabcikovo-Nagymaros Project;

Recognizing that the Parties concerned have been unable to settle these differences by negotiations;

Having in mind that both the Czechoslovak and Hungarian delegations expressed their commitment to submit the differences connected with the Gabcikovo-Nagymaros Project in all its aspects to binding international arbitration or to the International Court of Justice;

Desiring that these differences should be settled by the International Court of Justice;

Recalling their commitment to apply, pending the Judgment of the International Court of Justice, such a temporary water management régime of the Danube as shall be agreed between the Parties;

Desiring further to define the issues to be submitted to the International Court of Justice,

Have agreed as follows:

Article 1

The Parties submit the questions contained in Article 2 to the International Court of Justice pursuant to Article 40, paragraph 1, of the Statute of the Court.

Article 2

(1) The Court is requested to decide on the basis of the Treaty and rules and principles of general international law, as well as such other treaties as the Court may find applicable,

    (a) whether the Republic of Hungary was entitled to suspend and subsequently abandon, in 1989, the works on the Nagymaros Project and on the part of the Gabcikovo Project for which the Treaty attributed responsibility to the Republic of Hungary;

    (b) whether the Czech and Slovak Federal Republic was entitled to proceed, in November 1991, to the 'provisional solution' and to put into operation from October 1992 this system, described in the Report of the Working Group of Independent Experts of the Commission of the European Communities, the Republic of Hungary and the Czech and Slovak Federal Republic dated 23 November 1992 (damming up of the Danube at river kilometre 1851.7 on Czechoslovak territory and resulting consequences on water and navigation course);

    (c) what are the legal effects of the notification, on 19 May 1992, of the termination of the Treaty by the Republic of Hungary.

(2) The Court is also requested to determine the legal consequences, including the rights and obligations for the Parties, arising from its Judgment on the questions in paragraph 1 of this Article.

Article 3

(1) All questions of procedure and evidence shall be regulated in accordance with the provisions of the Statute and the Rules of the Court.

(2) However, the Parties request the Court to order that the written proceedings should consist of:

    (a) a Memorial presented by each of the Parties not later than ten months after the date of notification of this Special Agreement to the Registrar of the International Court of Justice;

    (b) a Counter-Memorial presented by each of the Parties not later than seven months after the date on which each has received the certified copy of the Memorial of the other Party;

(c) a Reply presented by each of the Parties within such time-limits as the Court may order;

(d) the Court may request additional written pleadings by the Parties if it so determines.

(3) The above-mentioned parts of the written proceedings and their annexes presented to the Registrar will not be transmitted to the other Party until the Registrar has received the corresponding part of the proceedings from the said Party.

Article 4

(1) The Parties agree that, pending the final Judgment of the Court, they will establish and implement a temporary water management régime for the Danube.

(2) They further agree that, in the period before such a régime is established or implemented, if either Party believes its rights are endangered by the conduct of the other, it may request immediate consultation and reference, if necessary, to experts, including the Commission of the European Communities, with a view to protecting those rights; and that protection shall not be sought through a request to the Court under Article 41 of the Statute.

(3) This commitment is accepted by both Parties as fundamental to the conclusion and continuing validity of the Special Agreement.

Article 5

(1) The Parties shall accept the Judgment of the Court as final and binding upon them and shall execute it in its entirety and in good faith.

(2) Immediately after the transmission of the Judgment the Parties shall enter into negotiations on the modalities for its execution.

(3) If they are unable to reach agreement within six months, either Party may request the Court to render an additional Judgment to determine the modalities for executing its Judgment.

Article 6

(1) The present Special Agreement shall be subject to ratification.

(2) The instruments of ratification shall be exchanged as soon as possible in Brussels.

(3) The present Special Agreement shall enter into force on the date of exchange of instruments of ratification. Thereafter it will be notified jointly to the Registrar of the Court.

[*Source*: (1993) 32 ILM p. 1293.]

F. Optional Clause Declarations

Peru (2003)

[*Translation from the Spanish*] In accordance with Article 36, paragraph 2, of the Statute of the International Court of Justice, the Government of Peru recognizes as compulsory ipso facto and without special agreement, in relation to any other State accepting the same obligation and on condition of reciprocity, the jurisdiction of the International Court of Justice in all legal disputes, until such time as it may give notice withdrawing this declaration.

This declaration does not apply to any dispute with regard to which the parties have agreed or shall agree to have recourse to arbitration or judicial settlement for a final and binding decision or which has been settled by some other method of peaceful settlement.

The Government of Peru reserves the right at any time by means of a notification addressed to the Secretary-General of the United Nations to amend or withdraw this declaration or reservations set out herein. Such notification shall take effect on the day on which it is received by the Secretary-General of the United Nations.

This declaration shall apply to countries that have entered reservations or set conditions with respect to it, with the same restrictions as set by such countries in their respective declarations.

Djibouti (2005)

[*Translation from the French*] Desiring, on the one hand, to reach a peaceful and equitable settlement of all international disputes, including those in which it may be involved, and, on the other hand, to make a contribution to the further development and consolidation of international law, the Republic of Djibouti, in accordance with Article 36(2) of the Statute of the International Court of Justice, hereby declares that it recognizes as compulsory ipso facto and without special agreement, in relation to any other State accepting the same obligation, the jurisdiction of the International Court of Justice in all legal disputes concerning:

(a) The interpretation of a treaty;
(b) Any question of international law;
(c) The existence of any fact which, if established, would constitute a breach of an international obligation;
(d) The nature and extent of the reparation to be made for the breach of an international obligation;

with the reservation, however, that this declaration shall not apply to:

1. Disputes in regard to which the parties to the dispute have agreed or shall agree to have recourse to some other method or methods of settlement;

2. Disputes in regard to matters which are exclusively within the domestic jurisdiction of the Republic of Djibouti, under international law;
3. Disputes relating to or connected with facts or situations of hostilities, armed conflicts, individual or collective actions taken in self-defence, resistance to aggression, fulfilment of obligations imposed by international bodies and other similar or related acts, measures or situations in which the Republic of Djibouti is, has been or may in future be involved;
4. Disputes concerning the interpretation or application of a multilateral treaty unless all the parties to the treaty are also parties to the case before the Court or the Government of Djibouti specially agrees to jurisdiction of the Court;
5. Disputes with the government of any State with which, on the date of an application to bring a dispute before the Court, the Government of Djibouti has no diplomatic relations or which has not been recognized by the Government of Djibouti;
6. Disputes with non-sovereign States or territories;
7. Disputes with the Republic of Djibouti concerning or relating to:
   (a) The status of its territory or the modification or delimitation of its frontiers or any other matter concerning boundaries;
   (b) The territorial sea, the continental shelf and the margins, the exclusive fishery zone, the exclusive economic zone and other zones of national maritime jurisdiction including for the regulation and control of marine pollution and the conduct of scientific research by foreign vessels;
   (c) The condition and status of its islands, bays and gulfs;
   (d) The airspace superjacent to its land and maritime territory; and
   (e) The determination and delimitation of its maritime boundaries.

This declaration is made for a period of five years, without prejudice to the right of denunciation and modification which attaches to any commitment undertaken by the State in its international relations. It shall take effect on the date of its receipt by the Secretary-General of the United Nations.

Japan (2007)

I have the honour, by direction of the Minister for Foreign Affairs, to declare on behalf of the Government of Japan that, in conformity with paragraph 2 of Article 36 of the Statute of the International Court of Justice, Japan recognizes as compulsory ipso facto and without special agreement, in relation to any other State accepting the same obligation and on condition of reciprocity, the jurisdiction of the International Court of Justice, over all disputes arising on and after 15 September 1958 with regard to situations or facts subsequent to the same date and being not settled by other means of peaceful settlement.

This declaration does not apply to disputes which the parties thereto have agreed or shall agree to refer for final and binding decision to arbitration or judicial settlement.

This declaration does not apply to any dispute in respect of which any other party to the dispute has accepted the compulsory jurisdiction of the International Court of Justice only in relation to or for the purpose of the dispute; or where the acceptance of the Court's compulsory jurisdiction on behalf of any other party to the dispute was deposited or notified less than twelve months prior to the filing of the application bringing the dispute before the Court.

This declaration shall remain in force for a period of five years and thereafter until it may be terminated by a written notice.

Germany (2008)

[*Translation from the German*] With reference to Article 36 of the Statute of the International Court of Justice I have the honour to formulate on behalf of the Government of the Federal Republic of Germany the following declaration:

1. The Government of the Federal Republic of Germany declares that it recognizes as compulsory ipso facto and without special agreement, in relation to any other state accepting the same obligation, the jurisdiction of the International Court of Justice, in conformity with paragraph 2 of Article 36 of the Statute of the Court, until such time as notice may be given to the Secretary-General of the United Nations withdrawing the declaration and with effect as from the moment of such notification, over all disputes arising after the present declaration, with regard to situations or facts subsequent to this date other than:
   (i) any dispute which the Parties thereto have agreed or shall agree to have recourse to some other method of peaceful settlement or which is subject to another method of peaceful settlement chosen by all the Parties.
   (ii) any dispute which
       (a) relates to, arises from or is connected with the deployment of armed forces abroad, involvement in such deployments or decisions thereon,
   or
       (b) relates to, arises from or is connected with the use for military purposes of the territory of the Federal Republic of Germany, including its airspace, as well as maritime areas subject to German sovereign rights and jurisdiction;
   (iii) any dispute in respect of which any other Party to the dispute has accepted the compulsory jurisdiction of the International Court of

Justice only in relation to or for the purpose of the dispute; or where the acceptance of the Court's compulsory jurisdiction on behalf of any other Party to the dispute was deposited or ratified less than twelve months prior to the filing of the application bringing the dispute before the Court.

2. The Government of the Federal Republic of Germany also reserves the right at any time, by means of a notification addressed to the Secretary-General of the United Nations, and with effect as from the moment of such notification, either to add to, amend or withdraw any of the foregoing reservations, or any that may hereafter be added.

[*Source*: ICJ website.]

G. WTO: Rules of Conduct for the Understanding on Rules and Procedures Governing the Settlement of Disputes (extract)

I. Preamble

Members,

Recalling that on 15 April 1994 in Marrakesh, Ministers welcomed the stronger and clearer legal framework they had adopted for the conduct of international trade, including a more effective and reliable dispute settlement mechanism;

Recognizing the importance of full adherence to the Understanding on Rules and Procedures Governing the Settlement of Disputes ('DSU') and the principles for the management of disputes applied under Articles XXII and XXIII of GATT 1947, as further elaborated and modified by the DSU;

Affirming that the operation of the DSU would be strengthened by rules of conduct designed to maintain the integrity, impartiality and confidentiality of proceedings conducted under the DSU thereby enhancing confidence in the new dispute settlement mechanism; Hereby establish the following Rules of Conduct.

II. Governing Principle

1. Each person covered by these Rules (as defined in paragraph 1 of Section IV below and hereinafter called 'covered person') shall be independent and impartial, shall avoid direct or indirect conflicts of interest and shall respect the confidentiality of proceedings of bodies pursuant to the dispute settlement mechanism, so that through the observance of such standards of conduct the integrity and impartiality of that mechanism are preserved. These Rules shall in no way modify the rights and obligations of Members under the DSU nor the rules and procedures therein.

III. Observance of the Governing Principle

1. To ensure the observance of the Governing Principle of these Rules, each covered person is expected (1) to adhere strictly to the provisions of the DSU; (2) to disclose the existence or development of any interest, relationship or matter that that person could reasonably be expected to know and that is likely to affect, or give rise to justifiable doubts as to, that person's independence or impartiality; and (3) to take due care in the performance of their duties to fulfil these expectations, including through avoidance of any direct or indirect conflicts of interest in respect of the subject matter of the proceedings.
2. Pursuant to the Governing Principle, each covered person, shall be independent and impartial, and shall maintain confidentiality. Moreover, such persons shall consider only issues raised in, and necessary to fulfil their responsibilities within the dispute settlement proceeding and shall not delegate this responsibility to any other person. Such person shall not incur any obligation or accept any benefit that would in any way interfere with, or which could give rise to, justifiable doubts as to the proper performance of that person's dispute settlement duties.

[*Source*: WTO Document WT/DSB/RC/1, 11 December 1996.]

H. Security Council Resolution 915, establishing UNASOG, May 1994

The Security Council,

Recalling its resolution 910 (1994) of 14 April 1994,

Welcoming the signing on 4 April 1994 at Surt (Libya), by the representatives of the Republic of Chad on the one hand and of the Great Socialist People's Libyan Arab Jamahiriya on the other hand, of the agreement relating to the implementation of the Judgment of the International Court of Justice of 3 February 1994,

Taking note of the letter dated 6 April 1994 from the Permanent Representative of the Libyan Arab Jamahiriya to the United Nations addressed to the Secretary-General (S/1994/402) and the letter dated 13 April 1994 from the Permanent Representative of Chad to the United Nations addressed to the Secretary-General (S/1994/424), and the Annexes thereto,

Noting that the agreement signed at Surt (Libya) provides that United Nations observers shall be present during all the Libyan withdrawal operations and shall establish that the withdrawal is actually effected,

Determined to assist the parties in implementing the Judgment of the International Court of Justice concerning their territorial dispute and thereby to help promote peaceful relations between them, in keeping with the principles and purposes of the Charter of the United Nations,

Having examined the report of the Secretary-General dated 27 April 1994 (S/1994/512),

A

1. *Takes note with appreciation* of the report of the Secretary-General on the implementation of the provisions of Article 1 of the abovementioned agreement (S/1994/512);
2. *Decides* to establish the United Nations Aouzou Strip Observer Group (UNASOG) and *authorizes* the deployment for a single period of up to forty days, starting from the date of the present resolution, of nine United Nations observers and six support staff to observe the implementation of the agreement signed on 4 April 1994 at Surt (Libya) in accordance with the recommendations of the Secretary-General (S/1994/512) and in accordance with paragraph 9 of resolution 907 (1994) of 29 March 1994;
3. *Calls upon* the parties to cooperate fully with the Secretary-General in verifying implementation of the provisions of the agreement of 4 April 1994 and, in particular, to grant UNASOG freedom of movement and all the services it requires in order to fulfil its functions;

B

Recognizing that UNASOG will need to travel to the Libyan Arab Jamahiriya by air and that this will require an exemption from the provisions of paragraph 4 of resolution 748 (1992) of 31 March 1992, and *acting*, in this respect, under Chapter VII of the Charter of the United Nations,

4. *Decides* that paragraph 4 of resolution 748 (1992) of 31 March 1992 shall not apply in respect of aircraft flying to or from the Libyan Arab Jamahiriya for the purpose of conveying UNASOG;
5. *Requests* the Secretary-General to inform the Committee established pursuant to resolution 748 (1992) of flights made to or from the Libyan Arab Jamahiriya in accordance with the present resolution;

C

6. *Invites* the Secretary-General to keep it informed as appropriate of the progress of the mission and to report at the time of its completion;
7. *Decides* to remain seized of the matter.

[*Source*: UN Document S/RES/915 (1994), 4 May 1994.]

I. Terms of Reference of the Trust Fund for the International Tribunal for the Law of the Sea (2000)

Reasons for Establishing the Trust Fund

1. Part XV of the United Nations Convention on the Law of the Sea ('the Convention') provides for the settlement of disputes. In particular, Article 287 specifies that States are free to choose one or more of the following means:
   (a) The International Tribunal for the Law of the Sea;
   (b) The International Court of Justice;
   (c) An arbitral tribunal;
   (d) A special arbitral tribunal.
2. The Secretary-General already operates a Trust Fund for the International Court of Justice (see A/47/444). The Permanent Court of Arbitration has established a Financial Assistance Fund. The burden of costs should not be a factor for States, in making the choices under Article 287, in deciding whether a dispute should be submitted to the Tribunal, or in deciding upon the response to an application made to the Tribunal by others. For these reasons, it was decided to create a Trust Fund for the International Tribunal for the Law of the Sea ('the Tribunal').

Object and Purpose of the Trust Fund

3. This Trust Fund ('the Fund') is established by the Secretary-General in accordance with General Assembly Resolution XXX and pursuant to the Agreement on Cooperation and Relationship Between the United Nations and the Tribunal of 18 December 1997 (General Assembly Resolution 52/251, annex).
4. The purpose of the Fund is to provide financial assistance to States parties to the Convention for expenses incurred in connection with cases submitted, or to be submitted, to the Tribunal, including its Seabed Disputes Chamber and any other Chamber.
5. Assistance, which will be provided in accordance with the following terms and conditions, should only be provided in appropriate cases, principally those proceeding to the merits where jurisdiction is not an issue, but in exceptional circumstances may be provided for any phase of the proceedings.

Contributions to the Fund

6. The Secretary-General invites States, intergovernmental organizations, national institutions, non-governmental organizations, as well as natural

and juridical persons, to make voluntary financial contributions to the Fund.

Application for Assistance

7. An application for assistance from the Fund may be submitted by any State Member to the Convention. The application should describe the nature of the case which is to be, or has been, brought by or against the State concerned and should provide an estimate of the costs for which financial assistance is requested. The application should contain a commitment to supply a final statement of account of the expenditures made from approved amounts, to be certified by an auditor acceptable to the United Nations.

Panel of Experts

8. The Secretary-General will establish a panel of experts, normally three persons of the highest professional standing, to make recommendations on each request. The task of each panel is to examine the application and to recommend to the Secretary-General the amount of the financial assistance to be given, the phase or phases of the proceedings in respect of which assistance is to be given and the types of expenses for which the assistance may be used.

Granting of Assistance

9. The Secretary-General will provide financial assistance from the Fund on the basis of the recommendations of the panel of experts. Payments will be made against receipts showing expenditures made in respect of approved costs. The latter may include:
   (a) Preparing the application and the written pleadings;
   (b) Professional fees of counsel and advocates for written and oral pleadings;
   (c) Travel and expenses of legal representation in Hamburg during the various phases of a case;
   (d) Execution of an Order of Judgment of the Tribunal, such as marking a boundary in the territorial sea.

Application of the Financial Regulations and Rules of the United Nations

10. The Financial Regulations and Rules of the United Nations will apply to the administration of the Fund, including the procedures for audit.

Reporting

11. An annual report on the activities of the Fund, including details of the contributions to and disbursements from the Fund, will be made to the Meeting of States Parties to the Convention.

Implementing Office

12. The Division for Ocean Affairs and the Law of the Sea of the Office of Legal Affairs is the implementing office for this Fund and provides the services for the operation of the Fund.

Offers of Professional Assistance

13. The implementing office also maintains a list of offers of professional assistance which may be made on a reduced fee basis by suitably qualified persons or bodies. If an applicant for assistance so requests, the implementing office will make the list of offers available to it for its consideration and decision; both financial and other assistance may be extended in respect of the same case or phase thereof.

Revision

14. The General Assembly may revise the above if circumstances so require.

[*Source*: UN General Assembly Resolution 55/7, Annex I.]

J. Ruling Pertaining to the Differences between France and New Zealand Arising from the Rainbow Warrior Affair (extract)

Introduction

1. On 10 July 1985 a civilian vessel, the 'Rainbow Warrior', not flying the New Zealand flag, was sunk at its moorings in Auckland Harbor, New Zealand, as a result of extensive damage caused by two high explosive devices. One person, a Netherlands citizen, Mr Fernando Pereira, was killed as a result of this action; he drowned when the ship sank.

2. On 12 July, two agents of the French Directorate General of External Security (DGSE) were interviewed by the New Zealand Police and subsequently arrested and prosecuted. On 4 November they pleaded guilty in the District Court in Auckland, New Zealand, to charges of manslaughter and wilful damage to a ship by means of an explosive. They were sentenced to ten years' imprisonment each; they are presently serving their sentences in New Zealand prisons.

3. A communiqué issued on 22 September 1985 by the Prime Minister of France confirmed that the 'Rainbow Warrior' had been sunk by agents of the DGSE upon instructions. On the same day, the Minister of External Affairs of France pointed out to the Prime Minister of New Zealand that France was ready to undertake reparations for the consequences of that action. He also declared he was ready, as the Prime Minister of New Zealand had already suggested, to meet with the Deputy Prime Minister of New Zealand on 23 and 25 September in New York. Such a meeting did take place for the purpose of discussing the possible ways to find a solution to the problems arising from the Rainbow Warrior affair.

4. A number of subsequent meetings took place between officials of the two countries in the months that followed, but it did not prove possible to reach a settlement.

5. In June 1986 I was formally approached by the Governments of France and New Zealand, who referred to me all the problems between them arising from the Rainbow Warrior affair for a ruling which both sides agreed to abide by. I then informed both Governments that I was prepared to undertake such a task. On 19 June, in Paris and in Wellington, both Governments made public announcements to that effect, and in New York on the same day I publicly confirmed that I was willing to undertake that task and to make my ruling available to the two Governments in the very near future . . .

Ruling

The issues that I need to consider are limited in number. I set out below my ruling on them which takes account of all the information available to me. My ruling is as follows:

1. Apology

New Zealand seeks an apology. France is prepared to give one. My ruling is that the Prime Minister of France should convey to the Prime Minister of New Zealand a formal and unqualified apology for the attack, contrary to international law, on the 'Rainbow Warrior' by French service agents which took place on 10 July 1985.

2. Compensation

New Zealand seeks compensation for the wrong done to it and France is ready to pay some compensation. The two sides, however, are some distance apart on quantum. New Zealand has said that the figure should not be less than US Dollars 9 million, France that it should not be more than US Dollars 4 million. My ruling is that the French Government should pay the sum of US Dollars 7 million to the Government of New Zealand as compensation for all the damage it has suffered.

3. The Two French Service Agents

It is on this issue that the two Governments plainly had the greatest difficulty in their attempts to negotiate a solution to the whole issue on a bilateral basis before they took the decision to refer the matter to me.

The French Government seeks the immediate return of the two officers. It underlines that their imprisonment in New Zealand is not justified, taking into account in particular the fact that they acted under military orders and that France is ready to give an apology and to pay compensation to New Zealand for the damage suffered.

The New Zealand position is that the sinking of the 'Rainbow Warrior' involved not only a breach of international law, but also the commission of a serious crime in New Zealand for which the two officers received a lengthy sentence from a New Zealand court. The New Zealand side states that their release to freedom would undermine the integrity of the New Zealand judicial system. In the course of bilateral negotiations with France, New Zealand was ready to explore possibilities for the prisoners serving their sentences outside New Zealand.

But it has been, and remains, essential to the New Zealand position that there should be no release to freedom, that any transfer should be to custody, and that there should be a means of verifying that.

The French response to that is that there is no basis either in international law or in French law on which the two could serve out any portion of their New Zealand sentence in France, and that they could not be subjected to new criminal proceedings after a transfer into French hands.

On this point, if I am to fulfil my mandate adequately, I must find a solution in respect of the two officers which both respects and reconciles these conflicting positions.

My ruling is as follows:

(a) The Government of New Zealand should transfer Major Alain Mafart and Captain Dominique Prieur to the French military authorities. Immediately thereafter, Major Mafart and Captain Prieur should be transferred to a French military facility on an isolated island outside of Europe for a period of three years.

(b) They should be prohibited from leaving the island for any reason, except with the mutual consent of the two Governments. They should be isolated during their assignment on the island from persons other than military or associated personnel and immediate family and friends. They should be prohibited from any contact with the press or other media whether in person or in writing or in any other manner. These conditions should be strictly complied with and appropriate action should be taken under the rules governing military discipline to enforce them.

(c) The French Government should every three months convey to the New Zealand Government and to the Secretary-General of the United Nations, through diplomatic channels, full reports on the situation of Major Mafart and Captain Prieur in terms of the two preceding paragraphs in order to allow the New Zealand Government to be sure that they are being implemented.

(d) If the New Zealand Government so requests, a visit to the French military facility in question may be made, by mutual agreement by the two Governments, by an agreed third party.

(e) I have sought information on French military facilities outside Europe. On the basis of that information, I believe that the transfer of Major Mafart and Captain Prieur to the French military facility on the isolated island of Hao in French Polynesia would best facilitate the enforcement of the conditions which I have laid down in paragraphs (a) to (d) above. My ruling is that that should be their destination immediately after their transfer.

4. Trade Issues

The New Zealand Government has taken the position that trade issues have been imported into the affair as a result of French action, either taken or in prospect. The French Government denies that, but it has indicated that it is willing to give some undertakings relating to trade, as sought by the New Zealand Government. I therefore rule that France should:

(a) Not oppose continuing imports of New Zealand butter into the United Kingdom in 1987 and 1988 at levels proposed by the Commission of the European Communities in so far as these do not exceed those mentioned in document COM(83)574 of 6 October 1983 that is to say, 77,000 tonnes in 1987 and 75,000 tonnes in 1988; and

(b) Not take measures that might impair the implementation of the agreement between New Zealand and the European Economic Community on Trade in Mutton, Lamb and Goatmeat which entered into force on 20 October 1980 (as complemented by the exchange of letters of 12 July 1984).

5. Arbitration

The New Zealand Government has argued that a mechanism should exist to ensure that any differences that may arise about the implementation of the agreements concluded as a result of my ruling can be referred for binding decision to an arbitral tribunal. The Government of France is not averse to that. My ruling is that an agreement to that effect should be concluded and provide that any dispute concerning the interpretation or application of the other agreements, which it has not been possible to resolve through the diplomatic channel, shall, at the request of either of the two Governments, be submitted to an arbitral tribunal under the following conditions:

(a) Each Government shall designate a member of the tribunal within 30 days of the date of the delivery by either Government to the other of a written request for arbitration of the dispute, and the two Governments shall, within 60 days of that date, appoint a third member of the tribunal who shall be its chairman;

(b) If, within the times prescribed, either Government fails to designate a member of the tribunal or the third member is not agreed, the Secretary-General of the United Nations shall be requested to make the necessary appointment after consultations with the two Governments by choosing the member or members of the tribunal;

(c) A majority of the members of the tribunal shall constitute a quorum and all decisions shall be made by a majority vote;

(d) The decisions of the tribunal, including all rulings concerning its constitution, procedure and jurisdiction, shall be binding on the two Governments.

6.

The two Governments should conclude and bring into force as soon as possible binding agreements incorporating all of the above rulings. These agreements should provide that the undertaking relating to an apology, the payment of compensation and the transfer of Major Mafart and Captain Prieur should be implemented at the latest on 25 July 1986.

7.

On one matter I find no need to make a ruling. New Zealand, in its written statement of position, has expressed concern regarding compensation for the family of the individual whose life was lost in the incident and for Greenpeace. The French statement of position contains an account of the compensation arrangements that have been made; I understand that those assurances constitute the response that New Zealand was seeking.

[*Source*: 74 ILR p. 256.]

K. CIS: Concept for Prevention and Settlement of Conflicts in the Territory of States Members of the Commonwealth of Independent States (1996)

Unresolved disputes and disagreements and the armed conflicts arising from them undermine the very foundation of the Commonwealth of Independent

States (CIS), affect the vital interests of every member State and constitute a real threat to international peace and security.

The maintenance of peace and stability is an essential condition for the Commonwealth's existence, ensuring the economic and socio-political development both of each individual member State and of the Commonwealth as a whole.

This Concept sets out the general approaches of States members of CIS to questions of prevention and settlement of conflicts, as well as possibilities for collective measures to resolve emerging disputes and disagreements. It provides for collective action to prevent and settle conflicts, including the conduct of multilateral peace-keeping operations, as an essential component of CIS policy to strengthen the national security and preserve the territorial integrity and independence of its member States.

Recognizing that the prevention and settlement of conflicts relating to security issues must be a matter of concern primarily for the conflicting parties, the States members of CIS are at the same time aware of their responsibility for security in the territory of member States and for deaths and casualties as a result of conflicts and will do all in their power to identify and to defuse any possible sources of tension. They also favour influential roles for the United Nations and the Organization for Security and Co-operation in Europe (OSCE) in efforts to settle conflicts in the territory of States members of CIS since such conflicts threaten not only regional but global security. As a rule, when conducting operations to prevent or settle conflicts in the territory of States members of CIS, there should be a mandate to do so from the United Nations Security Council. In this connection, the involvement of the international community in conflict resolution must be more significant and commensurate with the threat represented by such conflicts.

States members of CIS will strive to strengthen the role of the Commonwealth in the peaceful settlement of conflicts, considering this to be a highly important contribution to the maintenance of regional security and stability, as well as to enhancement of the Commonwealth's authority.

Action to prevent and settle conflicts in the territory of member States of CIS shall be governed by the Charter of the United Nations, the charter and other fundamental instruments of CIS, the universally accepted principles and rules of international law, pertinent resolutions of the United Nations Security Council, documents of OSCE, and agreements and protocols concluded between States members of CIS.

Such actions shall embrace a range of measures designed to facilitate the prevention, resolution and settlement of contentious issues and conflict situations, as well as the narrowing of differences between conflicting parties with a view to identifying mutually acceptable agreements. The nature of such action, and the choice of means and instruments for its implementation, shall depend on the scale and stage of development of conflict. The objective of the action shall be:

conflict prevention (measures to prevent conflict);
settlement of armed conflicts, and
post-conflict peace-building.

1. Conflict prevention

The pre-eminent means of resolving disputes and preventing conflicts is the use of preventive political and diplomatic efforts, collective measures and the authority of CIS to seek ways of reducing tension before it develops into a conflict.

Such action shall be based on an official request from the State whose security and sovereignty are threatened but shall not absolve the parties themselves of their responsibility and duty to show political will in settling their differences by talks and other peaceful means. Preventive diplomacy may be conducted by a special representative of CIS.

Preventive diplomacy may embrace a range of measures to identify reasons and warn of disputes between parties before they develop into conflicts, including good offices and mediation in the organization of consultations and talks between the parties to a dispute, as well as the provision of assistance to them in seeking mutual understanding and reaching agreement on the settlement of differences. Favourable conditions for the development of a negotiating process may be created by harmonizing steps to implement confidence-building measures, including agreement between the parties to the non-use of force or the threat of force, the settlement of differences exclusively by talks, the exchange of information on issues of concern, the dispatch of special representatives, mediation missions or observers from either neutral parties or the conflicting parties themselves, the use of early warning mechanisms, the imposition of economic sanctions, and the creation of demilitarized zones.

Certain cases may also give rise to the preventive (pre-emptive) deployment of police, civilian and military personnel from States members of CIS in the region of possible confrontations with a view to preventing the escalation of tension of the development of disputes, disagreements and crises into armed conflict. Preventive deployment and the creation of demilitarized zones shall take place at the request of those States whose security and sovereignty are threatened, and with the consent of the parties to the dispute. A decision on preventive deployment and sanctions shall be taken by the Council of Heads of State of CIS, which shall determine the nature and term of application of the sanctions and establish the Mandate for deployment, including the powers and composition of the CIS Collective Peace-keeping

Forces (CPF) and the tasks and length of stay of such personnel from CIS member States.

2. Settlement of armed conflicts

The Commonwealth of Independent States shall, in its capacity as a regional organization, take the steps required to settle conflicts in the territory of States members of CIS in accordance with Chapter VIII of the Charter of the United Nations.

The settlement of conflicts shall mean a range of political, socio-legal, economic, military and other measures designed to end conflicts, including those which take the form of armed combat. The settlement of conflicts may include a broad selection of means: from, on the one hand, efforts to bring about the immediate cessation of bloodshed, monitoring and verification of compliance with cease-fire or truce agreements and separation of warring parties to, on the other hand, assistance in the implementation of agreements concluded by the parties to a conflict in the hope of achieving a solid and lasting solution of the crisis which led to armed conflict.

The basic task at this stage is, with the participation of military, police and civilian CPF personnel, to keep the peace after the conflicting parties reach a cease-fire agreement in support of efforts to stabilize the situation in areas of existing conflicts, with a view to ensuring favourable conditions for talks between the parties on a peaceful settlement of the conflicts.

Provision may be made, in the settlement of armed conflicts, for the conduct of peace-keeping operations (PKO).

PKO shall mean political action over a limited period of time to keep the peace between parties to a conflict. Such operations shall employ military, police and civilian personnel trained for the purpose.

Essential conditions for the conduct of PKO are as follows:

The signature of a cease-fire agreement by the conflicting parties and a clear expression by the parties of political will to settle the conflict by political means;

The consent of the conflicting parties to the conduct of PKO by CPF performing their appointed tasks, and the establishment of close cooperation between the parties and the CPF command for the conduct of such operations;

The acceptance by the parties to the conflict of their obligations to honour the international status, neutrality, privileges and immunities of CPF personnel in accordance with international law;

The open, neutral and impartial nature of peace-keeping operations.

The collective peace-keeping forces shall be formed on a coalition basis by the States which have agreed to take part in PKO. Each State member of CIS shall independently determine the form of its participation in PKO. Any decision on the detachment of troop contingents, military observers, police and civilian personnel for participation in PKO shall be taken in conformity with national legislation.

The collective peace-keeping forces shall act under a single command, adhering strictly to the principles of impartiality, compliance with the laws of the host country, and respect for the traditions and customs of the local population. PKO may not be considered to be a substitute for settlement by means of talks.

In the conduct of PKO, the collective peace-keeping forces shall not take part in active combat. They shall make use, first and foremost, of peaceful means and instruments to promote appropriate conditions for the holding of talks and the reaching of mutually acceptable agreements on the settlement of conflicts. They shall refrain from the use of weapons except in cases of armed resistance to their discharge of the Mandate to conduct PKO.

Enforcement measures in the settlement of conflicts (peace enforcement) shall be permitted only if such powers have been mandated by the United Nations Security Council in accordance with the Charter of the United Nations.

3. Post-conflict peace-building

Peace-building shall mean the adoption of political, socio-economic and legal measures following the settlement of an armed conflict for the purpose of promoting the restoration of an atmosphere of trust, mutual relations and cooperation between the conflicting parties and preventing a renewed outbreak of conflict.

Measures in this connection may include the following:

Help in restoring the institutions of State authority;
Help with the return of refugees and displaced persons;
Assistance with mine clearance and restoration of the essential elements of State infrastructure;
Provision of humanitarian and other forms of assistance to the population;
Help in reintegrating former members of armed bands into civilian life;
Creation of the conditions required for free elections to the representative organs of civilian authority;
Help with efforts to defend human rights.

Military observers or individual CPF units may be temporarily deployed in certain areas, provided the parties so agree, to guarantee the fulfilment of agreements.

4. Interaction with the United Nations and OSCE

When working to settle conflicts in accordance with Chapter VII of the Charter of the United Nations, the Commonwealth of Independent States shall closely interact with other international organizations, and particularly with the United Nations and OSCE. Such interaction shall take the following forms:

> Preparations for and conduct of multi-level consultations between representatives of CIS, the United Nations and OSCE;
>
> Assistance to the peace-keeping efforts of different missions and representatives of the United Nations and OSCE;
>
> Cooperation in promoting the political settlement process, including assistance with talks between conflicting parties;
>
> Provision of information to the United Nations Security Council and the corresponding organs of OSCE on decisions relating to the conduct of PKO;
>
> Provision of necessary information to the Secretary-General of the United Nations and to OSCE for the purpose of increasing the effectiveness of preventive diplomacy and other forms of peace-keeping activity;
>
> Discussion in the United Nations Security Council and corresponding OSCE organs of issues relating to the settlement of conflicts in the territory of States members of CIS;
>
> Interaction, coordination of efforts and cooperation between CPF, the Group of Military Observers and observer missions of the United Nations and OSCE;
>
> Participation in the further elaboration of the international legal and conceptual foundations of peace-keeping activities.

With a view to refining and further developing the interaction of CIS with the United Nations and OSCE on a basis of complementarity of efforts and a reasonable balance between the political, moral and financial responsibilities of all involved in conflict settlement, the Commonwealth favours the conduct of full-scale PKO under United Nations auspices when resolving conflicts in the territory of States members of CIS, with CPF participation.

The States members of CIS shall adhere to an agreed collective position in their international contacts on issues relating to conflicts where CIS is pursuing a settlement in its capacity as a regional organization. They shall exchange information on such contacts and consult on issues requiring additional measures to ensure the success of CIS conflict-settlement efforts.

5. General issues

The collective peace-keeping activities of States members of CIS to prevent and settle conflicts shall be directed by the Council of Heads of State of CIS. The Council of Heads of State of CIS shall take the decision to conduct PKO, shall confirm the Mandate specifying the powers and composition of CPF and the tasks and duration of the operation, and shall appoint the Head of the Peace-keeping mission or Special Representative of CIS for settlement of the conflict, the Commander of CPF and also, where appropriate, the Chief of the military observer group. The Head of mission and the CPF Unified Command shall be responsible for drawing up proposals for extensions of PKO.

The Head of mission (or Special Representative) shall be a person invested by the Council of Heads of State of CIS with appropriate powers in the area of conflict, acting on behalf of and reporting to the Council. He shall bear full responsibility for political aspects of the peace-keeping operation and shall monitor discharge of the Mandate to conduct PKO.

The Commander of CPF (or Chief of the military observer group) shall be in direct command of the forces (military observer group) and ensure that they perform their appointed tasks in accordance with the Mandate. He shall, as a rule, be appointed by the State which contributes the largest (in terms of numbers) troop contingent or detachment of military observers to CPF.

For the purpose of managing action by CPF conducting PKO, a Unified Command shall be established, consisting of representatives of States participating in the operation.

The process of talks to prevent and settle conflicts shall be directed by the Council of Ministers for Foreign Affairs, which shall keep the Council of Heads of State of CIS regularly informed concerning the progress of such talks.

[*Source*: UN Document A/51/62, S/1996/74, 31 January 1996, Annex I.]

Index